Psychology Revivals

Adolescence: From Crisis to Coping

Originally published in 1996, *Adolescence: From Crisis to Coping* presented a unique collaborative study of perceived problems and coping strategies of young people from a variety of socio-economic and national backgrounds. It describes the 'culture-fair' research model and explains results in terms of national background, gender and socio-economic, racial and minority status.

Rather than portraying adolescence as a stage of crisis, the study describes this age group as coping with multiple external crises. While adolescents are frequently similar in the issues that concern them, it is significant that their gender and socio-economic backgrounds are often better predictors of their problems and coping strategies than their national backgrounds.

The thirteen nations in which the study was carried out are: Australia, Brazil, China, Greece, India, Israel, Kuwait, Netherlands, Philippines, Russia, Turkey, USA, Venezuela.

Adolescence: From Crisis to Coping

A Thirteen Nation Study

Edited by
Janice Gibson-Cline

Routledge
Taylor & Francis Group
LONDON AND NEW YORK

First published in 1996
by Butterworth Heinemann

This edition first published in 2026 by Routledge
4 Park Square, Milton Park, Abingdon, Oxon, OX14 4RN

and by Routledge
605 Third Avenue, New York, NY 10158

Routledge is an imprint of the Taylor & Francis Group, an informa business

Publisher's Note
The publisher has gone to great lengths to ensure the quality of this reprint but points out that some imperfections in the original copies may be apparent.

Disclaimer
The publisher has made every effort to trace copyright holders and welcomes correspondence from those they have been unable to contact.

For Product Safety Concerns and Information please contact our EU representative GPSR@taylorandfrancis.com. Taylor & Francis Verlag GmbH, Kaufingerstraße 24, 80331 München, Germany

A Library of Congress record exists under ISBN: 9780750626040

ISBN: 978-1-041-31164-5 (hbk)
ISBN: 978-1-003-77817-2 (ebk)
ISBN: 978-1-041-31231-4 (pbk)

Book DOI 10.4324/9781003778172

Adolescence: From Crisis to Coping

A Thirteen Nation Study

Edited by

JANICE GIBSON-CLINE

Professor of Developmental Psychology, University of Pittsburgh

International Series in Social Psychology

To my husband.
Thank you

First published 1996

British Library Cataloguing in Publication Data
Adolescence: From Crisis to Coping –
A Thirteen Nation Study – (International Series in Social Psychology)
I. Gibson-Cline, Janice II. Series
362.7083

ISBN 0 7506 2604 6

Library of Congress Cataloguing in Publication Data
Adolescence: from crisis to coping: a thirteen nation study/edited
by Janice Gibson-Cline.
p. cm. – (International series in social psychology)
Includes bibliographical references and index.
ISBN 0 7506 2604 6
1. Adolescent psychology. 2. Adolescent psychology – Cross-cultural studies.
I. Gibson-Cline, Janice, 1934– II. Series.
BF724. A257
155.5–dc20 95–25382 CIP

Printed and bound in Great Britain by
Biddles Ltd, Guildford and King's Lynn

Contents

Foreword

The foreword, in most professional and academic works, is designed to provide the reader with an introduction and outside expert's interpretation of what is to follow. Because of the interdisciplinary nature of *Adolescence: From Crisis to Coping*, it was difficult to find a single expert whose background and professional interests encompass all aspects of the project important to our readers. Instead, we have taken the unusual step of inviting, not one, but three experts in their fields to examine our work, each from his own speciality. Psychologist, Herbert L. Friedman, examines *Adolescence: From Crisis to Coping* from the perspective of a specialist on adolescence in an international helping agency; Educational Anthropologist and comparative educator Thomas J. LaBelle, provides a research-educator's interpretation of our methodology and the empirical evidence it has produced; finally, Hans Z. Hoxter, President of the International Round Table for the Advancement of Counselling, remarks on the role of multinational sharing of ideas, a mission to both IRTAC and the Energetic Research Team. The commentaries of these three experts follow.

Thomas J. LaBelle

Most researchers working across national boundaries in social science fields find that doing comparative and international research is extremely complicated. For this reason, they often settle for case studies rather than reaching for the strength provided in studies which juxtapose cases and lead to deeper levels of analysis. *Adolescence: From Crisis to Coping* is a cross-cultural study involving thirteen nations which reaches for the more profound comparative perspective.

The study makes several contributions to the field:

1. Drawing on personal statements of more than 5000 subjects, it provides empirical evidence to describe the problems and coping of adolescents.

2. A rather unique outcome is provided by the implications drawn for preparing counselors and counseling psychologists to assist diverse populations.

3. A third contribution lies in the methodology, which grounds the data in the social and cultural milieu of the populations being studied.

Six years in preparation, the study has built on the participation and consensus of the host national scholars involved and then used the language and culture of the subjects to build data collection methods.

Given the rapid expansion of schooling worldwide, it is perhaps not unexpected that formal education, along with family concerns, would constitute the majority of problems identified by the multinational interviewees. It is not surprising, either, that gender and socioeconomic background are important differentiators of the sample or that professional helpers are the last people whom youth seek internationally for assistance. That these conclusions are empirically verified internationally, however, is significant and constitutes an important contribution to the literature.

Through these and other results, the study also sheds light on the extent to which the concept of adolescence, as a socially constructed stage of life previously associated with industrialized nations, has spread internationally. Originally, adolescence was a concept restricted to nations where children were separated from adults through, among other means, compulsory schooling; the use of post-secondary education as an entry point to many occupations; enactment of labor laws restricting children from salaried employment; and other policies which restricted voting, marriage, military service and the like, to specific ages. By finding commonalities among 13 to 15 year olds from such a wide variety of nations, this study reinforces the notion of adolescence as a modern universal phenomenon. To that end, it has moved us toward the development of a knowledge base and thus a framework for understanding this segment of the world's population.

Thomas J. LaBelle, educational anthropologist and comparative educator, is Provost and Vice President of Academic Affairs and Research at the University of West Virginia

Dr Herbert L. Friedman

Recognition that adolescence is a period of life, crucial to the future of all societies, has increased in recent years. In the past this was due to growing numbers of young people - there are more than one billion adolescents between the ages of ten and nineteen in the world today - four out of five of whom live in developing countries. Perhaps more significantly, there is greater awareness that it is in this period of life that key behaviours begin, new relationships are formed, and decisions are made which will have a profound and lifelong impact.

Dramatic changes are taking place in many societies with important and sometimes unsettling effects on young people and their families. These include accelerating urbanization, increased travel, tourism, and migration; a spread of telecommunications across cultural boundaries; a shrinking family; and earlier puberty combined with later marriage. Yet the picture is a complex one. For example, while in the least economically developed countries poverty is a great problem, it is often in such societies that one also finds close family ties, and a spirit of community cooperation. In the industrially developed world, while there is, by and large, much greater opportunity for education and employment, there is also often more divorce, isolation, violence and suicide.

Despite problems, however, young people constitute perhaps the greatest resource of all. They have the energy, idealism and creativity which all societies need. But they often need help, especially at this crucial phase of life when body, mind and social relationships change in uneven and unexpected ways to the young people of both sexes who experience them. What kinds of help do they need? Who is best placed to provide that help? What kind of training is relevant? What should the goals of that help be? What kinds of characteristics will young people seek in the helpers? These are some of the questions raised by the findings which point to the importance of school, family and personal identity as key concerns to the thirteen- to fifteen-year-olds who participated in these studies.

The research described in this book is useful not only by providing valuable information for each of the thirteen countries involved, but also in its global perspective. By drawing on a multiplicity of cultures, recognizing differences within societies, using a careful and participatory methodology and giving voice to young people themselves, it will render a service to all those concerned about strengthening policies and programming for young people. As with all good research, it raises questions that it cannot answer but it shows what can be done, and will open the door to giving greater attention to young people in all societies.

Dr Herbert L. Friedman is Chief, Adolescent Health Division of Family Health, World Health Organization

Hans Z. Hoxter

This book about young people, their problems and their coping behavior provides crucial information for helping professionals. It helps us to understand youth across both socio-economic strata and national backgrounds. Developed through the multinational collaboration of scholars, it adds to our profession both in terms of theories regarding adolescent behavior and suggestions for improving intervention strategies.

The International Round Table for the Advancement of Counselling (IRTAC) has given wholehearted support to the International Research Team by accommodating its annual pre-conference seminars and has watched with satisfaction the growth of its study of adolescents worldwide. The international sharing of ideas has always been one of IRTAC's most important missions, and it now gives a warm welcome to this important product of international co-operation.

Hans Z. Hoxter is President of the International Round Table for the Advancement of Counselling

Preface – The Evolution of a Multinational Study

Young people are a commodity worldwide. They represent the future leaders of their nations, the determiners of economic and political policy, the builders of family life. In spite of this fact, social scientists know very little about this age group, its thinking and problem-solving approaches or the effects that the environments our generation has created have on them. At a time when collaboration among peoples is increasingly recognized as necessary for world survival, we know little about how the thinking of youth compares across nationalities and cultures.

This book about young people, their problems and their coping behavior is a first step at providing needed information. A collaboration by social scientists and practitioners from 13 countries, it began at the University of Calgary during the 1988 meeting of the International Round Table for the Advancement of Counselling (IRTAC). Our plan was to decide together on research questions that were equally important in all of our countries, develop a procedure to obtain answers and return home to gather data. We agreed that our multinational group was unique in providing expertise that would assist us in avoiding ethnocentric error and conducting culture-fair research.

The project begun in 1988 continued for six years. It was not a simple task. We designed research questions and instruments for data collection and analysis, gathered data, and collaborated on interpreting our results. We met together in Ireland (1989), Finland (1990), Portugal and Greece (1991), Hungary (1992), France (1993) and Germany (1994). We shared ideas and deliberated on a greater number of possibilities than any one of us had considered by ourselves; we had long and sometimes heated debates about each step of the process; between meetings, we continued impassioned arguments and debated each point through mailings, faxes, telephone calls and E-mail. This book is testimony to our reaching consensus on all phases of the process and, in doing so, creating a model for culture-fair cross-cultural research for others to use.

It is also testimony to the relationships we developed, friendships that transcended national, cultural and religious boundaries. Our group expended so much energy on our work and our relationships that we began to refer to ourselves with common affection as the "Energetic Research Team" (ERT) and agreed to use this name in our publications. We became an international ERT family as well as a team. The ERT family was delighted to celebrate the wedding in 1993 of two of our founding members, Semiha Arsoy and Peter de Weerdt, who met and courted as our project developed.

The six years of our study were not quiet or always happy years for our family. Events in the countries of ERT members ranged from earthquakes and volcanic eruptions in the Philippines and flood and other natural disasters in India to the Gulf War in the Middle East and the fall of the USSR. There were also personal tragedies.

Semiha Arsoy, author of the Turkish study, co-author of Chapters 2 and 3, and loving wife of Peter de Weerdt for only a year, died tragically in May 1994 following an automobile accident near their home in Odijk, the Netherlands. She was laid to rest by her husband in Istanbul. Semiha and Peter, the lovers, were an integral part of our ERT family. We grieve both for Peter and ourselves. We will miss Semiha's contributions to our work together. Above all, we will miss her spirit and vitality. As her family, we are grateful for having been given the opportunity to share a portion of her life.

Adolescence: From Crisis to Coping is presented as a work of love as well as of international effort and cooperation. We have created a database comprising responses of more than 5000 adolescent subjects from varied backgrounds in thirteen developed and developing countries to bridge the important gap between what this important age group perceives as its concerns and what theory and practitioners have assumed them to be. We have created a culture-fair methodology that has permitted us to make comparisons across socioeconomic strata and gender as well as national background. We have used these to construct a theory of adolescence as well as dramatic new intervention strategies to assist this age group with our problems. Semiha would have been proud to see the results of our project presented here, just as the rest of us. To the best of our knowledge, our multinational research is the first of its scope to be conducted by consensus!

Janice Gibson-Cline
University of Pittsburgh

Acknowledgements

The author-members of the ERT wish to thank the International Round Table for the Advancement of Counselling for making our Seminars part of the annual meetings of the IRTAC for the past six years, permitting us not only to begin our work together and to meet on regular bases to continue it, but also to share ideas annually with eminent world scholars participating in the IRTAC meetings.

We also acknowledge with gratitude the financial assistance for this project provided by the University of Pittsburgh, University of British Columbia, University of Kuwait, Royal Melbourne Institute of Technology, Sydney College of Advanced Education, University of Puerto Rico and the University of Utrecht as well as the computer and library facilities provided by the Institute of Education, London.

About the Authors

QASEM AL-SARRAF, a founding member of the Energetic Research Team, received his initial training in teacher-education in Syria, his BA from Kuwait University and his MA and PhD from the University of Colorado. A Professor of Educational Psychology, he has taught since 1980 at Kuwait University, where he has also served as Director of the Counseling and Instructional Development Center. He is a member of both the Advisory Committee for the Kuwaiti Society for the Advancement of Arab Children and the Board of Directors of the International Round Table for the Advancement of Counseling. Dr Al-Sarraf has lived and worked in Kuwait, Syria, Lebanon, England and the US.

SEMIHA ARSOY was a developmental educational psychologist who contributed to the training of counselors in Turkey as an associate professor in Bogazici University where she taught from 1985 to 1993. Her educational background includes a BA in English Language and Literature and an MA and EdD in Educational Psychology. Most of her professional life was dedicated to teaching and research in the area of human development, particularly adolescence. A founding member of the ERT, she resided in Holland as a freelance consultant while writing the manuscript for the Turkish study. Dr Arsoy died in 1994 following an automobile accident.

CAROL BAKER, member of the ERT Steering Committee, is Director of the Office of Measurement and Evaluation of Teaching at the University of Pittsburgh in the US. She also teaches courses in statistics, measurement and computer applications in the Graduate School of Education at the University. Her PhD is in research methodology and she provides consultation to faculty and students with respect to the design and analysis of research studies. Dr Baker conducted the primary data analysis for this thirteen-nation study of adolescents.

MARIA DIKAIOU was born in Arkadia, Greece. After receiving her BA with Honours from the University of Thessaloniki, she worked as Research Associate in the same Institute, where she currently holds the position of Associate Professor in Social Psychology. Dr Dikaiou received her PhD from the Department of Psychology at Stirling University, Scotland. She is a member of several professional organizations representing her interests in social-psychological problems of minority groups (such as migrants, refugees and gypsies) and time perspective. These interests are reflected in her publications.

MARION DRAGOON recently ended a long career in education and counseling as Professor at Teachers College, Columbia University. She began as a teacher and guidance counselor in the New York City public schools. Two Guidance Training Institutes changed her professional life by teaching her the power of group training to effect behavioral change and encouraging her to complete her doctorate. She turned to training guidance counselors and developed a counselor training program for Teachers College. She spent the remainder of her career in full-time teaching of graduate students.

MIKA HARITOS-FATOURAS is Professor of Clinical Psychology at the University of Thessaloniki. Born in Athens, she received her BA and MA from the University of London and her PhD from the University of Thessaloniki, and undertook further training in psychotherapy and behavioral psychotherapy at Oxford University and the University of London. Among her publications are cross-cultural and cross-national studies dealing with refugees and migrants as well as behavioral psychotherapy and counseling.

TATANYA GABAY, Professor of Psychology at Moscow State University and a close working colleague of NINA TALYZINA, worked with Professor Talyzina in gathering the responses of adolescent Muscovites in 1990 at a time of great upheaval in her country. Professor Gabay was responsible for the coding of the Russian data.

JANICE GIBSON-CLINE (Editor), director and founding member of the ERT, is Professor of Developmental Psychology at the University of Pittsburgh as well as an officer of the International Round Table for the Advancement of Counselling (IRTAC). She served in Greece, PRC, Philippines and the former nations of Yugoslavia and the USSR as Visiting Research Professor under the sponsorships of the Fulbright Foundation and the Academies of Science of the US and USSR. Dr Gibson-Cline has published eight books and numerous research articles related to cross-cultural study of child development and families. She currently serves as Director of IRTAC's International Research Seminar.

ISAURA ROCHA FIGUEIREDO GUIMARAES, a founding member of the ERT, served as a high-school counselor before becoming Professor of Counseling and Guidance at the Campinas State University—UNICAMP—in Sao Paulo State, Brazil. She received her Masters Degree at George Washington University in Washington DC and her PhD at UNICAMP. In addition to her cross-cultural research, she has been active in the development of sex education in Brazil. She served as Coordinator of the Counseling and Guidance Services of the Campinas Board of Education from 1984 to 1988 and was President of the Counseling and Guidance Association for Sao Paulo State from 1986 to 1988.

CARLOS JONES was a member of the Energetic Research Team while a doctoral student and research assistant at the University of Pittsburgh. His training includes a BA in criminology, MA in counseling and PhD in counseling psychology from the University of Pittsburgh. He has worked clinically with forensic and psychiatric inpatient and outpatient populations and has specialized in delivery of services to at-risk students in general and African-Americans in particular. Dr Jones is employed as a forensic clinical psychologist by the California Department of Mental Health.

LINA KASHYAP is a Reader and Acting Head of the Department of Family and Child Welfare at the Tata Institute of Social Sciences, Bombay, where she teaches social work with children and families. She currently serves on the executive boards of a number of child welfare organizations and is faculty coordinator for the Department's field action project, "The Bombay Child Welfare Coordinator Council." Dr Kashyap is Associate Editor of *Community Alternatives: International Journal of Family Care,* and has published in professional journals in India and abroad. Possessing a PhD in Social Work, she joined the Tata Institute after a decade as a professional social worker.

GRIGORIS KIOSSEOGLOU is Assistant Professor of Statistics in the Department of Psychology at the University of Thessaloniki. He received his BA in Mathematics from the University of Thessaloniki and his MA and PhD in Applied Statistics from the University of Pierre et Marie Curie in Paris, France. Professor Kiosseoglou's research has been primarily in the application of the multivariate statistical methods to social and psychological sciences. He is a member of the Hellenic Statistical Institute.

GEORGE ONDIS was an ERT member and graduate research assistant at the University of Pittsburgh at the time this study was conducted. He received clinical training in community mental health, college counseling, state psychiatric hospital, and inpatient neuropsychiatric settings in the US and was employed for several years as a case-manager in community mental health. He holds a BS in Psychology from King's College in Wilkes-Barre, Pennsylvania, an MA in Clinical Psychology from Indiana University of Pennsylvania and a PhD in Counseling Psychology from the University of Pittsburgh, and is currently a mental health therapist with Health America in Pittsburgh, Pa.

FREDDI DI PAULA is a Venezuelan educator who obtained his PhD in educational administration in 1984 at the University of Pittsburgh. He currently serves as Chief of the Department of Chemistry at Government High School "Francisco Espejo" in Caracas and Chief of Planning and Development of the "Centro de Investigaciones Especiales" (Center for Special Research) at the Instituto Universitario Politecnico de las Fuerzas Armadas (University and Technical Institute of the Armed Forces).

MARIA EUGENIA FELCE DE DI PAULA earned her Diploma in Clinical Psychology at the Hospital Central de las Fuerzas Armadas, Dr Carlos Arvelo in Caracas and her PhD in Educational Psychology at the University of Pittsburgh. Employed as a practicing clinical and child psychologist since 1987, she has served as Chief of the Child Development Department of the Civil Association of Ladies from the Armed Forces in Venezuela and Chief of Psychological Services at the Military Hospital "Dr Vicente Salias" in Caracas. Currently, she is also Professor of Graduate Studies in Counseling and Human Development at the National Experimental University Simon Rodriguez.

ELIZABETE MONTEIRO DE AGUIAR PEREIRA is Professor of Education and Coordinator of the Education Department at the Federal University of Sao Carlos in Sao Carlos City, Sao Paulo State, Brazil. She received her MA in counseling and guidance from Sheffield University and her PhD in Philosophy and History of Education at the State University of Campinas. Prof. Pereira has had 20 years of experience as a counselor and serves as a consultant in Brazilan Career Service. From 1986 to 1988 she served as Vice President of the Sao Paulo State Association for Counseling and Guidance.

MARGARET ROBERTSON, Director of the University Counseling Service of the Royal Melbourne Institute of Technology, has been employed as a counselor practitioner in educational settings in Australia for 25 years. She is a registered psychologist and member of the Australian Psychological Society. A founding member of ERT, she joined the project because of her commitment to the idea that good counseling practice must always be supported by sound research and the belief that the information it contributes toward improving the provision of appropriate counseling services to a multicultural student population is a key issue for Australian universities.

MOHAMED SALEH, a practicing psychologist who received his PhD in developmental psychology at the University of Pittsburgh and then returned to work in his home in Israel, was employed in therapeutic settings with Arab youth in Mesgave, Israel at the time that this research project was conducted.

BENJAMIN SHAFRIR, a founding member of the ERT, came to Israel from Rumania in 1940 at the age of twelve. He studied at L'Ecole des Hautes Etudes Sociales in Paris, later became Co-Director of the Tokayer Residential Treatment Home for Children and Director of the Institute for Special Education at Kibbutz Givat Haim Ichud. He has lectured at Tel-Aviv University and served as Representative of the World Zionist Organization and Senior Consultant to the Child and Family Guidance Clinic in Tel-Aviv. His 1985 book, *To Be Involved* (Tel-Aviv: Hakibbutz Hameuchad Publishers) conceptualizes counselors as crisis interventionists and educational therapists.

FANNY SUN was a member of the Energetic Research Team and a graduate student in the University of Pittsburgh School of Education during the time this study was conducted. She holds a master's degree in cross-cultural counseling from the University of Pittsburgh, and currently serves as Career Case Manager for the Bridge to Employment Program, Community College of Allegheny County, Pittsburgh, Pennsylvania. She received her BA degree from Beijing Normal University, Beijing, PRC and served as a middle-school teacher in Beijing for two years before coming to the US.

NINA FEODOREVNA TALYZINA, Professor and former Chairperson of the Department of Psychology at Moscow State University, joined the ERT in 1990 during its meeting in Helsinki, Finland and collected and coded data in Moscow together with her colleague, TATIANA GABAY. Professor Talyzina has been active for many years in cross-national studies. Many of her books and articles, originally written in Russian, have been translated into English.

GUNDELINA VELAZCO, a founding member of ERT and Associate Professor of Counseling at DelaSalle University in Manila, received her BS in nursing from the University of the Philippines and her MA and PhD in counseling from DelaSalle University. She was Visiting Scholar at the Universities of Pittsburgh and London, and has presented her work in psychology and health internationally. A pioneer in the study of adaptive competence of rural children and economics counseling, she has studied extensively the psychology of street children. Past Director of the Institutional Testing and Evaluation Office of DeLaSalle University, Dr Velazco now serves as a counselor-educator.

PETER DE WEERDT was educated as a vocational and organizational psychologist at the University of Amsterdam. A founding member of the ERT, he was one of the initiators of the first post-graduate training program for school counselors in the Netherlands, and has been a counselor educator since that time. Besides his involvement in training school counselors, he is committed to research and development in the field of school counseling. He is at present Counselor-Educator at ACTA Midden Nederland, an independent department of Teacher Training College Hogeschool van Utrecht.

Additional Co-authors and Contributors

IRINI BONI, Graduate research assistant at the University of Thessaloniki.

WILLIAM BORGEN, Professor of Counseling Psychology at the University of British Columbia, a founding member of the ERT and member of the ERT Steering Committee.

DAVID BOTWIN, Professor of Counseling Psychology at the University of Pittsburgh, member of the ERT Steering Committee.

LINA GUISTI, Professor of Psychology at the University of Puerto Rico and a founding member of the ERT.

ISHU ISHIYAMA, Professor of Counseling Psychology at the University of British Columbia, a founding Member of ERT and member of the ERT Steering Committee.

INDIA IVORY, research assistant and graduate student, Teachers' College, Columbia University.

ILONA LEE, counselor-educator, Sydney College of Advanced Education.

LISA NGUYEN, research assistant and doctoral student at the University of Pittsburgh.

KLARA POPP, research assistant, University of Utrecht.

CATHERINE PRETROWITO, research assistant and graduate student, Teachers' College, Columbia University.

XUAN SHEN, Middle school teacher, Beijing, PRC.

SUSAN SHOWALTER, research assistant and doctoral student at the University of Pittsburgh; co-author of Human Problems and Methods of Help-seeking: A Taxonomy, Pittsburgh: University of Pittsburgh, 1989 (with J. Gibson).

MARVIN WESTWOOD, Professor of Counseling Psychology at the University of British Columbia, a founding member of the ERT and member of the ERT Steering Committee.

Part 1

Introduction

Is adolescence a stage of life characterized inevitably by crises? Can we learn the answer from cross-national research?

Chapter 1 introduces our multinational project with an examination of adolescence from two theoretical positions, that of traditional psychoanalytic and the more modern social psychological perspective, the former focusing on age-related factors leading to crisis and the latter on the ability of young people to cope with support provided them by their environments. The chapter reviews the roles of factors such as gender, socioeconomic status and national background as well as cross-national effectiveness of current counseling approaches used as intervention strategies.

Chapter 2 begins our research with the collaborative model designed by the research team to produce culture-fair descriptions of adolescent problems and coping. The chapter then details each step of the project from development of research questions to publication of this book, describing their complexities, limitations and effectiveness.

1

From Crisis to Coping: Theories and Helping Practices

JANICE GIBSON-CLINE
University of Pittsburgh
MARIA DIKAIOU
University of Thessaloniki
with M. HARITOS-FATOURAS, B. SHAFRIR and G. ONDIS

Introduction

Young people are an important commodity worldwide—the future leaders of their nations who will determine economic and political policies and affect family structures, lifestyles and educational programs. Today, however, social, economic and political conditions in many nations are making it difficult for this age group to develop the skills they need to take on these tasks in responsible ways. At the same time, social scientists have provided little information about the thinking of this age group, its problem-solving approaches and the effects of their environments on their behaviour. When collaboration among peoples is becoming increasingly necessary for world survival, we know little about how the thinking of youth compares across nationalities and cultures.

This book about adolescents in Australia, Brazil, China, Greece, India, Israel, Kuwait, Netherlands, Philippines, Russia, Turkey, US and Venezuela is a first step in providing this information. It asks more than 5000 young people of varied backgrounds in their homelands to describe the problems that cause them the greatest anxiety as well as the strategies they use to cope and the persons to whom they go to seek help. It uses their responses, together with information concerning their backgrounds, to create a unique database for cross-cultural study of this age group. Our subjects, young people early in their transition from pubescence to full physical and emotional maturity, come from socioeconomically "advantaged," "nonadvantaged" and "poverty" backgrounds and dominant as well as minority racial or ethnic groups. They are males and females between 13 and 15 years of age. They are children of families with multigenerational histories in their countries as well as of immigrants. They have in common their adolescence, a stage of life that has been variously explained.

Theories of Adolescence: From Crisis to Coping

Adolescence: a stage of crisis

How do we best characterize the stage of adolescence? Until recently, psychologists regarded it primarily in terms of age-related storm, stress and crisis. Traditional psychoanalytic theory assumed that crisis is inevitable when adolescents, made particularly vulnerable to stressors by the biological changes of puberty, strive to develop self-identity and ego strength needed to deal with new stressors associated with preparation to take on adult roles (Erikson, 1968). According to traditional psychoanalytic theory, successful resolution of this struggle is crucial before young people can equip themselves to take on adult responsibilities.

Clinical case histories suggest that, when young people respond to their new anxieties with socially unacceptable defensive behavior such as challenge to adult authority, they create a vicious circle from which it is difficult to escape: Adult disapproval increases their discomfort and leads them to seek approval elsewhere, usually from same-aged peers in similar circumstances. While peers may increase adolescents' feelings of psychological wellbeing temporarily, they may also teach self-destructive behaviors, in turn creating new crises (Erikson, 1968; Jaffe, 1991). Typical adolescent reactions include excessively moody behavior, indecision, confusion and distress at one end of the continuum and, more ominously, disengagement, deep-seated anger, rebellion against authority and profound unhappiness at the other. In many countries, this age group is increasingly being characterized by suicidal behavior.

Adolescence: a psychosocial perspective

Two significant events in the history of modern psychology led recently to a broader approach toward adolescence that examines a variety of factors in addition to adolescent stress and vulnerability, and does not assume that crisis is inevitable. The first event was the increased interest by psychologists in lifespan human development which began in the 1960s and led to an experimental approach to research concerning all stages of life. The second emerged from early clinical studies of stress that used young patients as subjects, and directed research toward determining the extent to which these clinical findings held true for subjects facing "normal" day-to-day realities of family, school, etc. The result is a psychosocial approach that examines adolescents in terms of how they interact with their daily environments, as it does human beings at all stages of life (see Bosma and Jackson, 1990).

Although psychosocial theories agree that adolescents may be particularly vulnerable to stress, they argue that youth are nevertheless capable of participating actively in their own development, coping productively and working toward solutions that utilize resources available to them. The assumption is that the problems that these young people face are determined in large part by their experiencing of their own environments as well as by their stage of life. And, since environmental resources vary, the strategies they use to cope with their problems as well as the effectiveness of these strategies also vary (Gordon and Saa-Meroe, 1991; Powers, Hauser and Kliner, 1989).

Psychosocial approaches point to the environment as a major factor in adolescent decision-making, arguing that the developmental tasks of adolescence (tasks that they must accomplish to develop adult skills and to obtain social approval from the adult world) differ widely in content across cultures, and, further, that cultural values and traditions play potent roles in making some tasks more stressful than others (Garmezy, 1981). As an example, in modern industrialized countries, adolescents are expected to take responsibility for making academic decisions and choosing occupations. By contrast, their same-aged peers in Third World countries are "relieved" of this necessity by the societies in which they live. In traditional societies, although some youngsters are challenging the right of the adult world to make decisions for them, most still accept their prescribed roles and traverse adolescence with little overt evidence of increased anxiety. Within many nations, developmental tasks vary by socioeconomic status as well as the setting in which individuals live. Thus, while advantaged youth are expected to prepare for college training, poor minority youth are more often required to join the unskilled work force at early ages to help their families. In similar fashion, youngsters living in rural areas in developing countries are often expected to take on adult roles at earlier ages and with less education than their urban counterparts.

Behavioral and cognitive-behavioral theories contribute to the psychosocial effort to explain behavior through environmental factors by examining wide behavioral variations within cultures and microcultures. The work of Skinner (1953), Lazarus (1981), Meichenbaum (1977) and others demonstrates the importance of individualized reinforcement in affecting behavior, just as culturally induced reward and punishment.

Psychosocial approaches do not suggest that the classical notion of adolescent "storm and stress" has been abandoned completely. There has been an important change of emphasis, however: Most researchers today argue that difficulties or problems presenting themselves during adolescence should not be considered solely in terms of their disruptive nature and their contribution to crisis and storm, but also with regard to the coping responses they evoke in the young people concerned. The focus is on coping rather than crisis.

Adolescent Problems and Theories of Coping

Adolescent problems

Age-related problems associated with adolescence and predicted by psychoanalytic theory deal with issues such as preparing to take on adult responsibilities, creating new roles through which to interact with others and developing definitions of self that fit these roles. It is not surprising, given the developmental tasks of adolescence, that this age group tends to have difficulties with various aspects of their school and family lives as well as interacting with others. In an earlier study conducted by Gibson et al. (1991), this proved true for young people across a variety of nations and socioeconomic status (SES) backgrounds.

Adolescent problems are also related to environmental factors and changing of conditions within the environment, as psychosocial theory would predict: Adolescents in Ireland, for example, express much concern about increasing family breakdown in their country (Ryan, 1993); while Gibson et al. (1991) found few concerns related to inner-city violence in their surveys of urban American adolescents conducted in 1989, Maccarelli (1994) showed, from surveys conducted five years later in the same but now more violent city, that fears of gang violence dominated youngsters' thoughts.

Socioeconomic status (SES) is known to play a role in adolescent problems. Dragona (1983) showed that adolescents living in low SES settings are more likely to report problems such as feelings of isolation, loneliness and depression than in wealthier communities. SES probably interacts with other aspects of the environment in complex ways to affect coping strategies, as when joining gangs is used by poor urban youth to decrease these feelings.

Gender is related to adolescent concerns. Showalter (1992) found that females report more problems related to intimacy or interpersonal conflict while the anxieties of their male peers were tied to physical or intellectual competence.

Most importantly, what youngsters perceive as their most serious problems are not necessarily what professionals believe them to be: While experts expressed concern about teenage pregnancy and sexually transmitted diseases (Benson, Williams and Johnson, 1987; Carnegie Council on Adolescent Development, 1989), for example, the 1992 Gibson et al. study showed that these problems were only rarely mentioned by youngsters.

Theories of coping

Psychosocial theory defines "coping" as a special type of problem-solving that involves a transaction between individuals and their environments that has specific characteristics, e.g. demands, constraints and resources (Lazarus and Folkman, 1984). Individuals who cope most successfully are those who make best use of the resources offered by the environment and use them productively.

This is true regardless of their specific problems. Depending on circumstances, coping may be an individual or interpersonal act that includes help-seeking (finding an individual to provide assistance); it may be "problem-focused" (directly related to solving the problem) or "emotion-focused" (not directly related to solving the problem but rather to reducing unpleasant emotions associated with it); it may be active or passive in its activity (Lazarus, 1966). Bosma and Jackson (1990) suggested that the use of "active" coping strategies decreases with declining socioeconomic status and that the more "passive" coping of lower SES groups is dysfunctional. The extent to which different problems may evoke varying types of coping strategies is not clear.

Background factors and coping

Most research related to the coping of young people has studied older adolescents and young adults rather than young (13—15-year-old) adolescents, the age of our subjects.

National background

Studies of older adolescents and young adults show that concerns and coping strategies appear to vary with national background (Bronfenbrenner, 1977; Herr, 1987). Studies of students matriculating at universities outside their home countries, for example, show that nationality is directly related to which day-to-day issues are described as problematic as well as decisions concerning what to do about these issues. Schwartz (1987) showed that, while Chinese students in the US listed school grades as their most serious problem and coped by reacting inwardly and indirectly, their Saudi counterparts considered personal interactions most important and coped by diverting attention from the problems, relaxing, seeking spiritual support or eliciting emotional support from peers. By contrast, Americans who identified interpersonal conflict as their most serious problem, tended to employ direct action, such as confrontation.

People of differing nationalities often vary even in their physiological reactions to stress: Chinese students in the US report more somatic distress than other ethnic groups, while Puerto Ricans tend to develop depressive reactions to problems (Kuo and Spees, 1983).

Whether youngsters grow up in rural or urban communities often affects the types of choices they make in coping. Comparison of Greek traditional rural and modern urban communities found, for example, that rural individuals regularly solved their problems by seeking support from other community members whom they perceived as members of their "in-group." By contrast, their urban counterparts who lived in more impersonal settings tended far more frequently to cope by themselves with no outside support (Triandis and Vassiliou, 1967).

Socioeconomic background

Many specific coping strategies have been correlated with socioeconomic background. Actively confronting a problem, for example, is correlated positively with SES, with individuals higher on the SES scale more actively involved in solution of their problems (Pearlin and Schooler, 1978; Hallahan and Moos, 1987; and Billings and Moos, 1981). Impoverished minorities, by contrast, are reported in some research to use passive, defensive coping. This difference may be due to individuals' choice of how best to adapt to a problem, given restricted resources (Bond and King, 1985; Hallahan and Moos, 1987).

Minority and immigrant backgrounds

Young people of minority or immigrant background tend to be poor relative to their country-people. Researchers have associated poverty, minority and immigrant status with passive coping strategies such as giving up (Pearlin and Schooler, 1978; Billings and Moos, 1981; Dikaiou and Kiosseoglou, 1994). Disengaging from the situation, another passive coping response, occurs most frequently when both personal and contextual resources that would ordinarily provide help are scarce (Hallahan and Moos, 1987). Studies of immigrants to new cultures suggest that a complex relationship between many factors may determine choice of coping strategy. To new immigrants, for example, ethnic and national identity, general social-emotional adjustment, competence to satisfy basic needs in the host culture as well as what is considered the best choice of personal and social adaptation all play roles in determining behavior (Taft, 1977, 1986; Bond and King, 1985).

Gender and coping

Males and females appear to cope with their problems in different ways and their gender-specific behaviors are both expected and reinforced by social approval in societies throughout the world. Aggressive behavior is expected and reinforced in males while gentle responding is preferred in females, perhaps universally (Whiting and Edwards, 1973). It is not surprising, therefore, that these coping behaviors tend to vary by gender, with males behaving more aggressively and females more gently. Other coping strategies have been found to vary with gender throughout the world as well: Females, for example, tend to seek help from others and to elicit (or offer) physical contact, while males act out more aggressively and tend to seek attention (Whiting and Whiting, 1975; Kessler, Brown and Broman, 1981). Females, who tend to worry more about personal relationships, are also inclined to be more emotionally expressive in dealing with their concerns (Maccoby and Jacklin, 1974) while males are more likely to seek competitive interactions (Frydenberg and Lewis, 1991).

Psychological Counseling

A working definition

The practice of psychological counseling as a profession initially was developed to aid clients in coping with problems. A classical definition given by Hans Hoxter, President of the International Round Table for the Advancement of Counseling, described the process as an

> "interaction developing through the relationship between a counselor and a person in a temporary state of indecision, confusion and distress, which helps that individual to make his own decisions and choices, to resolve his confusion or cope with his distress in a personally realistic and meaningful way, having consideration for his emotional and practical needs and for the likely consequences of his behavior." *(Hoxter, 1981, pp. viii)*

The approach is used with adolescents by many practice-based "helping professionals," including physicians and other health care workers, social workers, teachers and others devoted to assisting individuals to solve problems. And, of course, informal counseling has always been provided by those who care for and are usually most responsible for young people: their families and friends.

Environmental backgrounds and counseling

Researchers have long noted a gap between counseling theories and what occurs when counselors and clients interact as well as between what professionals believe is needed in a situation and what clients perceive is the case. This appears to be especially true when backgrounds of counselors and clients vary considerably, as, for example, in the case of middle-class counselors and low-income, minority clients in the US. Wrenn (1962) and others advocated several decades ago that helping professionals need to take the backgrounds of their clients into consideration when designing interventions for them. Charging that counseling approaches developed by White Western psychoanalytically oriented thinkers was not productive with clients of other racial and cultural backgrounds, many psychologists began to stress a need for cultural matching between clients and counselors. Indeed, choosing helpers of similar ethnic, cultural and racial backgrounds has been shown since that time to be facilitative, at least in the early stages of helping.

Current approaches to counseling

Regardless of this concern, helping professionals in most countries today still work with limited information concerning client background. With most having received their educations in Western countries or from Western-educated professors, they tend almost exclusively to use counseling models that had been developed to counsel clients from Western majority cultures. Although attempts have been made in recent years to increase the numbers of professional helpers whose ethnic, cultural or racial backgrounds are more similar to those of their clients, few attempts have been made to alter approaches according to client background or gender (Ivey, 1990; McGoldrick, 1982; Pedersen, 1987). The traditional approach espoused by psychoanalytic theory remains one of the most popular approaches still used today, although psychosocial and behavioral theories are in increasing use. Other well-known techniques include non-directive counseling and group counseling, in which more than one client is seen at a time. In only a few of those listed below are background and gender given special consideration.

Psychodynamic approaches

Traditional psychodynamic (psychoanalytic) approaches to counseling emphasized personality organization, defense mechanisms and developmental stages. The primary contributors to the application of these approaches to adolescent counseling, Erik Erikson and Anna Freud, took the position that young people are alike in dealing with the crucial issue of identity formation and that adolescence is essentially a stage of turmoil created by increased sex drive and decreased ego strength. Current therapies are designed to reduce anxiety and maladaptive defenses, and to provide outlets for drive activity (Erikson, 1968; Jaffe, 1991). Environment is far less of a consideration.

Psychosocial and behavioral approaches

These approaches to counseling take the position that the emphasis should be on developing productive coping strategies. In these approaches, the emphasis is on coping with a focus on actions and behavior rather than on psychological defenses and drive states. Behavioral and cognitive behavioral approaches utilize reward systems to increase appropriate behavior, looking to the client's environment to determine what constitutes effective reinforcers. Systematic desensitization, in which feared stimuli are paired gradually with positive reinforcement, is used frequently to decrease conditioned fear responses. Behavioral assertiveness training has also been effective in some situations. And, in recent years, cognitive-behavioral approaches have been used to help change "maladaptive" thoughts as well as behaviors, sometimes taking into consideration background factors (Lazarus, 1981; Meichenbaum, 1977).

Non-directive client-centred therapies

These approaches, based on the work of psychologist Carl Rogers and his disciples (1966), utilizes the "curative" power of client/helper relationships to change behaviors and attitudes. Rather than considering "maladaptive" thoughts or behaviors, non-directive counselors assume that positive changes derived from their interventions are due to the empathy, congruence and unconditional positive regard they exhibit to their clients. Little emphasis is placed on background.

Group counseling

Counseling in groups is frequently used with adolescents today, particularly in Western nations. The approach provides therapy in group rather than individual situations and is used with a variety of counseling approaches. Common techniques include group psychotherapy offered by trained mental health professionals; occupational, art or dance therapy in which clients are encouraged to act out their feelings in ways that do not require them to express their emotions verbally; encounter groups and sensitivity training groups that provide individuals with little experience with peoples from other backgrounds to interact intensively with such people in close encounters; and self-help and mutual-help groups in which clients interact with other individuals with similar experiences. All of these are used in a variety of settings, including classrooms, mental health facilities and, even, private homes.

Do these techniques work effectively independent of client background and gender? The answer, according to many experts, is that they often simply exaggerate commonalities and ignore differences as well as the factors that govern them. The results are oversimplifications of what is taking place (Herr, 1987).

Coping as a Help-Seeking Process

The need to better understand the effects of environment may be one reason why people, regardless of national or cultural backgrounds, usually bring their problems to informal helpers, usually family members, close friends or neighbors, and only rarely seek aid from professionals (dePaulo, Nadler and Fischer, 1983; Veroff, Kulka and Douvan, 1981). Durlak reported (1977) that these informal helpers actually were more effective in helping clients solve problems of low to moderate severity. Whether this is true today or not, cultural values regarding what behaviors are appropriate remain a factor in choosing helpers, dictating whether or not youngsters cope with personal problems by seeking any outside help as well as the choice of person(s) to whom they go. In some traditional societies, it is appropriate to solve one's problems oneself; in others it is appropriate to seek help only within the privacy of one's family. Among many microcultures created by migration or poverty in larger societies, this poses the problem that those from whom help is sought by young people frequently do not possess or know where to obtain the resources to assist effectively.

From Crisis to Coping: An Overview

The ERT[1] believes that helping youth develop productive coping strategies requires more than descriptions of the crises characteristic of their stage of life. As a first step, it requires sophisticated understanding of the complexities

[1] Energetic Research Team, the name chosen affectionately by the team of researcher-authors of this book – to describe themselves.

inherent in adolescent concerns and coping behaviors. It also dictates that psychologists and other professionals in the helping professions take into consideration national, cultural and socioeconomic settings in which young males and females grow and develop. Providing this understanding through cross-national and cross-cultural study of young people and outlining interventions to assist their coping are goals of our book.

To avoid a gap between professional views of the issues and the perceptions of perspective clients as to what these issues are, *Adolescence: From Crisis to Coping* goes directly to adolescents from a variety of backgrounds for the answers.

Part 1, "Introduction," began this process. Chapter 1 reviewed existing theories to explain this stage of life as well as counseling theories and practice derivative of these theories. The next chapter, Chapter 2, describes the specific research questions and the culture-fair methodology developed by the ERT to answer them.

In Part 2, "Findings: A Multinational View of Adolescents," Chapter 3 describes the perceived problems and coping of youngsters across all the countries of the study, permitting us to make some generalizations about adolescent problems and behaviors across nationalities as well as by SES and gender. Results of SES comparisons are used to develop a model of culture defined by SES.

In Part 3, "Findings: Thirteen National Studies of Adolescents," Chapters 4—16 portrays the results of each separate national study conducted in Australia, Brazil, China, Greece, India, Israel, Kuwait, Netherlands, Philippines, Russia,[2] Turkey, US and Venezuela that created the multinational findings.

Part 4, "Minority Populations," gives special attention to groups of minority youngsters surveyed in several countries: Chapter 17 includes Arabs in Israel, Gypsies in Greece, Moroccan and Turkish migrants in the Netherlands and "non-advantaged" and "poverty" African-Americans and Hispanic-Americans in the US.

Part 5, "Conclusions and Implications for Theory and Practice," takes us to our final step. Chapter 18 assesses our reports from 13 nations and more than 5000 young subjects. In this last chapter, the Energetic Research Team evaluates our study and interprets our findings so as to enhance both theory and practice and provide the basis for effective intervention strategies that will move us in emphasis from crisis to coping.

[2] The Russia study and some minority group studies appear in national chapters but not in the multinational study.

2

Methodology for a Multinational Study

JANICE GIBSON-CLINE
CAROL E. BAKER
University of Pittsburgh
with
M. WESTWOOD, I. ISHIYAMA, W. BORGEN, S. SHOWALTER, Q. AL-SARRAF, S. ARSOY, D. BOTWIN, I. GUIMARAES, L. GUISTI, M. ROBERTSON, B. SHAFRIR, P. DE WEERDT, G. VELAZCO, M. DIKAIOU and the members of the multinational ENERGETIC RESEARCH TEAM

Introduction

This chapter describes the methodology used in our study, highlighting both advantages and limitations. Creation of the research model was a collaborative effort, with the authors acting in concert during every step of the project, from initial development of the team to defining research questions, analyzing data and interpreting and publishing findings. We did so in agreement with Berrien (1970) and others that true collaboration is a necessity for reducing the "cultural bias" that permeates much cross-national and cross-cultural research. (See Triandis, 1972; Hofstede, 1984; Herr, 1987; Pedersen, 1987; Ivey, 1990.)

Berrien argued that the ideal collaborative model begins with joint definition of problems in which research questions are of equal importance to all participants; studies employ comparable methods and pool data; and collaborators are both obliged to strive for interpretations acceptable to a world community of scholars and, at the same time, are free to report their own data to their own constituents (1970, pp. 33—4). He also pointed out the importance of institutional support in the countries of the researchers.

The authors worked in close collaboration with one another, gathering data for the national studies in their own home countries. The Energetic Research Team (the affectionate name we chose for ourselves) patterned the process to include Berrien's requirements: We began with the establishment of our multinational team and the specific obligations of each member regarding the project from designing the study to collecting, coding and interpreting of data. In our case, data consisted of the responses from 5067 young males and females from "advantaged," "nonadvantaged" and "poverty" environments in Australia, Brazil, China, Greece, India, Israel, Kuwait, Netherlands, Philippines, Russia, Turkey, US and Venezuela.

Method And Research Model

Figure 2.1 describes the team-developed model and the steps used to develop as "culture-fair" an approach as possible. Each step outlined in the model is discussed below.

1. Establishing the team

Collaborative efforts of individuals living, working and collecting data within their indigenous cultures require heavy commitments and a consistently high level of interaction over a prolonged period of time, both to provide necessary feedback and to maintain high morale. The 1988 International Research Seminar described in Chapter 1 offered our multinational group opportunity to collaborate in defining a research problem. In its two days of discussion, Seminar participants outlined what they perceived to be necessary commitments both for the Team as a whole and for its individual members so that the project could be carried out. These commitments are listed in Table 2.1. Because of the arduous responsibilities involved, approximately 50% of the Seminar participants felt unable to take on the task and left the project. Those who formed the fledgling

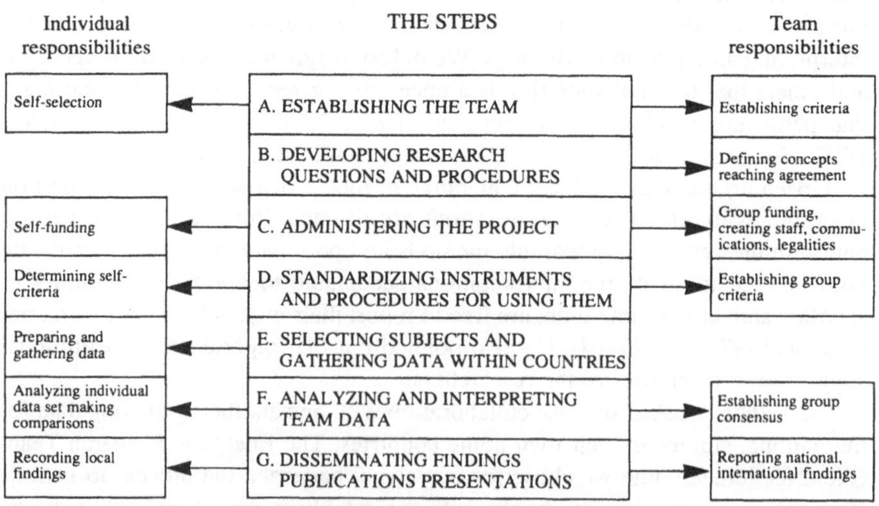

Figure 2.1: A model for the development of collaborative multinational research

TABLE 2.1 *Responsibilities of the research team and its members*

A. *The research team*

1. Reach consensus on criteria for group goals and methods.
2. Reach consensus on research questions and methodology.
3. Obtain necessary funding for communication, staff, assistancc to team participants, and preparing and disseminating team findings.
4. Establish staff, communications facilities, consultant services and computer access.
5. Establish legalities of international collaboration and insure that there are no ambiguities regarding responsibilities, rights to data and authorship of publications.
6. Utilize team input in developing and standardizing research instruments, procedures, data analysis and interpretation.
7. Share in preparation of multinational project publications.

B. *Individual team members*

1. Select self for team if agreeing with group goals, methods and required time schedule.
2. Seek self-funding if needed.
3. Determine self-criteria for developing instruments and methodology, and providing input to group through interactive communication.
4. Gather data in own country and prepare to project standards.
5. Analyze and interpret individual data set.
6. Provide input to group in developing larger analysis and in preparing dissemination of multinational results.
7. Disseminate self-study results locally and nationally.

team took on full responsibility to collaborate on developing group goals and procedures, preparing instruments and analyzing data as well as collecting and coding their own data according to a timetable set by the group ... a formidable and exciting task!

2. *Developing research questions and procedures*

The second step involved articulating research questions and data collection procedures that presented the same meanings to all researchers and that were feasible within all countries of the study. This process required extensive interaction of participants, and continued through several months before consensus was reached for a finalized questionnaire and procedures for developing an interview protocol for nonliterate subjects.

The ERT agreed that the study would "begin at the beginning" by describing what adolescents growing up in disparate national, cultural and socioeconomic environments perceive to be their most pressing problems and how they cope. The specific questions to be asked in a variety of countries and socioeconomic backgrounds (in wording approved by all ERT members) were:

(a) What problems do young people report as causing them to feel worried or pressured?
(b) What coping strategies do they report using to deal with these problems?
(c) When they seek help in coping, to whom do they go, and what helper qualities and forms of help do they desire?

We agreed that, for the reporting of data in each country, our respondents' answers would be compared according to nationality, socioeconomic background and gender.

The team developed a first draft of an open-ended questionnaire to be administered to the young subjects and procedures to be used for collecting data.

3. Administering the project

The Project Director[1] used the facilities of her university to develop the following:

(a) An administrative system to coordinate the project and permit systematic interactive communication among team members. Contact took place through:
   (i) annual team meetings held during subsequent IRTAC meetings;
   (ii) annual steering committee meetings, held between IRTAC meetings;
   (iii) communication via fax, E-mail, telephone and post in which ERT members contributed evaluations, suggested revisions and approved steps of the process;
   (iv) publication of a quarterly Newsletter that tracked study progress, provided a forum for discussion, kept researchers in contact, and provided continuous feedback and encouragement; and
   (v) circulation of findings and manuscript drafts for collaborative interpretation.
(b) Team staff, including secretarial and graduate student assistance as well as consultancy in research methodology.
(c) Financial support. Funding was provided by the University of Pittsburgh to administer the project. In addition, the home institutions of some ERT members provided funds to assist data gathering and coding within the home countries (see Acknowledgements).
(d) Formalized legal agreements. To ensure that no confusion existed among team members regarding how data collected by individuals would be used for a collaborative purpose, the ERT developed a formal agreement detailing the rights and obligations of all team members and describing precisely how data were to be used. The agreement, signed by all team members, included that:
   (i) all collaborators would be credited as co-authors of all reports in which their data is used;

[1] Janice Gibson-Cline

(ii) each collaborator would retain the right to publish his/her own data as author independent of the team so long as ERT contributions, including study design and instrumentation, are acknowledged appropriately;

(iii) each collaborator might use data collected by other ERT collaborators in independent studies provided that the appropriate researchers grant permission; and

(iv) collaborators might use the study instruments in new investigations and publish results so long as ERT contributions to instrument development are acknowledged appropriately.

4. Developing and standardizing instruments and procedures

(a) The questionnaire

To collect information from large numbers of subjects, our questionnaire needed to be both simple and efficient to administer. To provide data that was as "culture-fair" as we could make it, it also needed to

(i) accommodate written responses in diverse languages;

(ii) be adaptable in interview format for nonliterate subjects;

(iii) be readily translatable into a variety of indigenous languages; and

(iv) permit freedom of response.

Creating questions that mean the same in all countries of the study was accomplished in several steps:

(i) a first drafting, completed during the 1988 Research Seminar;

(ii) revision by a five-person steering committee;

(iii) review and repeated revision by the team.

The finalized open-ended questionnaire solicits descriptive information, including subjects' age and sex as well as education and country of birth of parents. Subjects are then asked to respond to the following seven questions which are repeated in sequence three times, creating a total of 21 questions:

Problems: Name one problem that causes you to worry or feel pressured; Please describe this problem in more detail;

Coping strategies: When you have this problem, what do you do about it? What are the things you would do in order to deal with this concern, pressure or difficulty? If you do not do anything to solve this problem, what do you do to make yourself feel better?

Desired helpers: If you were to discuss this problem with anyone, who would that be?

Desired helper qualities: What qualities **of helpers** allow (them) to help you?

Desired modes of helping: What would (they) say or do to help you?

The original questionnaire was prepared in English. To prepare it for use in each country, researchers whose subjects did not use English as their first language translated it into the appropriate first languages. This translated version was then back-translated into English by another person proficient in both languages. Translation and retranslation continued until back-translated versions matched the originals. For this study, the questionnaire was translated into Arabic, Chinese, Dutch, Greek, Hebrew, Portuguese, Russian, Spanish, Tagalog and Turkish.

Standardized directions to administer the questionnaire to literate subjects were developed and approved by the ERT. Special versions were also developed to be administered orally to the approximately 30% of "poverty" subjects who were nonliterate and who were questioned in their street environments, schools or youth centers by persons with experience with poverty populations who were specifically trained for the study.

(b) A coding scale to permit quantitative comparisons of responses

Because an international scale of human problems, coping strategies or choices of helpers was not available, the team prepared a scale of possible responses. To develop the scale, a sample of responses from different countries was used. These were translated into English if in another language. ERT members from the various countries of the team divided and subdivided them into classes and categories-within-classes. Successive drafts were disseminated to all team members for review and refinements until a "nearly finalized" draft and coding directions were submitted to all team members at the International Research Seminar held during the 1989 IRTAC meeting in Dublin, Ireland. Additional "final drafts" continued to circulate until consensus was reached as to classes and categories-within-classes of items and to standardized procedures for use of the scale (Showalter, 1990). The final step included development of a software program to permit entering of data onto computer disks, together with paper forms for coders who had no computer access to use in analysis of data.

The completed five-part scale included the following classes:

Problems: extreme poverty, war, catastrophe, material desires, family issues, schooling, personal identity/self-concept, sexuality, courtship and dating, interpersonal/socialization problems, concerns about emotions, self-fulfilment, altruistic (societal) concerns;

Coping strategies: seeking or giving assistance, interpersonal strategies, individual problem-solving (involving subject only), stress management, crying, religious response, resignation, disengagement, antisocial responding;

Desired helpers: family member, non-family, offender (source of problem), supernatural, animate creatures/inanimate objects;

Desired helper qualities: powerful, available, knowledgeable, appealing personal attributes (trustworthy, loyal, etc.); concern for others;

Desired helping modes: direct satisfaction of a need (gives something), counsels (gives advice), attends to, exercises power (solves problem), intercedes with others, assists client to evade.

These classes were subdivided into 102 categories-within-classes of problems, 37 within classes of coping strategies, 42 within desired helpers, 390 within desired helper qualities and 27 within desired helping modes. Classes and categories for all scales are listed in Appendix I.

Reliability of coding. To measure reliability of coding, responses of subjects from 15 countries were first coded by a team of faculty and graduate student researchers at the University of Pittsburgh to establish a "standard." Researchers from the various countries coded the same 15 sets of data; their results were then compared with those of the "standard" and the percentage of coded responses that agreed with those of the "standard" was obtained. The mean percentage of agreement between all national coders and the "standard" proved to be 95% for classes and 84% for categories-within-classes, with a range of from 91% to 97% for classes and from 80% to 90% for categories-within-classes. Appendix II lists the percentages of agreement obtained for each coder.

(c) A case history protocol

To supplement quantitative findings, a case history protocol provided standardized interview directions permitting each researcher to describe qualitatively the perceptions of a prototype subject.

5. Subjects and within-country data collection

ERT members chose male and female subjects within their own countries on the basis of age, socioeconomic status in those countries and, in some countries, several parental characteristics.

(a) Age: 13—15 years

(b) Socioeconomic status

Because conditions defining socioeconomic status vary greatly across nations, "advantaged," "nonadvantaged" and "poverty" socioeconomic grouping were determined within each country, taking into consideration national norms. Researchers selected samples in their countries that they deemed representative of the various SES groups and described the characteristics they used to make their decisions on an open-ended questionnaire designed for that purpose. The following general characteristics applied with minor exceptions (listed below) to all groups being studied:

"Advantaged" youngsters have literate, well-educated parents (above average according to national norms) who are employed in skilled professions that earn average-to-high per capita incomes in that country. Youngsters and their families reside in average-to-wealthy neighborhoods and generally expect to attain a minimum of at least a high-school education.

"Nonadvantaged" youngsters have parents, not all of whom are literate, with lower levels of education (below average according to national norms) and blue-collar or low-skill jobs that earn average-to-below-average per capita incomes in that country. Youngsters and their families reside in average-to-below-average economic neighborhoods, and expect to attain grammar/primary school educations on average.

"Poverty" youth have parents who often are not literate, have low levels of education, and either are unemployed or employed at the lowest paying jobs in that country. Youngsters and their families live in the most impoverished neighborhoods, with most expecting a maximum of grammar/primary school educations; these youth are distinguished from "nonadvantaged" in that they do not always have housing, enough to eat and adequate medical coverage.

The following exceptions to these definitions apply:

(i) Russian youngsters were surveyed while Russia was still a member republic of the USSR and were classified by the Russian researchers as "classless";
(ii) Chinese youngsters in the PRC, by contrast, were classified as "advantaged" and "nonadvantaged" on the basis of their admission or nonadmission to special schools for high achievers, which, according to the Chinese researcher, greatly enhanced their social status and provided opportunities for professional betterment;
(iii) Turkish youth were classified as "advantaged" or "nonadvantaged" on the basis of attendance at private or public schools for the same reason.

Youngsters from Russia are not included in the multinational sample, but those from the PRC and Turkey are.

While all national studies included "advantaged" subjects, only seven (Australia, China, Greece, Kuwait, Netherlands, Turkey and Continental US) included "nonadvantaged." Only five (Brazil, India, Philippines, Venezuela and the Continental US) included "poverty" subjects. Among these poverty groups, US Hispanic and African-American subjects were not included in the multinational sample both because of their size and fact that they were surveyed at a later time period than the rest of the multinational sample (see Chapter 17). Other "poverty" groups omitted in the multinational study because of their small sample sizes but that are included in the book are Greek Gypsies and Arab Israelis, both discussed in Chapter 17, Minority Populations.

(c) Parental characteristics

To ensure cultural similarity in background, youth who reported that one or both of their parents was born outside the country were eliminated from the study. Exceptions were Israeli youngsters, most of whose parents were born outside the country, and migrant populations such as Hispanic-Americans in the US and migrant youngsters in the Netherlands and Gypsies in Greece.

Data collection began for most groups in the early months of 1989, when questionnaires were distributed to small groups of literate subjects, usually within school classrooms, and from nonliterate subjects in one-on-one interviews. The goal for each researcher was to collect responses from 100 subjects per group representing each gender and SES grouping. Fewer were obtained, however, in some countries, for example, Russia, where political problems made it difficult both to collect data and to communicate effectively with the research team, and Kuwait, where data collection was interrupted by the Iraqi invasion. Sample sizes of "poverty" groups in some countries, including Brazil, Venezuela and the US were lower because of difficulties in data collection. Implications of the sample size discrepancies are discussed later in this chapter. Appendix III details specific numbers of subjects for all SES groupings and the two genders in both the multinational and national samples.

6. Analysis and interpretation of team data

To decrease errors caused by idiosyncratic cultural or language interpretations, each researcher coded the responses of his/her own subjects using the procedures outlined above. Coded data were then transferred to the University of Pittsburgh computer for analysis.

Results describing reported problems, coping strategies, chosen helpers and desired qualities of helpers across gender and socioeconomic boundaries were reported in quantitative form (in percentage of responses falling into classes and categories-within-classes) for the multinational study. These are cited in Chapter 3.

Results of national and minority studies were reported in the same fashion (Chapters 4—17). Each national study, in addition, presents qualitative results in case history format and compares its national findings to those of the larger sample, detailing those most significant to the situations **in those countries**. In interpreting the meaning of their results, the researchers in one study[2] utilized correspondence analysis in addition to descriptive analyses.

Interpretations of all results were shared by the ERT through E-mail communications, newsletters and faxed reports as well as in annual team meetings.

[2] The Greek Study

7. *Disseminating findings*

The ERT data suggest specific as well as general issues important to social scientists and helping professionals, regardless of nationality, ethnicity or SES backgrounds of their subjects. These include that

(a) frequently, problems that helping professionals consider important are not what adolescents themselves are concerned about or feel free to discuss;
(b) regardless of the many similarities among the problems and coping strategies of this age group, it is dangerous for helping professionals to consider them alike or expect them to behave in identical ways. Most importantly, our results suggest that, in considering important differences among youngsters, socioeconomic background may be more important than nationality.

Group presentation of these as well as more specific results in scholarly journals and national and international presentations has been our first step in dissemination of our findings (see Gibson *et al.*, 1990, 1991, 1992). Chapter 18 suggests our next steps to utilize the information obtained to improve intervention strategies.

Limitations

There are a number of limitations to our study that should be considered in interpreting our results. These include:

1. *Instruments*

(a) Questionnaire

Use of questionnaires and interviews to gather information have a number of general limitations, particularly in cross-national research. For one thing, although the ERT collaborated in the development of the instruments and directions for administration to make these as "culture-fair" as possible, we will never know whether some respondents were intimidated or, for other reasons, did not provide full information or that reported answers are not true perceptions of reality. Recent studies of German youth utilizing questionnaires have shown, for example, that youngsters who in reality commit socially nonacceptable acts are not likely to report this fact on questionnaires (Gille, Hoffmann-Lange and Schneider, 1993—4). Obviously, it is necessary to use caution in interpreting results.

The open-ended format of our questionnaire is another consideration. Although designed to reduce cultural bias inherent in the more frequently used checklist surveys, it may have affected our findings in other ways. In asking subjects to respond to open-ended questions regarding their problems without prompting them as to areas of concern, we may have elicited those worries that come to the surface immediately and, at the same time, failed to reveal less proximal, but equally or more serious problems. Maccarelli's (1994) comparison of open-ended and checklist formats in soliciting adolescent descriptions of their problems demonstrates that different formats can produce different results, and that these differences are affected by both the issues under consideration and the backgrounds of the subjects. In Maccarelli's study, problems of a sensitive personal nature, such as sexuality, and issues cited frequently by the news media, such as gang violence, were more likely to be elicited by checklist than by open-ended questionnaires; "advantaged" subjects appeared to be affected differently by the difference in format than "nonadvantaged."

Finally, because adolescents are normally concerned with more than one problem at a time, they probably have more than one coping strategy in their repertoires and rarely seek help from one individual exclusively. In order to sample as many of these as possible, the questionnaire asked for a description of three problems and coping strategies for each. Subjects were invited to present three problems, designating a coping strategy and up-to-three desired helpers, helper qualities and helping modes for each. Because not every subject provided all responses solicited, it was not possible to use other-than-descriptive statistics in interpreting results. (Comparison of responses to first, second and third problems revealed no differences in the percentage of responses reported in each class of problems. For this reason, the Greek study utilized responses related to problem 1 alone in examining possible relationships between problems reported and coping strategies and helpers chosen (see Chapter 7). In doing so, however, the researchers used a smaller number of responses in each cell for their analysis.)

(b) Coding scale

Classes and categories-within-classes of our scale were developed on the bases of sample responses submitted by researchers from each country. We were not able, however, to consider every response from every subject in the study and it was not possible to anticipate the views of every subject. To provide for unanticipated responses, each class on the five scales was provided a category, "Other." Responses placed in these categories were, unfortunately, lost for purposes of analysis.

2. Subjects

Because the ERT study was funded locally through the home institutions of the researchers rather than through larger grants obtained from international institutions, it was necessary to select subjects who could be accessed easily by the researchers. As a result, the ERT findings represent only the particular communities within those countries where subjects were accessed. Additionally, while

Berrien pointed out (1970) that multinational equal partnership benefits from the support of institutions in the respective countries of the researchers, one effect of having access to local support only in our study was that some countries were lost to the project, fewer minority samples were obtained and these sometimes included smaller numbers of subjects than desired.

3. Data collection

Timing is an important variable in all social science research. Our subjects were surveyed in 1989, during a period in which cataclysmic events ranging from war to natural disaster had direct impact on many of our subjects, probably affecting their responses. Maccarelli's (1994) study discussed above in which US youngsters reported an unprecedented amount of concern regarding gangs and violence, while this issue did not appear among the concerns of their 1989 counterparts, suggests that this is the case and that it is advisable to replicate all of our within-country studies after a sufficient time has passed.

Effectiveness of Our Model

Despite its limitations, we believe that the ERT model presents a number of important advantages:

1. It has met Berrien's criteria for the ideal model for successful multinational and multicultural collaboration described in the introduction. The study was developed by all team members in collaboration from the study inception to its conclusion. The team engaged the efforts of institutions and researchers in 13 nations in the design of research instruments, collection and analysis of data, and interpretation of potential biases in study design and in interpretation of findings. Many cultural values might not have been recognized without input from team members belonging to the indigenous groups studied.
2. Results are being disseminated widely. In addition to multinational data reports by the ERT in scholarly journals and presentations (see Gibson et al., 1990, 1991, 1992), each collaborator has analyzed and disseminated the data collected within his/her own country.
3. Our project has created a unique data base that can be used to determine relationships among national, cultural and SES background variables and client thinking and behavior—an important first step in the understanding of the thinking and understanding of young people worldwide.

The ERT achieved the goals determined at its first Seminar.

Part 2

Findings: A Multinational View of Adolescents

What did our young subjects tell us? Do their concerns match what the "experts" assume is causing them stress? How similar are these across the nations of our study?

Chapter 3 provides our results: a portrait of young people across multiple nations. The author-researchers use their intriguing findings to explain adolescent problems and coping in terms both of traditional and social-psychological theory as well as to develop hypotheses concerning factors that determine effectiveness of coping.

3

Results of a Multinational Investigation

JANICE GIBSON-CLINE, CAROL BAKER, QASEM AL-SARRAF, SEMIHA ARSOY, ISAURA GUIMARAES, MARGARET ROBERTSON, BENJAMIN SHAFRIR, PETER DE WEERDT, GUNDELINA VELAZCO, MARIA DIKAIOU, MARIA HARITOS-FATOURAS, LINA KASHYAP, MARIA DI PAULA, GEORGE ONDIS, FANNY SUN, CARLOS JONES, GRIGORIS KIOSSEOGLOU, FREDDI DI PAULA and ELIZABETE DE AGUIAR PEREIRA

Introduction

Chapter 3 describes the reported problems and coping strategies of 4367 male and female adolescents from disparate socioeconomic environments within Australia, Brazil, China, Greece, India, Israel, Kuwait, Netherlands, Philippines, Turkey, US and Venezuela.[1] Our specific research questions are:

1. What problems do these young people report as causing them to feel worried or pressured?
2. What coping strategies do they report using to deal with these problems?
3. When they seek help in coping, to whom do they go, and what helper qualities and forms of help do they desire?

Findings are presented across nationalities with respect both to gender and socioeconomic background as defined in Chapter 2. (Not all national or socio-economic groups surveyed by the ERT study are included in this chapter. Appendix III details those samples surveyed in this and other chapters.) Percentages of subjects' responses that fall into each class of problem, coping strategy, choice of helper, desired helper qualities and modes of helping are provided, together with categories-within-classes that represent 5% or more of

[1] Responses of 184 Russian subjects are not included in this chapter, but are reported in Chapter 13.

reported responses.[2] Highlights regarding similarities and differences among gender and socioeconomic groups are described. Implications are discussed.

Results and Discussion

Problems that cause worry or pressure

Similarities among the groups in our study

Table 3.1(a) describes the percentages of responses made by the three socioeconomic groups that have been coded into the various classes of reported problems; Table 3.1(b) provides the same information for the coding of categories-within-classes. With only one exception,[3] males and females, regardless of socioeconomic background, report **family**, **schooling** and **personal identity/ self-concept** concerns more frequently than others. These three classes account together for 57—67% of all responses. The single most frequently reported class, **schooling**, accounts for 16—35% of responses.

Among their schooling problems, concerns of our adolescent subjects centered about "academic failure," expressed by statements such as:

"What will I do if I don't get promoted?"

"No matter how hard I try, I don't pass my tests ..."

Most frequent among their identity problems are issues related to "self-confidence" and to the prospect of "growing up."

"I feel unsure of myself and am afraid that people will laugh at me."

"What will I become when I am an adult?"

"Will I ever be able to earn enough to support a family?"

The single most frequently reported **family** problem deals with "parental strictness" (reported by "nonadvantaged" youngsters):

"My parents always make me come home earlier than my friends. They don't trust me."

Adolescents in our study, by and large, appeared to be more concerned with their own problems and those of people close to them than of others. Few expressed anxiety about **altruism** (societal level concerns). **Extreme poverty** was a concern only of "poverty" youth.

These results might have been predicted by Erik Erikson and other traditional

[2] Because subjects reported multiple problems and strategies and sometimes gave more than one coping strategy per problem, the number of responses is greater than that of subjects in each subgroup and the number of coping strategies is higher than the number of problems reported. The 4367 subjects actually reported a total of 10 994 responses to the three problem questions and a total of 14 651 responses to the three questions related to coping strategies.

[3] Minority females, for whom **material desires** are ranked third and **identity** fourth.

TABLE 3.1 *Multinational study: percentages of total responses falling into classes and categories of problems*

(a) Classes

	Advantaged				*Nonadvantaged*				*Poverty*			
	Male		*Female*		*Male*		*Female*		*Male*		*Female*	
	%	*Rank*	%	*Rank*	%	*Rank*	%	*Rank*	%	*Rank*	%	*Rank*
Poverty	0.4	(14)	0.2	(14)	0.1	(14)	0.8	(12)	9.1	(5)	6.3	(7)
War	0.8	(12)	0.8	(12)	0.3	(13)	0.3	(13)	1.1	(10.5)	0.4	(11.5)
Catastrophe	0.5	(13)	0.6	(13)	1.0	(10.5)	0.9	(11)	0.1	(13.5)	0.3	(13)
Material desires	4.2	(6)	1.5	(10)	5.0	(5)	2.4	(7)	10.6	(4)	13.2	(3)
Family issues	12.6	(3)	20.2	(3)	16.5	(3)	25.0	(2)	26.2	(1)	30.1	(1)
Schooling issues	34.9	(1)	24.7	(1)	36.2	(1)	26.3	(1)	20.8	(2)	16.3	(2)
Identity	19.6	(2)	21.7	(2)	21.6	(2)	19.1	(3)	14.7	(3)	10.6	(4)
Sexuality	1.1	(11)	1.6	(9)	1.0	(10.5)	2.2	(8)	0.1	(13.5)	0.1	(14)
Courtship/dating	3.2	(9)	6.5	(5)	4.1	(6)	5.5	(5)	2.7	(9)	2.0	(9)
Interpersonal	8.7	(4)	9.5	(4)	6.3	(4)	10.8	(4)	4.3	(7)	7.4	(5)
Emotional	5.1	(5)	4.4	(6)	2.1	(9)	2.8	(6)	1.1	(10.5)	1.7	(10)
Self-fulfilment	1.2	(10)	1.2	(11)	0.5	(12)	0.2	(14)	0.8	(12)	0.4	(11.5)
Altruism	3.8	(8)	3.4	(7.5)	2.2	(8)	2.1	(9)	3.2	(8)	4.0	(8)
No problems	4.1	(7)	3.4	(7.5)	3.0	(7)	1.6	(10)	5.0	(6)	7.3	(6)

*(b) Categories**

	Male		*Female*	
	Category	%	*Category*	%
Advantaged	Academic failure	9.9	Academic failure	7.4
			Friendship	6.9
			Self-confidence	5.8
Nonadvantaged	Academic failure	9.8	Academic failure	8.3
	Academic achievement	6.3	Friendship	8.3
	Parental strictness	5.0	Parental strictness	5.8
	Growing up	5.4	Academic achievement	5.0
Poverty	Money	9.4	Money	12.5
	Extreme poverty	8.8	Extreme poverty	5.4
	Growing up	6.0	Domestic quarrels	5.4
	Academic failure	5.9	Growing up	5.0
	Inability to learn	5.2		
	No problems	5.0		

* Representing 5% or more of responses.

theorists who described adolescents as immersed in crises dealing with their preparation for taking on of future adult social and professional roles and defining their own identities, all associated specifically with their stage of life. Other results are not so easily explained: Almost no responses (0—3% of the total reported) of any group of youngsters in the study dealt with **self-fulfilment** (desire to understand and play a meaningful role in life). Even fewer (0—2% of the total) dealt with the very real threats to adolescents today associated with **sexuality**. Few (1—5% of responses) dealt with **emotions and feelings** (depression, stress, anxiety, loneliness, etc.).

What does the non-citing of these concerns mean? As regards lack of apparent concern regarding opportunities to create meaningful roles in adult life, this is a sad finding, perhaps reflective of a general disappointment by this age group in opportunities afforded them, awareness of the difficulties ahead and little expectation that the situation will change.

As regards the other rarely reported concerns, study limitations make it impossible to make conjectures. In the case of the very few reported problems of a sexual nature such as the dangers of AIDS or unwanted pregnancy, it may be that these issues are too sensitive for youngsters to be comfortable describing them in the format we provided, even if they are very much concerned. Maccarelli's (1994) comparison of questionnaire formats described in Chapter 2 demonstrated that problems of a personal nature, such as sexuality, are far more likely to be elicited by checklists in which adolescents mark the problems that concern them rather than describe the problems in their own words, as required in our study. As regards the few concerns related to adolescent emotions and feelings, the specific wording of the request made of our subjects, "Name one problem that causes you to feel worried or pressured," implies recognition of unpleasant emotions and may have precluded any discussion of these for many youngsters.

Differences among gender and SES groups: two intriguing trends

Two trends describe differences in the problems cited by the various groups of our study. Figure 3.1, comparing responses graphically by gender and socioeconomic status, shows that reported problems related to family issues increase with decreasing SES for each gender and that males within each SES group consistently report a lower percentage of family concerns than females. Figure 3.1 shows, further, that reports of school problems decrease from "advantaged" and "nonadvantaged" groups to the "poverty" group, with males continuing to report consistently more schooling worries than females within each SES group. Results of Chapters 4—16 indicate that these results tend to hold for most national studies as well.

It comes as no surprise that "advantaged" and "nonadvantaged" youngsters reported school as the major source of their concerns since responses of these groups were collected in classrooms and virtually all these children were attending school for long periods daily during our data collection period. It is also not astonishing that school appeared to be less of a concern for "poverty" youngsters, who often did not attend school and were questioned in other environments. It is intriguing, however, that our "poverty" subjects reported as many school problems as they did and that, even though these represented a lower percentage of responses than that of their more advantaged peers, it was second only to the percentage related to family issues.

Our Brazilian, Indian, Filipino and Venezuelan "poverty" youngsters included many street children as well as youth who live at home but have dropped out of school because they lack resources to obtain books or necessary clothing, enter

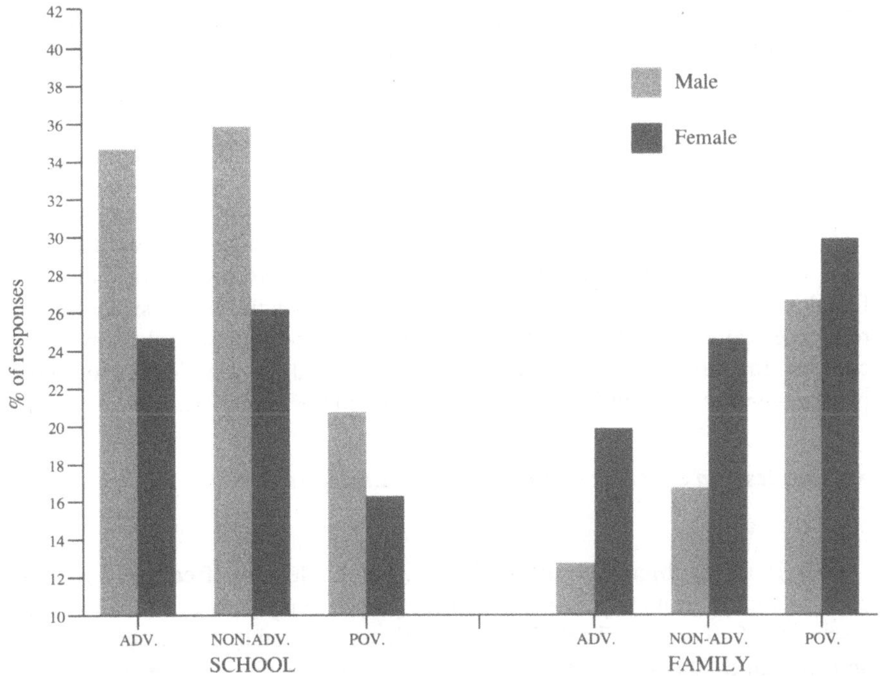

Figure 3.1 Multinational study: percentages of reponses referring to school problems and family problems.

the work force at early ages or are needed to help out at home. Their verbal descriptions of their problems provide a poignant reflection of youngsters unable to take advantage of educational systems in their countries and clearly aware of the importance of what they are losing.

> From Brazil: "I worry ... because I want to be a schooled person in the future. No one knows what can happen."

Descriptions of family and monetary problems of our "poverty" subjects provide indications of why obtaining education is difficult.

> From Venezuela: "If I don't struggle to help my parents, they may die ..."

> From Filipino street children victimized by armed conflict: "Everything we had is lost."

> "Poverty" males, alone among our subject groups, report a fear of being unable to learn.

That family problems increase with decreasing SES and that females report a greater percentage of problems related to family issues than males within each

SES group, with the poorest females reporting the highest percentage of problems of any group in our study is another indication of the important role of environment. In this case, it probably reflects increased family stress and disruption due to economic problems and cultural values that specify the feminine helping role in these matters.

That males report more school problems than females may be due to males actually having more problems, females worrying less about them or a combination of both. We cannot tell from this research. At the same time, we are aware that, although academic achievement is still valued more highly for males than females in most countries of our study, cultural values nevertheless continue to reinforce aggressive behavior in males that conflicts with school learning. By contrast, the more passive feminine behavior valued for females is more compatible with the types of learning that still take place in school.

Similarities and differences among coping strategies

Similarities

Individual problem-solving is, by far, the single most frequently reported class of coping strategy for all our subject groups, representing 36—52% of the responses of all groups (Table 3.2(a)).[4] Subjects reported that they "tried harder" and worked by themselves to "plan solutions" to their problems. **Seeking assistance** is the second strategy of choice. Those who reported **seeking assistance** most frequently sought helpers who would "provide information or social support" (Table 3.2(b)). These choices were made by subjects in each of the national studies as well.

Our subjects, regardless of their gender or SES backgrounds, are also similar in the coping strategies that they reported less often, such as **disengagement** and **antisocial responding**, a behavior expected of this age group by theorists espousing a crisis theory of development. While research shows that youngsters who commit antisocial acts are not likely to report them, even when guaranteed anonymity, the tendency to face their problems rather than to disengage from them by escaping or avoiding the situation behaviorally or distancing themselves psychologically is heartening. Chapters 4—16 reveal, however, that this is not true for youngsters in all our national studies; in some, in fact, high percentages of responses indicating disengagement have been noted and discussed.

Differences

Differences apparent among the groups of our study in coping strategies indicate another intriguing trend suggestive of environmental effects on adoles-

[4] In interpreting these results, it should be noted that there are fewer classes and categories within each class of coping strategy and chosen helpers, helping qualities and modes than in problem classes and categories. This increases the probability that actual percentages reported will be lower within problem classes and categories than in any of these other measures.

TABLE 3.2 *Multinational study: percentages of total responses falling into classes and categories of problems*

(a) Classes

	Advantaged				*Nonadvantaged*				*Poverty*			
	Male		*Female*		*Male*		*Female*		*Male*		*Female*	
	%	*Rank*	*%*	*Rank*	*%*	*Rank*	*%*	*Rank*	*%*	*Rank*	*%*	*Rank*
Assist	14.7	(2)	16.5	(2)	18.6	(2)	22.6	(2)	18	(2)	16.8	(3)
Interpersonal	12.9	(3)	14.6	(3)	9.2	(4)	14.4	(3)	12.4	(3)	17.9	(2)
Problem-solving	49.2	(1)	44.3	(1)	49.9	(1)	38.9	(1)	43.9	(1)	35.6	(1)
Stress-management	2.8	(6)	2.1	(6)	2.0	(6)	1.4	(7)	2.1	(7)	2.4	(7)
Crying	0.3	(9)	1.4	(7)	0.2	(9)	1.6	(6)	0.6	(9)	1.8	(8)
Religion	0.6	(8)	0.7	(8)	0.5	(8)	0.3	(9)	3.0	(6)	4.6	(6)
Resignation	10.3	(4)	11.6	(4)	10.0	(3)	9.8	(5)	10.3	(4)	13.8	(4)
Disengage	8.5	(5)	8.2	(5)	9.0	(5)	10.5	(4)	8.5	(5)	7.2	(5)
Antisocial	0.7	(7)	0.5	(9)	0.6	(7)	0.4	(8)	1.3	(8)	0.0	(9)

*(b) Categories**

	Male		*Female*	
	Category	*%*	*Category*	*%*
Advantaged	Try harder	22.0	Try harder	17.7
	Planning	17.4	Planning	16.2
	Seeking support	11.2	Seek support	13.4
	Assertive cope	6.8	Assertive cope	9.0
Nonadvantaged	Try harder	27.0	Try harder	19.7
	Planning	17.1	Seek support	18.2
	Seek support	11.6	Planning	11.8
	Offer help	6.3	Assertive cope	9.8
	Assertive cope	5.4	Escape/avoid	5.1
			Psychological distance	5.0
Poverty	Planning	18.3	Planning	14.2
	Seek support	15.2	Assertive cope	11.9
	Try harder	13.8	Seek support	11.5
	Assertive cope	8.2	Try harder	11.5
			Offer help	5.3

* Representing 5% or more of responses.

cent behavior. While **individual problem-solving** is the coping strategy of choice for both genders and all SES groups, Figure 3.2 shows graphically that the percentages of responses indicating **individual problem-solving** decrease with decreasing SES, with males from all three SES backgrounds reporting that they go about solving their problems by themselves more frequently than females. This finding appears also in our national studies, with few exceptions. Problem-solving by assessing and analyzing the situation to plan action and continuing to try harder also decreases with decreasing SES and is reported more frequently by males than females (Table 3.1(b)). In this regard, it is interesting that, while "advantaged" and "nonadvantaged" youngsters report solving their problems most frequently by trying harder themselves, their "poverty" peers more frequently engage in planning their activities. "Poverty" youngsters also seek support from others with greater frequency than their more advantaged peers.

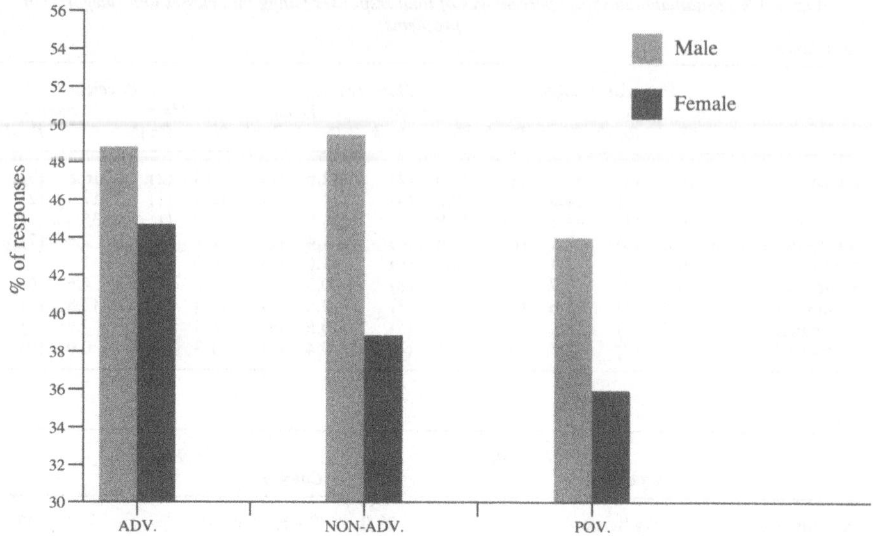

Figure 3.2 Multinational study: percentages of responses referring to individual problem-solving reported by gender and SES (advantaged, non-advantaged and poverty) for multinational subjects.

Help-seeking

When adolescents choose to seek help, to whom do they go and what do they desire from their helpers?

Desired helpers

Classes of desired helpers in Table 3.3(a) show that most groups chose some member of the **family** more frequently than any other source of helper.[5] However, Table 3.3(b) shows that, when classes of helpers are broken into categories, "personal friends" are the helpers of choice. Mothers are the first choice among family members and father the second.

While teachers were noted as desired helpers by all but "poverty" females, only "advantaged" females reported seeking help from a counselor. Results of Chapters 4—16 demonstrate that this tendency not to choose professional help occurs in nations in which professional help is easily available to this age group as well as in nations where it is neither easily available nor a culturally accepted resource. Very few exceptions can be noted in our data.

Helper qualities sought

Being **knowledgeable** (experienced in life, experienced in ways similar to the subject or having knowledge regarding the specific problem at hand) is reported most frequently by "advantaged and "nonadvantaged" youngsters, with this

[5] The one exception is "advantaged females."

TABLE 3.3 *Multinational study: percentages of total responses falling into classes and categories of desired helpers*

(a) Classes

	Advantaged				*Nonadvantaged*				*Poverty*			
	Male		*Female*		*Male*		*Female*		*Male*		*Female*	
	%	*Rank*	*%*	*Rank*	*%*	*Rank*	*%*	*Rank*	*%*	*Rank*	*%*	*Rank*
Family	52.5	(1)	46.2	(2)	59.6	(1)	53.3	(1)	51.3	(1)	55.2	(1)
Non-family	40.4	(2)	47.2	(1)	36.6	(2)	42.8	(2)	44.3	(2)	35.3	(1)
Offender	1.4	(5)	1.6	(4.5)	0.3	(5.5)	0.9	(4)	0.1	(6.5)	0.6	(6)
Supernatural	0.4	(6.5)	0.5	(7)	0.3	(5.5)	0.2	(7)	1.1	(4)	2.8	(4)
Creatures/objects	0.4	(6.5)	0.6	(6)	0.1	(7)	0.4	(6)	0.1	(6.5)	0.3	(7)
Non-specific	2.2	(4)	1.6	(4.5)	0.8	(4)	0.7	(5)	2.5	(3)	3.9	(3)
Nobody	2.6	(3)	2.3	(3)	2.3	(3)	1.7	(3)	0.7	(5)	2.1	(5)

*(b) Categories**

	Male		*Female*	
	Category	*%*	*Category*	*%*
Advantaged	Personal friend	17.3	Personal friend	24.0
	Mother	15.6	Mother	16.1
	Father	13.4	Father	6.6
	Teacher	6.7	Family member	5.9
	Family member	6.3	Sister	5.9
			Counselor	5.4
			Teacher	5.0
Nonadvantaged	Personal friend	21.4	Personal friend	24.3
	Mother	20.0	Mother	18.2
	Father	14.1	Father	7.0
	Teacher	6.0	Sister	6.8
			Teacher	6.0
			Schoolmate	5.7
Poverty	Personal friend	23.5	Personal friend	21.2
	Mother	12.7	Mother	14.2
	Father	8.6	Family member	7.9
	Family member	8.6	Father	7.2
	Teacher	7.3	Sister	5.3
	Brother	6.1	Aunt	5.2

* Representing 5% or more of responses.

quality apparently more important for "advantaged" than "nonadvantaged" subjects and for males rather than females. For "poverty" youngsters and females, by contrast, **concern for others** (being understanding, caring, loving and supportive), was paramount (see Table 3.4).

Desired modes of helping

Male and female subjects across all SES groups prefer most that helpers **counsel** them (give them help to solve the problem or provide directions or advice). Next, they want to be **attended** to (given comfort, reassurance and encouragement). Females in each SES group seek this type of attention more frequently than their male peers.

TABLE 3.4 *Multinational study: percentages of total responses falling into classes and categories of desired helper qualities*

(a) Classes

	Advantaged				*Nonadvantaged*				*Poverty*			
	Male		*Female*		*Male*		*Female*		*Male*		*Female*	
	%	*Rank*	%	*Rank*	%	*Rank*	%	*Rank*	%	*Rank*	%	*Rank*
Power	4.9	(4)	3.6	(4)	5.3	(4)	3.8	(4)	6.8	(4)	6.9	(4)
Knowledge	36.3	(1)	34.3	(1)	42.9	(1)	36.6	(1)	26.5	(2)	28.3	(2)
Availability	2.0	(5)	2.0	(5)	1.7	(6)	1.7	(6)	2.7	(5)	1.3	(6)
Person	30.3	(2)	30.5	(2)	26.8	(2)	29.4	(2)	27.1	(3)	24.5	(3)
Concern	24.6	(3)	27.6	(3)	19.4	(3)	25.1	(3)	35.3	(1)	35.8	(1)
Uncertain	0.8	(7)	0.8	(7)	1.5	(7)	1.1	(7)	0.4	(7)	0.8	(7)
No listing	1.1	(6)	1.2	(6)	2.4	(5)	2.2	(5)	1.2	(6)	2.6	(5)

*(b) Categories**

	Male		*Female*	
	Category	%	*Category*	%
Advantaged	Understanding	11.6	Understanding	14.8
	Experienced	10.4	Similarity	9.6
	Similarity	8.3	Approachable	8.9
	Caring	7.6	Experienced	8.4
	Trustworthy	6.5	Caring	7.6
	Approachable	6.4	Trustworthy	6.0
	Knowledgeable	6.4	Knowledgeable	5.5
	Generous	5.7	Gives advice	5.1
	Supportive	5.1		
Nonadvantaged	Similarity	13.1	Understanding	12.7
	Experienced	10.3	Approachable	9.9
	Understanding	8.9	Experienced	8.4
	Generous	7.6	Generous	8.3
	Approachable	7.3	Caring	8.2
	Caring	6.9	Gives advice	7.8
	Trustworthy	6.1	Similarity	7.4
	Gives advice	5.9	Trustworthy	5.8
			Knowledgeable	5.0
Poverty	Understanding	14.9	Understanding	19.9
	Caring	14.7	Caring	11.8
	Approachable	9.8	Supportive	10.3
	Gives advice	8.6	Generous	7.7
	Experienced	6.9	Experienced	5.9
	Supportive	5.6	Exercises authority	5.3

* Representing 5% or more of responses.

Conclusions

Similarities and differences

Adolescent concerns are age-related and remarkably similar when examining multinational data. This is true regardless of socioeconomic grouping or gender, just as traditional child and adolescent stage theorists might have predicted. At the same time, the fact that differences in the frequency of many reported problems and coping responses of our young subjects vary by SES suggests that psychosocial theories are also correct in their argument that adolescent problems and coping strategies are determined in large part by young people's experiences in their environments as well as by their stage of life. As Gordon and Saa-Meroe (1991) suggested, since environments of adolescents vary, so do their problems and coping strategies. Youth in this study, regardless of their SES backgrounds, appear to be participating actively in their development and working toward solutions that utilize many, if not all, resources available to them. Almost no youngsters reported passive coping such as disengaging from the situation.

The most frequently reported problems of the adolescent subjects in this study deal with schooling, family and identity/self-concept. Our subjects' school worries about learning are not surprising, since school takes up a large portion of every day for this age group. What is surprising is that this concern is important

TABLE 3.5 *Multinational study: percentages of total responses falling into classes and categories of helping modes*

(a) Classes

	Advantaged				*Nonadvantaged*				*Poverty*			
	Male		*Female*		*Male*		*Female*		*Male*		*Female*	
	%	*Rank*	*%*	*Rank*	*%*	*Rank*	*%*	*Rank*	*%*	*Rank*	*%*	*Rank*
Satisfy need	3.4	(6)	1.7	(8)	3.1	(7)	2.4	(7.5)	10.2	(4)	7.0	(5)
Power	9.0	(3)	7.4	(3)	9.1	(3)	6.6	(3)	16.9	(2)	11.6	(3)
Intercede	5.2	(4)	4.2	(4)	4.7	(4)	5.0	(4)	8.2	(5)	10.1	(4)
Counsel	47.4	(1)	44.2	(1)	48.5	(1)	43.3	(1)	44.9	(1)	46.1	(1)
Attend to	25.9	(2)	33.7	(2)	24.2	(2)	32.9	(2)	11.8	(3)	17.1	(2)
Evade problem	2.6	(8)	3.3	(6)	2.7	(8)	4.0	(5)	2.7	(7)	2.4	(7.5)
Uncertain	3.6	(5)	3.4	(5)	3.6	(6)	3.3	(6)	3.6	(6)	3.3	(6)
No listing	3.0	(7)	2.1	(7)	4.2	(5)	2.4	(7.5)	1.7	(8)	2.4	(7.5)

*(b) Categories**

	Male		*Female*	
	Category	*%*	*Category*	*%*
Advantaged	Advise	16.7	Advise	17.4
	Help	12.1	Help	11.8
	Direct	11.3	Comfort	11.8
	Comfort	9.7	Encourage	8.6
	Encourage	6.4	Direct	7.3
Nonadvantaged	Advise	19.5	Advise	16.4
	Help	12.9	Comfort	16.3
	Comfort	11.1	Help	12.8
	Direct	10.5	Direct	8.2
	Encourage	7.3	Encourage	7.0
	Solve problems	5.9		
Poverty	Advise	20.4	Advise	22.6
	Direct	16.1	Direct	14.3
	Solve problems	9.5	Mediate	9.3
	Give something	8.5	Help	6.8
	Mediate	6.1	Encourage	6.5
	Help	5.5	Comfort	6.2
	Encourage	5.4	Give something	6.2
			Solve problems	5.8

* Representing 5% or more of responses.

for "poverty" youth who may not be attending school. This finding suggests that youth today perceive education realistically as an important tool in today's society, whether or not they are able to attain adequate education. In a world that badly needs adults qualified for highly skilled jobs, it is a sad fact that schooling seems universally to be a painful process.

Support systems and coping

It should be noted that the coping strategies of youngsters in our study were probably affected by the support systems available to them in the urban communities in which they lived. Comparison studies of rural and urban communities have found that they tend to differ in the support available to inhabitants and, further, that coping strategies utilized by inhabitants reflect the type of support available. Triandis and Vassiliou (1967) found, for example, that individuals living in traditional rural Greek communities tended to seek support from other community members whom they perceived as members of their "in-group," while those in less personal modern urban settings tended to solve their problems by themselves.

Coping and socioeconomic status

Our results differ from those of previous studies (Pearlin and Schooler, 1978; Hallahan and Moos, 1987; Billings and Moos, 1981) that suggested that "poverty" subjects tend to cope more passively than their more advantaged peers. Although our urban "poverty" youngsters tended to seek outside support and engage in less problem-solving by themselves than their "advantaged" and "nonadvantaged" peers, the more frequent use by "poverty" youth of assessing and analyzing the situation as well as seeking support does not suggest passive coping. It may be that "poverty" youth are acknowledging their more limited ability to resolve their problems unless they change their method of attack and unless they are supported with help from others. In this regard, it is important that "poverty" youth seek help primarily from personal friends and family members who often are least able to provide the assistance needed and that, alone among the SES groups in our study, they choose helpers on the basis of their concern more frequently than their experience. The fact that "poverty" males report seeking some help from their teachers is encouraging. However, their female peers list no outside sources of help at all.

Our finding that "poverty" youngsters as a group differed in some of their concerns and coping strategies from both "advantaged" and "nonadvantaged" youth lends some credence to the hypothesis of a multinational "culture of poverty" of which the behaviors, attitudes and belief systems of impoverished peoples are predictable in many respects, regardless of other national or cultural characteristics. While the "poverty" sample described in this chapter includes only 663 subjects from four countries, additional data reported in other chapters corrobates these findings.

Comparisons of 207 "nonadvantaged" and 193 "poverty" minority Americans in Chapter 17 shows (Tables 17.1 and 17.2) that "poverty" Americans differed from their "nonadvantaged" counterparts in many ways similarly to their multinational peers: They reported a higher percentage of worries related to family problems with females reporting more such problems than males, a lower percentage of active individual problem-solving coping strategies and a higher percentage of seeking help from others and interpersonal coping (engaging others to share the problem and help arrive at a solution), again with females reporting the highest percentages than males. "Poverty" youngsters also reported more financial worries and concern about drugs and crime.

Coping and gender

It is interesting that our portrait of females as compared to males is so similar to that of "poverty" subjects as compared with their more advantaged peers. This similarity might provide some of the reasons that females are often considered minorities in their own countries!

Toward a new approach to coping in counseling

What do our findings suggest as to the relative roles of crisis and coping in the lives of adolescents today? Implications of our multinational, national and minority population findings for psychological theory and counseling practice are the subject of Chapter 18.

Do these suggestions hold across countries? This chapter has examined the data as a whole. What is now important is to consider the data from each separate country. This is the topic of Part 3.

Part 3

Findings: from Thirteen National Studies of Adolescents

Part 3 describes the results of each of 13 studies conducted in Australia, Brazil, China, Greece, India, Israel, Kuwait, Netherlands, Philippines, Russia, Turkey, United States and Venezuela. Authors of Chapters 4—16 have related highlights of their findings to social, political, educational and economic conditions particular to their homelands, compared them to those of the larger multinational study and discussed implications for their own nations. Authors have used their own presentation styles, choosing those results they wish to emphasize and presenting them in formats with which they are most comfortable. They have all focused on those highlights relevant in their own countries, and provided background descriptions of country and culture, including pertinent features such as families and childrearing, educational programs and the current status of counseling. Each has also described minor departures if any exist from methodology used in other national studies.

Although authors have gathered and analysed their data in the same manner, some studies have used additional analyses beyond those used in the multinational study (Greece, Australia and continental US). Some have emphasized different theoretical positions (minority populations).

While each chapter represents a separate "national" study, it needs to be noted that these studies represent responses of young people in specific local communities and cannot be generalized to youth in all areas of their countries.

4

Australia[1]

MARGARET ROBERTSON

Royal Melbourne Institute of Technology

A schoolgirl: "I want to be happy."

Sarah is fifteen. Her father completed high school and is employed as a manager of a corporation. Her mother completed eleventh grade and works as a claims officer in an insurance company.

"In the future, I imagine that I will have a job. I won't be married, and will be concentrating on working and saving money, maybe to buy a house or go on a trip. I want to be happy. I wouldn't want to be unemployed, sick or anything bad.

"My biggest problem right now is my appearance. I want to be thinner and prettier. How I look is important to what everyone thinks of me. To get my mind off of it, I exercise and do sports. And I do things to make myself look better, like doing my hair nicely or exercising. I realize that there isn't much I can really do, so I try not to think about it all of the time.

"Whom do I confide in? My close friends and maybe my mum and dad. My parents know me best and know what I am like. And my friends are my age and they can relate to my problems. When I talk to them, they give me confidence. They say things like, 'No, you're not fat' and make me feel better. And they tell me not to worry so much. I wouldn't want them not to listen or to put me down. And I wouldn't want them to tell me to shut up or anything like that.

"If I had three wishes, they would be to be healthy, to succeed in life in general and in a job and to be happy (with everything going the way I want)."

[1] Ilona Lee, counselor-educator at the Sydney College of Advanced Education, contributed data to this study.

Introduction

As a third-generation Australian from a family of Anglo-Celtic origins who has spent the majority of my life in my country, I base my particular interest in this study on the opportunity it provides to understand the problems and help-seeking behaviors of young people from such a variety of countries and cultures. In common with most Australian schools and universities, my workplace includes an increasingly multicultural student population. This is the result of both the growing numbers of immigrants in the community and the influx of students from overseas as temporary residents. The provision of culturally appropriate counseling services to this culturally varied population is a major concern, given that Australian counselors are trained in essentially Western monocultural counseling models. The information provided by the adolescents from the many countries in this huge project should be extremely helpful in improving the quality and relevance of the counseling processes we engage in with our clients. The local study reported in this chapter offers obvious immediate benefits in this regard.

Country and Culture

Geography

Australia is essentially a Western democratic industrialized nation, geographically situated at the bottom of Asia on the largest and driest of the continents. Despite the fact that popular tourist images often concentrate on vast outback, sweeping beaches and exotic fauna, it is actually one of the most highly urbanized countries in the world, the majority of the 18 million populace residing in cities established around the coastal fringe of the continent. This may seem a sparse population for a country that spans three time zones, but the land and its climate are harsh. Large tracts of the inland are dry, arid and inhospitable to life. The climate of the coastal fringe ranging from tropical to temperate is mostly equable, periodic extremes of heat being the only climatic intrusion. The subjects of this study are drawn from Sydney and Melbourne, the two largest cities, both situated on the coast.

History and identity

Australian culture has been described as a "transplanted" one (Horne, 1987) and dates from British colonization in the late eighteenth century. The original indigenous inhabitants, the Koories, had occupied the continent continuously for at least 50 000 years. However, their non-acquisitive, nomadic culture was no match for the land-hungry and profit-seeking Europeans, and they were violently displaced. Their continuance on the fringe of Australian society haunts the national conscience today, but satisfactory restitution is not easy to find.

The society that was established was basically British, and, until the 1950s, Australians regarded themselves as citizens of a far-flung outpost of the British Empire, going to Europe to fight for their mother country in the two world wars this century. The major social institutions in Australia today, of government, law, education and social organization all display these origins. Indeed, while republican sentiment is currently growing strongly in the community, the British monarch is still the head of the Australian government.

Commencing in the post-Second World War period, a major shift in national identity occurred however, weakening ties with Britain. Defence links with the USA in the Pacific produced a recognition of regional realities and a retreat from a Europe-centered world view. Pride in essentially Australian characteristics and cultural achievements began to expand. Simultaneously, the burgeoning Western (predominantly USA) consumer culture was eagerly embraced, as the explosion of communication technology made it accessible to every home. Perhaps most importantly, the post-war immigration program pursued by the government produced major changes in the demographic makeup of the population. Initially European, then Middle Eastern, and, latterly, Asian settlers have arrived and begun the process of assimilation, bringing a variety of cultural traditions and practices that have broadened and enriched the Australian culture enormously. Australia now has, with the exception of Israel, the most ethnically heterogeneous workforce in the industrialized world (Galvin and West, 1988). Immigration now accounts for the major proportion of population growth.

Family and social issues

As might be expected in such a pluralist society, there exist a variety of value systems, family patterns and childrearing practices. However, in common with most Western cultures, the dominant factors influencing families today are the increase in women's independence and participation in the workplace, the sharp reduction in the birthrate and size of families and a big increase in the marriage breakup rate. It is a disturbing reality that the social structures that have protected childhood have been weakened and the community is groping to find their replacements. The frequently linked problems of drug abuse and homeless young people are growing, usually the fallout of family disintegration. The previously hidden issues of family violence and sexual abuse of children are now in the open and their prevalence is proving to be greater than formerly believed.

Considerable tension exists in Australian society as changing power relationships between men and women are worked out. While Australian governments have generally taken a lead in legislating against sexual discrimination and harassment in the workplace, sexist attitudes are still strong in the community. Distinctively different male and female subcultures still exist, though the gulf between the two is lessening. Women are still vastly underrepresented in positions of power and prominence in the society, and overrepresented in poverty situations, dependent on social welfare.

Politics and economy

Politically, Australia is a stable parliamentary democracy. It is a small capitalist economy, too long reliant on natural resources and primary production as its base, and currently undergoing major restructuring in the attempt to become more industrially competitive. This fact, coupled with the recent worldwide recession, has plunged Australia into the most severe economic conditions experienced in 60 years. Recovery now is slowly underway. Considerable hardship and distress have been experienced in the community as unemployment and business failures soared. The recession was just beginning when the data for this study was collected, in late 1989.

Education

While free universal education was achieved last century in Australia when state-funded school systems were put in place, the level of educational attainment of the population compares unfavorably with that of comparable industrialized nations. Strenuous efforts are being made to increase school retention rates, and the Commonwealth government has recently exercised tighter controls over the universities to ensure they focus on producing graduates with the skills to meet the nation's economic goals.

While universities are publicly funded and administered, at primary and secondary levels a system of private, fee-charging schools has been established, operating parallel to the public one, though receiving some funding from governments. Better equipped than government schools and drawing their pupils from the articulate, privileged upper middle classes, the products of these schools tend to dominate the prestigious university faculties and later the positions of power and influence in the community. Thus, it must be acknowledged that the education system in Australia makes an unfortunate contribution to the preservation of inequalities and the maintainance of social divisions.

National characteristics

Indeed, Australia is a highly unequal society, in direct contradiction to the national myth of egalitarianism that has been revered since early settlement. In the words of recent social commentators,

> "In Australia there are vast differences between rich and poor, between men and women, between different ethnic groups ... they extend across the whole range of socially desired resources, economic security and power, health

and general wellbeing, educational opportunity, positions of prestige and esteem within the wider society." (Galvin and West, 1988).

When invoked, the egalitarianism myth operates most unfortunately to enforce mediocrity. It provides justification for Australians to distrust and belittle high achievers or the pursuit of special excellence. This attitude acts to the national detriment in Australians' unwillingness to be seen to excell or to take credit for achievement lest they be criticized as setting themselves up as a "tall poppy." Its counterpoint is the popularity of the Australian caricature, the "larrikin," the outspoken disruptive common man who debunks authority and scorns achievement. "Larrikins see themselves as having a special mission to cut down 'tall poppies.'"

Another related national characteristic, frequently decried, is Australians' alleged generally relaxed attitude toward hard work and effort. This is well captured in the catchcry, "She'll be alright, mate," the caricatured national response to challenge. Australia has been dubbed "the land of the long weekend" (Conway, 1978), its workers being credited with achieving more paid leisure earlier than any other country in the world (Horne, 1987). Certainly there is a belief among economists that Australians are going to have to work harder if the country is to recover from its economic predicament. Perhaps this stereotypic view of the Australian worker was expressed a little more kindly by the historian Ward, "He is a great improvisor, ever willing to 'have a go' at anything, but willing to be content with a task done in a way that is 'near enough' ... He is one who endures stoically rather than one who acts busily" (Ward, 1958).

Professional counseling services

Professional counseling services are not widely provided in the Australian community, and most Australians are unlikely to consult professional counselors. The only exception is in the universities, where counseling services are almost routinely established as a measure designed to prevent wastage and preserve students in their courses. The effect is that university-attending young people are uniquely advantaged in comparison to their peers in the wider community. In the public school system, a pool of counselors is usually available centrally, to be called in by schools for crises. Schools in the private system are more likely to employ counselors on staff, creating another group of young people advantaged with respect to counseling. Educational counseling services are well used, indicating strongly positive attitudes among the groups who have access to them. In line with trends in other countries, females are more likely to use counseling services than males.

The Study and Its Methodology

Subjects: an "atypical group of Australians"

Initially, when this study was designed, the decision was taken to choose subjects who were second-generation citizens in order to ensure that cultural background was as similar as possible within each country of the study. In the Australian context, this decision resulted in the selection of subjects of almost exclusively Anglo-Celtic origins. As the earlier discussion indicated, this makes the group reported upon here anything but a currently "typical" group of Australians in terms of ethnic background. It is a defensible decision, however, as they are the group for whom current counseling models have been fashioned and who have to date been the main clients of counseling services in Australia. If there are in Australia longstanding attitudes toward problems and help-seeking in adolescents, they will be found in this group.

Subjects were selected in the age-group 13—15 years from a range of schools. Five high schools in Melbourne and two in Sydney were chosen with a view to sampling a wide spectrum of the metropolitan community. Three were state public schools, two were high-status, high-fee private schools and two were relatively moderate fee-charging private schools.

The subjects were rated "advantaged" or "nonadvantaged" on the basis of socioeconomic status, defined primarily as related to the education and occupation of parents. The parents of "advantaged" subjects held professional or educated white-collar positions. Those of the "nonadvantaged" were blue-collar workers, unemployed or dependent on social welfare. It needs to be stressed that in Australia the universal social security net ensures that no-one lives in dire poverty, i.e. unable to secure minimal necessary levels of food, clothing and shelter. As expected, the subjects' socioeconomic status conformed quite closely to school type. For example, no "nonadvantaged" subjects attended either of the two high-status private schools.

The sample reported here totalled 154 males (99 "advantaged" and 55 "nonadvantaged") and 137 females (59 "advantaged" and 78 "nonadvantaged").

Procedure

Data collection

Data were collected between September and November 1989. Students were surveyed in their class groups during school hours. Appropriate school authorities were requested to make available classes of grade 8 students, the level matching the age group sought. The entire class was surveyed and the protocols of subjects meeting the nationality criteria for this study selected out. (The responses of the other students in the classes, i.e. immigrants, form the basis of another study.)

The questionnaires were administered, using the standardized instructions developed by the ERT (Chapter 2). In Melbourne, the author administered the questionnaire. In Sydney, administration was performed by an experienced cross-cultural researcher.[2] Subjects were permitted to ask questions and seek extra guidance in completing the task. Care was taken to ensure that assistance given did not influence answers.

In some schools, considerable efforts were required to ensure that subjects engaged in the task at hand rather than taking refuge in disruptive behavior. It proved necessary to discard several questionnaires because they were completed facetiously or in collusion with other students. This problem was experienced predominantly with male students and seems to have been a good example of Australian male "larrikin" behavior.

Coding

The questionnaires were coded using the standardized instructions and guide developed for the study. The author and the Sydney researcher were both trained by the Pittsburgh group in the manner described in Chapter 2. In Melbourne, another coding assistant was employed and trained by the author. The training was achieved by both coding ten problems and associated responses independently and then discussing codes on which they diverged until a common understanding of the coding scheme was achieved. Interrater reliability as measured by the percentage of agreement on coded responses between the two Melbourne coders on fresh procotols showed that a level of 96% agreement for both classes and categories-within-classes was eventually achieved. Interrater reliability as determined by percentage of agreement on coded responses between the author-researcher and the Pittsburgh master code showed 94% of agreement for classes and 84% for categories-within-classes. The coded data were entered into the specially designed database and dispatched to the databank in Pittsburgh.

The Study Results

For problem and coping strategies, results are reported as percentages of responses coded into classes and categories. They are also reported as percentages of subjects coded into classes. For the other variables, results are reported in terms of classes of responses.

While the small size and limited nature of this sample of Australian adolescents precludes any claim for national representiveness or definitive conclusions, nevertheless their responses provide an intriguing snapshot of the attitudes toward problems and help-seeking of a group of young Australians. In broad terms they respond in ways similar to the rest of the adolescents around the world, supporting the key finding of the study—the universality and age-relatedness of adolescent difficulties. On the other hand, there are some differences apparent and it is of interest to study how these link with national characteristics previously described.

[2] Ilona Lee.

Problems

As Table 4.1 and Chapter 3 indicate, the Australian adolescents conformed closely to the multinational sample in reporting their major problems to be related to **schooling, family issues,** concerns about **personal identity** and **self-concept**. Some typical problems of Australian subjects included:

"... getting good grades, too much homework."

"My parents are separated and I found out they were both having affairs when they were married."

TABLE 4.1 *Australian study: percentages of total responses falling into classes and categories of problems*

(a) Classes

	Advantaged				*Nonadvantaged*			
	Male		*Female*		*Male*		*Female*	
	%	*Rank*	*%*	*Rank*	*%*	*Rank*	*%*	*Rank*
Poverty	0.0	(13)	0.0	(12)	0.0	(12)	0.5	(10.5)
War	0.4	(11.5)	0.0	(12)	0.7	(10)	0.0	(12.5)
Catastrophe	1.3	(10)	1.9	(9.5)	1.3	(8.5)	0.5	(10.5)
Material desires	3.0	(8)	0.0	(12)	7.2	(5)	3.3	(8.5)
Family issues	14.2	(3)	21.5	(3)	20.4	(2)	27.6	(1)
Schooling issues	39.9	(1)	22.8	(2)	36.8	(1)	20.6	(2)
Identity	18.9	(2)	25.3	(1)	15.8	(3)	17.8	(3)
Sexuality	1.7	(9)	3.2	(7)	0.0	(12)	3.7	(7)
Courtship/dating	6.4	(5)	5.1	(5)	3.9	(7)	5.1	(5)
Interpersonal	6.9	(4)	11.4	(4)	7.9	(4)	13.6	(4)
Emotions	3.4	(6.5)	2.5	(8)	0.0	(12)	3.3	(8.5)
Self-fulfilment	0.4	(11.5)	1.9	(9.5)	1.3	(8.5)	0.0	(12.5)
Altruism	3.4	(6.5)	4.4	(6)	4.6	(6)	4.2	(6)

(b) Categories

Advantaged male	*%*	*Advantaged female*	*%*
Academic failure	9.9	Friendship	8.9
Academic achievement	9.4	Behavioral issues	6.3
Friendship	5.6	Acad failure	6.3
Domestic quarrelling	5.2	Time pressure	5.1
Time pressure	5.2	School (other)	5.1
		Confidence	5.1
		Appearance	5.1
Nonadvantaged male		*Nonadvantaged female*	
Time pressure	7.2	Friendship	11.2
Academic failure	6.6	Time pressure	7.0
School (other)	6.6	Domestic quarrelling	5.6
Money	6.6	School (other)	5.6
Personal health	5.3	Divorce	5.1

* Representing 5% or more of responses.

"... pressure by friends to do things that are not good—like shoplifting."

"fear that my friends are just one big lie and none of their feelings are genuine."

Concerns about drugs, alcohol and suicide among peers were often described, corroborating the earlier observations concerning Australian social issues. Fortunately, extreme poverty, war and catastrophe seemed rarely to be in these adolescents' experience. As in the multinational sample, concerns about **sexuality** formed a low proportion of the total problems described (Table 4.1(a) and 4.1(b)). However, examination of the proportion of respondents reporting these concerns puts the issue in a different light, revealing stronger concern. Table 4.2 shows that one in ten of the "nonadvantaged" Australian girls (and 8.5% of the "advantaged") reported concerns about sexuality of which the following is typical:

"Well, I love my boyfriend very much and he loves me, but I wish we hadn't of had sex because I think the love would be much stronger."

Gender differences were similar to those found in the composite multinational sample, with "nonadvantaged" more than "advantaged" and females more than males in each SES group more likely to focus on **family** concerns. In the Australian sample, "advantaged" and males were also more likely to report **schooling** concerns. Australian females also focused more than their male counterparts on **identity** and friendship matters. They were also likely to report worries about confidence and physical appearance, frequently about wanting to lose weight.

TABLE 4.2 *Australian study: percentage of subjects whose responses fall into each class of problem*

	Advantaged				*Nonadvantaged*			
	Male		*Female*		*Male*		*Female*	
	%	*Rank*	*%*	*Rank*	*%*	*Rank*	*%*	*Rank*
Poverty	0.0	(13)	0.0	(11)	0.0	(11)	1.3	(10.5)
War	1.0	(11.5)	0.0	(11)	1.7	(10)	0.0	(12.5)
Catastrophe	3.1	(10)	5.1	(9.5)	3.4	(8.5)	1.3	(10.5)
Material desires	7.1	(8)	0.0	(11)	18.6	(5)	8.9	(8.5)
Family	33.7	(3)	57.6	(3)	52.5	(2)	74.7	(1)
Schooling issues	94.9	(1)	61.0	(2)	94.9	(1)	55.7	(2)
Identity	44.9	(2)	67.8	(1)	40.7	(3)	48.1	(3)
Sexuality	4.1	(9)	8.5	(7)	0.0	(11)	10.1	(7)
Courtship/dating	15.3	(5)	13.6	(5)	10.2	(7)	13.9	(5)
Interpersonal	16.3	(4)	30.5	(4)	20.3	(4)	36.7	(4)
Emotions	8.2	(6.5)	6.8	(8)	0.0	(11)	8.9	(8.5)
Self-fulfilment	1.0	(11.5)	5.1	(9.5)	3.4	(8.5)	0.0	(12.5)
Altruism	8.2	(6.5)	11.9	(6)	11.9	(6)	11.4	(6)

Coping strategies

With regard to coping strategies, a possible Australian trend is discernible. Table 4.3 sets out the percentages of responses related to coping strategies. While in common with the adolescents in the multinational sample (Chapter 3), the Australians reported **individual problem-solving** as their favored strategy. Like their peers in the multinational sample, Australian "advantaged" youth reported a higher percentage of **individual problem-solving** responses than their "nonadvantaged" peers, with males reporting this approach to coping more frequently than females in each SES group. Australian youngsters were unique in reporting **disengaging from the problem** as their number-two choice. Frequent disengaging responses to a wide range of reported problems included:

TABLE 4.3 *Australian study: percentages of total responses falling into classes and categories of coping strategies*

(a) Classes

	Advantaged				*Poverty*			
	Male		*Female*		*Male*		*Female*	
	%	*Rank*	*%*	*Rank*	*%*	*Rank*	*%*	*Rank*
Seek assistance	9.5	(5)	15.6	(2)	17.4	(3)	18.6	(2)
Interpersonal	9.9	(4)	14.2	(5)	12.4	(5)	10.4	(5)
Problem solve	38.4	(1)	36.3	(1)	34.8	(1)	36.1	(1)
Stress management	4.8	(6)	1.4	(6.5)	2.5	(6)	2.2	(6.5)
Crying	0.7	(8.5)	0.9	(8)	0.0	(8.5)	2.2	(6.5)
Religious	0.7	(8.5)	0.0	(9)	0.0	(8.5)	0.0	(9)
Resignation	13.6	(3)	15.1	(3.5)	18.6	(2)	13.0	(4)
Disengagement	19.4	(2)	15.1	(3.5)	13.7	(4)	16.4	(3)
Anti-social	3.1	(7)	1.4	(6.5)	0.6	(7)	1.1	(8)

*(b) Categories**

	Male		*Female*	
	Category	*%*	*Category*	*%*
Advantaged	Try harder	15.6	Seek support	13.7
	Planning	10.9	Try harder	12.3
	Psychological escape	9.9	Planning	10.8
	Behavioural escape	8.5	Assertive cope	9.9
	Seek support	8.5	Psychological escape	8.5
	Do nothing	6.1	Behavioural escape	6.1
Nonadvantaged	Try harder	17.4	Seek support	17.0
	Seek support	16.8	Planning	13.7
	Planning	10.6	Behavioural escape	10.0
	Behavioural escape	8.7	Try harder	8.1
	Do nothing	6.2	Psychological escape	5.9
	Give up	5.6	Assertive cope	5.9
			Do nothing	5.6

* Representing 5% or more of responses.

"Eat and watch TV."

"Do nothing."

"Forget about it."

"Smoke."

It is tempting to interpret this, together also with their high use of **resignation** ("There is nothing I can do about it") as an early acquisition by these young Australians of the "she'll be alright, mate" attitude to grappling with the vicissitudes of life. Unfortunately, "advantaged" Australian males, previously described as destined to be society's leaders, were particularly likely to report **disengagement** in preference to **interpersonal** or **seeking or giving assistance**

TABLE 4.4 *Australian study: percentages of total responses falling into classes and categories of coping strategies*

(a) Classes

	Advantaged				*Nonadvantaged*			
	Male		*Female*		*Male*		*Female*	
	%	*Rank*	*%*	*Rank*	*%*	*Rank*	*%*	*Rank*
Family	58.9	(1)	39.4	(2)	61.2	(1)	48.5	(1)
Non-family	34.6	(2)	53.5	(1)	32.6	(2)	45.9	(2)
Offender	1.4	(4)	1.3	(5)	1.0	(4)	1.4	(5)
Supernatural	0.4	(7)	0.5	(6)	0.0	(6.5)	0.6	(6)
Creatures	1.2	(5)	1.6	(4)	0.7	(5)	1.8	(3.5)
Non-specific	1.0	(6)	0.0	(7)	0.0	(6.5)	0.0	(7)
Nobody	3.0	(3)	3.7	(3)	4.6	(3)	1.8	(3.5)

(b) Categories

	Male		*Female*	
	Category	*%*	*Category*	*%*
Advantaged	Friend/classmate	23.1	Friend/classmate	41.4
	Mother	21.5	Mother	12.9
	Father	17.5	Sister	8.7
	Sister	6.3	Brother	6.3
	Teacher	6.1	Counselor	5.2
	Brother	4.7	Father	5.2
	Family (non-specified)	3.7	Family (non-specified)	3.4
	Counselor	1.4	Teacher	1.8
Nonadvantaged	Mother	22.7	Friend/classmate	32.8
	Friend/classmate	20.1	Mother	16.3
	Father	13.5	Sister	11.7
	Sister	7.2	Father	6.2
	Teacher	5.9	Counselor	4.0
	Brother	4.9	Family (non-specified)	3.6
	Family (non-specified)	3.9	Brother	3.6
	Counselor	2.3	Teacher	3.4

strategies reported more frequently by the females and "nonadvantaged" males. These reports of strong reliance on basically avoidant and non-productive strategies in coping with problems seem cause for some alarm.

Chosen helpers

Table 4.4 contains the data concerning classes of helpers chosen. The Australian responses were similar to those of the multinational sample (Chapter 3). When these adolescents sought helpers, **family members** constituted the largest class of helpers (Table 4.4(a)). However, in common with the multinational sample, "friends" were the preferred single category when compared with individual family members. Table 4.4(b) shows the percentages of responses for the most commonly chosen categories. "Mothers" were the second choice, rated well ahead of "fathers."

There do seem to be gender differences apparent in the Australian data that do not appear in the data provided in the multinational study. The males reported far more reliance on "mothers," and to a lesser degree on "fathers," than did the females. The females overwhelmingly described "friends" and "classmates" as confidants, well ahead of parents. They were also more likely than males to turn to their siblings for assistance, most often their "sisters." The picture that emerges is of very different interpersonal worlds developing for males and females at this early stage of adolescence. Females appear to be moving into a supportive same-sex peer subculture, while males are still looking to their parents for support. These differences occur in both socioeconomic groups and are perhaps indicative of the Australian divided gender cultures in formation.

"Teachers" and "counselors" were clearly important sources of help. While they both accounted for quite low percentages of the total number of responses identifying helpers, nevertheless they were nominated by a substantial number of subjects. Table 4.5 shows that more than 34% of "advantaged" girls and 25% of "nonadvantaged" girls identified "counselors" among their helpers while similar percentages of males identified teachers. On the other hand, an average of 10% of males identified "counselors" and 17% of females identified "teachers." The stronger tendency of the males to report **schooling** problems probably contributes to their stronger reliance on teachers.

TABLE 4.5 *Australian study: percentages of subjects whose responses fall into the categories of 'teacher' and 'counselor'*

	Advantaged		*Nonadvantaged*	
	Male	*Female*	*Male*	*Female*
Teacher	32.0	12.1	31.6	21.5
Counselor	7.2	34.5	12.3	25.3

TABLE 4.6 *Australian study: percentages of total responses falling into classes of desired helper qualities*

	Advantaged				Nonadvantaged			
	Male		Female		Male		Female	
	%	Rank	%	Rank	%	Rank	%	Rank
Powerful	4.6	(4)	1.9	(5)	10.6	(4)	5.3	(4)
Knowledgeable	26.7	(3)	25.8	(3)	36.9	(1)	26.5	(3)
Available	2.9	(5)	0.0	(6)	1.1	(6)	0.6	(6)
Personal qualities	27.5	(2)	30.7	(2)	17.9	(3)	33.0	(1)
Concern	36.5	(1)	37.5	(1)	29.6	(2)	32.1	(2)
Uncertain/no list	1.8	(6)	4.2	(4)	3.9	(5)	2.5	(5)

Preferred helper qualities

As Table 4.6 and Chapter 3 illustrate, the Australians reversed the order of the top three qualities sought in a helper as described by the multinational sample and displayed more interest in finding a helper demonstrating **concern for others** and **personal qualities** (particularly caring, understanding and good listening skills) and less interest in being **knowledgeable** (having a particular expertise).

Is this another indicator of a less solution-focused concern among Australians or even an unwillingness to engage with "tall poppies"? Socioeconomic grouping did appear to make a difference. "Nonadvantaged" males placed more importance on being **powerful** and **knowledgeable** in a helper. They were seeking a more efficacious person than were their "advantaged" peers. Overall, finding an emotionally responsive helper was more important to the "advantaged" young people.

Preferred modes of helping

Table 4.7 sets out the data showing how the Australian subjects would like to be helped. In common with the multinational sample (Chapter 3), the Australians' top two preferences were being **attended to** and **counseled**. Overall,

TABLE 4.7 *Australian study: percentages of total responses falling into classes of desired helping modes*

	Advantaged				Nonadvantaged			
	Male		Female		Male		Female	
	%	Rank	%	Rank	%	Rank	%	Rank
Direct need satisfaction	3.9	(5)	0.5	(7)	5.9	(4.5)	1.3	(7)
Exercise power	7.4	(4)	2.7	(5.5)	5.9	(4.5)	2.5	(5)
Intercede	3.0	(3)	2.7	(5.5)	3.0	(7)	2.1	(6)
Counsel	40.0	(1)	32.1	(2)	43.0	(1)	30.1	(2)
Attend to	27.8	(2)	43.3	(1)	23.7	(2)	49.8	(1)
Evade problem	2.2	(7)	4.3	(4)	3.7	(6)	4.6	(4)
Uncertain/no listing	15.7	(3)	14.4	(3)	14.8	(3)	9.6	(3)

however, they were less willing or able to articulate precisely how they would like to be helped. Given their relatively high use of **disengaging** strategies and the fact that this question occured toward the end of the questionnaire it is perhaps not surprising. When they did respond, they also displayed a lower preference for receiving such instrumental modes of assistance as **direct satisfaction of a need** or **exercise of power** on their behalf. In the context of the rest of their responses, unfortunately, this seems more suggestive of a retreat from strategies to address the problem at hand than evidence of a sturdy independent stance!

Some gender differences are apparent in the responses to this question: The females were particularly likely to seek to be comforted, reassured and understood, presumably what they are accustomed to receiving from their preferred peer group helpers. Males were more likely than females to seek advice, also congruent with their preference for parents and teachers as helpers. These gender differences conform with the findings of another Australian study on adolescent coping strategies which drew the conclusion that females seek and utilize social support as a coping mechanism and males are more likely to ask for advice (Frydenburg and Lewis, 1991).

Implications for Counseling in Australia

Coping with problems: from age-related issues to modern crises

This study has invited a group of Australian adolescents to give voice to the problems that concern them. Many that they described can be categorized as the expected age-related concerns of their developmental stage of life. Succeeding at school is an overwhelming concern. These young people are more fortunate than some of their peers from other countries in the study in that they report virtually no exposure to dire catastrophic circumstances or extreme poverty. However, there is cause for concern in the frequency with which problems of drug and alcohol abuse and suicide in their peer group are described. In sexual matters, the most frequently elaborated problem was the helplessness many of these adolescent girls felt in resisting pressures to become sexually active. Feminist empowerment has apparently not impacted on this group of Australian young women. Most noteworthy were the high number of stories of families in conflict reported, adolescents propping up their warring parents, while negotiating minefields of divided loyalties and relationships. An indisputable need for counseling assistance to assist with these problems is the first message from this study.

Changing "national attitudes"

The second is an urgent need to assist Australian adolescents to enlarge their repertoire of coping strategies. Australians would appear to be at a definite disadvantage in this regard. In particular, they need to replace the perhaps national characteristic of disengaging or lapsing into resignation in the face of difficulties with more instrumental strategies of seeing a problem through to solution or seeking the intervention of expert assistance. Again, perhaps they need to modify a national attitude of devaluing possessors of power and expertise, if they are to access helpers who can offer them these qualities. The necessity for training programs for adolescents in problem-solving and when and how to ask for help is a major implication of this study in Australia.

Teachers and counselors might well be the most appropriate people to provide this training. However, it would be surprising if Australian professionals were not limited by their cultural context in the same way as their students. Specific training for both professional groups in enlarging their awareness of problem-solving strategies is definitely indicated.

Given the perceived importance of teachers to this age-group, particularly for the males, it would seem important to increase teachers' counseling skills generally. If males are to be encouraged to make more use of help from both teachers and counselors, both groups should bear in mind their lower preference for emotionally expressive approaches compared with females, and amend their counseling approaches accordingly.

As peers are clearly such an important source of assistance for this age group, classroom exercises and discussions to increase awareness of an expanded range of strategies for managing and solving problems seems highly desirable. In this manner, educated adolescents might be helped to provide even more valuable assistance to others than the emotional support and understanding they currently seem to be providing so well. This seems particularly true for females. It would be very desirable, particularly, for young males to assist each other.

Conclusions

With a small sample such as the one in this study, it is possible only to hypothesize possible issues in counseling Australian adolescents. Nevertheless, if we are to listen to these young voices, intriguingly reflecting their cultural context, some conclusions seem unwise to ignore. More counseling assistance, expanded awareness of a wider range of coping strategies, improved training for helpers and supporters—all are essential if Australian adolescents' management of their problems is to be improved. These are the key implications of this study for the counseling profession in Australia. Perhaps there is a message here for improving the nation's prosperity as well. Consider what Australia might achieve if we were able to make ourselves a nation of expertise-valuers and problem-solvers and finally lay to rest "she'll be alright, mate!" One way to start is with our adolescents.

5

Brazil

ISAURA ROCHA FIGUEIREDO GUIMARÅES
Campinas State University
ELIZABETE MONTEIRO DE AGUIAR PEREIRA
University of Sao Carlos

A slum boy: "I'm afraid of being unemployed."

Marcela is fifteen years old. His father works as a garbage man. His mother has died. His father is illiterate. So was his mother.

"When I'm older I would like to be working in Campinas at the Xerox Company as a copy boy, as I do today. I don't want to go back to the northwest (of Brazil) where my family came from. And I don't want to be a robber or a 'bad' person who commits crimes.

"I'm afraid of being unemployed. I try to forget about this as much as possible and leave the problem to the future. I prefer to think about my girlfriend and to go out with her.

"When I worry too much, I talk with my father, my cousins and my oldest brother. They teach me what to do and do their best to make things easier for me. They give me information. They guide me.

"My wishes? Just to be alive, to be married to someone I love and to be able to work."

Introduction: The Country and the Culture

National characteristics

Known as the "giant of South America," Brazil occupies 48% of that continent and is the fourth largest nation in the world. Its major regions each represent a distinct aspect of ethnic, historical, economic, political and cultural heritage

(Brazilian Institute for Geography and Statistics, 1992). Brasilia, the new capital in the central portion of the country, was constructed in 1960 in the best position to link the 24 Brazilian states, preserve unity and overcome regionalism. Our research on adolescents was conducted in Campinas, a city in the southeast state of Sao Paulo known for its industrial, commercial and cultural activities.

Brazil has a preponderance of young people: 38% of the population is under 14 years of age and 67% under age 29 (UNICEF, 1992). Although life expectancy has been increasing gradually, it is still below that of industrialized countries.

Brazilians represent a mix of ethnicities and races with the strongest influences coming from Portuguese, Indians and Blacks. Although Brazilian history is often described as having been free of racial discrimination, Ianni (1987) and others have pointed out that Blacks are more predominantly impoverished and less able to obtain adequate education or other social benefits than other Brazilians. Irregardless, African influence remains strong in Brazilian culture today, as seen especially in its music, religious rituals and literature.

Brazil's history of financial crisis

Since the First World War, Brazil has passed repeatedly through booms and financial crises. Immediately following the First World War, its average gross domestic product was one of the highest in the world. In the next 40 years, massive foreign investment helped continue its growth. Between the late 1970s and 1980s, however, increased petroleum prices and interest rates, coupled with cuts in financial flow to developing countries, led to a series of crises that Brazilians refer to as the "lost decade."

Brazil's per capita income now ranges from US$800 in the Northeast to US$ 4000 in the Southeast (*Annual Bulletin of the Mercantile Gazette*, 1994). Many Brazilians count on MERCOSUL (agreement for a Latin American common market) to improve the economy (Kanitz, 1994). In the meantime, Brazil remains one of the world's major food exporters and agriculture is the main source of the Brazilian economy. The area already cultivated for grain production is enormous, even at 56% of potential at the beginning of the decade (*Guide to Brazilian Economy*, 1991).

Politics and political problems

Brazil's legal political system is, today, a democracy with an elected president. With two long periods of dictatorship having ended only in 1988, however, the country is still struggling to create a true democratic government. There is general agreement that, to succeed, the elected government must improve the quality of life of its citizens. It will be a massive task to provide adequate housing, improve health conditions, make education accessible to all and reform both the judicial and taxation system. It is widely feared that the failure to do so will lead to increased political violence, crime and narcotics trafficking.

Religion

The Roman Catholic Church is one of the genuinely national institutions. Until the 1980s, some 90% of Brazilians declared themselves Catholic, a religiosity measured by the respect enjoyed by the church rather than by church attendance. Recent surveys have shown, however, that middle-class Brazilians are no longer so comfortable with Catholic doctrines, complaining primarily of restrictions on "modern" approaches to sex life such as contraception, abortion, sex before marriage, etc. as well as on divorce (Revista Veja, 1990). Pentecostal, Protestant and Spiritual churches are attracting growing numbers of converts annually. "Folk Catholicism," heavily influenced by African cults and the local religious habits of the back lands, continues to dominate the faith outside the large coastal cities.

Education and educational problems

Illiteracy, dropoutism and school failure are high in Brazil when compared either to developed or other Latin American countries. In 1990, the illiteracy rate was 18.5% (Brazilian Institute for Geography and Statistics, 1992; Jatoba, 1994).

The Brazilian education system includes eight years of elementary school and three of secondary school as well as college programs through doctoral degrees. Although the eight elementary school years are compulsory, however, only 39% of Brazilians actually complete eighth grade; the highest percentage of children leaving school early come from lower SES groups (Brazilian Institute for Geography and Statistics, 1992). There is, today, major concern regarding the increasingly large number of children and youth, especially among poverty populations, who fail or leave school—and agreement that the country's economic crisis will continue until it can provide both its poor and middle classes opportunities to develop the skills necessary to become useful citizens (Werebe, 1994).

Families and childrearing

The family plays a more important role in Brazilian society than in most "non-Latin" countries. The basic family unit has gradually evolved in the past 25 years or so from an extended family group of several generations to a nuclear unit of parents and children only (Brazilian Institute for Geography and Statistics, 1992). Among families in poverty communities, female-headed households with closely related families living in the same immediate vicinity and forming extended kin residence areas are common. This is particularly true in small towns or rural areas. Within all social classes, the most important family relationship exists between mothers and their children. Fathers tend to remain somewhat distant (Dauster, 1988). Brazilian youth generally remain at home until they marry.

While some young people today are adopting informal unions referred to as "living together" without formal ritual, marriage is celebrated by both civil and religious ceremonies for most. Divorce is a recent alternative, first permitted in the early 1970s, since which time its rate has grown annually. The new generation of young women differ from their mothers in seriously planning for careers. Among the lower classes, females begin working in their teenage years and in the upper classes they seek university education to enhance career opportunities.

Youth from "advantaged" families tend to be less interested than previous generations in power and money and more concerned with quality of life and fun. Known as "grunges" or "shopping center people," many spend their free time in the new shopping centers meeting with friends (Pompeu, 1990; Silveira, 1992). Their "poverty" peers, who enter the work force earlier, spend more time helping their families and working to gain needed money.

Counseling and guidance

"Counseling" and "guidance" have special meanings in Brazilian education. The latter term describes a process of assisting in instruction through placing students in programs appropriate to their abilities, teaching of study techniques, assisting in career planning, providing disciplinary intervention, etc. These services are provided by professionals who may or may not be trained in the processes involved in "counseling." The "true" counseling process, by contrast, refers to the process of helping others adjust to critical situations and doing so in intimate ways, touching the privacy of individuals in order to help them. This type of counseling is provided by psychologists and psychotherapists.

Brazilian counseling had its beginnings in the 1920s when the concept was imported from the US and Europe and expanded to meet the nation's public school needs (Grinspun, 1987). During the next four decades, counselors worked at assessing student abilities for placement purposes, making student needs, interests, aptitudes, abilities and attitudes—and standardized tests—important parts of a process designed to teach life skills to Brazil's impoverished. In the 1960s, the Brazilian government began actively encouraging educators to combat "negative influences of cultural privation" on learning. At the same time, official documents began referring to "educative guidance" and "assessment of vocational aptitudes" as important priorities.

Many Brazilian counselors question whether it is appropriate for school counselors to take on the role of helping others in their intimate lives. The feeling is that such an approach is elitist in that it directs the counselor's work to individual clients rather than the social causes of students' problems. Counselors taking this position suggest that a more appropriate use of counseling would involve curricular planning together with a participative role in school administrative decision-making, the ultimate goal being the improvement of education for the massive poor population. During the current critical economic recession, however, counselors unfortunately find that they are needed to provide day-to-day intervention for stress-related crises before taking on other tasks.

Research devoted to learning among poverty populations suggests both that characteristics such as self-esteem and self-awareness are important to the learning process and that socially improved conditions increase learning. At the same time that guidance counselors defend the value of increasing autonomy, independence and freedom for the future citizens of a democratic Brazil, however, phenomenological theorists argue that the "self" is the core for creating change. The authors of this study take the approach that the ultimate goal of counseling should be a joining of these two approaches in which counselors are permitted to help youngsters better their own personal lives and, at the same time, assist them to reach greater social goals of the country.

The Study and Its Methodology

Subjects

Two groups of 13—15 year olds from "advantaged" and "poverty" backgrounds were used in this study.

"Advantaged" subjects

The 224 "advantaged" youngsters (94 males and 130 females) came from middle- and upper-class backgrounds and attended three private schools located in residential areas situated 10—15 km from the center of the city. Children were transported to school in their parents' cars or by car pool or school bus. All schools have adequate facilities in attractive settings, with main buildings surrounded by green grass and large spaces provided for sports and recreation. The buildings include reception areas, administrative offices, large numbers of suitable classrooms and ample corridors and stairways. They have modern equipment, including video systems and computers. All have libraries. Students remain in school for four to five hours daily, so refectories are not needed; it is usual to carry or buy a snack in the school's bar. Both counseling and guidance services are provided with waiting rooms, small counseling rooms and multiple purpose rooms. Each school employs from two to six full-time counselors.

"Advantaged" subjects usually live with their families: mother, father and siblings. The majority of their parents have attended college and are well employed with good salaries. Fathers' professions include medicine, engineering, law, entrepreneurial, administration, academia, dentistry, banking and industrial management. The majority of mothers are housewives; many have college educations. Those who are employed outside the home include secretaries, teachers, librarians, lawyers, entrepreneuses, administrators, professors and authors. Family economic level is usually high, with most families possessing two cars, many household appliances, more than one tv, video, computer, "high tech" electronic sound, etc. They spent vacations on the beach once or twice per year and may travel abroad. The average annual income is approximately US$30 000 (*Newspaper on Economy*, 1994/5). The proportion of Black students in this group was approximately 1%.

"Poverty" subjects

The 65 "poverty" subjects (34 males and 31 females) live under hardship conditions and meet the requirements for "poverty" of the multinational sample, although they are not the "poorest of the poor" in Brazil. (The most impoverished students are not in school, being required to work at early ages (Cheniaux, 1988).) Our subjects attended public schools in old buildings situated in areas close to industrial complexes that were of poor condition and whose classrooms were overcrowded. Most buildings were surrounded by barriers designed to withstand attempts by delinquents to destroy them.

Parents of "poverty" subjects have low levels of education; many are illiterate. When employed, they work at the lowest paying jobs. They do not own their residences, which are in impoverished neighborhoods where there is no sewerage, running water or electric power. They manage with minimal medical care. Fathers, when employed, work as truck drivers, construction workers, waiters or clerical workers. The majority of mothers, whose levels of education are lower than fathers, are housewives. Those employed outside their home work as household servants, nurse attendants or saleswomen. The average annual income is approximately US$1500. Transportation is a major problem for "poverty" families with no automobiles and homes often 10—15 km from their work places. "Fortunate" "poverty" children spend 1—2$^1/_2$ hours on buses each day, going to work or to school; "Less fortunate" youngsters walk 3—4 km each day to reach their destinations. Leisure activities include folk festivals such as carnival and other traditional fests they can commemorate in the streets.

The small size of the "poverty" sample (N = 65) is due to the difficulty of collecting data in public schools: In some cases, public school administrators refused to permit the surveys to be conducted. In others, students did not complete the questionnaires properly so that their responses could not be used. (In one session, 50% of the completed questionnaires had to be thrown out.)

Procedure

Data collection

The Brazilian data was collected in the first semester of 1990. Questionnaires were translated into Portuguese at the University and administered in classrooms, taking approximately 40 minutes per session. Students were told the purpose of the project and were requested to answer the items on the questionnaires by themselves. Three trained researchers collected responses of "advantaged" youngsters in the private schools; Prof. Guimaraes surveyed the "poverty" youngsters in a public school.

Coding and analysis of data

Coding was accomplished by the procedures used for the multinational study (Chapter 2). Coded data was reported in terms of percentages of subjects' responses to classes and category-within-classes as described in that chapter. Interrater reliability, as described in Chapter 2 and reported in Appendix III, was .80 for classes and .89 for categories-within-classes.

Results and Discussion

The responses of both groups of Brazilian youngsters are compared in this chapter with the responses of their multinational peers. In addition, the responses of "advantaged" Brazilian youngsters are compared with those of "poverty" youngsters and the responses of males are compared with females within each SES group.

Brazilians and their multinational peers: similarities and differences in problems and coping

Table 5.1 and Chapter 3 show that, while the reported problems of Brazilian adolescents are frequently similar to those of their multinational counterparts, they differ at the same time in intriguing ways. For example, while both studies show that most frequently reported problems are related to **schooling, family** and **personal identity/self-concept**, usually in that order, "advantaged" Brazilians gave the highest single percentage of responses to **personal identity/self-concept**. While Brazilian "advantaged" youngsters reported fewer **family** problems than "poverty" youngsters, with "poverty" females reporting the highest percentage of **family** problems of any group, "advantaged" females reversed the multinational trend by reporting the lowest percentage.

Our subjects also did not show the trends reported by the multinational study regarding **schooling** problems. Although males within both Brazilian SES samples reported a higher percentage of problems related to **schooling**; within the "poverty" sample, this difference was enormous, with 44% of male responses and only 2% of female responses related to **schooling**. A typical "poverty" male described his problem:

> "I worry about school because I want to be an educated person in the future ... nobody knows what can happen tomorrow ..."

How might we interpret the gender difference? While, at first glance, one might assume that the low reporting of school concerns by impoverished females

TABLE 5.1 *Brazilian study: percentages of total responses falling into classes and categories of problems*

(a) Classes

	Advantaged				Poverty			
	Male		Female		Male		Female	
	%	Rank	%	Rank	%	Rank	%	Rank
Extreme poverty	1.0	(10.5)	—	—	—	—	—	—
War	1.0	(10.5)	0.7	(9)	—	—	—	—
Catastrophe	—	—	0.4	(10)	—	—	2.3	(7.5)
Material desires	1.0	(10.5)	1.4	(8.5)	5.6	(5.5)	4.5	(5.5)
Family issues	17.6	(3)	13.0	(3)	22.2	(2)	31.8	(1)
Schooling issues	25.6	(2)	17.0	(2)	44.0	(1)	2.3	(7.5)
Identity	26.3	(1)	37.5	(1)	11.1	(3.5)	15.9	(4)
Sexuality	1.9	(10.5)	1.4	(8.5)	—	—	—	—
Courtship/dating	2.9	(7)	8.7	(5)	5.6	(5.5)	4.5	(5.5)
Interpersonal	9.3	(4)	9.4	(4)	—	—	18.2	(2.5)
Emotions	2.0	(8)	—	—	—	—	—	—
Self-fulfilment	6.3	(5.5)	2.5	(7)	11.1	(3.5)	2.3	(7.5)
Altruism	6.3	(5.5)	7.9	(6)	—	—	18.2	(2.5)

*(b) Categories**

	Advantaged		Poverty	
	Category	%	Category	%
Male	Self-confidence	11.7	Academic failure	22.2
	Growing up	8.8	Time pressure	11.1
	Friendship	8.3	Inability to learn	11.1
	Academic achievement	7.8	Growing up	11.1
	Failure	7.8	Divorce/separation	11.1
	Time pressure	5.9	Welfare of family	11.1
			Good and evil	11.1
Female	Self-confidence	15.2	Growing up	11.4
	Growing up	13.7	Divorce/separation	11.4
	Friendship	9.4	Friendship	11.4
			World poverty	6.8

* Representing 5% or more of responses.

means that they are simply not interested in school, the authors' experience suggests that these females are actually better adjusted to school than their male counterparts. However, since almost none go on to further studies regardless of how well they do, it may be that they do not consider education as a serious factor affecting their futures and, for this reason, they do not discuss school concerns.

Female lack of reported concern regarding **schooling** might also be due to greater concern about other problems:

> "My main problem is with my family and life. I am afraid to be without house, food, school because many people outside are going to the streets, without food ..."

"If I don't struggle to help my parents, they may die and it can be heavy in my conscience because they depend on me. It can remain in my head as if I killed somebody."

In fact, the problems most frequently reported by "poverty" females dealt with **family issues**. This was followed by **interpersonal problems** and **altruism**, concerns that are no doubt exacerbated by the economic and social pressures on their lives.

Brazilian females, like their counterparts around the world, are more concerned about relationships than males and are given far more responsibility regarding their families. Categories-within-classes of responses chosen by "poverty" females reflect these gender-related concerns, with problems most frequently related to friendship, divorce, separation and family welfare. "Poverty" males, by contrast, who tend to believe that education is important if they are to change their lives in positive ways, evidenced strong preoccupation with academic failure.

"School is a problem for me because in my house is a mess ... they make such a noise fighting ... my parents, my uncle and my grandmother, that I have to go to a friend's house to study. Besides that, I don't understand much what the teachers say."

In comparison to the "poverty" subjects of this study, "advantaged" youngsters expressed a great deal of concern with problems regarding **personal identity and self-concept**. This group appears to have been affected greatly by family pressure to succeed. An upper-class girl put it this way:

"My problem is feeling confidence in myself. My parents keep stressing me with charges. I become depressed, but then I hold my head up and work hard to succeed."

Coping strategies

Considering the coping strategies of our Brazilian adolescents (Table 5.2) as well as the coping strategies of adolescents in the multinational sample (Chapter 3), it appears that adolescents generally seek solutions for their problems on their own and look for others to help only when they are not successful. The words of an "advantaged" adolescent:

"When I have a problem, I talk to my pillow, I swallow it quietly ... I keep it for myself until I find a light."

As Table 5.2 shows, **individual problem-solving** strategies such as planning toward a solution and trying harder were cited by the majority of both "advan-

TABLE 5.2 *Brazilian study: percentages of total responses falling into classes and categories of coping strategies*

(a) Classes

	Advantaged				*Poverty*			
	Male		*Female*		*Male*		*Female*	
	%	*Rank*	%	*Rank*	%	*Rank*	%	*Rank*
Seek/give assistance	5.8	(4)	10.8	(4)	19.4	(2)	10.5	(3)
Interpersonal	9.1	(2.5)	9.7	(5)	6.5	(5)	15.7	(2)
Individual problem solving	69.3	(1)	54.4	(1)	45.2	(1)	46.4	(1)
Stress management	1.2	(6)	1.3	(6)	—	—	3.9	(7)
Crying	—	—	.8	(7.5)	—	—	2.6	(8)
Religious	—	—	.8	(7.5)	—	—	5.2	(6)
Resignation	9.1	(2.5)	10.8	(3)	16.1	(3)	6.5	(5)
Disengage	5.5	(5)	11.0	(2)	12.9	(4)	9.2	(4)
Anti-social	—	—	.8	(7.5)	—	—	—	—

*(b) Categories**

	Advantaged		*Poverty*	
	Category	%	*Category*	%
Male	Planning	33.1	Planning	22.6
	Try harder	20.5	Reframing	22.6
			Seek support	19.4
			Psychological distancing	12.9
			Giving up	12.9
Female	Planning	24.6	Planning	17.0
	Try harder	14.6	Try harder	11.1
	Seek support	9.3	Psychological/distancing	9.2
	Psychological/distancing	8.7	Assertive cope	7.8
			Reframing	6.5
			Seek support	5.2

* Representing 5% or more of responses.

taged" and "poverty" males. These strategies were mentioned less frequently by females than males.

Interpersonal problem-solving and **seeking or giving assistance** followed, with the seeking support from others the most frequently reported category-within-a-class. This was true for both "advantaged" and "poverty" groups and for both genders.

The Brazilian data does not suggest the gender trend noted in the multinational study regarding **individual problem-solving** as a coping strategy, although "advantaged" subjects reported a higher percentage of this type of coping strategy than "nonadvantaged" youngsters. The data suggest only a few gender differences as regards coping: Females report crying and praying, strategies not reported by males.

> "When things don't work well, I feel a desire to revolt ... then I ask God to free me from that, so I pray, I sing, I do exercises, I talk to somebody."

Helpers

In contrast to their multinational peers, Brazilian adolescents selected their mothers as helper first and personal friend second (Table 5.3 and Chapter 3) in contrast to the subjects in the multinational study who chose friends before their mothers. This reinforces our previous comments on the closeness of family relations within Brazilian culture, especially the dyadic relationship between mother and child. Brazilian reliance on **family** is evidenced in the majority of responses of all groups.

The words of a poor adolescent:

> "I would look for my mother because, although she has nothing to give me [materially] ... she is older, she has experienced life, so she can give me a word, she can show me the way ..."

TABLE 5.3 *Brazilian study: percentages of total responses falling into classes and categories of desired helpers*

(a) Classes

	Advantaged				*Poverty*			
	Male		*Female*		*Male*		*Female*	
	%	*Rank*	*%*	*Rank*	*%*	*Rank*	*%*	*Rank*
Family	68.0	(1)	53.2	(1)	51.1	(1)	55.9	(1)
Non-family	27.2	(2)	40.9	(2)	48.9	(2)	36.3	(2)
Offender	0.8	(5)	—	—	—	—	1.0	(4)
Supernatural	—	—	0.3	(5)	—	—	1.0	(4)
Creatures/objects	—	—	0.9	(4)	—	—	—	—
Non-specific	1.6	(5)	—	—	—	—	1.0	(4)
Nobody	2.4	(3)	4.7	(3)	—	—	20.8	(3)

*(b) Categories**

	Advantaged		*Poverty*	
	Category	*%*	*Category*	*%*
Male	Father	22.5	Mother	17.8
	Mother	22.1	Personal friend	15.6
	Schoolmate	7.7	Gangmate	15.6
	Personal friend	6.9	Brother	13.3
	Parents/family	5.3	Schoolmate	8.9
Female	Mother	21.2	Personal friend	10.8
	Personal friend	15.2	Aunt	8.8
	Father	10.6	Mother	7.5
	Gangmate	8.9	Father	6.9
	Parents/family	6.8	Grandmother	5.9
	Sister	5.9	Teacher	5.9
	Schoolmate	5.0		

* Representing 5% or more of responses.

TABLE 5.4 *Brazilian study: percentages of total responses falling into classes and categories of desired helper qualities*

(a) Classes

	Advantaged				*Poverty*			
	Male		*Female*		*Male*		*Female*	
	%	*Rank*	*%*	*Rank*	*%*	*Rank*	*%*	*Rank*
Powerful	4.2	(4)	4.6	(4)	—	—	2.7	(5)
Knowledgeable	34.8	(1)	35.8	(1)	60.0	(1)	43.6	(1)
Available	2.3	(5)	1.7	(5)	—	—	1.3	(6)
Personal qualities	32.7	(2)	24.2	(3)	2.0	(3)	21.5	(3)
Concern	25.5	(3)	31.8	(2)	30.0	(2)	24.2	(2)
Uncertain	—	—	1.0	(6)	—	—	—	—
No listing	0.5	(6)	1.0	(7)	7.5	(4)	6.7	(4)

*(b) Categories**

	Advantaged		*Poverty*	
	Category	*%*	*Category*	*%*
Male	Understanding	12.1	Experienced	20.0
	Experienced	11.6	Content area knowledge	15.0
	Supportive	8.4	Understanding	15.0
	Trustworthy	6.0	Supportive	15.0
	Caring	5.1	Similarity	10.0
			Gives advice	5.0
			Caring	5.0
			Intelligent	5.0
Female	Understanding	15.9	Experienced	13.4
	Experienced	11.9	Similarity	13.4
	Caring	9.2	Gives advice	11.4
	Supportive	6.7	Supportive	9.4
	Mature	5.4	Understanding	8.1
			Caring	6.7

* Representing 5% or more of responses.

Most frequently reported desirable helper qualities included being **knowledgeable**, being **concerned** about others and possessing **personal qualities** such as experience and understanding, similar in general to those reported in the multinational study (Table 5.4 and Chapter 3). Adolescents in both the Brazilian and multinational studies reported that they most desired being **counseled** or **attended to**.

Conclusions

The important needs of Brazil's poor

We have surveyed both "advantaged" and "poverty" youngsters in this study, but emphasize our results here primarily in terms of what we found regarding our "poverty" population. The reason is that this group represents a significant and growing portion of the Brazilian population today in dire need of educational opportunity, health care, adequate nutrition and assistance in developing the skills needed for their and their country's progress. The fact that little help is currently available to meet these needs poses a major threat to Brazil citizens of all socioeconomic groups today.

Today, most of Brazil's impoverished youth who have homes have been fulltime workers since they were between 10 and 14 years old. In 1994, this population, when it worked fulltime, earned a quarter of the minimum guaranteed salary: US$40 per month! The country today faces a "street boy" phenomenon in its large cities: adolescents with no homes who have come to live in slums and earn their living by begging, robbing, assaulting and trafficking in drugs (Fischer-Ferreira, 1980).

The rise in poverty is not likely to stop with this generation. It has been estimated that 15% of the one million births a year in Brazil are from mothers 15—19 years of age, some 60% of whom live in families whose per capita income is less than half Brazil's minimum salary (Brazilian Institute for Geography and Statistics, 1992; Takiuiti, 1990). For today's impoverished adolescents as well as for those youngsters who will follow them, the universal and predictable problems related to their stage of development are increased by the contradictions offered in their lives: They will be obliged to choose between school and work at very early ages; they will have no realistic chance to succeed in school because of their circumstances and therefore will be unable to develop viable skills needed to improve their own lives. Without changing these conditions, the cycle of poverty will necessarily continue.

Creating change through counseling

To play a role in creating needed change, the counseling profession must first take note of its absence in the public schools that are the sole source of teaching viable skills needed by the poor. It is not surprising that our "poverty" youngsters showed little awareness of the help that counselors are able to provide or that they turned to their parents for assistance. It is ironic, however, that this group also noted the importance of knowledge in finding solutions to the problems that their parents were unable to solve.

It is important in this regard to discuss the perceived importance of schooling for our "poverty" males. While these adolescents perceive school as a means of increasing socioeconomic mobility, they must struggle far more than their "advantaged" peers in order to obtain education. They are under double pressures because of both the economic needs of their families and their own difficulties in following their school programs. This population would benefit heavily from a variety of counseling programs to help them deal with their stressors as well as to teach them learning skills.

Expectations for the future

Recently, a Brazilian magazine surveyed 600 adolescents aged 11—14 years from different regions of the country and asked what they viewed as their personal goals and expectations regarding quality of life for themselves as well as what they expected for the nation's political future (Almeida, 1993). The answers were pessimistic, focusing on the low quality of life, urban violence, poverty, pollution, corruption, drugs, ecological problems, abandoned children, kidnapping, corrupt politicians and inflation and unemployment as their major concern. A significant number of respondents reported that they had no belief that Brazil has a positive political future. However, when they discussed their own personal goals, they revealed traditional dreams: Improving society, earning money, having professional careers, marrying and raising families, becoming famous, preserving nature and improving the nation's judicial, political and economic systems. Brazilian adolescents still have some hope, creating the seeds for the work of counselors and academic teachers.

Using schools to "free the oppressed"

Paulo Freire (1983) described education as the means by which a nation may free its oppressed. To contribute to this goal, educators must begin by teaching that the nation's poor are human beings rather than "things" to be explored, used and considered incapable of learning and being loved. By enabling the impoverished to reach their human goals, education, in this sense, is "reinventing power" and creating a society in which human rights for all can be respected. To respond to Freire's challenge, counselors must utilize a constructivist approach, setting goals that free their clients from fear of their future, make them aware of their own self-value and, at the same time, free them of their own social prejudices. We believe that counselors need to go beyond concrete reality to accomplish these goals and agree with Freire that, to do so, we must "reinvent" with our clients the traditional dreams and perspectives that challenge injustices and respect human rights. If counselors play a role in enabling all Brazilian children to obtain education and to learn how to succeed in school, a major step will have been accomplished.

6

The People's Republic of China[1]

FANNY SUN

Allegheny Community College

JANICE GIBSON-CLINE

University of Pittsburgh

"I don't want to be someone who doesn't work hard for my country."

Her name is **Liyun**. She is fifteen years old and attends a Beijing middle school, *not* a Key school. Liyun's father had a high school education and works as a salesman; her mother, who graduated from elementary school, is a kindergarten teacher.

"When I think of what I will be doing ten years from now, I hope I will be a fashion designer. I don't want to be someone without a career who does not work hard for my country. I don't want to become a burden for the country.

"I worry a lot these days about young people ... Some of them do not treasure their opportunity to a free education. They only want to make money and to date. Many break the school rules; I do not, and I try to talk with those who do, so I can make them realize their mistakes.

"When I have problems myself, the only people I talk to about them are my best friends. Since we are about the same age, I can open up my heart to them without worrying that I will say wrong things. When we talk together, they comfort me. I wouldn't like them to take my worries lightly and they don't. My friends and I share the same worries. Our relationship is equal.

"If I could have three wishes come true? First I would wish for students to have a chance to take school examinations more than once. Then they could choose the best one. I think that the teachers would find out that way that there are many talented students.

"Second, I would wish for my teachers and my parents to be more like my best friends, so we could discuss things and I wouldn't always have just to listen to their lectures all the time ...

"I would also like to have more surveys of this type. Why? So I can say what I want about my feelings without worrying."

[1] The data for this study was collected by Xuan Shen.

Introduction

The Chinese study reports the results of surveys of Chinese young people who grew up in Beijing, an inland city in the northern portion of the socialist Peoples' Republic of China.

Characteristics of an ancient society

The Peoples' Republic of China (PRC), of which Beijing is the capital, is the world's most populous nation today with more than 1.2 billion people and 960 000 sq.km of land (Qu and Li, 1994). A feudal clan society for most of its 2000 year history, China entered the twentieth century impoverished. Following a series of calamitous wars and other disasters in the first half of this century, the nation found itself unable to provide adequately for its people. Massive upheaval followed throughout the country, ultimately bringing the 1949 Chinese revolution and the current socialist government whose goal it was to redistribute wealth to the starving masses through centralized control of all resources and manpower. What followed changed the lives of those living in China irreparably.

Despite limitations on personal freedom dictated by the PRC government since 1949, the Chinese people living in mainland China continue honoring their families, revering education and boasting of their history of scholarly thought. Even the efforts of the infamous Cultural Revolution of 1966—76 to remove cultural tradition through the closing of formal education programs and punishment of all behavior and thinking deemed inappropriate in a socialist country, did not change this tradition. The Chinese cultural legacy remains, regardless of whether Chinese live in mainland China as citizens of the PRC or have left their homeland to build lives elsewhere.

As a people, the Chinese tend to be characterized alternately as industrious but conservative; valiant but submissive (Gao, 1987). They are regarded as intensely private, placing strong value on beliefs developed over more than 2000 years. Referring to the intensity of the Chinese culture, an American writer once commented that, although it is possible for people to go to China, they can never become Chinese.

The Chinese family

The Chinese family was, historically, a large extended unit. It was self-sufficient, containing as many as 3—4 generations of family members living and working together in the same household at both production and consumption functions suited to the small scale production of feudalism. In most cases, women were in charge of domestic duties and men of outside activities. Chinese society has always been patriarchal, with the family line carried on only by descendants on the father's side and with only male offspring belonging to the clan community (Gao, 1987).

In present-day PRC, increased industrialization has diminished both the productive capacity and feasibility of large multigenerational family units. Approximately 90% of the country remains agricultural, and large extended families remain together today in some rural areas where they still serve economic purposes such as providing care for very young and old family members. In cities, other family configurations predominate, including nuclear families (husband, wife and unmarried children) as well as joint families (two or more nuclear families that include two generations or the nuclear families of siblings) and incomplete families (one spouse has died or is absent, or unmarried orphans live together) (Xiaotong, 1982).

At least 65% of Beijing residents now live in nuclear families (Ying, L. 1985; Women of China, 1987). This percentage might be higher were it not for the severe housing shortage in the PRC that makes it difficult for new young families to find ways to develop households. Even though young adults are establishing their own households independent of their extended families, however, they continue to find ways to retain their close kinship ties, with different generations relying on one another for support. This is part of their legacy.

Life within the family

One can learn much about Chinese family life today from the structure of the traditional Chinese home. Constructed of high walls that separated house and garden from the outside world with only rooftops visible from beyond, the home was private to all but family members. Within its confines, however, there was little privacy. Rooms were arranged in sequence similar to the cars of a train, one leading into the next, so that it was impossible to close a door on any family member or to have secrets from one another (Hsu, 1981, pp. 78—9). All those aspects of family life kept secret from outsiders were shared by each and every family member (Baker, 1979, pp. 1—21). (It is indicative of Chinese culture that the Chinese word for "privacy" alludes to domestic insulation from the outside world.)

With family members sharing work, grandparents often assumed responsibility for childrearing, as well as teaching family history and appropriate ways to behave. They served as the initial source of socialization, a process through which children learned not to ask questions or to have personal opinions, but to value kinship and hold the family, especially the elders, in esteem (Hsu, 1981). Children learned early to behave respectfully and obediently. They also learned that they represented the entire family rather than themselves in everything they said and did (Baker, 1979, pp. 26—8).

Today, in Beijing, grandparents still serve frequently as initial teachers of the next generation. In modern times, however, they rear their grandchildren while their daughters or daughter-in-laws work outside the home. The traditional ethical code that has always governed Chinese parent—child relationships is founded on reciprocal duty and the right of caring and being cared for. Parents take care of their children, and children, in turn, are expected to take care of their aged parents. This is true today, as it has been for some 2000 years.

Gender roles

An old Chinese saying suggests, "Raise sons to support you in your old age. The more sons, the more happiness." The Chinese kinship system stresses the importance of the male and of relationships traced through the male, with women's status firmly dependent on the production of male heirs.

Today, the PRC government mandates that both genders be treated equally and provides equal educational and work opportunities for males and females, the cultural value placed on male children—-and the effects on women's status—- still exists today.

China's "one child" policy

In 1979, the government of the PRC responded to a population explosion threatening to impoverish the country with a family planning campaign directed primarily to urban areas that pressured married couples to agree to having no more than one child. The highly controversial campaign, criticized in the West and resisted in China by families desirous of male heirs, has not yet succeeded in reducing China's dangerous population explosion to a workable level. Its system of social and economic rewards and punishments appears to be having some initial effects on urban populations, however. In 1986, the number of families with single children was reported to have reached 32 million or 3% of the population. Now, in some cities in the PRC, 80—90% of children are reported to be singletons (Pepper, 1991, p. 42; Naltao, 1986). If the increasing numbers of families with female single children become as ambitious for their daughters as traditional families were for their sons, their births may have important effects on the attitudes toward women and their roles in society. Research conducted in the PRC suggests that this is already beginning to happen: One-child families have been reported to have extremely high educational expectations for both male and female offspring, often requiring them to work long hours at their studies after school (Davin, 1991).

Single youngsters reportedly have some difficulty sharing with others and becoming independent. Chinese researchers hypothesize that this may be the result of overdoses of lavish attention and material rewards made available from government subsidies to one-child families. Surveyed parents in one-child families have reported spending as much as 25—50% of their joint incomes directly on their children (Davin, 1991).

Education in the PRC

The socialist education system of the PRC, thought to have been adapted from that of the former USSR, is designed to educate a proper citizen of the socialist country. It does so by providing models for students to emulate, by collective teaching in which all students play a role in critiquing their peers. To develop a sense of community (and possibly to replace the home as the most important community of the child), students normally remain with the same class and homeroom teacher *(banzhuren)* for several years. The homeroom teacher (*banzhuren*) is a powerful "mother figure," providing advice, helping solve problems, assisting in decision-making and evaluating progress. She also teaches moral education as well as academic subjects (Wang, 1987).

Moral education

Today in mainland China, moral education begins with daycare and kindergarten classes, where children learn through games and stories to distinguish between right and wrong, to follow the teacher's instruction step by step and accept what they see and hear. Political education follows in elementary school (Grades 1—6) with the teaching of morality, loyalty, honesty, collectivism and selflessness. The *banzhuren* teaches group responsibility through activities such as communal cleaning of classrooms, group decision-making on issues such as what pictures to put on the walls and what news to publish in the class newspaper and class competition for best decoration, cleaning, sports, singing and the like. The *banzhuren* also evaluates students' moral weaknesses and strengths, taking into consideration students' cooperation with classmates, enthusiasm, etc. (Wang, 1987).

Political studies continue throughout middle and high school and later, in higher education programs, via formal coursework and discussion groups. In middle school, the role of the *Banzhuren* extends from teaching and evaluating moral behavior to conducting courses and discussion groups concerning Communism. She also evaluates formally a variety of student behaviors, including attendance at political studies and self-expression of political views. It is the *banzhuren's* responsibility at this point to provide formal evaluation for the dossiers that follow students through their lives.

Academic education

While moral education is taught in similar fashion throughout the PRC, some schools are designed to provide more effective academic education than others and, at the same time, better opportunities to attain respected positions in Chinese society.

In 1977, one year after the end of the Cultural Revolution, the socialist government began a system of Key schools to ensure the best quality education possible to China's highest achievers. Today, the Key School system provides increased human, material and financial resources through higher education (White, 1987). Although graduates of any school can compete freely for university places, graduation from a Key School increases the probability of acceptance. With university places available to only the top 2% of students, admission to a Key School thus has important positive effects on career possibilities and status throughout life (Pepper, 1991; Sun, 1988).

Gender and education

The post-1949 PRC government made education equally available to males and females for the first time in Chinese history. During the next several decades, female participation in elementary schools increased an approximate 7% and in secondary and higher education an approximate 10%. By 1988, 46% of students in primary school, 41% in secondary and 33% in higher education were female (Hooper, 1991, p. 354).

Although more females are now obtaining higher education, however, they still tend to elect traditionally female fields of study such as pedagogy, languages and literature rather than traditionally male fields such as natural science. These gender-associated choices have been related both to Chinese females' feelings of intellectual inferiority and to generally held beliefs that women should be caring and provide service while men should be achievers. According to surveys conducted in 1987, the majority of Chinese males still accepted the traditional attitude, "It is virtuous for a woman to be untalented" (Hooper, 1991, p. 362). These same surveys showed that both males and females believe that females have lower intellectual ability than do males.

The Study and Its Method

The Chinese study provides results of our surveys of "advantaged" and "nonadvantaged" Chinese youth in Beijing. Because Key School admission has a major positive effect on career possibilities and status throughout life in the PRC, and because it is not possible to match socioeconomic classes in socialist and capitalist states, "advantaged" Beijing students have been defined in this study as those attending Key Schools, while "nonadvantaged" students are those attending regular schools. Our survey, matching that of the multinational study, asked what problems cause these young people stress, what strategies they use to cope and what types of helpers they seek. This chapter describes our subjects and their responses, and discusses those deemed to be of particular relevance to adolescence in Beijing.

Research questions

The general research questions posed in this chapter are:

1. How do our "advantaged" and "nonadvantaged" Beijing youngsters compare with their multinational peers in reported problems, coping strategies and helpers sought?
2. What role, if any, is played by gender differences among subjects?

Subjects

The 148 "advantaged" Beijing subjects (73 males and 75 females) attended a Key middle school; 90% of subjects came from families in which either or both parents had received college education or higher and were employed as college professors or researchers in national institutes.

The 149 "nonadvantaged" subjects (69 males and 80 females), were students attending a regular middle school. Approximately 75% came from families in which either one or both parents received a maximum of high school education (12 years) or lower and were factory workers.

Two of the characteristics distinguishing our Chinese subjects from those of the multinational study are that:

1. parents, by and large, belong to that special PRC generation who lost their own opportunities for education and pursuance of their life plans during the Cultural Revolution and for whom the only hope of attaining their life goals now lies with their children's educational achievements;
2. 25—30% of the subjects in each of our two groups of PRC were single children.

Procedure

Subjects were surveyed in their classrooms in January, 1990 by a middle school teacher using procedures that matched those of the multinational study (Chapter 3). Responses were sent to the University of Pittsburgh where they were coded by the principal author. The interrater reliability of coding, as measured by the percentage of agreement between responses of the coder and those of the standard for the multinational study (see Chapter 2), was .95 for classes and .81 for categories-within-classes.

The Study Results

Problems

Table 6.1(a) shows that **schooling**, **identity** and **family** problems ranked among the top three problem classes for most Chinese subject groups, just as in the multinational groups. The only exceptions include "nonadvantaged" males for whom family problems were ranked fourth.

The Chinese data supports one of the trends shown in the multinational study (Chapter 3) and partially supports another. Chinese females reported a higher percentage of **family** problems than their male peers. The Beijing data show, similar to the multinational results, that females also report a lower percentage of **schooling** problems than males. Our data did not demonstrate the SES trends noted in the multinational study, however. This finding is not surprising, given the difference in definition of SES in this and the multinational study.

Examination of categories-within-classes accounting for at least 5% of reported problems (Table 6.1(b)), shows that academic achievement, academic failure or both are prominent worries for all groups, with Chinese youngsters reporting more than multinational subjects (Chapter 3).

It is notable that our Beijing subjects recounted significant concerns related to self-expectations (demands on self/self-criticism of one's behavior and motivation). Some examples:

TABLE 6.1 *China study: percentages of total responses falling into classes and categories of problems*

(a) Classes

	Advantaged				*Nonadvantaged*			
	Male		*Female*		*Male*		*Female*	
	%	*Rank*	*%*	*Rank*	*%*	*Rank*	*%*	*Rank*
Extreme poverty	0.0	(11.5)	0.0	(11)	0.0	(11)	0.0	(11.5)
War	0.0	(11.5)	0.0	(11)	0.0	(11)	0.0	(11.5)
Catastrophe	0.0	(11.5)	0.0	(11)	0.0	(11)	0.0	(11.5)
Material desires	1.8	(8)	0.0	(11)	0.7	(7.5)	0.5	(9)
Family Issues	10.8	(3)	14.1	(3)	8.1	(4)	12.5	(3)
Schooling issues	41.0	(1)	39.3	(1)	27.2	(2)	23.9	(2)
Identity	25.9	(2)	31.9	(2)	44.1	(1)	42.4	(1)
Sexuality	0.0	(11.5)	0.0	(11)	0.0	(11)	0.0	(11.5)
Courtship/dating	0.6	(9)	0.5	(8)	0.7	(7.5)	1.6	(6.5)
Interpersonal	6.0	(4.5)	8.4	(4)	3.7	(6)	11.4	(4)
Emotions	6.0	(4.5)	3.7	(5)	5.1	(5)	4.9	(5)
Self-fulfilment	5.4	(6)	1.0	(6.5)	0.0	(11)	1.6	(6.5)
Altruism	2.4	(7)	1.0	(6.5)	10.3	(3)	1.1	(8)
No problem	0.0	(X)	0.0	(X)	0.0	(X)	0.0	(X)

*(b) Categories**

	Male		*Female*	
	Category	*%*	*Category*	*%*
Advantaged	Academic failure	10.2	Academic failure	12.0
	Self-expectations	9.6	Academic achievement	9.4
	Academic achievement	9.0	Individual vs conformity	7.9
	Growing up	6.0	Friendship	7.9
	Friendship	6.0	Self-confidence	6.8
	Teachers relationship	5.4	Self-expectations	6.8
			Growing up	6.3
			Time pressures	5.2
Nonadvantaged	Self-expectations	13.2	Academic failure	12.0
	Academic failure	11.8	Individual vs conformity	12.0
	Growing up	10.3	Self-confidence	9.8
	Self-confidence	9.6	Self-expectations	9.8
	Individual vs conformity	7.4	Growing up	8.7
	Parental strictness	6.6	Friendship	8.2
	Time pressures	5.1		

* Representing 5% or more of responses.

"I want to become a newspaper editor. But I worry very much that I do not study my Chinese language sufficiently, and my grade is not good enough to let me do what I want."

"I worry that I don't study hard enough and that my grades won't be good enough to let me do what I want. I don't want to become someone who has no job or friends, and who leads a boring life."

"I want to be a scientist and work in a laboratory. I worry that I am not working hard enough to gain knowledge to do these things."

"Nonadvantaged" and males gave a higher percentage of these reports than "advantaged" and females. By contrast, self-confidence was reported as a problem more by females and "nonadvantaged" than by males and "advantaged."

TABLE 6.2 *China study: percentages of total responses falling into classes and categories of coping strategies*

(a) Classes

	Advantaged				*Nonadvantaged*			
	Male		*Female*		*Male*		*Female*	
	%	*Rank*	*%*	*Rank*	*%*	*Rank*	*%*	*Rank*
Seek/give assistance	1.4	(6.5)	2.4	(5.5)	3.0	(4.5)	1.7	(5)
Interpersonal	5.5	(4)	2.4	(5.5)	3.0	(4.5)	4.1	(4)
Individual problem-solving	61.6	(1)	67.5	(1)	63.1	(1)	62.2	(1)
Stress management	2.3	(5)	2.7	(4)	1.5	(6)	0.7	(6.5)
Crying	0.0	(8.5)	0.0	(8.5)	0.5	(7.5)	0.7	(6.5)
Religious	0.0	(8.5)	0.0	(8.5)	0.0	(9)	0.0	(9)
Resignation	14.6	(2)	12.5	(2)	11.8	(3)	14.8	(3)
Disengage	13.2	(3)	11.8	(3)	16.7	(2)	15.5	(2)
Anti-social	1.4	(6.5)	0.8	(7)	0.5	(7.5)	0.3	(8)
Do nothing	0.0	(X)	0.0	(X)	0.0	(X)	0.0	(X)

*(b) Categories**

	Male		*Female*	
	Category	*%*	*Category*	*%*
Advantaged	Trying harder	35.6	Trying harder	32.5
	Planning toward solution	15.1	Planning toward solution	22.7
	Do nothing	7.8	Escape	5.9
	Psychological distancing	7.3	Psychological distancing	5.9
			Reframing	5.5
Nonadvantaged	Trying harder	31.5	Trying harder	30.9
	Planning toward solution	18.7	Planning toward solution	14.4
	Psychological distancing	11.8	Acceptance	8.6
	Acceptance	10.3	Do nothing	8.6
			Psychological distancing	8.6
			Escape	5.8
			Anxiety without solution	5.2

* Representing 5% or more of responses.

Coping strategies

Individual problem-solving by trying harder is the favored strategy of both SES groups, just as for their "advantaged" and "nonadvantaged" multinational peers (Table 6.2 and Chapter 3).

"I study as hard as I can."

Our results did not support the multinational trends that suggested that females and "nonadvantaged" youngsters are less likely than their male and "advantaged" peers to report **individual problem-solving** strategies.

Helpers

All groups reported seeking helpers from outside the family **(non-family)** more often than from within, with personal friends or classmates the favored choices (Table 6.3 and Chapter 3).

TABLE 6.3 *China study: percentages of total responses falling into classes and categories of desired helpers*

(a) Classes

	Advantaged				*Nonadvantaged*			
	Male		*Female*		*Male*		*Female*	
	%	*Rank*	*%*	*Rank*	*%*	*Rank*	*%*	*Rank*
Family	43.3	(2)	42.3	(2)	44.3	(2)	42.1	(2)
Non-family	52.9	(1)	53.5	(1)	52.8	(1)	56.0	(1)
Offender	0.3	(3.5)	0.0	(5.5)	0.0	(5.5)	0.0	(4.5)
Supernatural	0.0	(5.5)	0.0	(5.5)	0.3	(3.5)	0.0	(4.5)
Creatures/objects	0.0	(5.5)	0.2	(4)	0.0	(5.5)	0.0	(4.5)
Non-specific	0.3	(3.5)	0.4	(3)	0.3	(3.5)	0.0	(4.5)
Nobody	3.3	(X)	3.6	(X)	2.3	(X)	1.9	(X)

*(b) Categories**

	Male		*Female*	
	Category	*%*	*Category*	*%*
Advantaged	Friends	28.1	Friends	28.7
	Classmates	22.0	Classmates	19.8
	Mother	12.1	Mother	13.1
	Father	11.0	Father	10.2
	Brother	7.2	Family members Eldest sibling	7.3
Nonadvantaged	Friends	27.2	Friends	30.6
	Classmates	20.0	Classmates	20.9
	Mother	12.1	Mother	10.6
	Father	10.5	Father	8.6
	Family members	8.9	Sisters	5.6
			Family members	5.6

* Representing 5% or more of responses.

Our subjects distinguished themselves from their multinational peers by **not** reporting seeking help from their teacher! They also sought helpers who were **knowledgeable** and had appealing **personal qualities** (Table 6.4 and Chapter 3). It is significant that all Beijing subject groups want trustworthy helpers (discreet; not likely to tell another person what the subject has shared in confidence).

"I ask my best friends for help. I trust them."

They mentioned this desired quality two-to-four times more frequently in comparison to other attributes as their peers in other countries. "Advantaged" males mentioned it approximately twice as frequently as their peers in other Beijing groups.

TABLE 6.4 *China study: percentages of total responses falling into classes and categories of desired helper qualities*

*(a) Classes**

	Advantaged				*Nonadvantaged*			
	Male		*Female*		*Male*		*Female*	
	%	*Rank*	*%*	*Rank*	*%*	*Rank*	*%*	*Rank*
Powerful	0.5	(6)	0.0	(6)	0.0	(6)	0.3	(5.5)
Knowledgeable	36.1	(2)	50.4	(1)	45.6	(1)	42.6	(1)
Available	2.1	(4)	2.4	(4)	1.0	(4)	0.7	(4)
Personal qualities	42.9	(1)	23.8	(2)	32.0	(2)	30.5	(2)
Concern	16.2	(3)	19.0	(3)	18.0	(3)	23.8	(3)
Uncertain	1.6	(5)	0.4	(5)	0.5	(5)	0.3	(5.5)
No listing	0.5	(X)	4.0	(X)	2.9	(X)	1.7	(X)

*(b) Categories**

	Male		*Female*	
	Category	*%*	*Category*	*%*
Advantaged	Trustworthy	26.2	Similarity	21.8
	Similarity	10.5	Understanding	14.1
	Generous	9.9	Trustworthy	12.1
	Understanding	9.4	Experienced	11.7
	Experienced	8.4	Knowledge	7.7
	Informative	5.8	Advise	5.2
Nonadvantaged	Trustworthy	14.6	Trustworthy	15.1
	Similarity	13.6	Understanding	14.8
	Understanding	10.7	Knowledge	9.4
	Experienced	9.7	Informative	9.4
	Advise	8.3	Similarity	8.4
	Generous	8.3	Generous	8.1
	Informative	6.8	Caring	7.4
	Listener	6.8	Intelligent	5.4
	Caring	5.8	Experienced	5.0
			Advice	5.0
			Listener	5.0

* Representing 5% or more of responses.

Discussion and Conclusions

Of what relevance are these findings to life for adolescents in Beijing?

The importance of academic success

On a macro level, the concerns of our Chinese subjects tended to be similar; Beijing youngsters worried about typically adolescent issues regarding schooling, identity and family, just as their peers around the world and regardless of whether they grew up under a socialist or capitalist system. The fact that academic success and failure were prominent worries was not surprising, given:

1. the importance attributed to education by the Chinese culture;
2. the fact that individuals' personal success in China as well as in most developing countries today depends on academic success ("I think (academic) knowledge is everything"); and
3. within the Chinese culture, success or failure of an individual child represents the success or failure of the entire family.

"I want to make my parents proud and work hard for my country."

Societal change and cultural values

Our results suggest a number of hypotheses concerning the possible effects that societal change may have on cultural values. The concern regarding their self-expectations reported uniquely by Beijing youngsters is a case in point. This probably reflects two factors:

1. pressure by Beijing parents, most of whom had lost their own educational opportunities during China's Cultural Revolution and many of whom had only one child on which to place their hopes; and

2. official governmental encouragement of equal educational opportunities for both genders. That students enrolled in regular Beijing schools seemed to have greater difficulty than those in Key schools as regards both self-confidence and self-expectations may be indicative of already recognized loss of status because they already failed to gain entrance to the more prestigious Key schools.

Gender roles

Even though females are still more concerned with family and less with schooling than males, female concern with self-expectations reported in our Beijing surveys supports the hypothesis (Davin, 1991) that a change in attitudes toward gender roles may be beginning in the PRC. Parents, particularly those of single female children, may be treating daughters in ways they restricted to sons in the past, creating pressure on females to succeed academically and creating for them a conflict between traditional views of proper women's roles and abilities and what is now being required of them. Female adolescents deal with their day-to-day pressures with a belief in female intellectual inferiority still embedded deeply in their own, their families' and their teachers' minds (Hooper, 1991). That females seemed to have somewhat more of a problem as regards self-confidence than males lends support to this hypothesis. If correct, increasing numbers of single female children will face this problem as a result of the PRC One Child Policy.

Our results regarding help-seeking show that all our Chinese groups tended to seek helpers from outside more frequently than from within their families, unlike their multinational peers. The explanation may lie in the PRC educational system designed to develop proper citizens of a socialist country. Students in the PRC remain in the same class with their classmates and *banzhuren* for several years, permitting them to develop a sense of community reserved traditionally for the extended family in which they perceived their school friends in much the same way that their parents, coming from larger families, had traditionally considered their siblings.

That Beijing youngsters were unique in choosing **not** to go to their teacher with their problems suggests, however, that the system does not work as it was intended and that the *banzhuren* is still considered an outsider in a culture that traditionally has placed value on privacy from outsiders and not from the family. It is difficult for youngsters to entrust their most personal concerns to an authority figure who controls their reputations and opportunities for future education and careers through her evaluations of them, but who doesn't possess the concern of a parent.

Teachers as helpers: the importance of trust

The fact that the primary quality desired of helpers by Beijing students is trustworthiness supports the above argument. In elementary school, the *banzhuren* evaluated our subjects' moral strengths and weaknesses, taking into consideration her judgements of how well they cooperated with their peers, how enthusiastic they were about their work, etc. (Wang, 1987). By the time of our survey, when they had reached middle school, the *banzhuren*'s evaluations included her perceptions of their political views, attendance at and interest in political studies, etc. Students were well aware that the dossiers prepared by the *banzhuren* would follow them through their lives. Chinese students, as students in other countries, look for similarity to themselves in their helpers. In the PRC, how much more easy it is to confide in a classmate who has had similar experiences and faces similar problems and whom one has known well for a longer period of time than a teacher!

Suggestions for Counseling in a Nation in which the Profession Doesn't yet Exist

Our findings suggest a number of needs of youngsters growing up in urban PRC that could be met with counseling. With no counseling program currently in existence in the PRC, we suggest that training programs be established to educate professionals in understanding students and their developmental issues and to assist teachers to develop appropriate student services. We include among needed student services:

1. programs for youngsters, to provide skills in peer counseling;
2. provision of family education to deal not just with single children but with others as well, and to provide skills necessary in dealing with youngsters; begin with grandparents who already have developed the confidence of youngsters;
3. assistance for females to deal with gender-related conflicts;
4. counseling of teachers to reduce pressure on children created by fear of evaluation and administrators to develop a more flexible and less frightening system.

The question is not whether these services can be developed in China today, but rather with what speed. Help is needed for Chinese youth if the China is to take an appropriate place in the twenty-first century.

With no counseling program yet in existence in the PRC, there is much to be done. We suggest as early a start as possible.

7

Greece[1]

MARIA DIKAIOU

MIKA HARITOS-FATOURAS

GRIGORIS KIOSSEOGLOU

University of Thessaloniki

"I worry because I cannot decide what I want to be."

Petros is fifteen years old. His father is an unskilled factory worker and his mother's job is housekeeping. Both his parents completed elementary education.

"When I think of myself ten years from now, I have a profession and I am content with it. I don't see myself as being away from friends or not having a profession.

"Now I'm concerned about what my future occupation will be. I cannot decide what I want to be or what kind of academic studies would lead to it. I spend a lot of time worrying about this. Sometimes I imagine that I have solved the problem and am making the right choice, but then I become unsure again. I discuss this with people who are close to me and who are understanding, like my father or my friend who is well informed about career orientation. They both give me information and help me make my decisions. I don't want them to press me to take up studies I dislike and they don't.

"What do I wish? First, to decide what I want to be and then to able to become that type of professional person. And I wish to have a girlfriend."

[1] The authors wish to acknowledge the contributions of Irini Boni to this research.

Introduction

Country and culture

Greece, a nation of ten million people which forms part of the Balkan Peninsula in Southeastern Europe, has an ancient, byzantine and modern history of 4000 years. It is ethnically, culturally and religiously homogeneous, with small populations of Moslems, Jews, Armenians and Gypsies constituting less than 1% of the population. Having reaching the standards of a developed country, it is currently one of the twelve countries forming the European Community. Greece has a thriving tourist industry and is the third commercial naval power in the world. While for decades it exported migrants to richer parts of the world, increasing numbers of migrant workers and refugees from Eastern Europe, Albania and the former USSR now are entering the country with and without legal permits. At the time of writing, the estimated number had reached approximately 5000.

Data for the Greek study were collected in Thessaloniki (Salonica), the capital of the northern province of Macedonia and the country's second largest city. Thessaloniki has an urban history of 2000 years and a population of approximately a million people; a small but strong Jewish community, about 3000 Gypsies, the largest community of former and recent Greek USSR refugees and an unspecified but large number of Albanian refugees. It possesses important Byzantine monuments, a thriving commercial port and a rapidly developing industry. 31% of the population is under the age of 19, with 26% of this age group between 13 and 15 years (the age sample of our study) and found mainly in urban areas due to internal migration within Greece (Emke-Poulopoulou, 1994).

Greek adolescents and their families

The Greek family has always been a powerful institution characterized by strong attachments. This is still true today. Even though the traditional extended family is gradually giving way to nuclear-style units, great interdependence remains among parents and children in all stages of life and continues to provide important psychological support.

Greek adolescents and their families, like their counterparts elsewhere, are not without problems. Social changes of the past several decades, while they have created new individual freedoms especially for females, have also created new issues with which families have not been able to deal adequately: Sociologists, economists and psychologists, for example, point out that adolescence is often being prolonged at the expense of childhood, with children becoming sexually and socially active before they are sufficiently mature to cope with the consequences of their actions. (See Laslett, 1992; Gerris, 1992; Elgaard, Langsted and

Sommer, 1989.) Socioeconomic problems continue to increase the flight of families into cities, decrease the numbers of extended family units and, at the same time, add to the numbers of mothers in the workforce. One result is decreases in both the time and number of adults available to attend to the needs of children. Today, smaller numbers of busier adults are responsible for childrearing and single parent families consisting primarily of mothers and children are increasing.

Family turmoil resulting from these changes has been for several decades causing Greek youth to lose confidence in the adult world and, often, to become confused about what they want to be and passive rather than creative or imaginative. Parents who tend to vacillate in their child-rearing attitudes are contributing to increasing role confusion, problems of social adjustment and anti-social behavior. While modern urban youth are participating less in family activities, their parents, in the process of redefining their new own roles, are often creating ambiguous role models, making it difficult for their children to learn appropriate behavior. These trends reported by psychologists studying the Greek family more than a decade ago (Vassiliou and Vassiliou, 1982; Dragona, 1983) continue today.

The status of counseling in Greece

Counseling in Greece, as in most countries, has been designed to dispense services that previously were provided through families. The first serious efforts to introduce educational and vocational counseling and guidance in the country were made in 1953 almost simultaneously by the Ministries of Education and Labor which have since remained the main agents for such services (Haritos-Fatouros, 1981). However, widespread use of guidance and counseling has not yet been realized, because of both an inadequate number of trained counselors and a lack of available specialized training in these fields (Emke-Poulopoulou, 1986). Even so, vocational counseling is conducted today in all six grades of the state high schools of the country. Job description manuals have been prepared, "sandwich seminars" have been organized for high-school teachers and a limited number of counselor-trainees have been sent for post-graduate specialized training in England. One result is that school counseling and guidance in Greece today are concerned primarily with providing vocational and labor market information and much less with the teaching of coping strategies, stress management and decision-making processes.

Supportive counseling akin to psychotherapy is offered primarily in state and (rapidly expanding) private mental health centers and less frequently in psychiatric clinics and community centers, which deal primarily with drug addiction. The professional "counseling psychologist" is very rare in Greece.

The Study and Its Methodology

Research questions

The Greek study asks two questions:

1. How do Greek adolescents of "advantaged" and "nonadvantaged" SES backgrounds compare with their peers in the multinational study as to reported problems, coping strategies and choices of helpers and helping modes?
2. For the Greek adolescents of our study, what relationships, if any, exist among types of problems, coping strategies and choices of helpers across gender and SES groups?

Subjects

The subjects of our study were students in "nonadvantaged" low income urban areas and in "advantaged" suburban high-income areas. Children of divorced or separated parents were excluded from the study.

"Advantaged" subjects included 200 adolescents (100 males and 100 females), 13—15 years of age, whose parents were either university graduates with average-to-high-income or high-school or technical-school graduates with relatively high income from business or commerce. These youngsters usually lived in high-income suburban residential areas with average-to-wealthy housing conditions (one bedroom per person) and attended private and sometimes foreign private schools.

"Nonadvantaged" subjects included 200 youth (100 males and 100 females) of the same age from lower income families. Parents were blue-collar employees or low-skilled or unskilled workers who had attained lower educational levels than their "advantaged" peers. In most cases, at least one parent, usually the mother, had not gone beyond elementary school. "Nonadvantaged" youth lived in average-to-below-average neighborhoods and housing conditions (one room per 2—5 persons) and attended state schools.

Instruments and data collection

To reduce subjects' errors in interpreting questions as found in a 50-subject pilot study, the questionnaire used in the multinational study was given the following minor revisions:

1. The question, "Mention three problems, events, situations or persons which cause you difficulties or worries" was changed to "Mention three problems that are important to you and have consequences on your life; these may be events, situations or persons which cause you difficulties or worries";
2. When describing their coping strategies, subjects were asked to state the particular problem to which the coping strategies were applied in each case.

Revised questionnaires were distributed to students in their classrooms, using the standardized procedures described in Chapter 2.

Data Analysis and Results: A Two-Part Study

Data analysis and results are presented in two parts, designed to answer Research Questions 1 and 2.

Part I. A description of Greek responses to the three problems requested by the questionnaire and a comparison with those reported in the multinational study

Data analysis

Procedures matched those used in the multinational study and are described in Chapter 2.

Results

Results are reported according to classes and categories-within-classes of problems, coping strategies and choices of helpers.

A comparison of Greek and multinational gender differences is provided.

Problems: Problems related to **schooling, identity and self-concept** and **family issues** are the classes most frequently cited by Greek adolescents (see Table 7.1). This is true regardless of SES group or gender, just as in the multinational study. There are also differences with regard to the content of categories-within-classes. While "nonadvantaged" multinational concerns regarding

TABLE 7.1 *Greek study: percentages of total responses falling into classes and categories of problems*

(a) Classes

	Advantaged				*Nonadvantaged*			
	Male		*Female*		*Male*		*Female*	
	%	*Rank*	%	*Rank*	%	*Rank*	%	*Rank*
Poverty	1.7	(3)	2.0	(8)	0.0	(12)	3.0	(7.5)
War	0.3	(10.5)	0.3	(9.5)	0.0	(12)	0.3	(11)
Catastrophe	0.0	(12.5)	0.0	(11.5)	0.3	(9.5)	1.0	(9)
Material desires	8.0	(5)	2.0	(8)	9.0	(4)	5.4	(5)
Family issues	13.7	(3)	21.0	(2)	15.7	(3)	17.8	(3)
School issues	37.3	(1)	33.0	(1)	35.3	(1)	32.6	(1)
Identity	22.7	(2)	16.7	(3)	26.0	(2)	20.1	(2)
Sexuality	1.0	(9)	2.0	(8)	1.0	(8)	2.3	(8)
Courtship/dating	3.0	(6)	8.0	(5)	4.7	(6)	4.0	(6)
Interpersonal	10.7	(4)	11.0	(4)	6.3	(5)	9.7	(4)
Emotions	1.3	(8)	3.7	(6)	1.3	(7)	3.0	(7.5)
Self-fulfilment	0.3	(10.5)	0.0	(11.5)	0.0	(12)	0.0	(12)
Altruism	0.0	(12.5)	0.3	(9.5)	0.3	(9.5)	0.7	(10)

TABLE 7.1 (*continued*)
*(b) Categories**

	Male		*Female*	
	Category	*%*	*Category*	*%*
Advantaged	Growing up	13.3	Parental strictness	10.0
	Teacher related	8.7	Academic failure	10.0
	Academic failure	8.0	Growing up	8.3
	Schooling (other)	7.7	Friendship	7.0
	Money	6.3	Teacher related	6.7
	Parental strictness	6.3	Time pressure	5.7
Nonadvantaged	Growing up	12.7	Growing up	14.1
	Academic failure	10.7	Academic failure	10.4
	Parental strictness	9.5	Parental strictness	9.1
	Money	7.0	Teacher related	7.4
	Schooling (other)	6.7	Friendship	5.7
	Teacher related	5.7		
	Self-expectations	5.3		

* Representing 5% or more of responses.

schooling included both "academic achievement" and "academic failure," both "advantaged" and "nonadvantaged" Greek youngsters reported academic fears related primarily to "failure." This concern may be related to problems inherent in the Greek school system and/or to the fact that Greek culture is a highly education-oriented culture that pressures children in such a way that it produces strong fear (Moussourou, 1985). Alternatively, an emphasis on failure may be an artifact of language differences between countries. Nevertheless, the same concerns—and coping strategies to deal with them—were repeated from subject to subject:

"I discuss my failure with my father to give me some ideas about what to do."

"I work harder."

"I study more than I used to."

Coping strategies: Table 7.2 and Chapter 3 show that, in both the multinational and Greek samples, **individual problem-solving, seek/give assistance** and **interpersonal coping** are the three most common classes of coping strategies. This was true regardless of SES or gender. A single exception to this finding is the "nonadvantaged" multinational male group for whom **resignation** is ranked third and **interpersonal coping** fourth.

While the chosen coping strategy reported in the multinational sample was **individual problem-solving** (Table 7.2 and Chapter 3), Greek "nonadvantaged" females reported **seek/give assistance** more frequently than any other strategy. This is due, perhaps, to the encouragement by Greek families and social networks for females to support one another when facing problems, and, among low SES groups, provide help both within and outside families.

TABLE 7.2 *Greek study: percentages of total responses falling into classes and categories of coping strategies*

(a) Classes

	Advantaged				*Nonadvantaged*			
	Male		*Female*		*Male*		*Female*	
	%	*Rank*	*%*	*Rank*	*%*	*Rank*	*%*	*Rank*
Seek/give assistance	24.9	(2)	30.9	(2)	37.2	(2)	34.6	(1.5)
Interpersonal	13.1	(4)	15.2	(3)	7.1	(4)	13.2	(3)
Individual problem solving	45.9	(1)	40.2	(1)	50.0	(1)	34.6	(1.5)
Stress management	13.3	(3)	12.0	(4)	4.0	(5.5)	7.3	(4)
Crying	—	—	—	—	—	—	—	—
Religious	—	—	—	—	—	—	—	—
Resignation	2.4	(5)	1.5	(5)	8.0	(3)	3.0	(5)
Disengage	0.4	(6)	0.2	(6)	4.0	(5.5)	0.3	(6)
Anti-social	—	—	—	—	—	—	—	—
Do nothing	—	—	—	—	—	—	—	—

*(b) Categories**

	Advantaged		*Nonadvantaged*	
Sex	*Category*	*%*	*Category*	*%*
Male	Try harder	34.2	Try harder	35.4
	Planning	20.5	Planning	20.5
	Seek support	18.3	Offer help	17.9
	Assertive cope	10.3	Seek support	17.0
	Offer help	8.9		
Female	Try harder	23.7	Seek support	30.7
	Planning	23.0	Try harder	30.2
	Seek support	21.9	Planning	11.4
	Offer help	10.9	Offer help	11.2
	Assertive cope	10.7	Assertive cope	8.2

* Representing 5% or more of responses.

The most interesting finding regarding Greek coping strategies, however, is with respect to **resignation**, the class ranked among the top three of "nonadvantaged" males in the multinational study. Neither Greek males nor females report this strategy in any significant amount. We suspect that this is due to the fact that Greek society supplies more support for young people through its families and other reference groups than is usual in many other countries, and, as such, this compensates for other difficulties related to low SES backgrounds.

Helpers: Table 7.3 shows that Greek youngsters, as their multinational peers, reported seeking help from **family** before looking elsewhere. "Mothers" are the first choice of both males and females with "fathers" or "personal friends" second. We think that, in Greece, this reflects the strong parent—child relationship (Vassiliou and Vassiliou, 1970). Greek parents are usually willing to solve problems for their children who, by turn, look to them as a source of power. One Greek youngster said:

> "I discuss fears about my academic work with my father to give me some ideas as to what to do."

Apart from family members, personal friends and teachers, another source of perceived power for students seem to be preferred by adolescents. Counselors are referred to as a chosen source of help so rarely as not to appear in the table. At least in Greece, this may be due to their scarcity.

Gender and socioeconomic comparisons: Tables 7.1—7.3 show that gender differences noted in the multinational study occur also in the Greek study: Males within each socioeconomic grouping report a higher percentage of concerns related to **schooling** issues and a lower percentage of **family** concerns than females. Males also report a higher percentage of **individual problem-solving** strategies. This is not surprising in a society which, as discussed earlier, so

TABLE 7.3 *Greek study: percentages of total responses falling into classes and categories of desired helpers*

(a) Classes

	Advantaged				*Nonadvantaged*			
	Male		*Female*		*Male*		*Female*	
	%	*Rank*	*%*	*Rank*	*%*	*Rank*	*%*	*Rank*
Family	57	(1)	63	(1)	70	(1)	61	(1)
Non-family	43	(2)	34	(2)	30	(2)	26	(2)
Offender	—		3	(3)	—		13	(3)
Supernatural	—		—		—		—	
Creatures/objects	—		—		—		—	
Nonspecific	—		—		—		—	
Nobody	—		—		—		—	

*(b) Categories**

	Male		*Female*	
	Category	*%*	*Category*	*%*
Advantaged	Mother	34.6	Mother	50.2
	Personal friend	25.0	Personal friend	19.0
	Father	20.0	Child	13.5
	Sibling	8.5	Sister	9.1
	Grandmother	8.1	Father	8.1
	Sister	5.8	Sibling	7.7
	Teacher	6.0	Teacher	6.0
			Grandmother	5.7
Nonadvantaged	Mother	36.3	Mother	40.8
	Father	29.0	Personal friend	17.0
	Personal friend	17.0	Father	14.7
	Grandmother	9.7	Child	11.7
	Child	7.7	Sibling	9.7
	Sibling	7.0	Sister	8.0
			Grandmother	7.0
			Brother	5.4
			Boy/girl friend	5.0
			Teacher	5.0

* Representing 5% or more of responses.

strongly encourages these gender stereotypic responses. Greek youth also differ in interesting ways according to their socioeconomic backgrounds: Our results, just as the multinational findings, show that "advantaged" youth report a higher percentage of **schooling** concerns than do "nonadvantaged" youngsters, regardless of gender. Only males report correspondingly fewer **family** problems, however, which is probably related in part to parental strictness, the only category of concern reported by our subject groups that accounts for 5% or more of total responses.

Part II. Utilization of multiple correspondence analysis to examine possible relationships among problems, coping and choices of helpers

Whereas Part I described the responses of our subjects in terms of their percentages for each class and category-within-that-class, Part II utilizes multiple correspondence analysis (MCA) to explore possibilities of relationships among classes of problems, coping strategies and helpers.

Because this approach is effective only with a limited number of variables at a time and with higher frequencies than required in Part I (Benzecri, 1977; Lebart, Morineau and Warwick, 1984), our first step was to reduce the numbers of possible classes into which responses could be coded so as to increase the frequencies within those that remained. (As shown in Appendix I, data from the multinational study was originally coded into 13 classes of problems, 9 of coping strategies and 6 of desired helpers.)

In order to use subjects rather than responses as variables, we examined only the first problem reported, together with coping strategies used and helpers sought for that problem. (The multinational study permitted each subject to provide up to three problems, together with coping strategies and helpers for each. As noted in the limitations listed in Chapter 2, however, the same results were found for problems, coping strategies and helpers sought regardless of whether analysis was done for problem 1, 2 or 3. For this reason, while our strategy reduced the number of problems from the three reported in Part I, this procedure should not have affected our findings in any significant way.)

1. Data reclassification

Reclassification of subjects' responses took place in the following steps:

(a) We identified all "rare" classes of problems, coping strategies and desired helpers for which the percentage of responses as reported in Tables 7.1—7.3 did not exceed 5% of our total sample. Using this definition, "rare" classes included:

   (i) for problems: **extreme poverty, war, catastrophe, self-fulfilment, altruism, emotions/feelings** and **sexuality;**

(ii) for coping strategies: **religious responses, crying** and **antisocial behavior;** and
(iii) for desired helpers: **offender, supernatural and animate creatures/ inanimate objects.**

(b) Two independent trained judges reclassified responses falling into "rare" classes into the "next most appropriate" classes. For classes of reported problems, this meant identifying, first, the specific and then the wider situational contexts associated with each response, as suggested by Folkman and Lazarus (1980). (If, for example, a subject reported, "I am worried about my mother's illness," the specific context was "parents' health" and the wider situational context was "family.")

Then they classified each identified situational context into the next appropriate class. Using this process, they placed responses classified in the multinational scale as **extreme poverty** and **material desires** into a new class entitled **unsatisfied needs**; They enlarged the multinational class, **self-concept/identity**, to include **self-fulfilment**. They joined multinational classes **sexuality, courtship and dating** and **emotions and feelings** to form one new class, **relations with opposite sex**. They joined **interpersonal and socialization issues** and **altruism**, forming another new class, **socialization and societal concerns** which included problems ranging from inter-personal to inter-group relations, such as conflicts, human rights etc. They left unchanged two multinational classes, **family issues** and **schooling issues.**

For coping strategies, responses that fell into the "rare" multinational class, **religious responses** (seeking religious support), were added to other responses that dealt directly with seeking or giving support to others. This created a new class, **seeking assistance and social support**. Three multinational classes, **crying, disengagement** and **antisocial behavior**, were added to **stress management** to make a new, enlarged **stress management** class. Responses describing assertive, interpersonal and hostile-aggressive coping involving confrontations with person(s) with whom the subject disagrees became **interpersonal or confrontive coping** as referred to by Folkman and Lazarus (1980). The original class, **individual problem-solving or planful behavior** (similar to what the cognitive-behaviorists call "planful behavior"), remained as in the original classification with the exception that one category, "anxiety without a definite plan of action," was removed and added to a new class, **resignation**.

The newly formed coping classes may be organized according to whether they are "problem-focused" or "emotion-focused," according to the theoretical framework of Lazarus and his associates (Lazarus, 1966; Lazarus and Launier, 1978; Folkman and Lazarus, 1980, 1986). While both dimensions include cognitive and behavioral efforts to reduce stress that has resulted from a specific problem, they differ in direction of these activities: "Problem-focused" coping is directly related to solving the problems that caused the stress. This includes our classes, **seeking assistance or social support, interpersonal or confrontive coping, individual problem-solving or planful behavior**, with responses such as "I made a plan of action and followed it," "I stood on my ground," or "I spend much time thinking about it and trying to find alternative solutions." "Emotion-focused" coping, by contrast, deals with stress-reduction. This includes our classes, **stress management and disengagement, resignation**, with responses such as "doing sports," "listening to music," "thinking about something else," "dreaming," or "forgetting about the whole thing."

For helpers, the following classes were chosen: **family members, non-family** and **professionals** (including persons such as teachers, clergy and counselors who are not family members but who have positions of power regarding the subject).

The reclassification process resulted in the reduction of the original 13 multi-national problem classes to 6, the 9 original coping classes to 5 and the 5 helper

TABLE 7.4 *Greek study: definitions of problems, coping strategies and chosen helpers reclassified for multiple correspondence analysis*

Class	*Definition*
Problems	
1. Unsatisfied needs	Unsatisfied physical and/or psychological needs
2. Family issues	Problems associated with families or relations within families
3. Schooling issues	Problems related to school, learning and socialization
4. Identity and self-concept	Problems related to human development
5. Relations with opposite sex	Issues related to opposite sex
6. Socialization and societal concerns	Interpersonal and intergroup relations outside family and school (concerns about)
Coping strategies	
1. Seeking assistance and social support	Process of seeking and giving support
2. Interpersonal or confronting coping	Process of confronting another person
3. Individual problem-solving	Process of solving a problem by oneself
4. Stress management resignation	Process of reducing the impact of the problem
5. Resignation	Resigning oneself to problem
Helpers	
1. Family	Nuclear and extended family members
2. Non-family	Persons (friends, acquaintances or peers) who hold no position of power with regard to the subject
3. Professionals	Persons who hold or are perceived to hold positions of power with regard to the subject and are not family members

classes to 3, creating the 14 classes shown in Table 7.4. Agreement was reached by the judges on 85% of identifications made for each class.

2. Multiple correspondence analysis

Our next step used MCA to explore possible relationships among classes of problems, coping strategies and helper choices. The following procedures were used, as suggested by Lebart, Morineau and Warwick (1984):

(a) We described our subjects' responses in binary coding, creating a "response table" of 400 rows representing each of our 400 subjects and 14 columns representing each of the new classes of problems, coping strategies and helpers. We assigned each cell in the table a value of "1" indicating a choice of the corresponding class by the subject or a value of "0" indicating a non-choice of that class.

(b) We then transformed the binary table into a Burt Table in which each of our 14 classes was cross-tabulated both with itself and with all the others, indicating in its intersections of rows and columns the number of subjects whose responses demonstrated a simultaneous choice of two classes.

(c) We utilized two indices to extract factors that might explain relationships between classes: CTR to identify classes contributing to the creation of factors and COR to demonstrate for each factor those classes which are better represented. (CTR refers to "contribution" and indicates the proportion of variance contributed by each class to the factor; COR stands for "correlation" and indicates the proportion of variance in a class that can be explained by a given factor (Benzecri, 1973).)

(d) Taking into account only those classes with the highest CTR and COR values, we found that the first three factors extracted accounted for 43.1% (F1: 16.1%; F2: 14.6%; F3: 12.4%) of the total variance ("inertia" in MCA terminology). Figure 7.1 provides the factorial plan defined by F1 and F2, with the vertical axis corresponding to the first factor and the horizontal axis to the second and with each axis going from positive (F1 > 0; F2 > 0) to negative (F1 < 0; F2 > 0). The relative positions of the response classes projected on the plan in relation to the two axes reveals possible relationships among them.

Factor 1 represents 16.1% of the existing variance. Figure 7.1 shows that, on the positive side of the axis (F1 > 0), **professional helpers** (PR) appear in closest proximity with two types of problems, **identity/self concept** (IS) and **schooling issues** (SI) and one type of coping strategy, **seeking assistance and social support** (SA). In contrast, classes positioned in the negative pole of the axis (F1 < 0) are **non-family helpers** (NF) and **family issues** (FI) (see note to Figure 7.1 to interpret coding).

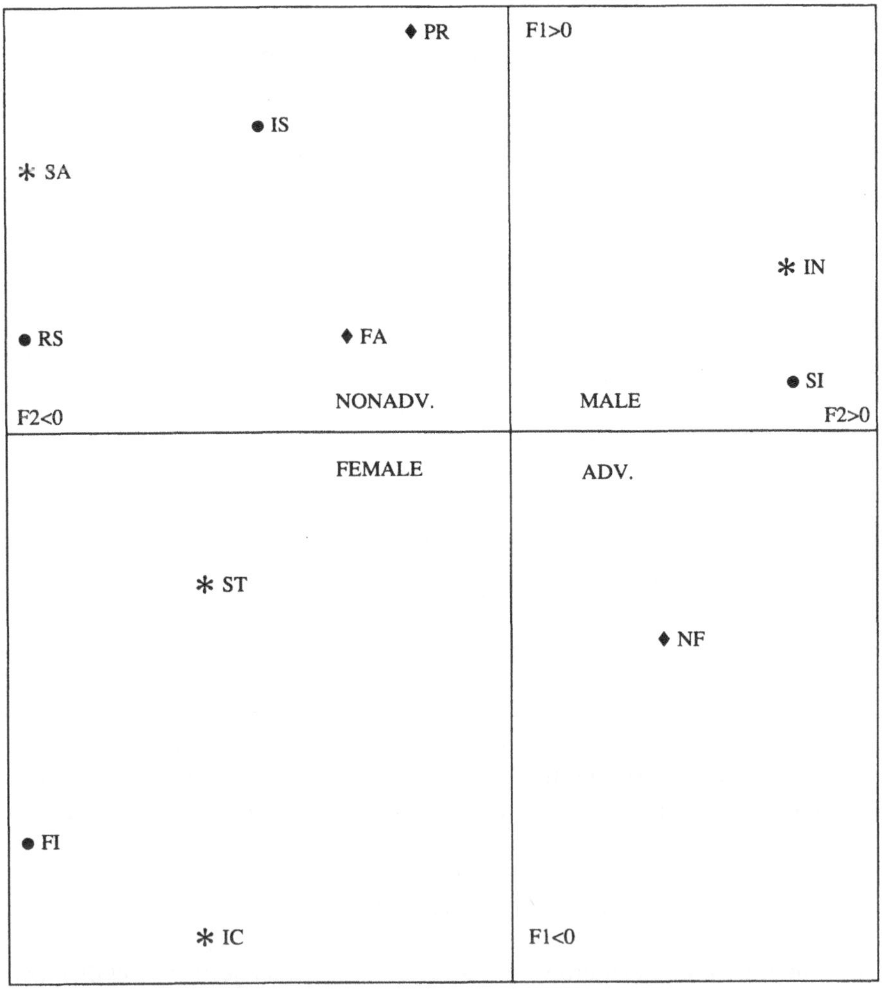

Figure 7.1 Greek study: multiple correspondence analysis of the classes of problems; coping strategies and helpers factorial plan (1, 2)
Vertical Axis: F1– Horizontal Axis: F2.
For each code the first symbol denotes the type of the question – ●: Problem, ✻: Coping ♦: Helpers – and the last two characters denote the type of class – FI: Family, SI: Schooling, IS: Identity and Self-Concept, RS: Relations with Opposite Sex, SA: Seeking Assistance and Social Support, IC: Interpersonal or Confronting, IN: Individual Problem Solving, ST: Stress Management, FA: Family, NF: Non-Family, PR: Professional – Underlined characters denote the supplementary elements – ADV: Advantaged group, NONADV: Nonadvantaged Group.

Factor 2, as illustrated in Figure 7.1 represents 14.6% of the variance and introduces two clusters. On the positive pole of the F2 axis (F2 > 0), **schooling issues** (SI) are in juxtaposition with **individual problem-solving** (IN). On the negative pole, **family issues** (FI), **identity/self-concept** (IS) and **relationship with the opposite sex** (RS) appear together with **seeking assistance and social support** (SA) and **stress management** (ST).

Factor 3 (not included in Figure 7.1) explains another 12.4% of the variance. On its positive side (F3 > 0), problems of **relations with opposite sex** are related to **stress management**. On its negative side, **socialization and societal concerns** appears closest to two types of coping strategies: **seeking assistance and social support** and **interpersonal or confronting coping.**

(e) As a final step, in order to reveal possible socioeconomic group differences, we added to the analysis the two subject groups, "advantaged" and "nonadvantaged" as supplementary elements (new variables that do not participate in the creation of the factors (see Benzecri, 1973)), and considered their proximity to the other classes on the factors. Figure 7.1 shows that "advantaged" and "nonadvantaged" subject groups are represented by the first two factors. The "advantaged" group (GR1) appears in quadrant F1 < 0, F2 > 0, in contrast with the "nonadvantaged" (GR2) which appears in the quadrant F1 > 0, F2 < 0.

3. Results and discussion of the MCA analysis

Overall, results of our MCA analysis suggested little evidence for a consistent pattern of relationships among reported problems, coping strategies and helpers of Greek adolescents. The only exception might be found in Factor 1 (F1 > 0) which tells us that those subjects who reported seeking help from **professional helpers** (PR) tended to report problems related to **identity/self concept** or **schooling issues** and to cope by **seeking assistance and social support**. Since very few subjects chose professional helpers, this represents a very small proportion of our results. Although dyadic relationships appeared between specific types of problems and coping strategies (second and third factors), no evidence was found that relates these to the type of helper chosen.

While these results may be due to lack of rational relationship between the problems and actions of our subjects, another explanation might be an artifact of this study. It may be that problems, as reported by our subjects, reflect their perceptions of reality rather than what exists and that coping strategies and choices of helper refer to actual behavior, i.e. what subjects actually do and to whom they turn for help in real life. The latter are more likely than the former to be influenced by situational determinants (what one can safely do, availability of and freedom of access to helpers) and normative beliefs (common conceptions held by both the subject and important others as to what can be done and when).

Our subjects, and probably adolescents in general, have a wide variety of perceived problems and do not use any one coping strategy exclusively in dealing with them. Any one type of problem, for example, **relations with the opposite sex**, may lead to different coping strategies depending on the context (coexistence of different types of problems occurring in the milieu). Figure 7.1 shows, in fact, that when **relations with the opposite sex** appear in juxtaposition with **identity** and **family** problems (i.e. all positioned on the negative pole of

Factor 2), two classes of strategies are more frequently used: **seeking assistance and social support** and **stress management** (both also positioned on the negative pole of Factor 2). In contrast, when **relations with opposite sex** appears on its own, a single coping strategy is more probable: **stress management** (positioned on the positive pole of the third factor). Finally, in cases where inter- and intrapersonal relations are involved, as for example, **socialization and societal concerns**, more than one coping strategy is indicated: **seeking assistance and social support** as well as **interpersonal or confrontive coping**. In line with studies by Lazarus and Folkman (1987), these findings may suggest that, depending on the type of problem(s) they deal with, adolescents may use classes of strategies that may be classified as either emotion- and/or problem-focused as described above.

In considering our findings regarding SES status, these suggest that "advantaged" Greek adolescents may tend to seek help from non-family members (friends, acquaintances or peers in general) when they have family problems, while their "nonadvantaged" peers apparently turn more frequently to their families for help. Does this mean that families of "nonadvantaged" as opposed to "advantaged" youngsters, have greater cohesion and, as such, facilitate the solving of their own problems? Or does it suggest that peer group relationships are stronger in the "advantaged" group? Either way, one thing is certain: For "nonadvantaged" youths, families can be both a strong source of difficulties as well as support.

Conclusions and Implications for Counseling

Similarities and differences: a need for research

What do the two parts of our study tell us about overall patterns of responding as well as patterns of gender and SES groups within our sample? When overall responding is considered, Greek adolescents tend to be both similar and different from each other and from youngsters in other countries. Trends implied in the gender stereotypic responses of our subjects, together with SES response differences, suggest the importance of reexamining the roles played by gender and SES in determining these as well as other behaviors. The fact that, in some ways, "advantaged" subjects respond in similar fashion to males in comparison to "non-advantaged" and females is tantalizing!

As to relationships among perceived problems, coping strategies and choices of helpers, although we found few relationships in our study, our results suggest the need for further research in an obviously complex area.

An ecological perspective in counseling

In terms of implications for counseling, at this stage, we suggest adopting an "ecological" perspective in counseling, following the line expressed by

Bronfenbrenner (1979), who stressed that counseling should be developed in a way that allows both for similarity and diversity of concerns and their resolutions as shown among our subject groups. An ecological perspective which is not directed solely toward individuals but toward young people of both genders, each in their own SES environments, seems most important in meeting this end.

With regard to Greece, we believe that the best role that can be played by counselors is that of mediator between children and their social environments. Young people need help, not only in resolving their problems but in utilizing the existing support systems in most effective ways. An important role of counselors in this regard is in enhancing relationships between children and their families as well as between children and their communities (school and otherwise). We believe this means recognizing the similarity of many concerns such as fear of academic failure and discomfort regarding parental strictness as well as uniqueness of others. We further believe that, in Greece, this can best be done through collective activities, group work and involvement in cultural activities.

8

India

LINA KASHYAP

Tata Institute of Social Sciences

"I want to come up in life."

Her name is **Anjana**. She is fourteen years old. Her father is a bus mechanic. He has a high-school education. Her mother is a housewife; she does not have any formal education.

"Thinking of myself ten years in the future, I suppose I will be married with a kid or two and living with my husband and his family. If I am allowed, I would also like to be working in an office. I would definitely not want to be sent away to work in the fields in the hot sun.

"I worry about not knowing English language well enough and not having adequate time to study it. I have to help with household duties. I also have to supplement the family income, so I work two hours a day as a part-time maid. This leaves very little time to study. Besides, no one at home believes that my studies are important, especially my English studies. I believe, however, that it is very important if I want to come up in life.

"As I am quite good in my studies except for English language, I have over and over again pleaded with my parents to allow me to take special courses in this subject, but they do not pay attention. I have subsequently asked my best friend. She helps me as much as she can, but it is not enough. I will just try harder on my own. The only person I can discuss this problem with is my best friend. She is always available and understands my feelings.

"My wishes for the future? I wish that I would be allowed to study as much as I am capable of doing, so I can have opportunity for a better life. I wish for happiness for all my family."

Introduction: India and Indian Life

A land of contrasts

India is a vast country of diversity, complexity and tradition. It is multicultural, multiethnic, multilingual and multireligious. Vast differences in food and clothing exist as well as in language and customs; bullock carts, primitive ploughs and oil lamps sit alongside nuclear reactors. This diversity is moderated by the strong artistic, cultural and religious traditions which unify the country.

India is poor, with an annual per capita income of US$300. According to UNICEF (1991), the number of unemployed Indian nationals in 1989 was approximately 13.5 million. By 1991—2, this figure had risen to 17 million (Datt, 1994).

The country today faces a population explosion of crisis dimension today, caused by a high fertility rate combined with an increase in life expectancy that, in turn, resulted from its improved health services. It is currently the second most populous country in the world, with a population estimated to touch the one billion mark by the end of the century. Approximately 39.6% of Indian nationals are under 15 years of age (Census of India, 1991). Twelve Indian cities presently have over a million people each and are facing unprecedented strain in terms of congestion, lack of basic amenities and poverty. An interesting feature in some cities is the presence of pockets of rural communities created by migrants which makes them not quite as impersonal as cities in many developed countries. A metropolitan center often replicates in miniature the cultural diversity of the country. Such is the case for Bombay, where this study was conducted.

India's caste system

India's caste system is characterized by division into superior and inferior classifications with members marrying within their group and each caste following ritual customs peculiar to itself. Traditionally, the system was a rural phenomenon in which higher castes tended to be landowners while the marginal farmers, landless laborers and craftsmen were from lower castes. The lowest castes still suffer social and economic deprivation, exploitation and outbursts of violence at the hands of the dominant higher castes, in spite of the national policy of positive discrimination designed to bring them into the mainstream of society (Roach, 1986). In urban areas, increased educational and vocational opportunities have blurred caste distinctions and facilitated upward economic mobility somewhat. However, by and large, individuals in higher status occupations and professions still come from higher rungs in the traditional caste hierarchy and distinctions tend to be based both on the age-old caste and a new one based on classes (Chauhan, 1989). The "advantaged" adolescents in the Indian sample come from the higher castes, whereas those comprising the poverty sample are from the lower castes.

Family life and gender roles

India represents the patriarchal form of society in general, with a few pockets of matrilineal arrangements. In the past, the "ideal" family pattern was three-generational with the eldest male member heading his family. Though this family system was not without strains, it provided a sense of solidarity and security against local troubles and has been a center of religious, cultural and socialization activities.

Relations among family members of different generations have usually been of deference toward elders. Though urbanization has promoted dispersal of extended families into nuclear family units residing in different places, family sentiment is still strong and the extended family unit still holds its significance. Norms of segregation of women are still rigid, though there are beginnings of a women's liberation movement which is more conspicuous in the urban areas, spearheaded by highly educated and articulate middle-class women.

Indian marriages are still generally arranged by the parents and members of the kinship group, although patterns of partner selection vary in terms of extent of choice given the young boy or girl. In urban areas, it is usually through mutual consultation between the parents and young people, especially the boys. Child-rearing is often a centrally shared task of female members of the extended family, and indeed of the local community as a whole.

Gender differentiation starts early, with boys considered economic assets. There is visible discrimination in rural areas and urban migrant pockets in favor of boys with regard to food, medical attention and education. In urban educated families, while there may be little discrimination with regard to these aspects, gender differentiation is implicit in the distribution of household tasks and in the concessions and freedom of behavior permitted to boys. There is emphasis on adjustability and submissiveness in the socialization of girls.

With violence against women a worldwide problem, in India, reported cases of harassment of married women over "dowry" by husband and in-laws leading to deaths and suicides have tripled in the last few years (Sriram, 1991). Other violence also exists: India serves as a major transit route of drug trafficking to the west. In Bombay, most drug addicts are under the age of 25 and are students, unemployed or unskilled laborers, including children who work as ragpickers. There are an estimated 154 880 addicts in Bombay alone (Gandevia, 1989). A few non-governmental organizations have started rehabilitation services.

Education and counseling

India's constitution provides free and compulsory education for all children from 7 to 14 years of age with primary education free in government schools. Currently, the government is implementing a single pattern of education with ten years of primary school followed by two years of higher secondary and three years of university. Though enrolment in primary education has gone up steadily, however, wastage is still high. Female enrolment in primary levels remains low: only 35% in 1987—88 (UNICEF, 1991). In fact, education is enjoyed by only half the Indian children of primary school age with a vast majority having never enrolled or dropped out. As far as secondary education is concerned, though the number of schools has increased in the last few decades, the resulting increase in enrolment has affected only the middle and upper classes and includes only 40% of boys and 20% of girls. There is sharp disparity between government and private schools with the latter being superior with regard to physical facilities, quality of teaching and suitability of curriculum and the former having lowest enrolment and highest drop-outism and stagnation. Children from low socioeconomic backgrounds usually attend government schools.

Indian education, in common with most other educational systems, has always given primacy to cognitive goals with an emphasis on teaching rather than on learning and seems to make little direct contribution to other than white-collar occupations (Gore, 1977). However, efforts are being made to draw more students to vocational and technical education after high school, so that a majority of students after the 10 + 2 stage can enter jobs.

The training of Indian counselors currently takes place in master's level curricula of psychology, education and social work. The profession has not held high status, however, in a country where the extended family has traditionally looked after its members' needs and, when advice has had to be sought outside the family, the village priest, teacher or *panchayat* (village elders) have been approached (Dave, 1984). Graduates of psychology and education have, by and large, restricted their work to testing and clinical diagnosis and have ventured into active counseling only in the area of educational-vocational guidance. The masters program in social work offers training in basic counseling skills as well as specialized courses related to counseling with specific target groups for social and personal adjustment. Currently, in the major cities, professional social workers are offering counseling services in a few schools and colleges, special schools for disabled children, children's institutions, child guidance clinics, family courts, hospitals and industries as well as in rehabilitation centers for alcoholics, drug addicts and, recently, AIDS victims. There is now growing recognition among the country's policy-makers of the need for these services (Bakri and Mukhoadyay, 1989).

Bombay, the site of the Indian study

Bombay, the capital of the State of Maharashtra on the west coast of India, is an intellectual and commercial/industrial center that attracts job-seekers from other States of India. It houses a highly cosmopolitan population of 9 900 000 inhabitants, representing every religion, caste, profession and linguistic group in India (Census of India, 1991). Its vast northern suburbs, where the adolescents surveyed in this study live, house upper, middle and lower socioeconomic classes and represent a variety of regional and linguistic groups from various parts of India.

The Study Methodology

Our subjects, their families and their schools

Subjects and their families

The 400 adolescents in this study were urban, with 200 subjects (100 males and 100 females) coming from upper and middle income "advantaged" backgrounds and 200 subjects (100 males and 100 females) living on the edges of "poverty."

"Advantaged" or "poverty" groups both matched the socioeconomic descriptions used in the multinational study (see Chapter 2). In the case of India, "advantaged" subjects had educated families with three-quarters of fathers and slightly less than half of mothers having university degrees. They lived in affluent localities in multistoried apartments or bungalows. Though all were studying in English medium schools, they represented many linguistic groups.

"Poverty" subjects, by contrast, tended to come from large, one-parent or female-headed families caught up in the daily struggle for survival. Most parents had a maximum of primary level education; 10% of fathers and 28% of mothers were illiterate. They lived in crowded, unhygienic single room tenements or huts with rudimentary household sanitary facilities. Most had to help their parents in household chores or other work before and after school, and many held small jobs to supplement their family's income. (Unlike "poverty" samples in some other countries of the multinational study, Indian adolescents do not represent the poorest of the Indian poor, as they had sufficient resources to allow their children public education.)

"Advantaged" and "poverty" schools

The Indian sample was drawn from six schools that offer pre-primary, primary and secondary level of education. The three private schools attended by "advantaged" subjects included a "boys-only" school run by a private trust, a "girls-only" convent school run by nuns, and a co-educational school run by Christian missionaries. Instruction in all three was conducted in English, though the co-educational school also had a Marathi section. Buildings were well-maintained and had large halls, gymnasia, adequately equipped science laboratories and libraries. They offered extra-curricular activities, monitored attendance and maintained regular contact with parents.

The three schools attended by the "poverty" subjects were co-educational public schools funded by government or charitable trusts that provide instruction in Marathi. Buildings were poorly maintained, large and impersonal structures situated in densely populated slum neighborhoods. Facilities were barely adequate with few facilities for extra-curricular activities. All three schools charged nominal fees. School dropout rate was high with a higher rate for girls than boys. The principals bemoaned the fact that their female pupils generally faced indifference if not open opposition toward their educational needs from their families. Student—teacher relationships were impersonal and little attempt was made to monitor attendance or maintain parent relationships.

Procedure

Data collection

Data collection procedures were similar to those of the multinational study (Chapter 2). Responses were collected by the author with the assistance of a trained social worker. The questionnaire was first field-tested on 13—15-year-olds from a school not selected for the study. It was translated into Marathi for use with the "poverty" sample. The questionnaire and study objectives were shared with the principals of the six schools chosen. One class period, usually the last of the day, was allotted for administering the questionnaire to students from classes VIII to X.

Data collection took about two months. For most children, the 45 minutes it took to fill in the questionnaire provided a first conscious experience in serious reflection. Some found it difficult to write down feelings and emotions. Others could mention only one or two problems. When we met some of the boys later, they told us that though they had found it difficult to write down deep or intense problems faced by them at the time of filling up the questionnaire, it helped in serious introspection later. However, a few "advantaged" youngsters voiced relief at this opportunity to express their innermost thoughts and concerns without fear of being identified or made subjects of fun.

Coding

The author and research assistant trained together in coding the data, using the standardized instructions developed for the multinational study (see Chapter 2). Interrater reliability as measured by the percentage of agreement between the two Indian coders on coded responses of the test data prepared in Pittsburgh was 98% for classes and 95% for categories. The same measure of interrater reliability between the author and the Pittsburgh "mastercode" was 93% for classes and 80% for categories.

Study Results

Reflecting on the cumulative results from the 13 countries in this study and comparing these with the Indian study brought out both common trends and differences.

Problems and coping

Problems

"Advantaged" and "poverty" subjects in the Indian and the multinational study both described problems related to **school**, **family** and **identity/self concept** more frequently than any other (see Table 8.1(a)). "Advantaged" groups also reported many concerns about **interpersonal and socialization issues**, whereas "poverty" groups cited problems related to **material desires**. Indian subjects demonstrated the trends shown in the multinational sample in which

(a) the percentage of **schooling** problems decreased and **family** problems increased with decreasing SES; and
(b) females reported more **family** and fewer **school** problems than males.

TABLE 8.1 *Indian study: percentages of total responses falling into classes and categories of problems*

(a) Classes

	Advantaged				Poverty			
	Male		Female		Male		Female	
	%	Rank	%	Rank	%	Rank	%	Rank
Extreme poverty	0.7	(7.5)	0.0	(12)	1.7	(6.5)	2.0	(6.5)
War	0.0	(12)	0.0	(12)	0.0	(12)	0.0	(12)
Catastrophe	0.3	(9)	0.0	(12)	0.0	(12)	0.0	(12)
Material issues	1.7	(6)	3.0	(8.5)	4.7	(4.5)	7.8	(4)
Family issues	5.7	(4)	9.4	(3)	28.0	(1.5)	30.2	(1)
Schooling issues	28.6	(1.5)	18.7	(2)	28.0	(1.5)	22.0	(2)
Identity	28.6	(1.5)	31.8	(1)	23.6	(3)	21.6	(3)
Sexuality	0.0	(12)	0.7	(7)	0.0	(12)	0.0	(12)
Dating/courtship	2.7	(5)	3.0	(5)	1.7	(6.5)	0.8	(8)
Interpersonal	6.1	(3)	4.0	(4)	1.0	(8)	2.4	(5)
Emotions	0.7	(7.5)	1.0	(6)	0.0	(12)	0.0	(12)
Self-fulfilment	0.0	(12)	0.3	(8.5)	0.0	(12)	0.0	(12)
Altruism	0.3	(9.5)	0.0	(12)	4.7	(4.5)	2.0	(6.5)

*(b) Categories**

	Male		Female	
	Category	%	Category	%
Advantaged	Inability to learn	10.4	Self-confidence	8.7
	Physical appearance	8.7	Physical appearance	8.3
	Behavioral issues	7.7	Behavioral issues	7.0
Poverty	Growing up	11.5	Growing up	11.8
	Studies	6.8	Lack of privacy	9.8
	Inability to learn	6.1	Parental strictness	9.0

* Representing 5% or more of responses.

Results of the Indian study suggest that adolescent males may be slightly more caught up with problems related to **courtship and dating** (such as dating restrictions and lack of freedom in choice of marriage partner) than their counterparts elsewhere. With Indian society in a stage of transition regarding this issue, it may be that educated urban youth are struggling to find a middle ground between traditional Indian norms such as segregation of the sexes and family arranged marriages and Western liberalism with its emphasis on individuality and self-arranged marriages. Studies by Mahale (1987) and others have reported that, though urban educated youth still accept arranged marriages, most feel they should have a final say in the choice of their life partner. This is not always the case in India today.

Indian "advantaged" and "poverty" subjects were similar to the comparable subject groups in the larger multinational study with respect to problems they did not cite such as **sexuality**, but the reasons for these omissions may differ from those of young people from Western countries where sex is discussed openly and youngsters become sexually active by age 13. In India, due to social and cultural restrictions and strict sex segregation, few adolescents engage in any form of sexual relationship!

Although concern with poverty appears to increase slightly as SES status decreases, this was not a major focus even for the poverty group in India. This is probably because, in India, poverty is accepted as a fact of life with which people learn to live. However, in the larger multinational study, "poverty" subjects have identified extreme poverty as a stressful area with males more concerned with this problem than females.

Examination of the three most frequent categories of problems reported by Indian subjects and subjects from the larger study (Table 8.1(b)) brings out more differences: "Advantaged" male and female subjects in the larger study reported a higher percentage of concerns related to academic achievement, whereas their Indian counterparts may not have been so much concerned about achieving academic excellence as with supposed "inability to learn." One reason for "advantaged" youngsters may be difficulty in comprehending and expressing English language which is the medium of instruction at school but may not be the language spoken at home. The second reason is more systemic and rooted in the malaise of the Indian education system. Basic education in India has made little direct contribution to the life of the community (Gore, 1977). The fact that students appeared to have no worries regarding academic success may well be that they viewed academic excellence as unimportant to success in life!

Coping

Regardless of SES group and gender, the most frequently reported class of coping strategy was **individual problem-solving**, with males reporting a higher percentage of responses indicating this coping strategy than females, as shown in the multinational study trend. The multinational trend regarding decreasing

TABLE 8.2 *Indian study: percentages of total responses falling into classes and categories of coping strategies*

(a) Classes

	Advantaged				Poverty			
	Male		Female		Male		Female	
	%	Rank	%	Rank	%	Rank	%	Rank
Give/seek assistance	12.1	(3)	12.2	(3)	17.3	(4)	14.2	(4)
Interpersonal	6.4	(5)	8.8	(4)	8.4	(5)	20.6	(2)
Individual problem-solving	45.3	(1)	44.7	(1)	56.0	(1)	38.5	(1)
Stress management	1.9	(6)	1.1	(7)	5.6	(6)	0.9	(6)
Crying	1.1	(7)	1.5	(6)	0.0	(9)	0.5	(7.5)
Religious	0.4	(8.5)	0.4	(8)	0.0	(9)	0.5	(7.5)
Resignation	24.2	(2)	28.2	(2)	20.2	(2)	19.7	(3)
Disengage	8.3	(4)	3.1	(5)	18.0	(3)	5.0	(5)
Anti-social	0.4	(8.5)	0.0	(9)	2.2	(7)	0.0	(9)

*(b) Categories**

	Male		Female	
	Category	%	Category	%
Advantaged	Try harder	24.8	Try harder	27.1
	Plan toward solution	13.5	Do nothing	13.7
	Do nothing	11.7	Seek support	11.5
Poverty	Try harder	16.4	Try harder	16.1
	Plan toward solution	16.4	Assertive coping	13.3
	Seek support	14.6	Seek support	11.9

* Representing 5% or more of responses.

responses with decreasing SES did not occur in the Indian sample, however. The least frequently reported strategies were **crying, religious responses** and **anti-social responses** (Table 8.2(a)). This suggests that adolescents may want to take personal responsibility and make an active attempt to resolve their own problems, which is heartening. The fact that adolescents have not sought religious support to solve their problems supports what a number of theorists have anticipated: that though youth have a strong belief in a God who watches and protects humanity, adolescence does involve a period of doubt and even rebellion against traditional components of religious beliefs and practices (Newman and Newman, 1986). It should be noted that, unlike Christianity, Hinduism (the religion of majority of people in India) does not provide individual guidance and counseling to the followers of the faith.

Females from both "advantaged" and "poverty" groups both in India and in the larger study are more likely to use **interpersonal coping** strategies than males (Table 8.2(b)). This confirms what developmental psychologists have been suggesting that is, though both boys and girls show increasing behavioral independence, this issue seems to be more salient for boys than girls (Newman and Newman, 1986).

"Trying harder" was the most frequently used strategy of all adolescents in the large study, regardless of SES and gender. However, "advantaged" Indian male and female subjects reported that they "give up," "do nothing" or "make no more attempt to resolve their problems." This is a significant finding. It suggests a feeling of powerlessness and doubts about the ability to handle situations independently and could be related to the fact that these advantaged Indian adolescents are neither expected or encouraged to take independent decisions or paid employment while still studying, resulting in prolonged economic and emotional dependence on their families.

Help-seeking

In response to the questions related to the persons to whom adolescent subjects were most likely to go for help with their problems, **family members** was the most frequent class of helpers chosen by all Indian subjects (Table 8.3) with one exception of "poverty" males, whose most frequent choice was **non-family**, specifically, "personal friend" or "teacher." Examination of categories of chosen helpers (Table 8.3(b)) shows, however, that the category, "personal friend" within the class, **non-family**, was the single most frequent choice of all adolescents regardless of SES group or gender. "Mothers" were chosen more frequently than "fathers" by all groups.

TABLE 8.3 *Indian study: percentages of total responses falling into classes and categories of desired helpers*

(a) Classes

	Advantaged				*Poverty*			
	Male		*Female*		*Male*		*Female*	
	%	*Rank*	*%*	*Rank*	*%*	*Rank*	*%*	*Rank*
Family	56.5	(1)	56.3	(1)	46.4	(2)	64.3	(1)
Non-family	33.6	(2)	37.2	(1)	52.1	(1)	33.7	(2)
Offender	0.2	(3.5)	0.3	(3)	0.1	(3.5)	0.0	(6)
Supernatural	0.0	(6)	0.0	(6)	0.0	(6)	0.0	(6)
Creatures/objects	0.0	(6)	0.0	(6)	0.1	3.5	0.2	(3)
Non-specific	0.2	(3.5)	0.0	(6)	0.1	(3.5)	0.0	(6)

*(b) Categories**

	Male		*Female*	
	Category	*%*	*Category*	*%*
Advantaged	Personal friend	22.0	Personal friend	31.1
	Mother	15.7	Mother	20.9
	Father	13.3	Sister	11.4
Poverty	Personal friend	30.2	Personal friend	21.9
	Teacher	12.1	Mother	15.6
	Mother	10.8	Father	11.6

* Representing 5% or more of responses.

TABLE 8.4 *Indian study: percentages of total responses falling into classes and categories of desired helper qualities*

(a) Classes

	Advantaged				Poverty			
	Male		Female		Male		Female	
	%	Rank	%	Rank	%	Rank	%	Rank
Powerful	0.9	(5.5)	2.9	(4.5)	7.2	(4)	11.5	(4)
Knowledgeable	41.2	(1)	31.7	(2)	25.2	(3)	26.4	(3)
Available	0.9	(5.5)	2.9	(4.5)	2.4	(5)	0.3	(6)
Personal qualities	28.0	(2)	20.9	(3)	28.5	(2)	27.2	(2)
Concern	25.2	(3)	38.4	(1)	35.4	(1)	33.2	(1)
Uncertain	1.9	(4)	1.5	(6)	0.7	(6)	0.5	(5)

*(b) Categories**

	Male		Female	
	Category	%	Category	%
Advantaged	Understanding	13.5	Understanding	22.7
	Experienced	12.9	Similarity	11.0
	Trustworthy	11.0	Trustworthy	10.2
Poverty	Caring/loving	18.5	Caring/loving	15.2
	Supportive	8.7	Understanding	14.7
	Understanding	8.0	Exercise authority	9.9
			Gives advice	9.9

* Representing 5% or more of responses.

Indian adolescents, as those from the larger study, cited **being knowledgeable** about the problem, **appealing personal qualities** and **concern for others** as desirable helper qualities (Table 8.4). "Poverty" subjects in both India and the larger study cited **concern for others** as the most important of these.

Implications of the Indian Study for India

Interpreting the responses of Indian youth

For a meaningful interpretation of the responses of Indian youth, categories within classes were examined for the five scales under study. The three most frequent categories above the 5% cut-off point were enumerated in part (b) of Tables 8.1—8.4 for this purpose and suggest the following:

1. Advantaged Indian adolescents may be more egocentric in nature as compared with their poverty peers, who, though also concerned with self-identity issues, had family related problems to contend with as well. "Poverty" groups had many more varied problems with which to contend.

2. Adolescents from the two Indian SES groups were concerned with different issues related to personal identity and self concept: "Advantaged" subjects were more concerned with physical appearance and behavioral issues such as inability to control temper, inner hostilities and having to cope with peer pressure. These young people are in a stage of transition between adjusting to traditional family norms and the pull of Western liberal ideas. The subjects in the poverty group were, by contrast, more concerned with issues related to growing up. This is hardly surprising, as these youngsters have to make relatively earlier transitions into adult roles and take over their share of family responsibility including contributing to the economic survival of their families, much earlier, as compared to adolescents from higher SES groups.

3. That schooling issues were not reported as frequently by female subjects as males could be related to the fact that girls in India are not socialized to view educational achievement as an important part of their lives.

4. "Inability to learn" is a major concern for Indian male subjects. While "advantaged" males reportedly had difficulty in coping with specific subjects, "poverty" males experienced a deteriorating interest in studies. This could be due to inadequate role models within the family land community and lack of relevance of current education programme to the student's aspirations and daily life.

5. "Trying harder" is a problem-solving method used by all the adolescents. Besides individual problem-solving strategies, other methods adopted by "poverty" subjects included seeking support from others and attempting assertive coping strategies. However, subjects from the "advantaged" group did not use any such alternate strategies, but tended to give up, do nothing more to resolve their problems. This is quite an alarming trend, even in developing countries. In India, the current occupational and economic life of urban industrialized cities demands initiative, certain aggressiveness, a capacity for making choices, a capacity to cope with tensions and above all, a readiness to accept consequences for one's actions. The traditional pattern of upbringing and socialization may not have equipped the young with these qualities.

6. When adolescents were asked to name their most preferred helpers, a personal friend was the most frequent choice of all the adolescents followed by their mother. The only exception were "poverty" males who, after their personal friend, turned to their teachers before seeking their mother's help. These "poverty" youth may not perceive their families, especially their parents, most of whom were illiterate, either as knowledgeable or powerful enough to be able to help. Just as the adolescents in the multinational study, adolescents in India did not mention counselors, most probably due to total lack of exposure to such professionals.

7. The young Indian subjects wanted their helpers to be understanding, the implication being that more than knowledge and skills, attitude of counselors toward the adolescent was considered most important. At the same time, they sought advice, direction and help in problem-solving. "Advantaged" males alone reported that they considered professional experience important in providing this assistance. In sum, Indian youth considered the counselors' role of "enabler" in assisting the adolescent in problem-solving as the key role.

Implications for counseling

The concerns and anxieties of Indian adolescents are indeed age-related and characteristic of their life-cycle stage. However, as we move from "advantaged" to "poverty" populations, results show that age-related problems decrease while the reverse is true for problems that are situation-related, for example, inability to cope with studies or with specific subjects like mathematics, science or language. An "advantaged" child confessed that he found it difficult to cope with English studies as no one at home or in the neighborhood knew the language. A "poverty" female worried about parental strictness:

> "It is most unfair, my parents are much more strict with me than with my brother and interfere in all matters. I feel helpless and frustrated."

The responses of the adolescents regarding their coping strategies and desired helper qualities suggest that these young people would appreciate active involvement on the part of their helpers on a range of transient problems of a psychosocial nature, and would benefit from a counseling service which is person-centered.

This study suggests that adolescent concerns need to be recognized by educational institutions as these constitute the major settings outside the family unit where these young people are being socialized. The school system can be an effective entry point for providing professional counseling services to youth. Currently, however, the few available school-based programs that exist in India are limited to vocational guidance. The concerns of adolescents in this study suggest the need for broadening the scope of these programs to include counseling for personal and social adjustment, aimed at building up a healthy self-concept and maximally developing an individual's potential.

The fact that individual problem-solving strategies are used by all adolescents is heartening, and they need to be enhanced. Development programmes in family life education need to become a regular aspect in Indian secondary school co-curricular activities.

The "do nothing" attitude of the "advantaged" group and the attempts at seeking support from others in problem-solving by the "poverty" group probably underline feelings of constraint, dependency, weakness and lack of confidence in ability to resolve problems. Counselors should work toward decreasing these feelings and empowering youngsters to make their own decisions.

> "My father interferes in everything I do, every decision I make. It is so frustrating because I can do nothing about it right now."

Our data point both to the fact that male adolescents feel constrained to seek help—or support—from others. An outreach program that meets youth on their own grounds may be an effective strategy. Counseling programs will need, also, to reach out to families, especially parents.

It is not surprising that adolescents go to family members for help, showing that parent—adolescent interaction need not always be conflictual and in fact can play an important part in sustaining an adolescent's sense of well-being. However, we also find that male subjects in the "poverty" group do not turn as readily to their parents for help as others, possibly because they perceive them as lacking in knowledge and power. This again suggests the need for family development programs in which parents are helped to understand their changing adolescent and build a good relationship with him/her. In the Indian context it is important that parents understand that different patterns of decision-making, disciplines and resource allocation will affect adolescents' opportunities to experience responsibility and to exercise autonomy, which are necessary for the development of his/her personal identity.

The fact that personal friends were reported to be a major source of support suggests the need for training adolescents in helping skills for initiating peer counseling.

Counselor training

The responses of these Indian subjects clearly point to the characteristics counselors will need in order to get in touch with adolescents. Indian youth are crying out to be treated as an individuals, are craving for helpers who will listen without being judgmental or controlling, who can be trusted and who are genuinely interested in them and who will not only be a guiding and directing force, but who will be actively involved in the helping process. Therefore, not only must counselors learn to be good listeners and communicators. They must learn to convey openness, genuineness and unconditional positive regard and be scrupulously honest.

Currently, India has very few professional counselors. To meet the needs of the vast youth population in the country, professional counselors as well parents, teachers and adolescents themselves need to be trained in basic counseling skills.

What type of training is needed for such counselors? The gender and SES differences found in this study make it obvious that there can be no one counseling model which can work for all. Counseling programs will need to be separately designed for each group and the counselor's repertoire of methods and skills will need to be adapted to meet the special needs of each. An important component of an appropriate training program therefore would be to provide sensitivity toward group needs through supervised field experience in working with various groups. Another important training input is understanding of the power structure of institutions and communities and the social processes of change which will equip trainees for working toward changing the institutional setting or community climate so that newer approaches and programs can be implemented. A final essential component is training in self-awareness and self-acceptance. This should include experiential sessions in which trainees are helped to see themselves and gain sensitivity to others.

As mentioned earlier, some universities in India currently offer master's courses in counseling. This will hardly meet the needs of a vast country like India which has a large youth population to cater to, however. The university departments of Education, Psychology or Social Work could offer intensive short-term training programs for training school teachers who show aptitude for counseling as auxiliary counselors. These short-term training programs should be certified and standardized so that a uniform program is followed throughout the country. These auxiliary counselors could be supported and provided consultations by professional counselors. A step in this direction is already being taken by the Tata Institute of Social Sciences, Bombay.

Centers to help families

The fact that family issues featured among the three highest ranking concerns and was the highest ranking class of problems for the "poverty" group strongly points to the need for family-based interventions. For Indian females, whose educational needs often are not considered important by their families, this intervention should involve increasing awareness of the right to receive education and the advantages it brings.

Because of the importance of helping families to help their children, the manner in the Indian national scheme for assisting family counseling centers, like those of other some countries, might be broadened to assist in the organization of family programs. This is one of the topics discussed in Chapter 18, which summarizes the implications of our multinational findings.

9

Israel

BENJAMIN SHAFRIR

Institute for Special Education, Kibbutz Givat Haim Ichud

"Will I reach my goals?"

Adam is fifteen years old and lives on a kibbutz. His father is a qualified electrical engineer and his mother is a nurse with a master's degree in nursing.

"In the future, when I have finished my military service and I have traveled two years in the Far East and in South America, I will be studying oceanography in Florida. I wouldn't like to be sitting on my ass, working twelve hours a day, and ask myself every day, 'What should I learn? What should I do?'

"I'm worried about the future. What does it hold for me? Will there still be constant danger of war? Will I perform as expected — by myself, by my mates — in the army? Will I be able to achieve and reach my goals?

"I talk a lot about this with my father and my best friend. And there is this guy, twenty-six years old, who was an officer in the army, spent a year in the Far East, worked for another year and now is studying in the States. They all are supportive and on the same wave length as me. They are experienced and mature. They encourage me and share with me their thoughts and experiences. I don't want people to treat me like a child. Otherwise, I spend as much time as I can in under-sea diving. In the end, I believe there isn't a thing that can stand against will power and determination. Most of it depends on me.

"Three wishes? I wish to achieve my goals. I want to be accepted into the commandos when I join the army. And I wish good health for my family."

Introduction

The Israeli study reflects the problems and coping of two characteristic segments of the Israeli adolescent population who live on "kibbutzim" (Israeli farming collectives) and in urban and suburban areas. It includes Jewish adolescents only, not because of disregard of the Moslem and Christian Arab population in the country, but because of the Jewish population's availability to the author and of his professional involvement with the groups studied.

Israel's historical background

The problems that preoccupy Jewish Israeli youth as well as the coping strategies preferred by them must be understood within the unique context of an emergent society in a new and changing nation. The modern State of Israel was established in 1948 as a result of the millennia-old Jewish aspiration to return home. This historical process was revitalized at the end of the last century by Theodor Herzl, father of the modern Zionist Movement and a massive immigration of Eastern European Jews homeward began as early as 1882. These first Jewish pioneers lived in the Era of Enlightenment, a brief period in history, when national aspirations for the peoples of Europe were at long last being realized. For the displaced Jews it, too, was time to go home.

By 1917, Zionism had achieved its first significant goal toward self-realization when Great Britain issued the Balfour Declaration recognizing the right of the Jewish people to their homeland in Palestine. The next three decades witnessed the rise of fascism which led to a Jewish migration of fear for those who were able to leave Europe before the deluge destroyed them. Even when fleeing Jews from Nazi Europe were denied access by Great Britain to this one last refuge, they kept coming. The modern State of Israel was born from the ashes of 6 000 000 Jews. On November 29, 1947, two years after the end of the Second World War, the United Nations declared the Partition of Palestine. On that day 671 900 Jews were living in this land, 453 000 of whom were immigrants who had settled in Israel since 1919.

The legitimate right of Israel to exist as a nation was actively rejected by seven Arab states, beginning a war that was to last for one and a half years. During the ensuing War for Independence, more than 200 000 new immigrants arrived at Israel's shores. Most of them, recent survivors from Nazi persecution, were immediately sent into battle. More than 6000 Jewish Israeli youth died in that war. Hardly a family remained untouched. The question of how to cope simultaneously with awesome security problems remains an urgent issue in Israeli society today (Israeli Statistical Abstracts, 1993; Israeli Ministry of Education and Culture, 1991).

Israel today: a country of immigrants

During its first six years, the State of Israel more than doubled its population through migration. This trend of unconditional absorption still continues: In the 1950s and '60s, Israel absorbed more than 100 000 Jews from North Africa and a wave of Jewish immigration from Rumania and other Balkan countries. During the 1980s and '90s, it is absorbing new waves of Ethiopian and Russian immigrants (Israeli Statistical Abstracts, 1993).

The main problem in integrating most of these new peoples into Israeli society has been vastly dissimilar cultural backgrounds. While those who initially arrived from European or English speaking cultures reflected cultural norms and traditions similar to those already living in Israel, others, from countries such as Morocco, Iraq, Yemen, Algeria, Tunisia, Libya, Iran and Egypt, embraced a variety of different values. Bridging cultural gaps was made more difficult by the "absorbers" of that time— Jews of European origin (54.8% of Israel's total population)— who were devoid of any cultural point of reference or understanding of these newcomers and unconsciously reflected an "anthropological patronizing nature" according to which "they knew everything better." In attempting to expedite absorption, they often ignored cultural sensibilities, with disastrous effects.

One of the psychosocial problems that arose from this "melting pot" approach was the attenuation of parental authority. The patriarchal pattern of immigrant families, characteristic of the oriental cultures in particular, was contested and broken. Children learned Hebrew in school, for example, while their parents struggled with severe economic problems and had neither time nor energy to learn Hebrew. The result was not only communication problems within the resettlement communities but also within families. (Any similarity between Israel and the US in this regard is not coincidental. The United States was long a "melting pot" of different cultures, where it often took two to three generations to close the gap between the indigenous population and the newcomers.)

Another issue faced by Israeli youth is related to their encounters with survivors of the Holocaust. From the time of their arrival in Israel it was expected of survivors to repress their most traumatic experiences. They arrived after the Second World War in a country that was in the process of achieving statehood; despite all its hardships, Israel's youth was in a state of euphoria following its long War of Independence. Joy and exultation, together with feelings of strength and victory, charged the emotional climate. The Holocaust survivors symbolized and represented everything that Zionism was trying to forget: the image of the homeless, the weak, the apologetic, the Jew surrendering Jew to humiliation.

Only today, after 48 years of silence, are many formerly displaced persons beginning to share those feelings hidden deep in the past. Their absorption into Israeli society was particularly difficult, all the more so because they felt they could not complain. They felt a contempt by those who absorbed them, a sense of personal anger and accusation in the question they were asked:

"How could you surrender and not fight back?"

Survivors felt that no one wanted to listen to their tales of horror and that they had, at whatever cost, to hide their shame from their children—children who were born free. This was the collective repression of a whole nation that could not confront the horrors of its past. The children of the Holocaust survivors, in turn, had to grow up knowing but not knowing, seeing but not seeing, all the shadows of their parents' hidden secrets. Only in recent years have support groups emerged for the second generation of "survivors of survivors" of the Holocaust; only now has the terrible damage become evident of what this second generation suffered from their parents' terrible silence— a silence of absolute alienation from the past.

Adolescents in this study represent the third generation after the Holocaust. Their awareness and degree of insight are greater and deeper than that of their parents, and yet, there are still reports about difficulties and problems deeply rooted in the Holocaust.

There is, however, a positive aftermath to this "end of silence": The Israeli family of today is actively seeking out greater stability as can be seen in its relatively lower divorce rate, when compared to families in other Western societies. There is an unconscious wish to establish large and stable families as a form of compensation for the traumatic destruction of their parents' and grandparents' families— a wish to make things right again.

National identity: questions and doubts

Max Weber, the prominent sociologist and political economist, claimed that a distinct and dynamic relationship existed between revolutions and religion. Zionism, the ideology upon which the State of Israel was reborn and rebuilt, was a revolution in the patterns of thought, behavior and way of life for the Jewish people. It required commitment and sacrifices characteristic of religion, while it simultaneously sought social and political renewal. It drew upon the traditional mythology of "David vs. Goliath—the few against the world"—in order to sustain and strengthen a people in all of Israel's wars. The native born Israeli, the Sabra, identified with the State of Israel.

This national identity is not taken for granted today, however. For many, there exists an identity crisis. While the generation that had fought and founded the State struggled with the ideological crossroads concerning Israel's future, the generation of the Yom Kippur War (1973) struggled with the question of how much should the individual sacrifice for the group. In the last two decades, the development of international communication has strengthened contacts with Western culture (note the answers of the interviewed adolescent, Adam, p. 119, stating his goals in ten years). The earlier acceptance of Zionist values is now being questioned. A political awareness concerning the Palestinian people is more openly being expressed, and this generation of youth is more politically involved. There are more extreme shifts within the youth culture, both to the left and to the right.

Youth culture, army service and high school

It may be concluded that today, Israeli youth is in the same situation as most of the adolescents in the West. The need to cope with rapidly changing technological and social developments in the world is leading many to doubt their parents' values as well as to increase a tendency toward individualism and hedonism. An independent "youth culture" has arisen, marked by negative phenomena similar to that of the West, such as joining esoteric cults in the search for meaning, drugs, alcohol and expressions of violence. It is only the compulsory army service (for men between the ages of 18 and 21 and for women between the ages of 18 and 20) and other frameworks of obligatory values that compel most of these young people to leave the hedonistic search and to become a part of accepted organized social groups.

High school, as a dynamic and integrative framework of scholastic and social achievement, is still perceived as an important motivation of adolescents to prove themselves.

Kibbutzim

This study describes urban and rural youngsters. Approximately 50% of Israeli subjects grew up in urban areas similar to other cities in the Western world in which the nuclear family remains the important socializing agent during the first critical years until formal schooling takes over (Ziv, Guttman and Green, 1980). Another 50% were raised on "kibbutzim" (farming collectives), a type of rural community unique to the State of Israel that provides a different socialization process.

Understanding the meaning of the *kibbutz* to its residents is important in understanding this latter group. Martin Buber (1958) called it "the bold Jewish undertaking of the twentieth century ... a utopian socialism that finally works." Bruno Bettelheim (1969) referred to its inhabitants as "children of the dream." Psychologists, sociologists and educators worldwide continue to be intrigued by its physical, socioeconomic and educational qualities. Only the *kibbutz* appears to take itself for granted.

The *kibbutz's* original premise remains at the center of its philosophical being: individuals give to and receive from the community according to their special intellectual and physical abilities, all within the framework of an elevated regard for the value of productive manual labor. The realization of this ideology lies in a precarious balance between the struggle of the individual's need for self-fulfilment and communal need for social cohesiveness, equality, and conformity. While the *kibbutz* does absorb new immigrants, its selection of new members requires that, first and foremost, individuals accept and adapt to a very precise set of social and cultural norms. The result is that *kibbutz* society in general is far more homogeneous demographically than that of the cities or villages in Israel.

The socializing process within the *kibbutz* is singular, based on an ideology that reinforces cooperation and embraces all aspects of life. While the *kibbutz* is a stable and consolidated society, however, the social, cultural, and educational changes made over the past 35 years show that it is not irrevocably trapped by dogmatic ideology. To the contrary, it is proving itself capable of meeting the changing needs of its coming generations. In recent years it has become increasingly tolerant and responsive to outside influences.

"*Kibbutzniks*" understand that the future of their unique society lies with their children; nowhere does the *kibbutz* invest more energy than in the education of its next generation. One of the principal characteristics of this collective education is the provision of coordinated care of children while both mother and father work full time as equals. To accomplish this, the *kibbutz* created a unique social-educational personality, the "*metapelet*" or "mothering caretaker." Over the years "fathering caretakers" have also emerged.

A literal translation of the *metapelet's* role is nearly impossible, since it has had over the years a multi-faceted and interdisciplinary function. In the first generations of *kibbutz* youth who ate and slept away from their parents' home in their own "children's house," the *metapelet* had enormous overlapping responsibilities involving many aspects of informal learning and socialization. She was not quite a parent surrogate, but much more than an educational staff person— perhaps the first "general guidance specialist." Since the 1980s, many *kibbutzim* have returned to more traditional approaches to childrearing in which children eat, sleep, and spend much of their informal time in their parents' homes, and the *metapelet's* role has been redefined in function to that of "general counselor."

Today, the vast majority of "*metaplot*" (plural of "*metapelet*") are fellow members of the community and, as such, have a shared and mutual interest in the best possible education of their children. In working and rearing collectively, these parents provide for their children a system of maximal care, including material comforts, which as individuals they could not afford. The *kibbutz* "Children's House," in which children spend their time with their peers and *metaplot*, is not a daycare center: It is an organic part of their lives and identities, together with their biological homes. While "classmates" often assume the importance of sibling relationships, the biological home and the Children's House are partners in the shared process of childrearing, and, in a way unique unto this community, the entire *kibbutz* is, in effect, an extended family for the child. For this reason, it is often easier for *kibbutz* children to seek support and guidance outside the strict parameters of their own homes.

In *kibbutzim*, where personal financial success is neutralized, social involvement and social acceptance assume primary importance. To grow up an outsider from within, however, brings with it social alienation and loneliness. It is not surprising, therefore, that "to belong or not to belong" becomes the essential preoccupation of the child growing up in this unique society. This can be one of the most reinforcing or painful imperatives of *kibbutz* life.

The status of counseling

Counseling in Israel is highly integrative in role definition and in function. The school counselor interacts both intensively and extensively not only with students, but also with the principal, teachers, psychologists, social workers, school nurses and special needs staff as well (Fishman and Stuftal, 1978).

The functions of the school counselor were initially defined in the recommendations of the Central Committee for Reform in High Schools in 1969. However, the role has since developed from the relatively simple assignment of fulfilling a function in "continuing education" into what has become a full and comprehensive profession that concerns itself with many related areas, among which individual counseling has achieved a special prominence (Fishman and Stuftal, 1978). In 1991, Israel's Ministry of Education employed 1821 counselors, most of whom were placed in the country's elementary, junior and high school systems (Israeli Ministry of Education and Culture, 1991). In addition, many other professional help-providers such as social workers and *metaplot* have formally or informally taken on counseling roles. Today, most child and family guidance clinics of the *Kibbutz* Movement include staff counselors who function much as "guidance counselors" in the United States. "Counseling" has been given a centrality of function of many professional help providers throughout the Israeli educational community and the counselor has emerged as ... a first among equals, a person for all seasons.

By making counseling readily available to children and their parents from within the school systems, Israel has gone beyond the preconceived fears of social stigma to an open and meaningful dialogue between children, parents, teachers and counselors.

The Study and Its Methodology

The Israeli study compares the responses of "advantaged" Israeli youth with their "advantaged" counterparts in the multinational study. It does not include a "nonadvantaged" or "poverty" group.

Subjects

Subjects were 305 adolescents (160 females and 145 males) aged 13—15 years. Approximately 52% came from *kibbutzim* communities and the other 48% from urban communities and their suburbs.[1] Because of the following similarities between *kibbutz* and urban subcultures as regards socioeconomic status, all youngsters were placed together in one "advantaged" group:

[1] These figures greatly overrepresent the percentage of Israelis who live on *kibbutzim*, but are reflective of the adolescent populations with whom the author has professional involvement and to whom he has access. In this sense, they are typical.

1. all youngsters bear cultural characteristics similar to the modern, middle-class norms of Western European societies;
2. occupations of heads of families in both groups fell at approximately the midpoint on a scale from unskilled to highly skilled;
3. all parents in both groups were literate;
4. standards of living were similar, with family and per capita income classified as slightly higher than the national average;
5. living arrangements were comparable, with most urban housing similar to condominium living in the West and *kibbutz* housing in duplex or triplex buildings; and
6. schooling levels were comparable, with both groups attending junior high and high school.

Subjects are expected to attain the educational level of 12 years of schooling (high school graduation).

Data collection and coding

Data were collected during the years 1989—91 using the procedures detailed in Chapter 2. Questionnaires were translated into Hebrew. All data were collected exclusively by the author.

Potential subjects were provided group introductions to the multinational study by the author in the presence of their teachers, school counselors or group leaders. Sites for these meetings included two regional *kibbutz* schools (one junior high school and one high school), two non-*kibbutz* schools (one urban and one semi-urban high school) and one urban youth scout movement (analogous to the Boy Scouts in the US).

The introduction stressed anonymity of answers but did not disclose the questions to be asked. Subjects participated on a voluntary basis; approximately 50% offered to answer the questionnaire after hearing the introduction. Appointments were scheduled for those who agreed to participate to meet in groups of four to five youngsters after school hours in one of three locations (the author's home, office, or subjects' school).

Approximately 10% of the volunteer group dropped out after viewing the questionnaire. Of the 305 youngsters who completed the questionnaire, 32 were known to the author previously; of these, 8 were known on a counselor—counselee basis.

An observation of the author while reviewing written responses of subjects was that, in more than a few cases, the oldest adolescents responded to the first question evasively, mentioning the "defeat of their favorite soccer team" or other such trivialities. Their "real" problems appeared to emerge on the second or third page. Conversely, those subjects who answered the first question with responses marked by significant anxiety or distress demonstrated a tendency to avoid reporting further problems either by leaving blank questions or writing "no problem."

Coding of data, conducted by the author, followed the procedures outlined in Chapter 2. Interrater reliability as measured by the percentage of agreement between the author and Pittsburgh mastercoder was .95 for classes and .83 for categories-within-classes.

Study Results

Problems

Table 8.1(a), comparing the multinational data with those of the Israeli study, clearly shows that among the reported problems the three most frequently cited

TABLE 9.1 *Israeli and multinational studies compared: percentages of total responses falling into classes and categories of problems*

(a) Classes

Multinational Study				Problems	*Israeli Study*			
Male		*Female*			*Male*		*Female*	
%	Rank	%	Rank		%	Rank	%	Rank
0.4	(14)	0.2	(14)	Extreme poverty	0.3	(13)	0.0	—
0.8	(12)	0.8	(12)	War	4.6	(6)	5.3	(7)
0.2	(13)	0.6	(13)	Catastrophe	1.5	(12)	2.1	(10)
4.2	(6)	1.5	(10)	Material desires	3.4	(8)	2.1	(10)
12.6	(3)	20.2	(3)	Family issues	18.6	(2)	23.7	(1)
34.9	(1)	24.7	(1)	Schooling issues	27.8	(1)	18.9	(2)
19.6	(2)	21.7	(2)	Identity	14.7	(3)	16.1	(3)
1.1	(11)	1.6	(9)	Sexuality	3.1	(9)	4.1	(9)
3.2	(9)	6.5	(5)	Courtship/dating	2.3	(11)	5.5	(6)
8.7	(4)	9.5	(4)	Interpersonal	10.6	(4)	7.4	(5)
5.1	(5)	4.4	(6)	Emotions	6.7	(5)	8.3	(4)
1.2	(10)	1.2	(11)	Self-fulfilment	2.6	(10)	4.6	(8)
3.8	(8)	3.4	(7.5)	Altruism	3.6	(7)	0.9	(12)
4.1	(7)	3.4	(7.5)	No problem	0.3	(X)	1.1	(X)

*(b) Categories**

Male Category	%	*Female* Category	%
Multinational Study			
Academic failure	9.9	Academic failure	7.4
		Friendship	6.9
		Self-confidence	5.8
Israeli Study			
Male		*Female*	
Social success/failure	5.4		
Self expectations	5.2		

* Representing 5% or more of responses.

classes for all groups of adolescents are **schooling**, **family** and **personal identity/self concept**, with **schooling** the highest ranked concern for most groups. Israeli females, who reported a higher percentage of **family** than **schooling** problems, were an exception.

Concerns regarding **family** frequently reflected generation gaps exacerbated by inability of parents to adjust to life in a new country as quickly as their children. The **family** problem of a 13-year-old Russian immigrant to Israel:

> "My parents ... They are old, not in their age but in their thinking. They are old-fashioned."

The Israeli data provide another confirmation that adolescent concerns are age-related and remarkably similar, regardless of national background and gender, as reported in Gibson *et al.* (1991). Our data concurs, also, with those collected by Friedman in a 1989 study in which that author reported that the most frequently reported problem of 1700 ninth and eleventh grade students in Israel was related to schooling and studies.

Table 9.1(a) also confirms the gender trends reported in the multinational study in which males reported a higher percentage of responses related to **schooling** and a lower percentage related to **family**.

There is a marked difference between the Israeli study results and those of the multinational study, however, in respect to reported concerns regarding **war**. In the Israeli study, **war** is ranked 6—7, representing between 4.6% and 5.3% of all reported responses, as compared to a ranking of 12 in the multinational results, representing less than 1% of responses. Increased concern regarding **war** emphasizes the particular reality in which young Israelis grow up. The categories shown in Table 9.1(b) of "social success/failure" and "self-expectation" are also represented prominently, probably reflecting the competitiveness, social involvement and resultant stress among adolescents in the study.

Another recurrent concern noted by the author in many responses of Israeli youth that does not appear in Table 9.1 is related to required military service. This worry, unique in the multinational study to the Israeli subjects and corroborated by Friedman (1989) as one of the most important concerns reported by Israeli youth, was not provided a class in the coding manual and was therefore coded, under a variety of available categories, depending on the subjects' wording and context in which the worry appeared.[2] Its omission in the coding manual represents an important limitation to the multinational and Israeli studies.

Review of Israeli subjects' written reports produced varied responses regarding war and military service which often reflected questions and doubts regarding the Holocaust in Europe as well as Israel's political situation today.

[2] These included self-expectation (a category-within-the-class, **personal identity and self-concept**), role conflict (**interpersonal and socialization issues**), stress (**emotions and feelings**) and fear of war (**war**).

"After visiting concentration camps in Poland, I can't understand and I am angry that my parents didn't fight and the Jews were slaughtered like sheep." (15-year-old boy from a *kibbutz*)

"The Intifada ... Are we Israelis right or wrong in our relationships with the Arabs?" (15-year-old boy from Haifa)

"The Arabs have many countries to live in. We have only Israel ... They want to throw us into the sea..." (15-year-old girl from Tel Aviv)

"Will there always be war? What kind of a life is this?" (15-year-old girl from France who had lived three years in Israel)

TABLE 9.2 *Israeli and multinational studies compared: percentages of total responses falling into classes and categories of coping strategies*

(a) Classes

Multinational Study				*Coping strategies*	*Israeli Study*			
Male		*Female*			*Male*		*Female*	
%	*Rank*	*%*	*Rank*		*%*	*Rank*	*%*	*Rank*
14.7	(2)	16.5	(2)	Seek/give assistance	16.8	(3)	15.7	(3)
12.9	(3)	14.6	(3)	Interpersonal	22.6	(2)	22.4	(2)
49.2	(1)	44.3	(1)	Individual problem solving	45.7	(1)	42.7	(1)
2.8	(6)	2.1	(6)	stress management	4.4	(5)	3.7	(6)
0.3	(9)	1.4	(7)	Crying	0.4	(7)	2.8	(7)
0.6	(8)	0.7	(8)	Religious	0.1	(8)	0.3	(9)
10.3	(4)	11.6	(4)	Resignation	4.2	(6)	7.7	(4)
8.5	(5)	8.2	(5)	Disengage	5.3	(4)	4.2	(5)
0.7	(7)	0.5	(9)	Anti-social	0.4	(7)	0.6	(8)
0.0	(X)	0.0	(X)	Do nothing	0.0	(X)	0.0	(X)

*(b) Categories**

Male		*Female*	
Category	*%*	*Category*	*%*
	Multinational Study		
Try harder	22.0	Try harder	17.7
Planning	17.4	Planning	16.2
Seek support	11.2	Seek support	13.4
Assertive coping	6.8	Assertive coping	9.0
	Israeli Study		
Male		*Female*	
Try harder	15.4	Seek support	14.0
Seek support	12.1	Try harder	13.4
Assertive coping	8.6	Assertive coping	9.3
Hostile aggressive	8.3	Planning	7.9
Seek company of others	5.0	Hostile Aggressive	7.6
		Seek company of others	5.0

* Representing 5% or more of responses.

Their own required military service was on the minds of two 15-year-old boys from *kibbutzim:*

"In two years, I will be in the army. Will I have physical and mental strength to be accepted into the paratroopers, like my father's older brother?"

"I want to be strong and am determined to distinguish myself in the army."

They weren't alone. A same-aged male peer from Tel Aviv:

"I will be prepared for whatever challenges I will have
to meet in the future."

Coping strategies

Results of the multinational and Israeli studies as shown in Table 9.2 demonstrate that both the classes and categories within classes accounting for more than 5% of total responses to the question of coping strategy are remarkably similar. **Individual problem-solving**, the strategy of choice in terms of percentage of reported classes of responses for both studies, represents an expression of confidence in adopting decision-making strategies and a manifestation of initiative in selecting alternatives. The Israeli study confirms the gender trend reported in the multinational study in which males report a higher percentage of **individual problem-solving** strategies.

Israeli subjects differed from those in the multinational study in reporting a sufficient number of strategies that are defined in the coding manual as "hostile aggressive" and "seeking company of others" to appear in Table 9.2(b). Both reflect **interpersonal coping**, a strategy reported with greater frequency in the Israeli data than in the multinational study.

Helpers

Table 9.3(a) shows that, while the multinational data suggests that **family** members are more often chosen as helpers than **non-family**, the reverse was true for Israeli subjects. (One exception is the multinational female group in which the percentages of **family** and **non-family** responses are similar.) Examination of categories of chosen helpers (Table 9.3(b)) suggests that this finding was probably caused by the high percentage of Israeli responses indicating professional counselors as desired helpers. In the Israeli study, this includes social workers, *metaplot* and youth leaders as well as counselors.[3]

[3] While, by definition, all of these professional helpers are not strictly counselors, they function in counseling roles and are readily approached by Israeli adolescents in search of guidance counseling and crisis intervention. Because there were no categories for each of these professionals listed in the multinational coding manual, they were coded by the author under the category, "professional counselor."

TABLE 9.3 *Israeli and multinational studies compared: percentages of total responses falling into classes and categories of desired helpers*

(a) Classes

Multinational Study Male %	Rank	Female %	Rank	Helpers	Israeli Study Male %	Rank	Female %	Rank
52.5	(2)	46.2	(2)	Family	33.9	(2)	32.0	(2)
40.4	(2)	47.2	(1)	Non-family	58.2	(1)	59.5	(1)
1.4	(5)	1.6	(4.5)	Offender	5.6	(3)	5.6	(3)
0.4	(6.5)	0.5	(7)	Supernatural	0.5	(5)	0.7	(5)
0.4	(6.5)	0.6	(6)	Creatures/objects	0.7	(4)	1.1	(4)
2.2	(4)	1.6	(4.5)	Non-specific	0.3	(6)	0.0	(7)
2.6	(3)	2.3	(3)	Nobody	0.9	(7)	1.1	(6)

*(b) Categories**

Male Category	%	Female Category	%
Multinational Study			
Personal friend	17.3	Personal friend	24.0
Mother	15.4	Mother	16.1
Father	13.4	Father	6.9
Teacher	6.7	Parents/family	5.9
Parents/family	6.3	Sister	5.9
		Counselor	5.4
		Person with desired qualities	5.2
		Teacher	5.0
Israeli Study			
Professional counselor	14.7	Professional counselor	17.7
Personal friend	14.3	Personal friend	13.7
Teacher	8.7	Parents/family	7.3
Parents/family	7.8	Other	7.3
Father	7.0	Teacher	7.0
Source of problem	5.5	Mother	6.4
Mother	5.4	Boyfriend	5.2

* Representing 5% or more of responses.

Probable reasons for the preference for these professional helpers are twofold:

1. kibbutz adolescents (who comprise approximately 50% of Israeli subjects) prefer the guidance and intervention of the *metapelet*, who is readily available on a daily basis and highly approachable to help with schooling problems; and
2. students in regular schools and youth groups are intensely involved with professional helpers counseling tied both to classroom and teaching, often on one-to-one bases.

TABLE 9.4 *Israeli and multinational studies compared: percentages of total responses falling into classes and categories of desired helper qualities*

(a) Classes

Multinational Study				Helper qualities	Israeli Study			
Male		Female			Male		Female	
%	Rank	%	Rank		%	Rank	%	Rank
4.9	(4)	3.6	(4)	Powerful	7.9	(4)	7.1	(4)
36.3	(1)	34.3	(1)	Knowledgeable	38.2	(1)	34.5	(1)
2.1	(5)	2.0	(5)	Available	2.6	(5)	2.4	(5)
30.3	(2)	30.5	(2)	Personal qualities	30.3	(2)	32.8	(2)
24.6	(3)	27.6	(3)	Concern	19.6	(3)	21.1	(3)
0.8	(7)	0.8	(7)	Uncertain	0.8	(6)	1.1	(6)
1.1	(6)	1.2	(6)	No listing	0.0	(X)	0.0	(X)

*(b) Categories**

Male		Female	
Category	%	Category	%
Multinational Study			
Understanding	11.6	Understanding	14.8
Experienced	10.4	Similarity	9.6
Similarity	8.3	Approachable	8.9
Trustworthy	6.5	Experienced	8.4
Content knowledge	6.4	Caring/loving	7.6
Approachable	6.4	Trustworthy	6.0
Generous	5.7	Content knowledge	5.5
Supportive	5.1	Gives advice	5.1
Caring/loving	5.0		
Israeli study			
Experienced	12.1	Experienced	10.3
Similarity	9.9	Similarity	8.4
Supportive	8.6	Understanding	8.0
Content knowledge	7.8	Supportive	7.2
Understanding	6.9	Content knowledge	6.8
Authority	6.1	Caring/loving	5.7
Loyal	5.4	Authority	5.6

* Representing 5% or more of responses.

With **schooling** issues most prominent among the problems of Israeli youngsters, this involvement of professional helpers with their young charges appears to have created successful working relationships. In many cases, these professional helpers bridge the generation gap between the youth culture and the authoritative figures which loom above the adolescent's daily life experiences. Israel represents the only national study of our multinational analysis in which professional helpers are preferred by adolescents before any other helper.

The fact that in the Israeli study there was a higher preference for the person who is the source of the problem corresponds with the assertive coping and hostile— aggressive strategies noted in Table 9.2(b). This might confirm a consistent determination to confront (at any price), rather than to avoid issues.

Desired helper qualities

Consistent with the multinational study, Table 9.4(a) showed that **experience** ranked #1 for both genders in the Israeli study and for males in the multinational study (#2 for multinational females). Similarly, **understanding** ranked #2 for both genders in the Israeli study and for males in the multinational study (#1 for multinational females). Authority appeared as a significant factor in the Israeli study, while it did not reach the required 5% threshold in the multinational study to appear in Table 9.4(b)

TABLE 9.5 *Israeli and multinational studies compared: percentages of total responses falling into classes and categories of desired helping modes*

(a) Classes

Multinational Study				*Helping modes*	*Israeli Study*			
Male		*Female*			*Male*		*Female*	
%	*Rank*	*%*	*Rank*		*%*	*Rank*	*%*	*Rank*
3.4	(6)	1.7	(8)	Direct need satisfaction	2.0	(6)	0.8	(7)
9.0	(3)	7.4	(3)	Exercise power/solve	12.4	(3)	12.5	(3)
5.2	(4)	4.2	(4)	Intercede	4.6	(4)	4.1	(5)
47.4	(1)	44.2	(1)	Counsel	39.3	(1)	37.1	(2)
25.9	(2)	33.7	(2)	Attend to	35.7	(2)	21.1	(3)
2.6	(8)	3.3	(6)	Evade problem	4.3	(5)	1.1	(6)
3.6	(5)	3.4	(5)	Uncertain	0.7	(7)	5.1	(4)
3.0	(7)	2.1	(7)	No list	0.9	(X)	1.4	(X)

*(b) Categories**

Male		*Female*	
Category	*%*	*Category*	*%*
	Multinational Study		
Advise	16.7	Advise	17.4
Help solve problem	12.1	Comfort	11.8
Direct	11.3	Help solve problem	11.8
Comfort	9.7	Encourage	8.6
Encourage	6.4	Direct	7.3
	Israeli Study		
Help solve problem	11.7	Help solve problem	10.6
Share	9.7	Share	8.1
Comfort	9.2	Advise	6.7
Encourage	7.0	Comfort	6.2
Advise	6.6	Understanding	5.6
Direct	5.8	Listening	5.6
Solve problem	5.2	Prevent problem	5.0

* Representing 5% or more of responses.

Desired helping modes

While there were no significant differences between the results of the two studies as regards classes of helping modes (Table 9.5(a)), there were some interesting differences in the categories (Table 9.5(b)) which should be noted. Israeli adolescents report that they want help to solve their problems almost twice as frequently as they suggest direct (authoritative) counseling. The preference of Israeli adolescents for sharing (... the helper offering information about himself, his/her experiences, thoughts, and feelings, without any attempt to judge or direct ...) reinforces the first premise of seeking help rather than relying upon the authoritative imposition of a solution. Both of these preferred positions indicate these adolescents' high degree of independence.

Summary

A study of similarities and differences

The world of adolescents, despite national, cultural, socioeconomic and gender differences, represents a unity of remarkably similar classes of problems. Israeli youngsters matched their multinational peers in demonstrating concerns regarding schooling, family and identity/self concept, much as their peers in the other countries of the multinational study and much as traditional psychoanalytic theory would have predicted. They also matched their peers in most frequent coping strategies and many aspects of helpseeking as well as in trends that describe gender differences in problems and coping.

The Israeli study demonstrates, also, the importance of environmental factors, as social psychologists would predict. The high percentage of problems related to self-expectations and hostile aggressive coping strategies most probably reveal a reality in which Israeli adolescents grow up. Coping, not crisis, is the hallmark of their age.

Problems and coping unique to Israel

Of particular note are the choices of seeking professional help for problems and the emphasis on problems related to war and military service. The former, unique in any of the multinational studies, provides an important demonstration of the success of Israel's counseling system. The fact that the latter could not be demonstrated quantitatively because it was not included in the multinational coding scale provides a limitation to both the multinational and Israeli studies. This does not preclude the importance of this qualitative finding, however, but demonstrates the important interactive role of adolescents and the world in which they live as well as the complexities involved in multinational research.

Implications for counseling

Implications of the study results reinforce the conclusions that:

1. The counselor's role should be perceived not as a specialist, which is overly confining, nor as a generalist, which is vague and misleading, but rather as a "specialized generalist," who acts as an agent fostering change in adolescent coping.

2. While the preference of professional counselor among the helpers chosen reveals the depth and breadth of educational services in which Israeli adolescents develop, consideration should be given to a problematic duality of the "school counseling image." To reduce conflicts inherent in interdisciplinary and interpersonal relationships among counselors, teachers and other related professionals, awareness of appropriate roles of all these professionals needs to be cultivated.

3. The counselor's role should be perceived as a "crisis intervention agent" based on ego-supportive principles, keeping in mind that adolescents expect experience, similarity, understanding, and above all, unconditional acceptance.

4. The preference of choosing personal friends as helpers suggests that counseling should consist not only of individual consultation, but of group guidance techniques as well.

5. The family possesses an inherent duality, which is both highly complex and complicated. While adolescents turn to the family as a preferred helper, they also target it as one of the primary sources of their problems. The family as both subject/helper often requires active intervention of counseling and guidance.

6. Finally, this study has endeavored not only to provide answers but to raise equally important questions as well, the most pressing of which is the future perception of counseling. The question that remains is, should it be confined to the strict parameters of professional specialization, or should its role be further expanded into an extensive and comprehensive "way of life"?

10

Kuwait

QASEM AL-SARRAF

University of Kuwait

"I want to be my own person."

Fatima is the fourteen-year-old daughter of a physician/father and a business-woman/mother. Her parents both studied in the United States; her father passed his Medical Board exams there; her mother received her BA degree in English literature. She wants very much to succeed so that her "parents will be proud," and imagines herself going to the United States to study as they did. Fatima was interviewed after the Gulf War.

"Ten years from now, I will be at a US university getting a master's degree in journalism. I don't want to be at a job that is routine. And I want to be my own person ... not dependent on my parents or anyone else.

"The problem that worries me most now is keeping up my grades. I know that my future depends on them. If I don't do well in high school, my choices will be limited. When I think about it, I spend more time working and stop putting off my work or saying to myself, I've just started high school, I still have plenty of time. I'll pull up my grades later.

"When I worry a lot, I go to my parents, my sisters and one of my teachers. They encourage me and help me to be a better student. They have been through this already themselves; they have more experience than I do; and they are all people I respect. I don't want them to be angry with me; I just want them to understand and help me. My parents pressure me to do better, but it's good that they do because I've been improving.

"What are my three wishes? First, I want world peace, because everyone in all countries needs it. Next, I want my family to be happy and healthy throughout their lives. Finally, I wish our Kuwaiti society could become more open and liberal."

Introduction

Country and culture

The modern State of Kuwait, situated on the Arabian Persian Gulf, is a small country with a frontier of approximately 685 km and a land area of 17 818 sq.km, much of which is desert. During its cool season from October through April, low vegetation covers most of the land and temperatures range from 40 to 70°F. During May through September, its hot season, temperatures range from 100° to 120°F.

The country traces its origins to the early eighteenth century when the Utban clan of the Anaza tribe settled in the area. As a sign of their influence and the respect with they were viewed, the Sabah family were elected in 1752 as the hereditary ruling family. Rulers of Kuwait since that date have been members of the Sabah family. Kuwait was affiliated with Great Britain by treaty in 1899 and gained full sovereignty in 1961. In 1962, the current Kuwaiti Constitution was promulgated and the government became a democracy (Al-Ebraheem, 1984, p. 8). Today, executive power is vested in the Head of State, the Amir, and is exercised through a Council of Ministers under the leadership of the Prime Minister. Legislative power is vested in a National Assembly of fifty elected members who serve four years. Adult Kuwaiti male citizens (individuals who are not naturalized and whose ancestors dwelled in Kuwait prior to 1920) are eligible to vote. The subjects of this study are Kuwaiti citizens.

Economics, government and the presence of war

The modern Kuwaiti economic system includes both government-owned and private enterprises: The government owns all petroleum, natural gas and derivative industries, while the private sector operates building materials, constructions, trade and finance companies. Government spending priorities include education, housing, roads, public utilities, telecommunications, transportation and medical care. The Kuwaiti economy grew by 5% in 1989, reaching a gross national product of approximately US$30 billion (Al-Ebraheem, 1991). Kuwait's principal exports are crude petroleum and refined products, natural gas, chemicals, machinery, and transport equipment.

Kuwait today is a welfare and tax-free state. One of the most wealthy countries in the world, it had an annual per capita income of $20 250 in 1981 which made it the highest in the world that year (Hakim, 1984, p. 4). This figure has since decreased somewhat. In 1989, during the time our interviews were conducted, annual per capita income was $15 308.

The population of Kuwait in 1989 was approximately 2.2 million, approximately 123.1 persons per sq. km. Of this number, Kuwaitis constituted approximately 40%, other Arab nationalities approximately 37.9%, Asians 21% and Europeans and Americans 0.9% (Al-Ebraheem, 1991, p. 4). The population is

95% Muslim, of which 70% are Sunni and 30% Shi'ite Muslems. Of the non-Muslim expatriates, the majority are Christian, although there are Hindus as well as adherents of other faiths present. Although Friday is the holiday for all government offices and private businesses, the Kuwaiti Constitution guarantees freedom of religion and protects this freedom in accordance with established customs (Al-Ebraheem, 1991, p. 5). A Catholic church is situated in downtown Kuwait City.

In 1986, severe internal pressures in Kuwait caused by the Iran—Iraq war brought a dissolution of the National Assembly and suspension of elections. This was followed in 1990 by the seven-month Iraqi invasion of Kuwait until the country's liberation by the allied forces under the leadership of the US.

Kuwaiti family life and childrearing

The extended Kuwaiti family is central to Kuwaiti life. Decisions relating to family patterning, childrearing methods and other activities which carry significance for the extended family involve parents, grandparents and other relatives.

In recent years, childrearing methods have been affected not only by the changing social structure of the culture, including marriage, living conditions and socioeconomic status, but also by the social content of the society, including learning styles and individual perceptions as they are being affected by increasing contact with other societies (Al-Sarraf, 1991, p. 6). With Kuwaiti mothers entering the workforce in increasing numbers, families frequently depend heavily on household maids or nannies to take care of their children while they are away at work. This appears to be posing many of the same problems for Kuwaiti families as for families in other parts of the modern world. It has been hypothesized, for example, that surrogate parenting by maids or nannies may be damaging mother—child relationships. As in other countries, when increasingly busy Kuwaiti parents are at home, other activities often engage their time sufficiently to weaken personal interactions. The divorce rate among Kuwaitis is now 30%, affected in part by changing relationships between males and females (Kuwait Ministry of Planning, 1990).

Family problems

With 1.5 television sets per family and increased opportunity to travel abroad and observe television programming from around the world, Kuwaiti adults and children are learning about both the good and the bad outside their country, and sometimes use their knowledge to their own detriment. Drug abuse has become a problem; according to a recent police report, there were 343 reported cases of drug abuse in 1989. 62.8% of these cases were schoolchildren, and 6.5% were females (*Arab Times*, 1992).

Education and literacy

Education is considered one of the most important factors that can be used to assess the development of a country. Among developing nations, in which sometimes three out of four young people remain illiterate, Kuwait stands out as a nation in which education is available and free to all from kindergarten to university (Shaw, 1976). According to a UNESCO report (1960) concerning the state of education in the Arab countries, there were 10 532 schoolchildren enrolled in the first six grades for every 100 000 Kuwaitis. This ratio was the highest achieved at that time by any Arab state. Illiteracy is now limited almost exclusively to the most senior adult population.

Opportunities for women

Kuwait today is rated first in the Arab world in terms of opportunities for women. Females began to attend school for the first time in 1937 when some 140 female students joined the 620 males in pursuit of an education, but in strictly segregated classes. During the 1987—88 school year, there were 372 000 students in government-operated schools, of whom 191 000 were males and 181 000 females (*Annual Statistical Abstracts*, 1989). Fully 41% of Kuwait University degree holders are women (Kuwait University Statistical Bulletin, 1990). A breakdown of the 1991 programs of university study demonstrates the diversity of women's interests: Women undergraduates formed 80% of the student body in the College of Arts; 87% in the College of Education; 60% in the College of Commerce, Economics, and Political Science; 65.6% in the College of Shari'at and Islamic studies; 64.7% in the College of Science; 50% in the College of Medicine; 80% in the College of Allied Health and 40% in the College of Engineering.

With this rapid advancement of women in Kuwaiti society, a sense of duality has come to be realized. While traditional beliefs regarding the roles within society that are appropriate for women remain strong, particularly among the older generation, there is also a strong and growing element advocating modernization among those who have come into contact with Western ideas. It appears that education in Kuwait society is undergoing a critical period as regards modernization: To fulfil the needs and aspirations of this new generation of Kuwaitis, many Kuwaitis believe that education will have to be modernized so that it can permit updated educational strategies. Whether the government will take steps to make these changes remains to be seen.

Status of counseling

Professional counseling had its beginnings in Kuwait in 1966 in the form of social services provided in schools with social workers serving as counselors. In

1978, guidance and counseling programs were established to prepare educational counselors for responsibilities for school-related activities previously conducted by the social workers. These included educational counseling, social and psychological counseling, and career counseling (Abu-Eita and Sherif, 1990).

The current counseling movement began in 1980 when several trainees with academic degrees in psychology were recruited to undergo a one-year training program in counseling in which in-service training was provided with special emphasis on administering tests and interpreting results for educational placement purposes. At present, the primary function of the school counselor in Kuwait is to administer tests for educational counseling. The Ministry of Education is the only source of counseling services in schools, and not all high schools have yet been provided with such services. The Ministry is planning to expand counseling services to all high schools and, later, to middle and primary schools. At present, however, counseling programs are limited to school counseling in schools with credit-course systems.

The role of school counselors is defined in the Ministry of Education decree of 1980 as helping students to

1. know themselves, their aptitudes and their interests, and to understand the educational and vocational opportunities available within the society;
2. understand human interactions within school settings, acquire skills, habits, and positive attitudes that enable them to deal with others in good manners inside and outside school;
3. make appropriate decisions concerning their future educations and careers;
4. overcome their social and psychological problems through individual and group counseling; and
5. adjust both mentally and psychologically by providing preventative developmental and remedial counseling.

A recent survey of credit-system secondary schools in Kuwait found that students viewed counseling within schools as

1. advising them how to adhere to school scheduling and avoid absenteeism;
2. encouraging them to select majors that meet their interests;
3. helping some students reduce absenteeism; and
4. encouraging them to build proper relationships with their teachers (Al-Sarraf, 1991).

It can be assumed from their responses that students perceived that counseling does not help students to know themselves, to acquire skills, habits, and positive attitudes, or to overcome their psychological problems as indicated by the 1980 Ministry decree.

The Study And Its Methodology

Subjects:

The subjects of this study were 120 Kuwaiti students attending government secondary schools. Of these, 68 were males and 52 females. All were Kuwaiti nationals who lived in modern neighborhoods in or near Kuwait City and who had received free education from the age of four years when they had entered kindergarten.

Two subject groups were chosen, each based on a different background: "Advantaged" students (N = 97) came from "urbanized" families who made their livings in the city. They resided, together with their families, in private villas or mansions; their parents had employment positions considered higher than the average for the Kuwaiti population and tended to have above-average education levels. "Nonadvantaged" youngsters (N = 23), by contrast, came from families who represented the old desert tribal culture or working class. They tended to live in smaller houses or in public housing, and had parents with education and income lower than average in Kuwait.

A word on sample size

The size of the Kuwaiti sample is small when compared to samples in other national studies reported in this book. Sample size was reduced originally when a high proportion of youngsters surveyed (43 of the initial 150 subjects) failed to complete all portions of the questionnaire and were dropped from the study. Subsequent opportunity to survey additional subjects was removed by the 1990 Iraqi invasion of Kuwait, which effectively stopped all normal activities, including schooling, for seven months while the Iraqi army controlled the country. Later, after the Iraqi army was vanquished, it was no longer possible to obtain a comparable sample of youngsters unaffected by war. For this reason, although the Kuwait sample is small, its importance as a unique picture of Kuwaiti adolescence that cannot be duplicated makes it important. This small sample may represent the last "innocent" Kuwaiti adolescents.

Procedure: data collection and coding

Data collection

Three steps were taken in data collection:

1. Permission was obtained from the Ministry of Education to choose the male and female subjects for the study among the student populations of Kuwaiti public high schools.
2. The questionnaire developed by the Energetic Research Team was translated into Arabic—the language of the country—by the author. This translation

was then back-translated into English using the procedure described in Chapter 2. To correct for any unanticipated administration problems, the translated questionnaire was then piloted on a small group of students with the same characteristics as the sample-to-be.

3. The questionnaire was distributed in ten high schools situated in five governates that constitute the State of Kuwait. It was administered by assistants trained by the author, who were aided in the task by teachers and administrators in the schools.

Data collection took place during a three-month period, from February through April 1989.

Coding

Data was coded by two trained assistants under the supervision of the author-researcher. Both assistants had more than five years' experience in research and computer analysis at the College of Education, Kuwait University.

To measure reliability of coding among Kuwait coders, responses of each of the two assistants were compared with those of the author-researcher to determine the percentage of responses that were in agreement. During training of the coders, whenever there were disagreements, the assistants and the researcher-author discussed the responses until the researcher and at least one assistant reached agreement on the right response. (Unfortunately, the data used to obtain the mean percentage of agreement was lost with other laboratory material when the Psychological Laboratory was destroyed during the Iraq invasion of Kuwait. The researcher and the assistants are certain, however, that they reached concurrence a minimum of 90% of the time using this procedure.)

Reliability as determined by percentage of agreement between the responses of the author-researcher and the "master-code" at the University of Pittsburgh, as described in Chapter 2, was .95 for classes and .84 for categories-within-classes.

Study Results

The Kuwait study results showed Kuwaiti youth to be similar in many respects to their peers in the multinational study. At the same time, it demonstrated a number of potentially important differences that showed Kuwaiti youth to be unique. Highlights are reported below.

Similarities to multinational youth: age-related problems, goal-directed coping and peer-oriented help-seeking

Table 10.1(a) and Chapter 3 show that, for both Kuwait and multinational subjects, the paramount perceived problem is **schooling**, ranked first for males and females of both "advantaged" and "nonadvantaged" groups." Among cate-

TABLE 10.1 *Kuwait study: percentages of total responses falling into classes and categories of problems*

(a) Classes

	Advantaged				*Nonadvantaged*			
	Male		*Female*		*Male*		*Female*	
	%	*Rank*	*%*	*Rank*	*%*	*Rank*	*%*	*Rank*
Extreme poverty	0.0	(11)	0.0	(10)	0.0	(10)	0.0	(7)
War	0.0	(11)	0.0	(10)	0.0	(10)	0.0	(7)
Catastrophe	0.0	(11)	0.8	(8.5)	0.0	(10)	0.0	(7)
Material desires	3.1	(8)	0.8	(8.5)	0.0	(10)	0.0	(7)
Family issues	6.9	(5)	20.6	(3)	12.1	(2.5)	19.4	(3)
Schooling issues	44.3	(1)	29.2	(1)	39.4	(1)	44.4	(1)
Identity	9.9	(3.5)	23.3	(2)	6.1	(5.5)	22.2	(2)
Sexuality	1.5	(9.5)	0.0	(10)	6.1	(5.5)	0.0	(7)
Courtship/dating	4.6	(7)	8.3	(5)	9.1	(4)	5.6	(4.5)
Interpersonal	12.2	(2)	9.2	(4)	6.1	(5.5)	5.6	(4.5)
Emotions	9.9	(3.5)	6.7	(6)	12.1	(2.5)	0.0	(7)
Self-fulfilment	1.5	(9.5)	0.0	(10)	3.0	(9)	0.0	(7)
Altruism	6.1	(6)	1.7	(7)	6.1	(5.5)	2.8	(6)
No problem	0.0	(X)	0.0	(X)	0.0	(X)	0.0	(X)

*(b) Categories**

	Male		*Female*	
	Category	*%*	*Category*	*%*
Advantaged	Academic failure	11.4	Behavioral issues	10.8
	Schooling (other)	9.1	Teacher related	10.0
	Stress	8.3	Inability to learn	9.2
	Time pressures	7.6	Intergenerational disagreements	6.7
	Teacher related	7.6	Self-confidence	6.7
	Altruism (other)	5.3	Parental strictness	5.8
			Stress	5.0
Nonadvantaged	Stress	12.1	Teacher related	13.9
	Time pressures	12.1	Behavioral issues	13.9
	Teacher related	9.1	Academic failure	8.3
	Domestic quarrels	6.1	Time pressures	8.3
	Academic failure	6.1	Inability to learn	8.3
	Language barrier	6.1	Intergenerational disagreements	5.6
	Altruism (others)	6.1	Domestic quarreling	5.6

* Representing 5% or more of responses.

gories-within-classes (Table 10.1(b)), most reported problems accounting for 5% or more of responses fell into the category of **schooling**. The multinational trend for females to report a higher percentage of **family** problems than males within their own socioeconomic grouping held true for the Kuwaiti youngsters.

Also similar to the multinational subjects, **individual problem-solving** was the most frequently cited class of coping strategies for Kuwaiti youth, with "trying harder" and "seeking support" among the three most frequently reported categories-within-classes (Table 10.2 and Chapter 3).

Table 10.3(a) and Chapter 3 show that adolescents in both the Kuwait and multinational study, described **family** (some member of the family) more often than **non-family** when reporting the person(s) they would most like to have help

TABLE 10.2 *Kuwait study: percentages of total responses falling into classes and categories of coping strategies*

(a) Classes

	Advantaged				Nonadvantaged			
	Male		Female		Male		Female	
	%	Rank	%	Rank	%	Rank	%	Rank
Seek/give assistance	25.3	(2)	12.7	(3)	26.3	(2)	14.3	(3)
Interpersonal	3.8	(5.5)	8.5	(4)	0.0	(7)	2.0	(6.5)
Individual problem-solving	33.5	(1)	36.6	(1)	52.6	(1)	46.9	(1)
Stress management	3.8	(5.5)	1.4	(8)	2.6	(5.5)	2.0	(6.5)
Crying	0.0	(9)	7.0	(5)	0.0	(7)	6.1	(4.5)
Religious	3.2	(7)	2.1	(7)	2.6	(5.5)	2.0	(6.5)
Resignation	19.6	(3)	26.8	(2)	7.9	(3.5)	20.4	(2)
Disengage	9.5	(4)	4.9	(6)	7.9	(3.5)	6.1	(4.5)
Anti-social	1.3	(8)	0.0	(9)	0.0	(7)	0.0	(9)
Do nothing	0.0	(X)	0.0	(X)	0.0	(X)	0.0	(X)

*(b) Categories**

	Male		Female	
	Category	%	Category	%
Advantaged	Seek support	20.3	Trying harder	17.6
	Trying harder	12.7	Seek support	12.7
	Plan toward solution	10.1	Do nothing	11.3
	Mental preoccupation	7.0	Plan toward solution	9.9
	Take fatalistic view	5.7	Anger or depression	8.5
	Do nothing	5.7	Crying	7.0
	Escape/avoidance	5.7	Assertive coping	6.3
	Offer help to others	5.1		
Nonadvantaged	Trying harder	31.6	Trying harder	20.4
	Seek support	18.4	Seek support	14.3
	Accept responsibility	10.5	Plan toward solution	14.3
	Offer help to others	7.9	Anger or depression	10.2
	Plan toward solution	5.3	Do nothing	8.2
	Mental preoccupation	5.3	Crying	6.1
	Escape/avoidance	5.3	Psychological distancing	6.1

* Representing 5% or more of responses.

them with their problems. According to Table 10.3(b) and Chapter 3 that show listings by categories-within-classes, however, it is clear that, for both groups, young people go first to a "personal friend" and that "mother" is likely to be a second choice.

As for the helper qualities preferred by adolescents, Table 10.4 and Chapter 3 reveal that **personal qualities, knowledgeable** and **concern for others** are the most frequently cited classes of helper qualities for both Kuwait and multinational youngsters. Regardless of sex or socioeconomic group, subjects of both the Kuwait and multinational studies were similar, with respect to qualities of a helper they did not cite. "Distant," "patient," "good sense of humor," "stable," "objective," "moral," "religious" and "spiritual" went unreported.

Finally, adolescents of both Kuwait and the multinational study were similar

TABLE 10.3 *Kuwait study: percentages of total responses falling into classes and categories of desired helpers*

(a) Classes

	Advantaged				*Nonadvantaged*			
	Male		*Female*		*Male*		*Female*	
	%	*Rank*	*%*	*Rank*	*%*	*Rank*	*%*	*Rank*
Family	49.7	(1)	58.5	(1)	51.9	(1)	63.7	(1)
Non-family	44.9	(2)	37	(2)	42.9	(2)	31.9	(2)
Offender	1.0	(3.5)	1	(3)	0	(4)	0	(4)
Supernatural	0.0	(5)	0.3	(4.5)	0	(4)	2.2	(3)
Creatures/objects	0.0	(5)	0.3	(4.5)	0	(4)	0	(4)
Non-specific	1.0	(3.5)	0	(6)	1.3	(3)	0	(4)
Nobody	3.4	(X)	2.4	(X)	3.9	(X)	2.2	(X)

*(b) Categories**

	Male		*Female*	
	Category	*%*	*Category*	*%*
Advantaged	Personal friend	18.2	Personal friend	19.4
	Mother	11.5	Mother	18.7
	Father	11.1	Cousin	6.6
	Brother	7.1	Sister	6.6
	Teacher	5.4	Father	5.9
	Schoolmate	5.1		
	Person possessing desired qualities	5.1		
Nonadvantaged	Personal friend	24.7	Personal friend	22.0
	Mother	14.3	Sister	19.8
	Father	9.1	Mother	15.4
	Brother	7.8	Father	7.7
	Schoolmate	5.2		

* Representing 5% or more of responses.

in choosing desired modes of helping. **Counsel, attend to** and **exercise power/solve the problem** were the three most frequently cited classes of helping modes, with **counsel** consistently ranked first among classes and "advise" ranked first among categories for all subject groups (Table 10.5 and Chapter 3).

Differences from multinational youth: teacher-related problems, fear of inability to learn and coping by resignation

Table 10.1 and Chapter 3 also suggests potentially important cultural differences between Kuwaitis and youngsters in the other countries of the multinational study. Examination of the percentages of reports of **family** and **school** problems (classes) shows that while problems are reported with lower frequency by Kuwaiti subjects than by their multinational peers, among **schooling** problem categories, "teacher"-related problems are significant for Kuwaitis, with females more than males in both socioeconomic groups reporting a higher percentage of

TABLE 10.4 *Kuwait study: percentages of total responses falling into classes and categories of desired helper qualities*

(a) Classes

	Advantaged				*Nonadvantaged*			
	Male		*Female*		*Male*		*Female*	
	%	*Rank*	*%*	*Rank*	*%*	*Rank*	*%*	*Rank*
Powerful	7.4	(4)	1.8	(5)	3.1	(5)	3.8	(4)
Knowledgeable	30.9	(2)	30.3	(2)	32.3	(2)	41.3	(1)
Available	0.4	(5)	3.3	(4)	0.0	(6)	2.5	(5)
Personal qualities	41.2	(1)	39.1	(1)	50.8	(1)	40.0	(2)
Concern	8.1	(3)	22.9	(3)	9.2	(3)	12.5	(3)
Uncertain	0.0	(6)	0.7	(6)	4.6	(4)	0.0	(6)
No list	3.1	(X)	1.8	(X)	0.0	(X)	0.0	(X)

*(b) Categories**

	Male		*Female*	
	Category	*%*	*Category*	*%*
Advantaged	Good listener	11.5	Caring/loving	11.8
	Similarity	9.5	Trustworthy	11.1
	Understanding	8.2	Understanding	8.9
	Can exercise authority	7.0	Knowledge	8.1
	Caring/loving	7.0	Similarity	6.6
	Knowledge	5.8	Good listener	6.3
	Intelligent/wise	5.8	Generous	6.3
	Trustworthy	5.8	Intelligent	5.5
	Experienced	5.3		
	Generous	5.3		
Nonadvantaged	Honest	9.2	Experienced	8.8
	Intelligent	7.7	Similarity	7.5
	Good listener	7.7	Knowledge	7.5
	Generous	7.7	Gives advice	7.5
	Experienced	6.2	Trustworthy	7.5
	Similarity to subject	6.2	Loyal	7.5
	Trustworthy	6.2	Intelligent	6.3
	Loyal	6.2	Honest	6.3
	Mature	6.2	Caring/loving	6.3
			Good listener	5.0
			Generous	5.0
			Understanding	5.0

* Representing 5% or more of responses.

concerns. Kuwaiti females, unlike their multinational peers, also report concern with "inability to learn," which appeared in the multinational sample only among "poverty" subjects.

As regards classes of coping strategies (Table 10.2 and Chapter 3), Kuwaitis (with the exception of "nonadvantaged" males) gave a far lower percentage of reports of **interpersonal** coping, a slightly higher of **religious** coping and far higher of **resignation** coping responses than their multinational counterparts.

TABLE 10.5 *Kuwait study: percentages of total responses falling into classes and categories of desired mode of helping*

(a) Classes

	Advantaged				Nonadvantaged			
	Male		Female		Male		Female	
	%	Rank	%	Rank	%	Rank	%	Rank
Direct need satisfaction	1.9	(7)	0.6	(6)	0.0	(6)	0.0	(5)
Exercise power/solve	8.8	(3)	3.5	(3.5)	4.7	(3.5)	1.7	(3.5)
Intercede	4.4	(4)	3.5	(3.5)	4.7	(3.5)	1.7	(3.5)
Counsel	58.1	(1)	66.5	(1)	65.1	(1)	78.3	(1)
Attend	16.9	(2)	20.2	(2)	20.9	(2)	16.7	(2)
Evade problem	3.1	(5.5)	1.2	(5)	0.0	(6)	0.0	(5)
Uncertain	3.1	(5.5)	0.0	(7)	4.7	(3.5)	0.0	(5)
No list	3.8	(X)	4.6	(X)	0.0	(X)	1.7	(X)

*(b) Categories**

	Male		Female	
	Category	%	Category	%
Advantaged	Advise	28.0	Advise	32.4
	Help solve problem	14.3	Direct	17.9
	Direct	10.6	Comfort/reassure	12.7
	Comfort/reassure	8.7	Help solve problem	9.8
	Solve problem	5.6		
	Encourage	5.6		
Nonadvantaged	Advise	37.2	Advise	40.8
	Help solve problem	14.0	Direct	16.7
	Direct	9.3	Help solve problem	13.3
	Encourage	9.3	Encourage	10.0
	Comfort/reassure	7.0	Share	6.7
			Comfort/reassure	5.0

* Representing 5% or more of responses.

It is notable that while multinational youngsters chose "teachers" fairly frequently as their helper, teachers were chosen only by Kuwaiti advantaged males. No Kuwaiti group chose "counselors"!

Importance of the Kuwait Findings

Few family worries, more school and teacher-related worries and no seeking of professional help!

While the small size of the Kuwaiti sample makes it impossible to make more than a conjecture, the fact that Kuwaiti youngsters, regardless of whether their backgrounds were "nonadvantaged" and rooted in the desert culture or "advantaged" and part of the new urban culture of Kuwait, are as similar as they are to each other and to their multinational counterparts in so many respects may attest to the importance of adolescence as a stage of life in which important life decisions are being made.

The fact that Kuwaitis reported fewer family problems than their counterparts in other countries may be reflective of the Kuwaiti economy and its high standard of living even for those classified as "nonadvantaged"; within the countries of the multinational study, family problems increased with decreasing SES. This was not true in the Kuwaiti study. The fact that concerns regarding schooling are paramount among youngsters whose family background is of the uneducated desert culture may be reflective of Kuwait's effectiveness in teaching the importance of education and then providing it free to all its people.

It is worrisome, however, that Kuwaitis reported teacher-related problems with relatively high frequency when their multinational counterparts did not. If this is attributable to the inability of the school system in Kuwait to deal effectively with the needs of this generation of Kuwaitis, this suggests closer examination. The fact that "nonadvantaged" females report this type of problem most frequently among the four groups of Kuwaitis, and, at the same time, report a greater percentage of concerns related to inability to learn, suggests that this group of young people needs help. Since Kuwaiti females do not choose teachers to provide assistance, they may not be getting the help they need at a time when this help is very important.

Kuwaitis tend to report a lower percentage of family worries than do youngsters in the other countries of our study. When they do report them, however, the highest percentage include intergenerational disagreements, parental strictness and for, "nonadvantaged" females, domestic quarreling.

What do these findings suggest for Kuwait?

Since Kuwaiti adolescents report their problems to be largely related to schooling, it is suggested that counseling activities in this area be improved. If, as Kuwaiti students have reported, counselors' primary goals are to advise them on issues related to school scheduling, selection of majors and reducing absenteeism (Al-Sarraf, 1991), it might be advisable to return to the 1980 Ministry of Education decree and establish programs to help students understand themselves, their interactions within school settings, and overcome their social and psychological problems, areas in which it appears Kuwaiti counselors are not now functioning.

Teachers might also be used more effectively than they are now in the conducting of educational counseling, including advising students and their parents on the choices available in coursework, meaning of test scores, teachers' assessments over a period, classroom performance, emotional adjustment and the importance of raising levels of aspiration. To do this effectively, however, teacher images will need to be improved so that students will want to come to them for help. Family members, ranked first as choice of helper for all, may also be used as paraprofessional to assist their children if they are taught to do so (Al-Sarraf, 1990). In fact, programs have been considered which would train such people as paraprofessionals in counseling (Soliman, 1990).

There are many questions that need to be answered before direction is taken. First, how does the teacher-counselor or parent-counselor fit into the system? School administrative personnel must be convinced that these new roles are important and be prepared to make quite significant adjustments. Second, on what bases should we select parents and teachers for these new roles? What would be the stand of the Ministry of Education on such issues? Third, where can we obtain sufficient teachers to teach and to counsel simultaneously in such a country where there are tremendous teacher shortages? Whatever changes are made must be accomplished in light of the clear answers to these questions.

A final question relates to understanding of counseling as a profession. How can we improve the climate of opinion as regards the advantages of counseling? Without positive regard for the profession in the country, few changes are likely to take place. This is not likely to occur so long as counselors continue spending more time dealing with paper work than with students.

A Postscript: Effects of the Gulf War on Kuwaiti Youth

On August 2, 1990, after the subjects of this study were interviewed, Kuwait was overrun by the Iraqi army. The country remained under occupation until February 26, 1991. Throughout the seven-month occupation, young people in Kuwait were exposed daily to terror and violence, bombing and executions. Many experienced injuries or death of family members. During the occupation, many adolescents hid together with their frightened family members, their fears for those they love compounded by fear of being arrested themselves. The fact that Kuwaiti families were separated both inside and outside Kuwait during the ordeal increased loneliness and contributed to the anguish.

There is growing concern that these experiences will have long-term damaging effects on the psychosocial development of this population, changing their attitudes toward society, their relationships with others, and their general outlook on life (Mansour, 1992). Research suggests that prior experience with trauma increases vulnerability to future trauma. On the surface, while it may produce adaptations which permit the adolescent to function in daily life, in the long term it may decrease overall well-being. Recent findings on armed conflict show that individual war experiences are often diverse, can occur repeatedly over a long period of time and can affect many aspects of a young person's development, including mental health symptoms and adaptational outcomes (Garbarino, 1991; Macksoud, 1992).

Since the end of the Gulf War, Kuwaiti young people have reported a variety of problems quite different from those reported in our study. For many, powerful personal experiences and images of death and torment remain, creating high levels of stress. Others still suffer from trauma of separation from loved ones during the occupation. There has been movement toward helping youth through training of professional help providers and through enhancing public awareness of the problem.

Training workshops have been established to assist mental health workers, social workers, counselors, and psychologists in both the education and health sectors. Training has also been provided to others who work directly with young people such as parents, teachers, childcare workers, nurses and pediatricians. Public awareness campaigns have been initiated through different media forms such as the press, radio, and TV, periodicals and general public lectures.

Psychologists and counselors plan the development of Resource Centers in the future to collect materials dealing with violence, trauma and conflict and their effect on individual development in general as well as specifically related to the Kuwaiti experience for use by both the academic community and general public. Research is being directed toward development of new intervention procedures to provide help for Kuwait's next generation of citizens. Appropriate counseling has never been so important in Kuwait's history.

11

The Netherlands[1]

PETER A. DE WEERDT[2]

Counselor-Educator, Acta Midden Nederland, Teacher Training College, Hogeschool van Utrecht

"What worries me is my mother ..."

Mascha is fourteen years old. Both her parents are teachers in adult education.

"Ten years from now, what will I be doing? I will have moved out of my parents' house and have a room of my own. I'll be working with people: taking care of old people or working with children at a daycare center. Not a bum. Not office work.

"What worries me now is my mother. Some time ago she had a brain hemorrhage and now she still smokes and drinks secretly when she's not allowed to. It worries me very much; I cannot sleep at night and I am late in the morning. I can't concentrate at school.

"Most of the time, I do nothing. I keep it to myself. Then I get a headache or cramps in my stomach. I sit quietly and think, and try to sort things out. I talk about this to my father, my boyfriend and someone at school, the school counselor. My father knows about the situation; he explains things to me. My boyfriend comforts me, he reassures me. The school counselor listens and keeps things confidential. I would not want anyone to laugh at me.

"I have some wishes for the future: They are, first, to have a good job I like. I want to be happy. And I want to be living in Den Haag where my boyfriend lives."

[1] This study was completed with the aid of a grant from the Department of Counseling Studies, University of Utrecht.

[2] With the assistance of Klara Popp who coded the data.

Introduction

About the country

Background

The small country of the Netherlands, with a population of approximately 15 000 000, has one of the highest population densities of any country in the world—440 persons per sq. km—and a large population of immigrants. Its ethnic composition as of January 1, 1990 was 85% Netherlanders and 15% immigrants. Among the latter, 9% were Turkish and 7.5% Moroccan immigrants, together accounting for 2.5% of the Dutch population and the largest Islamic proportion of immigrant groups (Roelandt et al., 1991).

The most important religious affiliations are Roman Catholic, Dutch Reformed Church, Reformed Churches and Islamic, with approximately one-third of Netherlanders reporting no religious affiliation. Although still a small percentage of the population, inhabitants whose affiliation is Islamic appear to be increasing.

Counseling in schools

School counseling and vocational guidance are well established in Dutch secondary education with subject matter teachers providing counseling services. Although not all teacher-counselors have received formal training in guidance and counseling, most have acquired—or are in the process of acquiring—professional status through national certification programs. One basic assumption of the profession (Stern, 1985) is that counseling should be an integral part of the approach to students rather than an activity separate and isolated from other school activities. It is recommended that large teams of teachers (ideally speaking, the entire school staff) be involved in a humanistic approach to students and in the creation of schools with healthy developmental emphases and ample opportunity for staff to deal with student problems. The formal certification training model is based on four principles:

- counseling is a need of all school students, whether it be educational, emotional, developmental or career counseling;
- counseling is a task of every teacher in the school and should be supported by a trained colleague-counselor;
- counseling can improve the school climate and support for each student if it is expressed in a total approach to school students;
- the teacher-counselor model is a helpful one in the Dutch context (Stern, 1985).

Today, in all Dutch secondary schools, some form of counseling is available to all students upon request. In addition, an increasing number of schools are adopting a policy of integrating counseling and vocational guidance into the curriculum (Watts, Dartois and Plant, 1987). This is not a Dutch development only; a study of the Commission of the European Communities on the state of educational and vocational guidance services in the European Community found the following trends common its member states (Watts *et al.*, 1987):

- Guidance is more and more being seen not as an adjunct to schools but as an integral part of the educational process.
- This is resulting in the growth of specialist guidance roles within the schools.
- It is also producing recognition of the need to involve **all** teachers in guidance to some extent, and to develop ways of supporting them in their guidance roles.
- Guidance elements are increasingly being built into the curriculum, in the form of career education programs, work-experience programs, etc.
- Where external agencies work with schools, their role is now viewed increasingly as properly that of a partner or consultant to the guidance services within the school itself.

These trends do not suggest that the accessibility of counseling services is self-evident to all students, unfortunately. In a study concerning expectations and outcomes of school counseling (De Weerdt, 1988), it was found that, while teacher/counselors and students do not differ considerably in what they consider students' most urgent problems, they show a considerable variety in their view of the effectiveness of counseling. In those cases when students had made use of school counseling, they were more optiministic than the counselors as to the outcome. However, a majority of students had not seen a school counselor, partly because of ignorance of the service and partly because of conflicting anticipation of its effectiveness. The findings of the current study shed some new light on these issues.

The Study and Its Methodology

The Netherlands study describes the reported problems, coping strategies and desired helpers of "advantaged" and "nonadvantaged" groups of male and female adolescents in the Netherlands and, where appropriate, compares their responses to those of their multinational peers.

Subjects

Our 451 adolescent subjects, from both indigenous Dutch and minority immigrant backgrounds and from a lower vocational and junior high school, were divided into two groups as follows:

"Advantaged" subjects

This group consisted of 171 males and 183 females who attended a junior high school. All subjects were indigenous Dutch with characteristics that match those of "advantaged" subjects of the multinational study, as described in Chapter 2.

"Nonadvantaged" subjects

This group included 33 males and 64 females who attended vocational school and had the following characteristics in addition to those of the "nonadvantaged" subjects of the multinational study (Chapter 2):

1. subjects often have a poor mastery of Dutch language and a poor knowledge of the labor market situation;
2. parents tend to have relatively poor employment opportunities (often based on their minority status) and often have attained only low levels of education;
3. ethnic backgrounds include both indigenous Dutch (74 subjects) and immigrants of minority status (23 subjects).

(While this study does not distinguish among the various ethnic minority backgrounds of children making up our subject pool, we know that the parents of this population came from (were born in) Turkey (approximately 50%), Morocco (20%), Surinam and the Antillian Islands (15%), as well as other nations (15%). The immigrant group constitutes approximately 5% of the total Dutch sample, which makes it fairly representative of immigrant ratio in the nation's population.)

(The Dutch study does not compare the indigenous Dutch and immigrant adolescents in the "nonadvantaged" sample as to their reported problems, coping strategies and help seeking behaviors. A comparison of these two micro-groups appears in Chapter 17, Minority Populations.)

Procedure

The procedure used in the Netherlands study matches, by and large, that of the larger multinational study (see Chapter 2). The questionnaire standardized for use in all countries of the multinational study was translated into Dutch and back-translated for accuracy. Data collectors were secondary school teachers enrolled in a two-year postgraduate training program for school counselors, all of whom were well known to the students as their subject teachers. Data collectors were instructed by the author as to procedures for administering the questionnaires and for providing assistance in cases where the students had difficulty answering the questions.

Data collection took place under conditions comparable to the larger study. Minor differences in procedure include the following:

1. because it was feared that "possible answers" could be construed as "desirable" and because some immigrant adolescents tended to follow given examples (and, in some cases, actually used them), teacher/counselors were instructed not to provide illustrations of the types of possible answers;
2. some immigrant subjects needed—and received—encouragement by the teacher/counselors to express their concerns in writing on the forms provided. (See Chapter 17 for discussion of this issue.)

The time period of data collection was November 1989 through January 1990. Questionnaires were distributed and responses collected in the classroom during one teaching hour. (It is interesting to note that many data collectors reported that some students unexpectedly started to talk to them later about the problems and concerns which they had described in the questionnaire. Feeling "flooded," these teacher/counselors felt need to discuss their recent experiences in their counseling training classes!)

The data were coded by a trained assistant. Training began with a thorough analysis of all distinctions between classes and categories within the six scales of the manual used for coding (see Chapter 2 and Appendix I). The author and his assistant compared definitions of classes and categories-within-classes to assist in establishing distinguishable coding choices. (This is not to say that in some cases the distinction between two or more categories within one class did not remain somewhat ambiguous.)

As in all countries of the multinational study, reliability of coding was measured by comparing the author's coded responses to a series of 15 completed questionnaires with "correct" responses provided on a master code by the initial ERT research team at the University of Pittsburgh (see Chapter 2). Interrater agreement, as measured by percentage of agreed-upon choices when the author's coded responses were compared with those of the master code, was .94 for classes and .83 for categories-within-classes. The author's coded responses were also compared to those of the assistant responsible for coding on the same 15 questionnaires and found to be higher.

The Study Results

The findings of the Dutch study as regards each question on the questionnaire are presented in terms of the percentages of responses falling within each class and category-within-that-class. Responses of "advantaged" and "nonadvantaged" subjects are compared with those of the same socioeconomic groupings in the multinational study and also with each other.

Problems

For "advantaged" subjects, this study confirms what Dutch counselors have believed to be true (De Weerdt, 1988): **schooling** issues are at the top of the list of worries of both multinational and Dutch "advantaged" youngsters (Table 11.1(a)).

With Dutch "nonadvantaged," however, **interpersonal concerns** are ranked first for males and **family concerns** are ranked first for females (Table 11.1(b)).

Dutch **family** problems often deal with conflict: Typical reports included issues such as:

"disagreement with siblings"
"poor relationship with parents"
"disagreements with the extended family"
"parental strictness"
"divorce/separation."

With many Dutch migrant "nonadvantaged" youngsters, family problems often relate to discrepancies between their parents' cultural values and those of their host country. The reported family problem and possible coping strategy of a "nonadvantaged" migrant girl:

> "I do not want to be arguing with my family, especially my parents. But I'm afraid to be married off, to be forced to marry someone I don't know at all".

Dutch "nonadvantaged" males constitute the only Dutch (or multinational) group reporting "being pestered by peers" and the "well-being of friends" (coded as **interpersonal**-"other").

"Advantaged" males have a relatively high percentage of "concerns for the environment" (Table 11.1(b)). This **altruistic** attitude is quite common among Dutch pupils, since both childrearing practices and education pay a considerable amount of attention to pollution and waste in the Dutch environment.

Just as in the multinational sample, **poverty, war, catastrophe** and **self-fulfilment** are not issues for Dutch adolescents (Table 11.1). Neither are life-endangering events and intellectual or spiritual pursuits areas of concern to them.

The multinational trends that show that

1. the percentage of reporting of **family** problems increases with decreasing SES and from males to females within each SES bracket, and
2. the percentage of **schooling** problems, conversely, decreases with decreasing SES and from males to females, holds true for the Netherlands study.

Coping strategies

The universal choice of coping strategy in our multinational study is **individual problem-solving**. Table 11.2(a) shows that Dutch adolescents are no exception. It shows, in addition, that the multinational trend in which the per-

TABLE 11.1 *Netherlands study: percentages of total responses falling into classes and categories of problems*

(a) Classes

	Advantaged				*Nonadvantaged*			
	Male		*Female*		*Male*		*Female*	
	%	*Rank*	*%*	*Rank*	*%*	*Rank*	*%*	*Rank*
Extreme poverty	0.0	(0)	0.0	(0)	0.0	(0)	0.0	(0)
War	0.0	(0)	0.0	(0)	0.0	(0)	0.0	(0)
Catastrophe	0.0	(0)	0.0	(0)	0.0	(0)	0.0	(0)
Material desires	5.8	(7)	2.1	(8)	1.7	(7.5)	2.3	(8)
Family issues	11.1	(4)	21.3	(2)	20.3	(3)	40.2	(1)
Schooling issues	26.9	(1)	22.9	(1)	22.0	(2)	15.2	(2)
Identity	19.1	(2)	16.9	(3)	10.2	(4)	11.4	(3)
Sexuality	0.3	(9)	1.6	(9)	0.0	(0)	0.8	(9)
Courtship/dating	1.9	(8)	5.5	(7)	1.7	(7.5)	3.8	(6)
Interpersonal	10.2	(5)	9.1	(5)	23.7	(1)	9.1	(4)
Emotions	9.7	(6)	7.0	(6)	3.4	(6)	3.0	(7)
Self-fulfilment	0.0	(0)	0.0	(0)	0.0	(0)	0.0	(0)
Altruism	13.1	(3)	11.2	(4)	5.1	(5)	5.3	(5)
No problem	1.9	(X)	2.6	(X)	11.9	(X)	9.1	(X)

*(b) Categories**

	Male		*Female*	
	Category	*%*	*Category*	*%*
Advantaged	Academic failure	17.5	Academic failure	14.3
	Concern for environment	8.9	Self confidence	5.5
	Interpersonal (other)**	7.5	Concern for environment	5.5
			Time pressures	5.5
Nonadvantaged	Interpersonal (other)***	15.3	Family issues (other)****	9.1
	Academic failure	13.6	Academic failure	6.1
	Friendship	5.1	Parental strictness	6.1
	Schooling (other)	5.1	Friendship	5.3
	Behavioral issues	5.1	Divorce/separation	5.3

* Representing 5% or more of responses;
** criticism of homework; criticism at school;
*** being 'pestered'; concerns about friends;
**** disagreements with siblings, parents, extended family.

centage of reports of **individual problem-solving** decreases with decreasing SES and from males to females within SES brackets holds true for the Dutch. For Dutch youngsters, **individual problem-solving** is managed through a variety of strategies, and frequently includes "planning," "trying harder," "seeking support" and "assertive coping" (Table 11.2(b)).

More than multinational adolescents (Chapter 3), Dutch youngsters are inclined to withdraw from solving their problems and report "doing nothing" about them. This is less the case with Dutch "nonadvantaged" females who prefer to "seek support" from someone else when dealing with their main problems

(problems within the **family**). The "nonadvantaged" migrant girl whose problem (described earlier) was fear of being forced by her parents to marry someone she didn't know, reported:

> "When you can't do anything about it, there is no way to feel better. So if my parents decide to do that, I will try to make it clear that they cannot. I will also ask help from my sister and my best friend."

Only when all else failed would this youngster consider going outside her close cultural network:

> "Maybe the (Dutch) Institute for Child Protection. They must be trustworthy and should give me good and comfortable advice."

TABLE 11.2 *Netherlands study: percentages of total responses falling into classes and categories of coping strategies*

(a) Classes

	Advantaged				*Nonadvantaged*			
	Male		*Female*		*Male*		*Female*	
	%	Rank	%	Rank	%	Rank	%	Rank
Seek/give assistance	13.6	(3)	18.7	(2)	15.0	(4)	24.8	(2)
Interpersonal	8.1	(5)	11.3	(4)	18.3	(2.5)	22.1	(3)
Individual problem-solving	50.0	(1)	43.9	(1)	40.0	(1)	27.5	(1)
Stress management	2.0	(6)	2.3	(6)	0.0	(0)	2.7	(6.5)
Crying	0.3	(8)	0.6	(7)	0.0	(0)	2.7	(6.5)
Religious	0.0	(0)	0.4	(8)	0.0	(0)	0.0	(0)
Resignation	13.9	(2)	12.7	(3)	18.3	(2.5)	12.8	(4)
Disengage	10.9	(4)	9.4	(5)	3.3	(6)	7.4	(5)
Anti-social	1.3	(7)	0.6	(7)	5.0	(5)	0.0	(0)

*(b) Categories**

	Male		*Female*	
	Category	%	*Category*	%
Advantaged	Planning a solution	22.2	Planning a solution	21.5
	Try harder	21.5	Seek support	15.8
	Seek support	12.9	Try harder	15.0
	Do nothing	11.1	Do nothing	10.7
	Escape/avoidance	6.1	Assertive coping	9.0
	Assertive coping	5.3		
Nonadvantaged	Planning a solution	20.0	Seek support	24.8
	Assertive coping	16.7	Assertive coping	16.1
	Seek support	15.0	Planning a solution	12.8
	Try harder	13.3	Try harder	10.1
	Do nothing	13.3	Do nothing	6.0
	Anti-social (other)**	5.0		

* Representing 5% or more of responses;
** shooting the offenders;
beating them up; rioting.

Dutch "nonadvantaged" males take a different and unique position: They are the only group in the Dutch study to report their wish to have their problems (mainly "being pestered") solved by:

"shooting them" (their offenders)
"beating them up"
or
"rioting" (**antisocial**-"other").

This will be discussed later in the chapter.

Another interesting difference between Dutch "nonadvantaged" and "advantaged" youth is the greater inclination of the former to seek out the persons who are part of the problem ("assertive coping"). This result, found in both male and female youngsters, may be affected by cultural difference since the 97 Dutch "nonadvantaged" group includes 23 migrant adolescents from other countries.

TABLE 11.3 *Netherlands study: percentages of total responses falling into classes and categories of desired helpers*

(a) Classes

	Advantaged				*Nonadvantaged*			
	Male		*Female*		*Male*		*Female*	
	%	*Rank*	*%*	*Rank*	*%*	*Rank*	*%*	*Rank*
Family	57.1	(1)	49.2	(1)	45.2	(1)	47.2	(1)
Non-family	35.9	(2)	42.3	(2)	44.3	(2)	44.2	(2)
Offender	1.0	(4)	3.3	(3)	0.0	—	1.8	(4)
Supernatural	0.0	—	0.2	(6)	0.0	—	0.0	—
Creatures/objects	0.5	(5)	0.6	(5)	0.0	—	0.0	—
Non-specific	2.4	(3)	1.9	(4)	7.8	(3)	6.3	(3)
Nobody	3.0	(X)	2.6	(X)	2.6	(X)	0.6	(X)

*(b) Categories**

	Male		*Female*	
	Category	*%*	*Category*	*%*
Advantaged	Mother	18.4	Personal friend	24.0
	Father	18.3	Mother	19.1
	Personal friend	16.2	Father	11.5
	Teacher	6.6	Parents/family	7.1
	Parents/family	5.8	Sister	5.0
Nonadvantaged	Personal friend	26.1	Personal friend	23.3
	Father	13.9	Mother	11.3
	Sister	8.7	Teacher	8.7
	Nonspecific	7.8	Nonspecific	6.3
	Aunt	5.2	Father	5.7

* Representing 5% or more of responses.

Helpers

When they turn to helpers to solve their problems, Dutch adolescents show a unanimous strategy in choosing **family** members before persons not in the family (Table 11.3(a)). A different picture emerges, however, when **family** and **non-family** groups are broken down into separate persons (Table 11.3(b)). With one exception ("advantaged" males), all Dutch groups turn to their "personal friend" as the single person to whom they go in the first place and "mother" as their single helper choice in the second place. Compared to "advantaged" Dutch youngsters, Dutch "nonadvantaged" youth give much higher priority to personal

TABLE 11.4 *Netherlands study: percentages of total responses falling into classes and categories of desired helper qualities*

(a) Classes

	Advantaged				*Nonadvantaged*			
	Male		*Female*		*Male*		*Female*	
	%	*Rank*	*%*	*Rank*	*%*	*Rank*	*%*	*Rank*
Powerful	3.5	(4)	2.6	(4)	7.8	(4)	2.3	(5)
Knowledgeable	32.0	(2)	27.6	(2)	29.4	(2)	11.6	(3)
Available	0.7	(6)	0.5	(6)	0.0	(0)	0.0	(0)
Personal qualities	42.7	(1)	46.6	(1)	45.1	(1)	53.2	(1)
Concern	18.3	(3)	20.3	(3)	9.8	(3)	26.6	(2)
Uncertain	1.6	(5)	1.1	(5)	5.9	(5)	5.2	(4)
No listing	1.2	(X)	1.3	(X)	2.0	(X)	1.2	(X)

*(b) Categories**

	Male		*Female*	
	Category	*%*	*Category*	*%*
Advantaged	Approachable	12.5	Approachable	21.6
	Experienced	11.6	Trustworthy	12.0
	Trustworthy	9.3	Understanding	11.3
	Content knowledge	8.8	Similarity	8.4
	Generous	8.8	Content knowledge	6.9
	Caring/loving	8.6	Generous	6.5
	Understanding	8.4	Experienced	5.5
	Similarity	6.5	Gives advice	5.5
	Patient	5.8		
Nonadvantaged	Trustworthy	19.6	Approachable	24.9
	Approachable	15.7	Generous	13.3
	Experienced	11.8	Trustworthy	12.1
	Similarity	11.8	Caring/loving	10.4
	Exercise authority	7.8	Understanding	8.1
	Generous	7.8	Gives advice	5.2
	Understanding	5.9	Supportive	5.2
	Does not know	5.9	Does not know	5.2

* Representing 5% or more of responses.

friends as their helpers than to any one individual family member. Dutch "advantaged" males, the sole exception to the general tendency to turn to personal friends for help, prefer "mother" or "father" in the first place.

Desired helper qualities

What are the qualities of selected persons that adolescents believe make them able to help? Just as multinational subjects, Dutch adolescents are looking mainly for three qualities in their helpers: having some desirable personal qualities, being knowledgeable concerning the problem and demonstrating concern for others (Table 11.4(a) and Chapter 3).

There are potentially important differences between the Dutch and their multinational peers, however: Unlike both the "advantaged" and "nonadvantaged" multinational youngsters for whom knowledge about the problem or the problem situation is ranked first, the Dutch tend to search first personal qualities that are

TABLE 11.5 *Netherlands study: percentages of total responses falling into classes and categories of desired helping modes*

(a) Classes

	Advantaged				*Nonadvantaged*			
	Male		*Female*		*Male*		*Female*	
	%	*Rank*	*%*	*Rank*	*%*	*Rank*	*%*	*Rank*
Direct need satisfaction	4.1	(6)	1.5	(6.5)	2.2	(6.5)	2.4	(6)
Exercise power	4.4	(5)	4.2	(4.5)	4.3	(4.5)	1.6	(7)
Intercede	5.1	(4)	4.2	(4.5)	4.3	(4.5)	12.2	(4)
Counsel	45.9	(1)	45.9	(1)	37.0	(1)	37.4	(1)
Attend to	24.7	(2)	34.2	(2)	19.6	(2)	26.0	(2)
Evade problem	2.5	(7)	1.5	(6.5)	2.2	(6.5)	3.3	(5)
Uncertain	10.4	(3)	6.0	(3)	15.2	(3)	15.4	(3)
No listing	2.8	(X)	2.5	(X)	15.2	(X)	1.6	(X)

*(b) Categories**

	Male		*Female*	
	Category	*%*	*Category*	*%*
Advantaged	Advise	18.7	Advise	21.2
	Help problem solve	14.9	Comfort	14.5
	Comfort	13.6	Help problem solve	13.2
	Encourage	6.3	Encourage	9.7
	Counsel (other)**	6.0		
Nonadvantaged	Advise	19.6	Advise	17.1
	Comfort	13.0	Comfort	16.3
	Help problem solve	8.7	Mediate	12.2
			Help problem solve	8.9

* Representing 5% or more of responses.
** talk to me; check on me.

desirable to them, the most desired being "approachable" (having the capacity to listen to their problems). ("Nonadvantaged" males constitute the one exception; For this group, "approachable" is ranked second.) (See Table 11.4(b).)

Table 11.4(b) also reveals interesting gender differences: Considering the percentage of reported responses, Dutch males seek helpers on the basis of their "experience" somewhat more frequently than do Dutch females, similar to their multinational peers (Chapter 3), while Dutch females tend to search for "approachable" helpers more than their male counterparts, a trend also noted in the multinational study.

"Nonadvantaged" males and females both reported they "do not know" what qualities they want their helpers to have in at least 5% of their responses. This was not true for their "advantaged" peers.

Desired modes of helping

The manner in which multinational and Dutch adolescents want to be helped shows both a remarkable resemblance and a surprising difference. As far as classes of desired helping modes (Table 11.5(a) and Chapter 3), all groups in both the multinational and Dutch study put the highest priority on some kind of **counseling** (provides counseling assistance). Next (ranked second for all groups), they want a helping mode that demonstrates attention and care (**attend to**).

All Dutch groups—"advantaged" and "nonadvantaged," male and female—placed highest emphasis on the desire to be "advised" by their helpers, like their multinational peers (Table 11.5(b) and Chapter 3). Among Dutch groups, only "nonadvantaged" females reported a wish for someone to "mediate" between themselves and others.

Conclusions and Implications

Dutch problems: schooling and relational

Dutch "advantaged" groups, like their multinational peers, worry about school. By contrast, Dutch "nonadvantaged" boys are mainly concerned about their relationship with peers and "nonadvantaged" girls similarly worry about their relationships with family members.

These findings suggest that Dutch "nonadvantaged" youngsters may be more relationship-oriented than "advantaged" youth and that their perceptual horizon is determined greatly by their position among their most important reference groups: friends and family members. Sadly, for this group, societal opportunities are limited, considering their relatively low academic qualifications. Among migrant youth accustomed to operating within their own cultural milieu, opportunities for help may be even more limited. Should the migrant girl described earlier actually seek help from the Institute for Child Protection, she would be most unusual, indeed!

Dutch "advantaged" boys are unique among both their Dutch and multinational peers in putting a relatively high emphasis on environmental issues.

Coping

In their reported problem-solving behavior, Dutch boys and girls do not appear very different from adolescents in the multinational study. In general, they try to cope with their problems individually in the first place, just as the multinational adolescents. However, compared to the multinational subjects, the Dutch are more inclined simply to do nothing about their problems and wait for future events to change the situation.

In the case of Dutch "nonadvantaged" males, one of the reported ways to resolve problems is violent, for example, having the offender(s) "beaten up" or even shot. Recent research suggests that those who practice violence are not likely to report it on questionnaires. (See, for example, the report by Gille *et al.* (1993—4) regarding violence among German youth.) The antisocial coping responses reported in thus study were not reported in any other national study including the US (where violence is often practiced but is reported by US adolescents as serious problems with which they must deal rather than strategies they use [Maccarelli, 1994]). Quite possibly, the small number of Dutch youngsters who made these reports are indicating a phantasy of violent revenge rather than a real intention of acting it out. This and other possibilities are important and need to be examined.

Compared to multinational and Dutch "advantaged" adolescents, the Dutch "nonadvantaged" show a greater tendency to cope by dealing directly with persons who are part of the problem. (This is called "assertive coping" in Table 11.2(b).) This is an interesting difference that may be related to the fact that the Dutch "nonadvantaged" group includes many second generation immigrant youth of Islamic origin.

Here, two factors should be kept in mind: First, their major concerns are related to family members and friends or peers. Second, Islamic cultures are cultures of relatedness; issues arising in the lives of young people are normally discussed within the network of personal relationships. For these Islamic youth, it is customary that problems evolving from their personal relationships are resolved within the same network.

Dutch helper choices: a systems theory interpretation

In general, the Dutch are not very much different from the multinational adolescents in the sense that they tend to view their personal friends as their first eligible helping resource. In terms of percentages of total responses, the females in all groups show an almost identical preference for personal friends as their first choice of helper—a truly universal reference!

Given the fact that problems related to school are listed first ("advantaged" adolescents) and second ("nonadvantaged") by Dutch youngsters, it is significant that teachers are so infrequently named as helpers. However, this is not as surprising as it may seem. The most important school-related problem expressed by Dutch adolescents is "academic failure"—not the event of failure, but the fear of failure. When failure anxiety occurs, it is possible that any attempt to talk with a teacher responsible for evaluating achievements, or even to invoke an image of talking to that teacher, is likely to increase the anxiety.

The systems theory approach (Watzlawick, Weakland and Finch, 1973) asserts that the solution contributes to the problem by creating "more of the same." According to this approach, groups as well as individuals can be seen as a collection of elements called a system. A system has an inherent tendency to maintain and stabilize itself and, by doing so, resist change. When change cannot be avoided any longer, there are two possible alternatives: The first, a "first order change," attempts to vary the composition of the elements within the system. In the case of fear of academic failure as reported in this study, the most widely used change option is to increase familiar efforts to solve the problem ("try harder"). Without clear evidence of its effectiveness, however, this strategy simply produces a repetition of the old strategy. The individual maintains a "more of the same" scenario: The solution produces the problem and fear of academic failure is unaffected. The system itself—the individual with a fear of failure—remains unchanged.

For this reason, a "second order change" is needed. The solution can be found by considering the system itself as an element of a larger collection of elements. Second order changes require dealing with a group problem—not numerous individual problems—of a system defined by boundaries, as, for example, classes, schools or educational systems. This view has considerably different implications for helping interventions.

Given that Dutch adolescents hardly ever seek help from teachers (who are responsible for judging and evaluating their achievements), it may be only natural for youngsters to seek helpers whom they perceive as non-judgmental. And this is exactly what the data show: Dutch youngsters turn to someone (usually a friend) who has the desired personal characteristics to deal with their worries: being friendly, inviting and ready to listen. The desired helper also must be trustworthy. Finally, he or she must have knowledge and experience related to the problem or the problem situation. With so few Dutch adolescents turning to counselors for help, these attributes need to be given serious consideration by the profession.

Dutch adolescents: an (unreported) problem of learned helplessness?

In comparing the two Dutch groups, it is clear that "nonadvantaged" youngsters seek relationship-related qualities more so than their "advantaged" peers.

They are also the only subjects to report (above the cut-off point of 5% of total responses) that they do not know what helper qualities they desire or what they want their helpers to do.

In explaining these results, it is illustrative to relate them to the reported coping strategies in Table 11.5. Unlike their multinational peers, a relatively large proportion of Dutch adolescents (both "advantaged" and "nonadvantaged") report that they do nothing about their problems. In this case, both findings ("do nothing" and "don't know about helper's qualities and behaviors") are most probably interrelated: Those youngsters who make no attempt to solve their problems do not involve helpers and may not have considered what they might want of them. In this case, the responses, "Do nothing" and "Don't know" probably express the same position, that of "learned helplessness."

Learned helplessness: a definition and a solution

"Learned helplessness" has been defined as a state in which people typically tend to attribute failure to global, stable, and internal factors (Abramson, Seligman and Teasdale, 1978). Youngsters who have learned to be helpless do not perceive that they have control over the outcomes of their efforts. They "do nothing" and "don't know." They are prone to feeling depressed about their academic chances of success. They are likely to develop low self-esteem, making it more difficult for them even to attempt finding solutions.

What can be done to help these youngsters? One remedy is a change process in which unrealistic attributions for failure are directed toward specific external factors. In the case of students with fear of academic failure, counselors could determine what external circumstances (family life, social position of the student in peer groups, etc.) contribute to inability to focus on the task and then make their clients aware of available help.

Students need to know that they are not alone with this problem and that others share the problem as well as the way to solve it. Counselors could invite students who share the same fear to deal with this problem in groups. Efforts should be aimed at changing the students' internal monologues, which typically say something like:

"I can't ever do this, I'm too stupid"

into something such as:

"Right now, this task is too difficult for me."

Counselors can help students learn study skills. Tasks to be completed can be broken down in smaller sub-tasks, a strategy that allows them to start with a success experience and increase their self-esteem.

Dutch adolescents' preference for accepting advice

Finally, given the preference for accepting advice from counselors, it might be advantageous for counselors to train groups of students in a directive and structured way to develop problem solving strategies, without giving specific prescriptions as to what they should do. To be effective, this approach would require a delicate balance between a directive-authoritarian and a structured developmental approach based on self-exploration and individual responsibility. These counseling dimensions remain important, but should not be considered at all times and for all groups as the critical target. As always, counselors can be effective only when they take client expectations seriously.

12

The Philippines

GUNDELINA VELAZCO
DeLaSalle University, Manila

A streetboy: "It is my dream to be a detective."

Marlon is a former child prostitute. He is fourteen years old. His mother is a laundry woman. He does not know his father.

"In the future, it is my dream to be working as a detective. I do not want to be stealing. I don't have a right place in this world. I don't know where to go. I have no home.

"I try not to think about it. I go to an institute for homeless street children. I talk to a social worker or to Brother Francisco. (He's an administrator for street children.) He's nice. And he gives me advice. I don't like people who shout at me.

"My three wishes? A tee-shirt. Shoes. And pants."

Introduction

The country

One of the world's largest archipelagoes, the Philippines includes 7109 islands, all of which lie about 600 miles from mainland Asia on the western edge of the Pacific Ocean. Throughout its three geographic regions of Luzon, Visayas and Mindanao, the temperature averages about 80° F at sea level, decreasing approximately 10° for every 300 ft rise in elevation. The country is able to grow both tropical and temperate-zone fruits and vegetables (*The Encyclopedia Americana*, 1991).

Natural problems

Many natural causes contribute to a high level of poverty among both rural and urban Filipinos. Approximately 15—20 typhoons lash the country in the months from June to November, causing considerable damage annually to crops as well as to life and property. The many volcanoes that dot the islands have also been for centuries another natural cause of destruction.

Finally, lying within the Pacific Seismic belt, the Philippines has consequently experienced severe earthquakes on frequent bases throughout their history. Going back for just the past fifty years, in addition to the recent quake of 1990 that totally destroyed northern villages on Luzon, are the famous quakes of 1976 which triggered a tidal wave claiming thousands of lives and millions of pesos worth of property, of 1968 when hundreds of people were killed in Manila, and of 1955 when hundreds of lives and millions of pesos were lost (Agoncillo, 1990).

The culture

Religion

The Filipino people are deeply religious, with the majority observing faithfully the rituals of their religion. Approximately 86% of Filipinos are Roman Catholics, 5% Aglipayans (Philippine Independent Church), 4% Muslims, 2.5% Protestants, 2.5% animists (*The Encyclopedia Americana*, 1991). Filipinos tend to have a "theocentric" frame of mind (Timbreza, 1982) that leads to the general tendency, especially among the poor, to depend on and attribute most things to a supreme being.

Population

With a high birth rate and a low rate of mortality, the population rose from 19 000 000 in 1948 to 60 000 000 in 1990, producing a rate of natural increase well above the world average (NEDA, 1992). The high birth rate is sometimes attributed to the resistance of the Catholic Church to birth control. But a more likely cause can be found in the rural orientation of Filipino folk ways and the low productivity of the agricultural system (*The Encyclopedia Americana*, 1991). Traditional rural Filipino communities, which up to now have comprised 80% of the population, exist on the land, much as they did when the first islands were settled hundreds of years ago. If they do not own the land, rural Filipinos are tenants or farmhands whose survival, nevertheless, depends upon the land. Filipinos tend to believe that this type of economy necessitates as many hands as possible and thus gives rise to large families. Hence, the Filipino family system is also extended (Velazco, 1993). Given the authoritarian tendencies among Filipino parents, this means that aunts, uncles, and grandparents also play authoritarian roles in the life of the child.

Family life

The Filipino observes very close family ties. The family is the unit of society and everything revolves around it (Agoncillo, 1990). Dependency on others provides the extended family structure a reason for being, perpetuates it and creates a sensitivity to the responses of others.

The following points are emphasized in childrearing: suppression of aggression, responsibility for reciprocating favors, sociability, shame, and dependency on others (Morais, 1980). All can be explained in terms of the cultural necessity within the Filipino extended family system. Suppression of aggression wards off conflict that would normally arise in interacting with such diverse and numerous personalities as in a clan; reciprocating favors and sociability assists in creating acceptance in large communities in which tensions can arise easily; shame is deemed necessary in consideration of the welfare and feelings of others, especially considering that the sensitivity of Filipinos is reciprocal. There are innumerable minute actions that are a cause of shame, so that the Filipino child grows up worrying constantly about what others are saying and thinking about him and experiencing shame to some degree all the time.

Filipino parents are extremely authoritarian; the "tyranny of the elders" is a phenomenon which persists to this modern day. Respect for elders is a trait that has remained in the book of unwritten laws and the Filipino parent exercises almost absolute powers over the children (Agoncillo, 1990). One result, for the Filipino child, is a self-concept defined in terms not only of personal worth but also on whether he/she is a "good" child, a "good" nephew/niece, a "good" brother/sister (Velazco, 1993).

Among Filipinos, a close friend is often considered a member of the family. As such, he or she is expected to come to one's aid and to share in the family's sufferings as well as its happiness (Agoncillo, 1990).

Politics, armed conflict and trauma

Complex politics have also contributed to the problems of the Filipino people. At the time of data collection, in 1989, it had been three years since President Corazon Aquino had snatched power from then-President Ferdinand Marcos and restored democracy. The bicameral legislature had been restored and a new constitution ratified. These developments coincided, however, with continued unemployment and interest on the national debt (which the Marcos government had incurred) that used up 40% of government expenditures. One result was that Aquino's administration, in 1989, was seriously challenged by military extremists as well as by the Communist rebel New Peoples' Army (NPA).

At the time of the study, five coups had already been attempted and guerilla attacks by the NPA that had been occurring for some years in the rural areas were increasing (*The Encyclopedia Americana*, 1991). During the continuing conflict between the Philippine government and the NPA, large numbers of Filipinos, especially those from rural areas, were suspected of crimes and picked up for interrogation and imprisonment. Many simply "disappeared" and were declared missing. Others, although eventually returned to their families, suffered severe trauma. Large numbers of impoverished rural Filipinos fled to urban areas, hoping both to escape the strife and improve their chances of earning livings. Unfortunately, adults who were not equipped with skills necessary for working in the cities found only overcrowded slums or squatters' communities and little work to sustain them.

No dramatic political or economic changes occurred when Fidel Ramos assumed the presidency in 1992.

Education

Education is prized highly by both rich and poor Filipinos. Public and private schools, from elementary through university, are available in the Philippines. Elementary schooling lasts for six years, high school for four. The system, patterned after that of the US, has an individualistic orientation which encourages competition. Tuition for public school is free. For private school, it can be quite expensive.

Although available to all, formal education varies considerably for children from "advantaged" and "poverty" backgrounds. Impoverished children may begin public school at age six or seven; their more advantaged peers often begin as early as four or five years old as private nursery and kindergarten students, entering private prep schools at age six. While public and private schools appear "on the books" to provide similar curricula, private schools supply better instructional materials and facilities, and teachers are usually better trained. Public school classes are crowded, and, in urban areas, often provide fewer hours per day of instruction. For these reasons, Filipino children whose families are not impoverished (i.e. are able to meet their basic needs) are sent to private schools. This is true even when it is difficult to meet the cost of tuition. No "advantaged" child in this study attended public school.

While impoverished families realize the value of education and struggle to send their children to school, many "poverty" youngsters are forced to drop out because they must use their time to gain extra money for their families by entering the work force or begging at early ages. Many also take on added responsibilities in their homes while their mothers work. Because the medium of instruction in all Philippine schools—both public and private—is English, impoverished children, who cannot attend for a time and whose parents are unschooled themselves and do not speak English the language, usually do not learn English sufficiently well in the early school years to be able to continue their studies. For these reasons, few "poverty" youngsters reach high school. Only a very few of the "poverty" youth in this study attended school.

The status of counseling

Counselors serve in schools as well as in clinical and industrial settings in the Philippines. At the time of the study, a total of 75 educational institutions, 22 of these in Metro Manila, offered different degree programs in guidance and counseling; twenty-two offered master's degrees and seven doctoral degrees (Salazar-Clemena, 1987). The curricular offerings in these programs were patterned after the prescriptions of the American Association for Counseling and Development and the American Psychological Association (Salazar-Clemena, 1987).

For some years, the rallying cry among Filipino practitioners has concerned professionalization of counselors and accreditation of counselor education programs. This clamor has yet to be fully realized. One issue is that counseling has a low priority among the elements of the educational system and of the other systems that employ it. It is the last to be instituted in many schools and the first to go when funds are low. Often, the guidance counselor is any teacher in the school who lacks a teaching load or who seems to have the personality for it, because there is no one who has actual training in guidance and counseling. Guidance and counseling in the Philippines still have some way to go in establishing a distinct and recognized niche among the professions.

The Study and Its Methodology

Subjects

The 400 adolescent subjects of this study have been categorized as "advantaged" or "poverty," according to the definitions provided in Chapter 2. They are all residents of Manila, the capital of the Philippines and its largest city.

"Advantaged" sample

The 200 "advantaged" subjects (100 males and 100 females) were students of exclusive and expensive private schools in Manila.

"Poverty" sample

Only a very few of the 200 "poverty" subjects (100 males and 100 females) attended school. Those who did attended public schools. None was sufficiently literate to complete a written questionnaire. All "poverty" subjects resided either in slums as squatters or in some other poor pockets of the metropolis. Most were jobless, although some worked as household help, fish vendors or garbage scavengers. Many were homeless street-children.

Data collection

Data was collected from September 1988 to November 1989 by means of the multinational questionnaire for "advantaged" youngsters and interview guideline for "poverty" youth. Questionnaires and interview protocols were translated into Tagalog (the indigenous language of Luzon) following the procedure outlined in Chapter 2.

"Advantaged" youngsters were surveyed in groups in their classrooms by the author-researcher.

"Poverty" youngsters were surveyed by the author-researcher and a hired assistant who lived near the slums. Slum residents, who could not read, were interviewed individually, as were all nonliterate groups in the multinational study (see Chapter 2). Additional specialized techniques employed for interviewing Filipino subjects and the rationales for these techniques are as follows:

1. Social science researchers have long recognized that, because Filipinos are sensitive to issues that might produce shame and because Filipino children grow up worrying constantly about what others are saying and thinking about them, the responses that can be gathered from Filipino subjects in interviews are strongly dependent on the relationship between the researcher and the subjects. A researcher who is a stranger will likely elicit superficial data only; on the other hand, a deeper relationship between the researcher and subject can generate more personal data. Because of this phenomenon, the author carefully established close rapport and friendship before conducting interviews of "poverty" subjects.

2. Many Filipino street adolescents, some of whom suffered through the armed conflict in the country, had been picked off the streets and institutionalized. They had not led "ordinary" adolescents' lives, even when compared with "poverty" youngsters from other countries. Suspicion, fear and antagonism were common among these subjects, so that outright questioning would have produced poor results. For this reason, the author used her interview time to discuss all issues that the subjects raised, "weaving" her questions into the subject's chosen topics, rather than conducting interviews that dealt only with the research questions.

3. Finally, because many "poverty" youngsters had previously suffered severe trauma during the armed conflict that was prevalent in their country, one-on-one questioning often brought frightening memories of interrogations and torture. For these youngsters, the author conducted group interviews that permitted youngsters to respond to the same questions while in the safety of their friends. In these cases, while it is possible that some information deemed too confidential for their friends to hear went unreported, feelings of being threatened by an adult were minimized and they could talk about fears that they and their friends knew and understood. (In cases in which the author-researcher used group interviews, these sessions evolved into a form of group dynamics with the researcher as facilitator.)

Coding

All data were coded by the author herself, using the procedure developed for the multinational study (Chapter 2). The interrater reliability of coding, as measured by the percentage of agreement between the responses of the author and those of the standard for the multinational study for a sample of test responses (see Chapter 2) was .89 for classes and .97 for categories-within-classes.

Results and Conclusions

Problems

Filipino "advantaged" and "poverty" subjects gave very different descriptions of their problems. These are therefore described separately.

Problems of "advantaged" youngsters

Table 12.1(a) shows that, as in the multinational "advantaged" findings, **family, schooling** and **personal identity/self-concept** are the three most frequently cited classes of problems for the Filipino "advantaged" group, accounting for approximately 65% of the responses of males and 69% of those of females. In the case of the Filipino "advantaged" youngsters, this is not surprising, especially considering the important role played by both family and school in the lives of these youngsters as well as the importance of both these factors in determining the Filipino self-concept.

As earlier mentioned, Filipinos observe close family ties and are enmeshed in an extended family system. Problems cited by Filipino "advantaged" youngsters that are related to this trait and that suggest effects of the close interaction of many people within the household include:

"missing family members when they are away or working abroad"

"interference by members of my extended family"

"quarreling within my extended household."

Dependence of extended family members, irresponsibility of some family members, and favoritism were also expressed by some "advantaged" youngsters.

Among **schooling** problems reported by "advantaged" youngsters, the category, "academic failure," accounts for the highest percentage of responses of both males and females (Table 12.1(b)). Failing exams or grade levels can cause feelings of shame for these adolescents, particularly because tuition in private school is expensive and repeating grades often means a considerable slice of even "advantaged" families' budgets.

Many problems concerned with **personal identity/self-concept** or **schooling** reported by "advantaged" youngsters also dealt with parents' expectations and demands:

"being misunderstood by my parents"

"having to conform to my parents' wishes"

"pressure by my parents (for me) to succeed."

As pointed out earlier, Filipino children who fail to meet their authoritative parents' expectations also fail in developing positive self-concepts.

TABLE 12.1 *Philippine study: percentages of total responses falling into classes and categories of problems*

(a) Classes

	Advantaged				*Poverty*			
	Male		*Female*		*Male*		*Female*	
	%	*Rank*	*%*	*Rank*	*%*	*Rank*	*%*	*Rank*
Extreme poverty	0.0	(12.5)	0.0	(11.5)	19.2	(3)	10.7	(4)
War	0.4	(10.5)	0.0	(11.5)	0.0	(12)	0.8	(10)
Catastrophe	0.9	(8.5)	0.7	(8)	0.0	(12)	0.0	(12.5)
Material desires	11.5	(4)	5.0	(7)	19.6	(2)	26.9	(1)
Family issues	16.7	(2)	32.4	(1)	22.0	(1)	22.9	(2)
Schooling issues	32.1	(1)	25.5	(2)	13.2	(4)	15.8	(3)
Identity	15.8	(3)	10.8	(3)	10.0	(5)	5.1	(6)
Sexuality	0.9	(8.5)	0.0	(11.5)	0.0	(12)	0.0	(12.5)
Courtship/dating	7.3	(6)	8.6	(5)	4.0	(7)	3.6	(8)
Interpersonal	8.1	(5)	10.4	(4)	7.6	(6)	7.9	(5)
Emotions	6.0	(6)	5.4	(6)	2.4	(8)	4.3	(7)
Self-fulfilment	0.4	(10.5)	0.4	(9)	1.2	(9)	0.4	(11)
Altruism	0.0	(12.5)	0.0	(11.5)	0.8	(10)	1.6	(9)
No problem	0.0	(X)	0.7	(X)	0.0	(X)	0.0	(X)

*(b) Categories**

	Male		*Female*	
	Category	*%*	*Category*	*%*
Advantaged	Academic failure	15.4	Academic failure	11.2
	Money	10.7	Domestic quarrels	9.7
	Friendship	6.9	Friendship	9.4
	Time pressures	6.4	Money	5.0
	Self-confidence	5.1	Parental strictness	5.0
Poverty	Basic needs	18.8	Money	25.3
	Money	18.4	Basic needs	10.3
	Academic failure	5.6	Domestic quarrels	6.3
	Inability to learn	5.6	Friendship	5.5
			Academic failure	5.1
			Divorce	5.1

* Representing 5% or more of responses.

For both genders, "friendship" ranks among the top three categories of problem (Table 12.1(b)). Friendship, to a Filipino, is sacred (Agoncillo, 1990). Friendship implies mutual help under any circumstances, including those which a person thinks are not morally right. That is why many adolescent subjects expressed the problem of "pressure from bad company." Other expressed problems in the area of friendship include:

"being gossiped about"

"disagreement with friends."

These also underscore the sensitivity of the Filipino.

Problems of "poverty" youngsters

For Filipino "poverty" subjects, just as for their "advantaged" counterparts, **family** concerns were ranked at or near the top of their list of problems in terms of frequency of reporting. "Poverty" subjects, however, also reported a high percentage of concerns related to **extreme poverty** ("unmet basic needs") and **material desires** ("money"). The former was less frequently reported by their "poverty" peers in the larger multinational sample (Table 12.1(a) and (b)). Examples of Filipino problems include:

"not enough money for food"

"no decent clothing"

"leaking of roof of shanty house"

"overcrowded slum dwelling"

"everything we had is lost."[1]

In comparison to **family** problems, **schooling** and **identity** concerns appear less significant for Filipino "poverty" youth, although "academic failure" is often reported as a problem by "poverty" youngsters, especially females, even though they are not attending school (Table 12.1(b)).

Why should youngsters who do not attend school report "academic failure" as a problem? In the case of this sample of "poverty" youngsters, "failure" refers to "not getting into desired school." It appears that, although most of these "poverty" youngsters are not students, they do want to attend. In many cases, failure probably is caused by failure to learn English, the medium of instruction. Youngsters who fail at this task for any number of reasons, including being forced to be absent from school for periods at a time, stand little chance of achieving and are forced to drop out.

The Philippine study confirms the multinational trends that suggest that **schooling** problems decrease and **family** problems increase with decreasing SES. It also confirms the gender trend in which females tend to report a higher percentage of **family** problems within each SES group. The same multinational trends regarding **schooling** and gender does not hold true for the Philippine study.

Coping

As in the multinational findings, the first choice of coping strategy of both "advantaged" and "poverty" subjects' first choice of coping strategy was **individual problem-solving**, with the percentages of responses higher for males than females (Table 12.2(a)). Within this class, "planning toward a solution" consistently shows the highest percentage of responses (Table 12.2(b)).

Seeking or giving assistance and **interpersonal coping** follow, as does **resignation** (with the percentage of responses higher for females than males).

Unlike their "poverty" counterparts in the multinational sample, both Filipino

[1] Expressed by street-children and child victims of armed conflicts.

TABLE 12.2 *Philippine study: percentages of total responses falling into classes and categories of coping strategies*

(a) Classes

	Advantaged				Poverty			
	Male		Female		Male		Female	
	%	Rank	%	Rank	%	Rank	%	Rank
Seek/give assistance	17.7	(2)	13.4	(3)	16.0	(2)	15.6	(2)
Interpersonal	13.8	(3)	17.3	(2)	11.0	(3)	12.3	(4)
Individual problem-solving	46.2	(1)	35.9	(1)	40.2	(1)	35.2	(1)
Stress management	1.9	(7)	1.9	(8)	2.1	(7.5)	2.0	(7)
Crying	0.4	(8)	2.5	(7)	0.0	(9)	1.0	(8)
Religious	4.6	(6)	4.1	(6)	7.1	(6)	10.6	(5)
Resignation	10.0	(4)	13.2	(4)	10.7	(4.5)	15.0	(3)
Disengage	5.4	(5)	11.5	(5)	10.7	(4.5)	8.3	(6)
Anti-social	0.0	(9)	0.3	(9)	2.1	(7.5)	0.0	(9)

*(b) Categories**

	Male		Female	
	Category	%	Category	%
Advantaged	Plan toward solution	21.9	Plan toward solution	17.3
	Try harder	18.8	Seek support	13.4
	Seek support	16.2	Assertive coping	12.9
	Assertive coping	11.9	Try harder	12.6
	Do nothing	5.0	Passive acceptance	7.1
			Escape	7.1
			Take no action	5.5
Poverty	Plan toward solution	24.2	Plan toward solution	20.9
	Seek support	13.9	Seek support	14.6
	Try harder	11.7	Prayer	10.6
	Prayer	7.1	Assertive coping	9.6
	Escape	7.1	Try harder	8.3
	Passive acceptance	5.7	Passive acceptance	8.0
	Take no action	5.0	Take no action	7.0

* Representing 5% or more of responses.

and Filipina (male and female) youth frequently use "prayer" as a coping strategy. "Prayer," in fact, figures as one of the top categories of coping strategies among these Filipino groups, probably reflecting the "theocentric" frame of mind of the Filipinos, especially the poorer ones.

While the Philippine study confirms the multinational trend that suggests that **individual problem-solving** decreases with decreasing SES, it does not confirm the multinational gender trend in which females report a lower percentage of responses describing this coping strategy than males.

Desired helpers

In both the multinational and Philippine data, regardless of gender and SES, while most subject groups seek help from a **family** member before going outside the family (Table 12.3(a)), "personal friends" are the most frequent single choice

TABLE 12.3 *Philippine study: percentages of total responses falling into classes and categories of desired helpers*

(a) Classes

	Advantaged				Poverty			
	Male		Female		Male		Female	
	%	Rank	%	Rank	%	Rank	%	Rank
Family	45.6	(1)	37.4	(2)	45.3	(1)	43.5	(1)
Non-family	41.6	(2)	48.2	(1)	45.0	(2)	36.8	(2)
Offender	0.4	(5)	1.0	(5)	0.2	(5)	0.6	(5)
Supernatural	3.2	(4)	2.7	(4)	2.6	(4)	7.3	(4)
Creature/objects	0.0	(6)	0.3	(6)	0.0	(6)	0.0	(6)
Non-specific	8.9	(3)	9.6	(3)	6.1	(3)	10.7	(3)
Nobody	0.4	(X)	1.0	(X)	0.8	(X)	1.0	(X)

*(b) Categories**

	Male		Female	
	Category	%	Category	%
Advantaged	Plan toward solution	21.9	Plan toward solution	17.3
	Try harder	18.8	Seek support	13.4
	Seek support	16.2	Assertive coping	12.9
	Assertive	11.9	Try harder	12.6
	Do nothing	5.0	Passive acceptance	7.1
			Escape	7.1
			Take no action	5.5
Poverty	Plan toward solution	24.2	Plan toward solution	20.9
	Seek support	13.9	Seek support	14.6
	Try harder	11.7	Prayer	10.6
	Prayer	7.1	Assertive coping	9.6
	Escape	7.1	Try harder	8.3
	Passive acceptance	5.7	Passive acceptance	8.0
	Take no action	5.0	Take no action	7.0

* Representing 5% or more of responses.

of helper. The single exception is the Philippine "poverty" female group. These females chose God!

It is significant that "professional counselors" were not mentioned sufficiently often to be listed as a choice by any group of Filipino youth (Table 12.3(b)).

Desired helper qualities and modes of helping

"Concern," "understanding," "caring" and "loving" describe the helper qualities most popular among the Filipino subjects (Table 12.4(a) and (b)). While **concern** and "understanding" also rank first among multinational "poverty" groups, however, **knowledge** is given greater importance by multinational "advantaged" subjects.

TABLE 12.4 *Philippine study: percentages of total responses falling into classes and categories within classes of desired helper qualities*

(a) Classes

	Advantaged				*Poverty*			
	Male		*Female*		*Male*		*Female*	
	%	*Rank*	*%*	*Rank*	*%*	*Rank*	*%*	*Rank*
Powerful	3.4	(4)	1.6	(5)	6.1	(4)	4.3	(4)
Knowledgeable	22.0	(3)	20.0	(3)	19.1	(3)	18.3	(3)
Available	1.9	(5)	2.8	(4)	2.9	(5)	1.5	(5)
Personal qualities	28.0	(2)	31.6	(2)	29.5	(2)	28.0	(2)
Concern	43.5	(1)	43.5	(1)	41.5	(1)	47.3	(1)
Uncertain	0.0	(6)	0.2	(6)	0.0	(6)	0.0	(6)

*(b) Categories**

	Male		*Female*	
	Category	*%*	*Category*	*%*
Advantaged	Understanding	25.2	Understanding	28.5
	Caring/loving	11.8	Caring/loving	9.1
	Generous	11.5	Approachable	8.5
	Gives advice	7.1	Generous	6.7
	Experienced	5.3	Gives advice	6.3
	Supportive	5.3	Supportive	5.7
Poverty	Understanding	23.1	Understanding	30.0
	Generous	16.8	Caring/loving	14.5
	Caring/loving	15.2	Generous	13.5
	Gives advice	9.8	Gives advice	7.8

* Representing 5% or more of responses.

It is noteworthy that all Filipino groups want and expect their helpers to "give advice" (Tables 12.4 and 12.5). For both the multinational and Filipino samples, regardless of gender and SES, **counseling** and "advising" (Table 12.5(a) and (b)) are the most desired modes of helping, comprising the highest percentage of responses of all groups.

Implications of These Findings for Counseling in the Philippines

Issues for discussion

The findings of this study suggest several issues that need to be considered by Filipino counselors and teachers of counselors. These include:

1. Potential new counseling roles. It is significant that, regardless of the importance of the family to Filipino youth, personal friends were the most fre-

TABLE 12.5 *Philippine study: percentages of total responses falling into classes and categories of desired helping modes*

(a) Classes

	Advantaged				*Poverty*			
	Male		*Female*		*Male*		*Female*	
	%	*Rank*	%	*Rank*	%	*Rank*	%	*Rank*
Direct need satisfaction	4.9	(3)	0.6	(7)	10.8	(4)	7.0	(3)
Exercise power/solve problems	2.4	(4.5)	3.0	(4.5)	14.7	(2)	6.7	(4)
Intercede	2.0	(6.5)	3.0	(4.5)	6.5	(5.5)	5.7	(5)
Counsel	56.9	(1)	54.7	(1)	47.0	(1)	55.9	(1)
Attend to	26.0	(2)	32.4	(2)	12.2	(3)	18.1	(2)
Evade problem	2.0	(6.5)	3.3	(3)	6.5	(5.5)	4.0	(6)
Uncertain	2.4	(4.5)	1.5	(6)	0.4	(7)	1.7	(7)
No listing	3.3	(X)	1.5	(X)	2.2	(X)	1.0	(X)

*(b) Categories**

	Male		*Female*	
	Category	%	*Category*	%
Advantaged	Advise	27.6	Advise	28.5
	Direct	17.1	Direct	13.5
	Comfort/reassure	11.0	Comfort/reassure	12.9
	Encourage	7.7	Encourage	11.4
	Help solve problems	6.1	Help solve problems	10.2
Poverty	Advise	31.9	Advise	37.8
	Solve problem	10.0	Comfort/reassure	8.4
	Give something	9.7	Help solve problems	8.0
	Help escape	6.5	Direct	7.4
	Help solve problems	5.7	Give something	7.0
			Encourage	5.4

* Representing 5% or more of responses.

quently sought helpers of our young respondents. This might suggest the possibility of utilizing peer counseling in dealing with many types of adolescent problems. Advantages of such an approach are obvious when few counselors are available, although peer counselors would have to be given effective training. This approach might be particularly useful with "poverty" youth whose backgrounds might make it difficult for them to discuss their problems with adults. If peer counseling should be undertaken seriously, one new role of counselors should be that of preparing peer-paraprofessionals for the task.

2. Need for a Philippine counseling philosophy. Our Filipino "advantaged" and "poverty" groups reported problems and coping strategies different from each other as well as from their multinational counterparts. For example, "poverty" groups reported concerns regarding unmet basic needs and money, when "advantaged" subjects were more concerned with school. "Poverty" subjects

used religious coping strategies, including prayer, far more frequently than their "advantaged" and multinational counterparts.

It is significant, also, that our Filipino subjects wanted and expected their helpers to give them advice. (This is true of their multinational peers as well.) However, Philippine counseling textbooks hold that counselors should not advise clients on how to behave. The fact is, training and practice of counselors in the Philippines have been closely patterned after US models and consequently are bound up with certain key features of US culture, which are different from and sometimes oppositional to that of the Filipino culture.

If counseling of Filipinos by Filipinos is to be effective, the necessity for an indigenous Philippine counseling philosophy that is culturally consistent with the needs and expectations of Filipino counselees of all SES backgrounds is clear.

3. Consideration of counseling skills needed in the Philippines. It is significant that Filipino counselors were not mentioned by the youth in this study as persons who are considered as sources of help. For counselors to change this view, they must demonstrate to their clientele that they can provide useful services. To accomplish this end, they must augment their current skills and contribute to the struggle against the most prevalent difficulties of their place, time, and people (Velazco, 1991). The reports of our Filipino subjects suggest need for:

Economics counseling

For the "poverty" youngsters of this study, economic problems, expressed in terms of money, unmet basic needs and inability to attend school, are predominant concerns. A large percentage of the problems reported by "advantaged" youngsters also dealt with material desires and money. These issues are likely to continue in the minds of youth so long as serious economic problems beset Philippine society. For this reason, Filipino counselors, as counselors in other Third World countries, need to develop techniques to assist clientèle in dealing effectively with economic problems. Unfortunately, most counselors do not today have this capability (Velazco, 1991).

One solution to this and other problems associated with the many needs of clients, discussed in Chapter 18, is the creation of a multidisciplinary approach to client problem-solving. As part of such an approach, counselors would work together as one part of a human resource team to assist clientèle with diverse needs.

Counseling strategies are designed to increase effectiveness of client coping. In many cases, the problems of potential Filipino clients are tied not only to economic crises but to political situations fostering them. Gibson-Cline et al. argue (Chapters 1 and 18) that counselors need to assist their clients to increase the effectiveness of their coping strategies and that, to do so, they must first make them aware of the role of those variables that create the problem. Brazilian author-researchers Isaura Guimaraes and Elizabete de Aguiar Pereira (Chapter 5) make use of Freire's arguments (1983) to suggest that counselors might best accomplish this goal by teaching impoverished youth in the schools the "true" causes of their poverty in order to help them use this information to increase their socioeconomic mobility.

Whatever use Filipino counselors make of these approaches, their possibility poses a great challenge to the profession and suggests the efficacy of counselors building the appropriate skills to create a truly **Philippine approach to counseling**.

13

Russia

NINA F. TALYZINA

TATIANA GABAY

Moscow State University

JANICE GIBSON-CLINE

University of Pittsburgh

From Moscow: "I am frightened about my future."

Dima lives in Moscow. He was fourteen years old in 1990 when he was interviewed, before the fall of the former USSR. His parents are an architect and a clerk. Both have higher education.

"Ten years from now I want to be a farmer. I want to have my own dacha and grow vegetables. By that time, I do not want to be living in Moscow or any other large city, because by then all cities will be even larger than they are now. ... I don't want to go the office every morning.

"I am frightened about my future. I am not sure I will be able to be what I want. I am not really sure how to make it happen. But I know that it is necessary to prepare for such labor both morally and physically. Therefore I try to get up early and to work hard at everything I do. I think that, somehow, no matter what happens, I will be able to work on the land.

"I talk about my dream with my father and mother, and my grandfather and grandmother. They have knowledge of life and they give me advice. They help me think over my possible strategies to realize my dream, even when it seems impossible to achieve. They don't answer, 'Dima, you are a citizen. It is impossible for you to be a farmer.'"

Prologue

The Russian study examines the problems and coping of adolescents living in Moscow, the capital of Soviet Russia in 1989, the year during which Eastern Europe threw off Soviet rule and less than two years before the Russians shattered irrevocably the old Communist order in their own country. Although these young people were surveyed at the same time as others in the multinational study, they were not included in the larger study because the Russian authors deemed it inappropriate to place them in any of the study's delineated socioeconomic groups. Today, their responses stand as a unique description of adolescent concerns at a critical time in the history of their country.

The data described in this chapter were collected and coded by the first two authors. During the several years that followed, the chaotic disintegration of the USSR forced the Russian educational system to the bottom of its priorities. University student stipends were withdrawn because of financial exigencies, students were dismissed, faculties were closed and many institutions shut their doors. While the authors agreed that the manuscript for the Russian study would be prepared by the third author and that draft versions would be shared by the three colleagues, contact between the Moscow State University and the University of Pittsburgh was lost. No response to draft versions of this chapter had arrived from Russia by the date the book was sent for publication.

Although not a resident of Moscow during the time of data-gathering, I have utilized my pre-1989 experiences as research professor in that city, my study of the Russian family and reports of scholars as well as Soviet emigrés to the west to describe life and conditions in Moscow and to interpret the responses of our young subjects. As third author, I hope that my interpretations would have met with the approval of my Russian colleagues. I accept responsibility if they do not.

Janice Gibson-Cline
Pittsburgh, 1995

Introduction

In years prior to this study, Soviet Russian children were taught to be proud of their country, one of the largest (one-sixth of the world's land mass) and most powerful nations in the world. Before Eastern Europe's precipitous withdrawal from Soviet rule, the USSR comprised of more than 100 nationalities; its core—and the center of its government—was Moscow. While most Russian children lived under spartan conditions, they expected better lives than previous generations of their families had had. Their parents, accustomed to government control of most aspects of living and insulated from information about life outside their nation, looked to—and expected—better futures for their children.

By the mid-1980s, however, increasing shortages of food and other goods were critically eroding the quality of day-to-day life. In the late 1980s, "glasnost" brought the Russian people information regarding life in other countries as well as government corruption and inequities in the,distribution of goods within the USSR. Most important, it decreased hope for bettering the life of the next generation. When the data in this study were collected, the setting was ripe for what has been since been called the "second Russian revolution" (Smith, 1990).

Soviet Russian family life

Some historical background

Explaining the historical events leading to the fall of the USSR does not fall within the purview of this study. Suffice it to say here that the Soviet regime that followed the 1917 revolution dramatically affected every phase of life of the Russian people as well as of the peoples of its other republics. Among the many important changes brought by Communism was the provision to women of equal social and political rights with men, including the right to join the nation's work force. The effects of just this one provision changed Russian family life and with it, the lives of young people, irrevocably.

In Russia, women had always played the major roles of raising children and passing on Russian values and culture to the next generation. By the 1970s, under the Soviet regime, they also made up 51% of the nation's workforce. While sharing the same workloads as males, however, they continued to carry all the responsibilities at home. Inadequate housing, shortages of food and other goods, lack of consumer services and almost no modern household amenities, hwever, made child-rearing sufficiently difficult that birthrate fell. The government tried to encourage pregnancy by providing guaranteed maternity leave and child allowances. However, by the 1970s, more than half of Russian families had decided to have no more than one child (Gibson, 1988; Leus, 1992). At the same time, divorce increased and almost 50% of marriages were failing (Smith, 1976).

Other demographic trends in the 1980s portended difficulties for the Russian family. While Russia's birthrate was falling below the national replacement rate, her pension-aged population was increasing rapidly as were mortality rates and decreasing life expectancy (the latter due in large part to alchohol abuse). The government was losing ability to care for its people.

Life in Moscow: 1989

Home life

By Western standards, life at home in Moscow in 1989 was exceedingly harsh. The national housing shortage kept most families crowded together in tiny one- or two-room apartments, often sharing kitchens and bathrooms with other families; shortages of food and other necessities required long searches to meet basic needs, difficult for adults working full-time outside the home.

Despite these hardships, life was still excellent for Russian children in many ways that youngsters in many more economically advantaged countries often missed: Russians love children, and the same tiny apartments that ensured a lack of privacy to all family members provided opportunity for extensive social interaction among adults and children and for parents to serve as role models for their children. The fact was that, although life was difficult for adults, growing up in a Soviet Moscovite household could be quite happy for small children, especially so for the increasing numbers of singletons with two parents and, often, a grandparent or two to dote on them continually.

Until about the age of 12, Russian children occupy center stage—the true "czars" of the Russian family. This is still true today. Even when both parents work away from home, mothers and fathers take time to be with them after working hours. (In 1989, this meant fathers teaching their children to skate or to play chess and mothers cooking and cleaning up after them.) Research studies have shown that Russian parents actually spent more time caring for and interacting with their children than did parents from most other countries. They were affectionate and demonstrated their affection more openly than parents in many other countries, both toward each other and their children. Children under the age of ten were never left unsupervised (Gibson, 1988; Markun, 1973).

Although Russians are solicitous, Russian parental authority is strong. Our young subjects had likely been checked daily by their mothers to ensure that they had eaten enough, moved their bowels, done their homework, tied down the earflaps on their winter hats. Studies showed them generally to be acquiescent to parental demands (Pearson, 1990). At the same time, Russian parents didn't usually require their children to do chores. The most they usually requested of preschool children might have been to pick up their toys after play and of older children to go to the store for a few items. At the time of our study, Muscovite children were rarely given any more responsibility at home than the child of a Tsar a hundred years before, although this "royal" service had been criticized by Soviet educators who warned that children would become "wastrels" (Digest of the Soviet Press, 1977). If "spoiling" was a real danger, however, it appeared to be so only within the purview of the family: The same youngsters who were indulged at home by their parents were given heavy responsibility at school, often performing tasks for their teachers as a reward for performing well at their schoolwork.

Schooling

Schooling in Soviet Russia reflected Communist ideology. In 1989, ten years of schooling was compulsory for all. In Moscow, as elsewhere in the USSR, students began classes in September and continued until the end of May, with primary- and secondary-school students usually sharing the same buildings.

The Soviets created different schools for different purposes. In Moscow, in addition to regular schools, these included a wide range of "special schools" with curricula standardized for youngsters throughout the USSR and, in addition, intensive training in one subject such as maths, science, music, drama, foreign language or sports. Some were open to all students from a particular city district; others were open to those who passed entrance examinations. There were also "special schools" for physically handicapped and mentally retarded children as well as schools for children with emotional and disciplinary problems. There were experimental schools in which researchers from the Soviet Academy of Pedagogical Sciences tried out new teaching aproaches (Gibson, 1984; Leus, 1992).

Curricula, textbooks and learning materials were selected by the central Ministry of Culture and identical for all schools. (Minor variations were permitted in some Soviet republics, as for example, Georgia, where the native language was Georgian and Russian was taught as a second language.) Each year, beginning in first grade, additional subjects were introduced and the total lesson time was increased. By the time students were 13—14 years old, the age of our ERT subjects, they were attending classes 34 hours a week (six hours a day from Monday through Friday and four hours on Saturday). Students who were having difficulty in any of their studies were tutored after school, usually by their better-prepared peers under the supervision of the teachers. Pioneer programs provided additional organized daily activities in after-school hours. Often tied to the curriculum, these activities added subject matter for which there was no time during school hours (Levin, 1963).

Second grade was the official year in which students began evening homework—two or three hours a week.

Children who enrolled in the special schools that provided intensive training in a particular subject matter often had their area of specialization determined for them when they entered at age six. Others were expected to make their decision by grade eight; those who delayed were considered procrastinators.

Rote memorization was a principal method of teaching in all schools; accurate repetition (aloud or in writing) was the principal method of testing. (In 1978, all ninth graders were required to transcribe in longhand the full text of the new 173 page constitutution of the USSR.) Only in mathematics and science classes did problem-solving play a significant role (Smith, 1976). Despite rigidities, however, many students excelled in their studies, often performing in mathematics, sciences and foreign languages at higher levels when they graduated than did students in many other countries. They were taught how to study and were prepared to expend effort. It was presumably these attributes that had brought a nation that was 70% illiterate at the time of the Soviet Revolution to 99.7% literate at the end of the 1970s (*Newsweek*, 1977).

Muscovite students were evaluated in a variety of ways:

1. day-to-day teacher evaluations written in students' notebooks that became part of their permanent records;
2. examinations prepared by the central Ministry sent simultaneously to all schools;

3. ministry-prepared oral and written examinations on all subject matter given at the ends of both eighth and tenth grades.

These were most important because they determined all future educational endeavors. Eighth graders, usually 13—14 years of age, who received poor grades were strongly "advised" not to go on to ninth grade, but to apply to vocational schools or technical colleges. Those who failed at the end of tenth grade could not apply to take the entrance exams to institutes or universities. This was a problem for both sexes but more seriously so for males, who faced military service at the age of 18.

An unresolved dilemma for Soviet educators was created by the need for unskilled laborers in a country in which education was free to all and high-achievers theoretically had the right to education through university level. The problem was that not everyone who wanted to go on to higher education and who had good academic records could do so. There was room for only a very small percentage of hopefuls.

As Leus (1992) described it:

"The well educated graduate of the Soviet school who had studied Checkov and Dostoyevsky and knew Pushkin by heart did not want to work as janitor or waitress—the low prestige jobs."

Our 13—15-year-old subjects were in grades seven to nine when they were interviewed, these grades marked decision-making time.

The state of counseling

There was no counseling as we know it in the USSR in 1989.

The Study and Its Methodology

Subjects

The 184 Russian subjects included 78 males and 106 females between the ages of 13 and 15 years. As Soviet citizens, they were placed in one group not described by socioeconomic background. They lived in apartment buildings situated in "average" neighborhoods in Moscow. All parents were reported to be literate. All subjects attended regular schools and were expected to attain at least a high school education.

Procedure

The procedure matched that of the larger multinational study (Chapter 3). Surveys were administered in students' classrooms. Responses were coded and sent to the University of Pittsburgh for analysis. Reliability of coding as measured by a comparison of Professor Gabay's coding of the sample set of responses compared with those of the "master" code was .89 for classes and .70 for categories-within-classes.

Results and Discussion

Results are reported in terms of percentages of responses that fall in each class and category-within-class of problems, coping strategies and help-seeking for males and for females. These are described below and compared with the findings of the multinational study ("advantaged" and "nonadvantaged" groups) in Chapter 3.

Problems

Table 13.1(a) shows that **schooling** is the major problem causing stress for Russian adolescents. A higher percentage of responses indicated worries about **schooling** for males than for females, just as in the multinational study (Chapter 3). These included primarily, issues related to "achievement" and "failure" (Table 13.1(b). The fact that academic "achievement" and "failure" was expected. The fact that these worried males so much compared with females is also not surprising given the threat of Army service as a penalty for not succeeding.

Just as in the multinational study, also, **identity** problems fall among the top three worries. However, while **family** concerns make up the second ranked problem for females (who also reported a higher percentage of problems than did males as in the multinational findings), reporting of **family** problems was replaced among the top three concerns of males by **altruism**. Table 13.1(b) explains the source of these male concerns, which includes worries about "environmental issues" (taught in school) as well as the Soviet Union's moral health (altruism (other)) at that time.

Examination by the researchers of subjects' written responses showed **altruism** (other)[1] concerns such as the following:

> "It is not fair that there is lack of food and that some people have more than others in our society."
>
> "Government officials should not live better than the people for whom they are supposed to be working."
>
> "People should be free to think and act as they want."
>
> "There needs to be opportunity for all to obtain education."

[1] (Other) refers to a response not provided for in the coding manual for the study.

TABLE 13.1 *Russian study: percentages of total responses falling into classes and categories of problems*

(a) Classes

Problems	*Male* %	*Male* Rank	*Female* %	*Female* Rank
Extreme poverty	—	—	—	—
War	3.1	(9)	—	—
Catastrophe	—	—	—	—
Material desires	3.6	(8)	2.8	(9)
Family issues	6.7	(4)	14.2	(2)
Schooling issues	36.3	(1)	30.6	(1)
Identity	11.9	(3)	13.5	(3.5)
Sexuality	1.0	(12)	.7	(11)
Courtship/dating	1.6	(11)	5.3	(7)
Interpersonal	4.7	(6)	13.5	(3.5)
Emotions	2.1	(10)	6.8	(6)
Self-fulfilment	5.2	(5)	1.1	(10)
Altruism	19.7	(2)	7.1	(5)
No problem	4.1	(7)	4.3	(8)

*(b) Categories**

Male Category	%	*Female* Category	%
Achievement	14.0	Friendship	11.0
Altruism; other	11.4**	Growing up	10.7
Failure	10.4	Failure	8.2
Growing up	7.8	Intergenerational dispute	8.2
Environmental concerns	6.7	Achievement	6.4

* Representing 5% or more of responses.
** Problems related to inequalities in the Soviet system; corruption of government officials; desire for increased freedom; desire for educational opportunity.

It is fascinating that females reported a far higher percentage of **family** problems related to "intergenerational disputes" than did males. Despite the attempts of the Soviet regime to create equality of the sexes, Russian culture in 1989 had not changed very much as regards the role of women at home. It also had not changed considerably as regards the upbringing provided by the home: Parents were far more strict with females than males and met demands for more freedom differently for females, giving in to their sons on issues on which they stood firm with their daughters.

In fact, according to Leus (1992):

TABLE 13.2 *Russian study: percentages of total responses falling into classes and categories of coping strategies*

(a) Classes

Coping strategies	*Male* %	*Male* Rank	*Female* %	*Female* Rank
Seek/give assistance	1.1	(7)	2.7	(6)
Interpersonal	12.8	(3)	19.3	(2)
Individual problem-solving	50.5	(1)	41.9	(1)
Stress management	3.7	(5)	4.0	(5)
Crying	—	—	.7	8.5
Religious	—	—	.7	8.5
Resignation	19.1	(2)	15.6	(3)
Disengage	11.2	(4)	13.3	(4)
Anti-social	1.6	(6)	2.0	(7)
Do nothing	—	—	—	—

*(b) Categories**

Male *Category*	%	*Female* *Category*	%
Try harder	37.8	Try harder	30.2
Do nothing	14.9	Do nothing	11.3
Psychological distancing	7.4	Assertive coping	10.0
Planning	6.9	Seek company	7.0
Seek company	6.4	Escape/avoidance	7.0
		Psychological distancing	6.0

* Representing 5% or more of responses.

"It was all right for teenage boys to hang out in the streets, but not teenage girls."

"The first glass of vodka was offered the boy, most often at home (by his father). Again, to the boy and not to the girl."

These social attitudes existed even though more than half of Russian youngsters are singletons suggesting that the One-Child Policy in China may not change parental attitudes toward their female children as easily in social as in educational spheres. (See Chapter 6.)

Coping strategies

Individual problem-solving was the top-ranked class of coping strategy of both Russian males and females (Table 13.2(a)) and "try harder" the top-ranked category-within-class (Table 13.2(b)) with a higher percentage of responses given to both by males, just as in the multinational study. It is not surprising, given the political situation in Russia at the time of the study that so many responses indicated **resignation** and **disengagement**, but it is significant that, at

TABLE 13.3 *Russian study: percentages of total responses falling into classes and categories of desired helpers*

(a) Classes

	Male		*Female*	
	%	*Rank*	*%*	*Rank*
Family	47.7	(1)	47.7	(1)
Non-family	43.7	(2)	45.1	(2)
Offender	—	—	—	—
Supernatural	—	—	—	—
Creatures/objects	.3	(5)	—	—
Non-specific	.9	(4)	.2	(4)
Nobody	7.9	(3)	6.8	(3)

*(b) Categories**

Male		*Female*	
Category	*%*	*Category*	*%*
Personal friend	29.7	Personal friend	29.1
Parents/family	15.2	Mother	14.6
Mother	10.5	Parents/family	10.2
Father	9.6	No one	6.8
No one	7.4	Teacher	6.2
		Father	5.6

* Represents 5% or more of responses.

that time, even a small percentage of youngsters—both males and females—reported **anti-social** coping. This might have been "wishful thinking," as was suggested for the small percentage of **anti-social** coping responses given by migrant Dutch youth (Chapter 11). It might also be a reflection of increasing adolescent crime and a portent of the political violence that was to come shortly.

Help-seeking

When they needed help, Russian youngsters, like their multinational peers, selected a family member to go to for help first (Table 13.3(a)). If only one person was chosen, it was a "personal friend" (Table 13.3(b)).

While their multinational peers sought **knowledge** more frequently than any other attribute, however, Russian youngsters sought **concern** with far greater frequency (Table 13.4(a)). Similarly, while multinational youngsters sought "experienced" helpers, Russian youngsters sought helpers who were "understanding" and "concerned" (Table 13.4(b))[2].

[2] Unfortunately, the written responses of these youngsters are not available to permit determination of the exact meaning given by the Soviet researchers to this term.

TABLE 13.4 *Russian study: percentages of total responses falling into classes and categories of desired helper qualities*

(a) Classes

	Male		*Female*	
	%	*Rank*	*%*	*Rank*
Powerful	1.9	(5)	1.8	(5)
Knowledgeable	25.8	(2)	29.1	(2)
Available	.6	(7)	.4	(7)
Personal qualities	11.9	(3)	18.4	(3)
Concern	48.4	(1)	43.3	(1)
Uncertain	10.1	(4)	5.7	(4)
No listing	1.3	(6)	1.1	(6)

*(b) Categories**

Male		*Female*	
Category	*%*	*Category*	*%*
Concern: other	19.9	Understanding	25.2
Understanding	18.6	Concern: other	14.9
Don't know	9.9	Experience	9.6
Experience	8.7	Don't know	5.7
Caring	7.5	Caring	5.3
Intelligent	5.0		
Personal characteristic: other	5.0		

* Representing 5% or more of responses.

Table 13.5 shows that Russian youngsters wanted to be **counseled** (Table 13.5(a)) and to be "advised."

Why do Russian youngsters appear to have been searching less for **knowledgeable** helpers than their multinational peers? We can only conjecture. The fact that they chose to cope through **resignation** and **disengagement** so frequently suggests, however, that they might believe that they understand the sources of their problems, but that there is nothing that individual helpers can do. Their desire to be **counseled** ("advised") would suggest conflict. This is reinforced by the relatively high percentage of responses indicated by "don't know" (what they would like a helper to do) and "nothing."

TABLE 13.5 *Russian study: percentages of total responses falling into classes and categories of desired helping modes*

(a) Classes

	Male		Female	
	%	*Rank*	*%*	*Rank*
Direct need	14.0	(4)	16.0	(2.5)
Exercise power/solve	7.8	(6)	2.5	(7)
Intercede	2.3	(7)	1.3	(8)
Counsel	28.7	(1)	43.3	(1)
Attend to	16.3	(3)	16.0	(2.5)
Evade problem	1.6	(8)	6.7	(5)
Uncertain	17.1	(2)	8.4	(4)
No list	12.4	(5)	5.9	(6)

*(b) Categories**

Male		Female	
Category	*%*	*Category*	*%*
Advise	18.6	Advise	26.9
Don't know	17.1	Direct need satisfaction: other	13.0
Nothing	12.4	Don't know	8.4
Direct need satisfaction: other	10.1	Help solve problem	7.1
Encourage	7.0	Comfort	6.7
Comfort	6.2	Nothing	5.9
Help solve problem	6.2	Share	5.9
		Help escape	5.9

* Representing 5% or more of responses.

Implications of Our Findings

Our findings add to previous literature that suggests the disillusionment of youth with the Soviet system in the 1980s, one of the symptoms of which was increasing adolescent delinquency (Pearson, 1990; Shipler, 1989). To attempt to stem the tide, Moscow schools added extracurricular activities to their already full curricula—parties, dances, celebrations of political events, all designed to keep young people occupied. Government-sponsored "coffee houses" catered to young people in the evenings and were planned to keep them off the streets. Just as the attempt by the Soviet government to raise the birthrate by providing financial incentives to families with more than one child, however, these attempts, like many others offered in those years appear to be more of the same ... too little ... too late.

Our subjects were more clear in describing their problems than in providing solutions. Given the chaos that is Russia today, it is unlikely that professional helpers will guide them. Fortunately, Russian youngsters have one important source of support. The Russian family that has already survived generations of wars and difficulties will be sorely needed in the years ahead to direct its children toward a better future in a democratic society.

14

Turkey

SEMIHA ARSOY[1]

Utrecht, Netherlands

"I would like to have fun ..."

Nihal is thirteen. Her father is a university graduate; her mother has a master's degree. Both parents are architects.

"In my future, I could be living in England. I really want that. If I'm in Turkey, I will be working. Doing my best in a good job. I would like to have fun. To enjoy being young. I would not want to be still studying at a university like some people. I wouldn't like to be without a job or friends. And I wouldn't like to be married.

"We live on a street with a lot of traffic. I am an only child and my parents are too interested in me, too concerned. My mother allows me to get out to play only if my girlfriend is there. My girlfriend has a boyfriend ... well, sort of a boyfriend. When he is around, she doesn't treat me well. When I talk with her about this, she denies it. So, when her boyfriend comes around, I just go away and spend time with other friends.

"In whom do I confide? If I have problems, I go to my grandmother. She is always there for me. When I talk with her about my friends, she tells me what she thinks about them, both their good and bad sides. Something that upsets me is when my mother or grandmother compares me with my friends. I'm a good student. I got on the honors list, but my best friend got highest honors. My grandma said, 'You could be a high honors student like her.' This got on my nerves.

"My wishes are to graduate from the university—I want the two-year program. I want to get to England. And I want to be successful in sports."

[1] The author wishes to thank Nur Sucuka for her assistance in data coding.

Introduction

The Turkish study was undertaken, as part of the larger ERT project, to investigate Turkish adolescents' problems, coping strategies and choices of helpers as well as preferred qualities of helpers and desired modes of helping and to interpret this information so as to provide effective and culturally relevant counseling services in Turkish middle and junior high schools.

Country and culture

Turkey is situated in two continents of the world: Europe and Asia. This remarkable position makes the country a passage land with a rich diversity of climate and culture. The largest portion of the land consists mainly of the large peninsula of Asia Minor (Anatolia) with the Black Sea in the North, the Aegean in the West, and the Mediterranean in the South. A small region of the land is European Turkey (Thrace), containing the beautiful old city of Istanbul, once the capital of the Byzantine and Ottoman Empires. Istanbul is spread out on both sides of the Strait of Bosphorus which forms a natural border between Asia and Europe. Thus, during the course of a day, residents of this city often travel between two continents.

Cradle to many a civilization, Anatolia has seen the rise and fall of various empires and dynasties, among which are the Hittites, Phrygians, Lydians, Byzantians, Seljugs and Ottomans. The earliest written records found in Asia Minor date back to the second millennium BC indicating the existence of Assyrian trading colonies.

The modern Republic of Turkey is a relatively young state founded on the ruins of what was the Ottoman Empire. Following the 1918 Mudrice armistice after the Ottomans fought the First World War on the side of the Germans, what remained of the empire was occupied by the French, British, Italian and Greek forces. The Turks' reaction to loss of their homeland was strong. Although the nation was exhausted by war, people of all classes were energized and determined to fight for independence. Mustafa Kemal Atatürk emerged as their leader and organized the national liberation movement. In 1923, the homeland was freed from the invaders and on October 29 was declared a republic.

Mustafa Kemal Atatürk, as the first president of the Republic of Turkey, started rebuilding the country and introduced a series of reforms which changed the basis of society. In 1928, the constitution was amended to make Turkey a secular state. Furthermore, the Islamic law of the Ottomans was replaced by civil and criminal codes adapted from Europe and the Latin alphabet replaced the Arabic script. Women were declared equal to men in all rights as citizens and in 1934 given the right to vote.

The Republic of Turkey today is a multiparty democracy covering an area of 779 452 sq. km. The 1990 census indicated the population to be 56 473 035, an increase of 2.2% from 1985. The rural—urban distribution is estimated to be

54% (rural) versus 45% (urban) with a steady migration from the rural areas to the three major cities of Istanbul, Izmir and the capital, Ankara. The *Statistical Yearbook of Turkey* shows a very young population with 60% being under the age of 30. Of these, 20% are between the ages of 10 and 19. The majority of citizens are Muslims (99%) and the ethnic composition is mainly of Turkish origin (86%). Of the total population, 77% are literate, with the literacy rate of males 86% and females 68%. Although elementary school education is compulsory, only 55% of the male literate population and 56% of the female literate population have completed it. The percentage of the population who complete secondary education is less than 7% and less than 4% complete higher education (Statistical Institute of Turkey, 1992).

Yıldıran's (1990) comprehensive report on educational issues and problems in Turkey draws attention to the rate of failure to pass competitive examinations for entrance to junior high schools, particularly in public schools (estimated to be 29%). The same report also points out that between 1985 and 1989, 45% to 60% of the appropriate age cohort (12—15 years) were attending junior high schools. These schools provide the first three years of secondary education which are then followed by three additional years of senior high school education. Compared to 98% of the appropriate cohort (7—12 year olds) attending compulsory elementary schools, this is quite a drop in enrolment ratios.

Turkish society continues to undergo the social changes that began with the reforms introduced during the early years of the Republic. Various lines of historical-cultural influence have molded attitudes and belief systems. Kağıtçıbaşı (1982) names the main ones as nomadic Turkish, Anatolian, Islamic Middle Eastern and the Mediterranean. The diversity and complexity of the sociocultural backgrounds prevent making generalizations. Nevertheless, in comparison to Western cultures, Turkish culture is one of relatedness with close-knit kinship ties rather than a culture valuing individuality. Socialization practices often emphasize loyalty to family and respect for authority. Childrearing practices can be described as largely authoritarian. However, show of affection to children is not restricted. Because parents are attributed a high degree of legitimate power by the children, conformity and dependence are not necessary indicators of low self-esteem in such a system.

Counseling in Turkey

The history of counseling in Turkey dates back to the 1950s and, as Öner (1992) pointed out, has been basically influenced by American models and theories. Between 1950 and 1965, as part of the plan of the Ministry of National Education to improve the quality of education, a number of educators were sent to the USA and several US educators and psychologists were invited to Turkey. In the late 1950s, the interest of Turkish educators in the study of guidance and counseling in the US led to the establishment in Ankara and other major cities of

Guidance and Research Centers. The seventh (1962) and eighth (1970) National Education Conventions and State Development Plans underlined the importance of school guidance services which were subsequently made constitutional by the National Education Law in 1973. Implementation of the decision was in the form of weekly guidance classes in the secondary school curricula. The two hours of guidance were conducted by homeroom teachers under the supervision of the school counselor. Counseling hours were compulsory in all secondary schools until 1987 when a new by-law made them optional.

As can be concluded from the preceding summary, guidance and counseling in Turkish schools were established through decisions taken at top levels in a centralized system of education. What was the actual practice in schools and how did educators respond to the idea of guidance and counseling?

Initially, administrators and teachers were enthusiastic about school guidance and counseling, but this interest did not continue except in a few private and public schools. Thus, "Guidance never really attained a functional status within the Turkish education system" (Öner, 1992, p. 8). A major factor for the negative outturn was the shortage of professionally trained counselors. School guidance counselors were appointed to the position from among teachers of the school or from among university graduates with degrees in psychology, education, sociology and social work without any special training. After the counseling hour became optional, school guidance services became available only in large cities. On the positive side, since 1982 undergraduate programs in Guidance and Counseling have been instituted in several universities. Also, some major universities such as Boğaziçi University in Istanbul have been conferring masters degrees after two years of training in guidance and counseling. These professional graduates from these universities are committed to practicing preventive and culturally appropriate modes of counseling.

The Study and Its Methodology

Detailed information concerning the methodology used in all countries of our multinational study, including instrumentation, is provided in Chapter 2. In this chapter, only the Turkish sample description and those data collection procedures specific to Turkey are presented.

Subjects

The sample of Turkish adolescents consisted of 195 "advantaged" subjects (96 males and 99 females) and 233 "nonadvantaged" subjects (121 males and 112 females). All were Istanbul junior high-school students between the ages of 13 and 15 years.

"Advantaged" subjects

"Advantaged" youngsters attended a private school located in an upper-class section of the city. There were 25—30 students in each class and students could enjoy gyms, computer labs and various club rooms. The fathers of "advantaged" students tended to be professionals, executives or financially successful entrepreneurs. Most had achieved secondary or higher education. Approximately 46% of subjects were "advantaged."

"Nonadvantaged" subjects

"Nonadvantaged" youth, by contrast, attended a public school located in a poor area. This school provided few amenities; even basic necessities such as running water were often not available and students sat three-in-row chairs in crowded classrooms of at least 60 students. "Nonadvantaged" students came from lower-class families. Their fathers worked at occupations that brought either low pay or low prestige, often employed as drivers, clerical and blue-collar workers or small shopkeepers. The majority of parents had achieved primary educations only.

Procedure

Subjects were surveyed in 1989 by the author-researcher, using a Turkish translation of the multinational questionnaire developed according to project guidelines (see Chapter 2). Arrangements were made with the schools to administer the questionnaire during one class period, the counseling hour.

The data-collection procedure used with both groups of subjects was as follows:

First, a brief description of the research project and its purpose was presented to students. Students were assured of the confidentiality of their responses and provided the standardized instructions for filling out the questionnaire. After all questions raised by students were answered, students were administered the instrument and given the allotted time period for completion. (It is interesting to note that students in the public school displayed a more serious attitude during administration of the instrument and remained silent, while the private school students often joked with each other and were often distracted from their task.)

Coding was completed by the author with the assistance of her trained assistant. To determine the reliability of coding, two measures were taken. First, the author-researcher coded a data set of 15 completed questionnaires provided by the University of Pittsburgh ERT. The percentage of agreement between the coded responses of the author-researcher and that of the ERT master code was computed and found to be .95 for classes and .83 for categories-within-classes of responses. The percentage of agreement between the coded responses of the author-researcher and the trained assistant to a sample set of data was computed and found to be .87 for all responses.

TABLE 14.1 *Turkish study: percentages of total responses falling into classes and categories of problems*

(a) Classes

	Advantaged				*Nonadvantaged*			
	Male		*Female*		*Male*		*Female*	
	%	*Rank*	*%*	*Rank*	*%*	*Rank*	*%*	*Rank*
Extreme poverty	0.0	(0)	0.0	(0)	0.3	(11.5)	1.2	(10)
Catastrophe	0.8	(9)	0.4	(10.5)	1.5	(8.5)	0.0	(0)
Material desires	2.1	(8)	1.1	(9)	7.0	(6)	3.4	(6)
Family issues	15.4	(3)	25.5	(2)	20.9	(2)	33.4	(1)
Schooling issues	37.8	(1)	25.9	(1)	34.2	(1)	29.1	(2)
Identity	19.9	(2)	23.7	(3)	13.0	(3)	8.9	(4)
Sexuality	0.0	(0)	0.4	(12)	0.3	(11.5)	0.3	(11.5)
Courtship/dating	3.7	(6)	6.6	(5)	4.8	(7)	5.2	(5)
Interpersonal	6.6	(5)	8.8	(4)	8.2	(4)	9.8	(3)
Emotions	3.3	(7)	1.8	(7.5)	1.5	(8.5)	2.8	(8)
Self-fulfilment	0.0	(0)	0.4	(10.5)	0.0	(0)	0.3	(11.5)
Altruism	0.4	(10)	1.8	(7.5)	0.9	(10)	2.5	(9)
No problem	10.0	(4)	3.6	(6)	7.3	(5)	3.1	(7)

*(b) Categories**

	Male		*Female*	
	Category	*%*	*Category*	*%*
Advantaged	Academic failure	17.0	Physical appearance	13.1
	No problem	10.0	Parental strictness	10.9
	Academic achievement	7.1	Academic failure	10.2
	Physical appearance	7.1	Friendship	7.7
	Parental strictness	6.2	Self confidence	5.1
	Domestic quarrels	5.5		
	Friendship	5.4		
	Self confidence	5.0		
Nonadvantaged	Academic failure	10.0	Academic failure	11.3
	Parental strictness	8.5	Parental strictness	11.3
	Teacher related	8.5	Friendship	8.3
	Friendship	7.3		
	No problem	7.3		
	Academic achievement	5.2		
	Domestic quarrels	4.9		

* Representing 5% or more of responses.

While the Turkish data was being coded, the author-researcher remained available to the assistant to answer questions concerning ambiguous responses which could fit more than one class.

Coded responses to questions contained in each scale of the study were organized by gender and socioeconomic class so that results could be examined across the four groups of subjects.

Results

Results are presented in terms of percentages and rankings of responses falling into all classes of each of the study's five scales. They also appear as categories within each of these classes which account for 5% or more of the total number of responses. (See Appendix II.)

Problems

The most frequently reported problems of Turkish adolescents were related to **schooling, family** and **identity/self-concept**. These were the highest ranking three problems across the groups and together accounted for approximately 60—84% of all responses in the separate samples (see Table 14.1(a)).

Although **schooling, family** and **identity** were the most commonly reported problems for all groups, there is some variation within both gender and socioeconomic grouping: The percentage of reported **school** programs decreased with decreasing SES, while that of **family** problems increased. At the same time, a higher percentage of the responses of adolescent boys than of girls for both SES groups were related to **schooling** issues while a higher percentage of the responses of girls than of boys dealt with **family** issues.

Percentages of responses related to **identity** issues indicated possible SES group differences, with percentages higher for the "advantaged" boys and girls than for the "nonadvantaged."

Table 14.1(b) shows the frequently occurring concerns described by categories-within-classes. Among **schooling** concerns, "academic failure" was the most frequently reported category by all Turkish groups, with the exception of "advantaged" girls. "Academic achievement" was also a **schooling** concern for boys.

"Parental strictness" was a major **family**-related problem for all groups. Again, gender seemed to be an influencing factor in the frequency of reports, with girls in both "advantaged" and "nonadvantaged" groups reporting higher percentages in this category than boys in the same SES groupings.

Identity/self-concept concerns in general were more significant for the "advantaged" groups. Categories within this class in which the percentage of responses was above the 5% cut-off point showed up only among "advantaged" youngsters, with reported problems related to "physical appearance" and "self-confidence" with a higher percentage for girls than for boys (13% versus 7%). Concerns regarding "friendship" were reported by all groups.

Coping strategies

With respect to the question of how they deal with their problems (what they do to cope), Turkish adolescents' most frequently reported **individual problem-solving** (ranging within the four groups from 38% to 50% of responses), **resignation** (ranging from 18% to 20%), and **interpersonal coping** (interacting with another person in order to work out a problem) (9—14%).

TABLE 14.2 *Turkish study: percentages of total responses falling into classes and categories of coping strategies*

(a) Classes

	Advantaged				Nonadvantaged			
	Male		Female		Male		Female	
	%	Rank	%	Rank	%	Rank	%	Rank
Seek/give assistance	9.7	(4)	9.1	(4)	7.2	(5)	12.3	(4)
Interpersonal	10.5	(3)	13.1	(3)	9.2	(3)	14.1	(3)
Individual problem-solving	49.0	(1)	49.1	(1)	49.6	(1)	38.1	(1)
Stress management	2.4	(6)	2.5	(6)	2.0	(8)	2.9	(6)
Crying	0.0	(8)	0.9	(7)	0.0	(9)	1.3	(7)
Religious	0.8	(7)	0.3	(8)	0.9	(7)	0.5	(8)
Resignation	17.8	(2)	18.1	(2)	20.7	(2)	19.6	(2)
Disengage	9.3	(5)	5.6	(5)	8.9	(4)	11.2	(5)

*(b) Categories**

	Male		Female	
	Category	%	Category	%
Advantaged	Trying harder	23.5	Trying harder	23.4
	Planning a solution	18.2	Planning a solution	19.4
	Do nothing	8.9	Do nothing	7.8
	Seek support	8.1	Assertive coping	7.8
	Escape/avoidance	5.9	Seek support	6.9
Nonadvantaged	Trying harder	25.3	Trying harder	19.6
	Planning a solution	17.2	Do nothing	11.0
	Do nothing	11.5	Planning a solution	10.7
	Assertive coping	5.5	Seek support	10.4
	Seek support	4.9	Assertive coping	8.6
			Psychological distancing	5.5

* Representing 5% or more of responses.

Individual problem-solving ranked as the first strategy for all groups, although "nonadvantaged" girls were less likely to use this approach than other groups of Turkish youngsters. No differences were shown between SES groupings (Table 14.2(a)). Among categories-within-the-class, **individual problem-solving**, Turkish adolescents cited "making plans toward a solution" and "trying harder" as their most frequently used strategies. For "nonadvantaged" girls, the percentage of responses was slightly lower than for others (Table 14.2(b)).

Responses indicating **resignation**, the second ranking coping strategy, did not indicate discernible class or gender differences. **Resignation** was defined as concluding that one may not be able to solve the problem. Interestingly, the most frequent responses of Turkish adolescents in this class fell into the category, "do nothing" (make no attempt to find a solution), rather than under categories such as "anger or depression," "taking a fatalistic view" or "giving up" (after trying) (Table 14.2(b)). Responses of Turkish youngsters were expressed in statements such as:

"I just hope time will take care of it."

TABLE 14.3 *Turkish study: percentages of total responses falling into classes and categories of desired helpers*

(a) Classes

	Advantaged				*Nonadvantaged*			
	Male		*Female*		*Male*		*Female*	
	%	*Rank*	*%*	*Rank*	*%*	*Rank*	*%*	*Rank*
Family	54.6	(1)	47.1	(2)	55.1	(1)	48.4	(1)
Non-family	42.0	(2)	47.9	(1)	41.0	(2)	47.6	(2)
Offender	0.2	(5.5)	0.2	(6)	0.0	(5)	0.4	(5.5)
Creatures/objects	0.2	(5.5)	0.8	(4.5)	0.2	(4.5)	0.4	(5.5)
Non-specific	0.4	(4)	0.8	(4.5)	0.2	(4.5)	0.5	(4)
Nobody	2.6	(3)	3.3	(3)	3.4	(3)	2.6	(3)

*(b) Categories**

	Male		*Female*	
	Category	*%*	*Category*	*%*
Advantaged	Personal friend	27.9	Personal friend	34.7
	Mother	23.4	Mother	23.3
	Father	14.7	Teacher	7.8
	Teacher	8.9	Father	5.3
Nonadvantaged	Personal friend	27.4	Personal friend	30.3
	Mother	22.3	Mother	19.8
	Father	11.0	Teacher	12.0
	Teacher	7.6	Father	4.8
	Brother	5.4		

* Representing 5% or more of responses.

"I leave it to time."

"I hope it will all work out in the end."

This type of passive but, perhaps, somewhat optimistic view of existing problems was more frequently the coping strategy for "nonadvantaged" than "advantaged" youth.

Girls' reports of **interpersonal** coping appeared to be slightly more frequent than those of boys.

Choice of helpers

Table 14.3(a) shows that, in describing to whom they would turn for help when they experienced problems, more Turkish youth cited a **family-member** rather than a **non-member**, with a slightly higher percentage of responses appearing from boys.

When considering the specific individual, however, personal friend was the number one choice of helper (Table 14.3(b)). Among family members, mothers were chosen as helpers more frequently than fathers in all groups. Teachers were

TABLE 14.4 *Turkish study: percentages of total responses falling into classes and categories of desired helper qualities*

(a) Classes

	Advantaged				Nonadvantaged			
	Male		Female		Male		Female	
	%	Rank	%	Rank	%	Rank	%	Rank
Powerful	4.1	(5)	3.0	(5)	3.9	(5)	5.0	(5)
Knowledgeable	25.3	(3)	29.6	(2)	17.7	(3)	23.8	(3)
Available	4.6	(4)	3.2	(4)	5.3	(4)	2.9	(6)
Personal qualities	30.7	(2)	35.5	(1)	38.3	(1)	28.4	(2)
Concern	33.4	(1)	26.8	(3)	31.7	(2)	32.7	(1)
Uncertain	1.4	(6)	0.0	(7)	0.5	(7)	1.0	(7)
No listing	0.5	(7)	1.9	(6)	2.7	(6)	6.2	(4)

*(b) Categories**

	Male		Female	
	Category	%	Category	%
Advantaged	Understanding	12.2	Approachable	16.5
	Caring/loving	12.2	Understanding	13.3
	Approachable	11.7	Similarity	11.4
	Similarity	8.7	Supportive	7.2
	Supportive	8.4	Content area knowledge	7.0
	Trustworthy	6.5	Generous	6.6
	Generous	5.7	Caring/loving	6.1
			Experienced	5.5
Nonadvantaged	Caring/loving	12.0	Understanding	16.4
	Approachable	11.4	Generous	9.5
	Generous	10.7	Similarity	9.3
	Understanding	10.7	Approachable	8.5
	Trustworthy	9.0	Supportive	8.5
	Supportive	9.0	Caring/loving	7.9
	Similarity	5.6	Nothing	6.2
			Gives advice	5.6

* Representing 5% or more of responses.

also mentioned as helpers by all groups, but "nonadvantaged" girls were more likely to seek out **teachers** for help compared to others.

Desired qualities of helpers

What qualities led Turkish adolescents to choose the people they did to help them with their problems?

Appealing personal qualities as well as ability to show **concern** or to be **knowledgeable** about the problems of the subject appear to have been most important. "Advantaged" youngsters, more than their "nonadvantaged" peers, and girls of both SES groups more than boys, sought **knowledge** regarding the particular problem. "Nonadvantaged" girls were more likely than others to be unable to list any helper qualities (**no listing**) (Table 14.4(a)).

TABLE 14.5 *Turkish study: percentages of total responses falling into classes and categories of desired helping modes*

(a) Classes

	Advantaged				*Nonadvantaged*			
	Male		*Female*		*Male*		*Female*	
	%	*Rank*	*%*	*Rank*	*%*	*Rank*	*%*	*Rank*
Direct need satisfaction	2.3	(6)	0.8	(8)	1.1	(7)	1.0	(8)
Exercise power/solve	9.1	(3)	5.1	(4)	8.5	(3)	5.4	(4)
Intercede	4.2	(5)	1.9	(5)	2.8	(5)	3.2	(5)
Counsel	47.1	(1)	42.3	(1)	44.9	(1)	42.2	(1)
Attend to	29.7	(2)	39.4	(2)	35.8	(2)	38.3	(2)
Evade problem	6.1	(4)	7.3	(3)	4.1	(4)	6.4	(3)
Uncertain	0.4	(8)	1.6	(6.5)	0.3	(8)	1.2	(7)
No listing	1.1	(7)	1.6	(6.5)	2.5	(6)	2.2	(6)

*(b) Categories**

	Male		*Female*	
	Category	*%*	*Category*	*%*
Advantaged	Direct	16.7	Comfort	22.4
	Comfort	15.6	Advise	13.5
	Advise	14.8	Help solve problem	11.9
	Solve problem	9.1	Direct	8.1
	Help solve problem	8.4	Help escape	7.3
	Share	6.1	Listen	5.9
	Help escape	5.7	Share	5.7
			Encourage	5.7
Nonadvantaged	Comfort	19.0	Comfort	21.5
	Advise	17.4	Advise	14.6
	Direct	11.6	Help solve problem	12.1
	Help solve problem	9.9	Direct	9.6
	Encourage	7.4	Help escape	6.4
	Share	5.0	Encourage	6.4

* Representing 5% or more of responses.

For those who did list helper qualities, particular qualities such as "similarity" to the subject, being "understanding," "approachable," "generous," "caring/loving," "supportive" and "similar to the subject" were high on the list of all groups (Table 14.4(a)). "Trustworthiness," in the sense that the helper would honor confidentiality and "caring/loving" seemed more important for boys than for girls.

Desired modes of helping

When the Turkish adolescents responded to the question of how they would like to be helped, most boys and girls in both SES groups indicated a preference for being **counseled** (ranked first) or **attended to** (second), with boys apparently wanting to be **counseled** more than girls, and girls displaying somewhat greater preference for being **attended to** than boys (Table 14.5(a)).

Categories listed in Table 14.5(b) indicate that desired helping modes consisted of those helper behaviors directed at being "comforted " (soothed), "advised" (given directions on request) or "directed" (given authoritative instructions directions). In general, boys tended to prefer being "advised" or "directed" more than did girls. Conversely, girls appear to value "being comforted" slightly more than did their male counterparts.

Comparison of the Turkish Findings with Those of the ERT's Multinational Study

The findings of this and the multinational study show remarkable similarity, suggesting a number of commonalities of human development regardless of cultural experience, as would have been predicted by the traditional psychoanalytic theories described in Chapter 1. At the same time, as social psychological theories (also described in Chapter 1) would have predicted, there were findings particular to the Turkish sample that can be related to the specific context of experience of these adolescents.

Problems

Like the problems of their age-mates around the world, major concerns of adolescents revolved around schooling, family and identity issues. Moreover, the same gender and socioeconomic class trends reported in the multinational study were evident: A higher percentage of school-related problems were reported by boys, and family concerns by girls within each socioeconomic grouping. In addition, the percentage of schooling problems tended to decrease and family problems increase with decreasing socioeconomic grouping.

As regards Turkish youngsters, that schooling is the first concern is not surprising, given that most of the adolescents were in school and under extreme pressure to achieve. The trend for females in Turkey as well as multinationally to be more concerned about family issues has been explained in Western psychological literature in terms of gender-associated socialization in which females learn to be more concerned about relationships than males (Maccoby and Jacklin, 1974). The same pattern is true for Turkish females.

With regard to emphases placed by Turkish adolescents on fear of failure and parental strictness (strictness unrelated to issues of dating or courtship is perceived by youngsters as inappropriate), these represent a far higher proportion of responses than in the multinational study. Fear of academic failure is consistent with Turkish reality: Approximately 30% of Turkish students enrolled in junior high school fail annually. Problems related to parental strictness are also consistent with reality and have been related by psychologists to extremely authoritarian child-rearing practices associated with high expectations for conformity and respect for parents (Kağıtçıbaşı, 1982).

Identity issues appeared less important for the "nonadvantaged" than "advantaged" Turkish youngsters, unlike their multinational counterparts. There are two possible explanations: First, it may simply be that "nonadvantaged" Turkish youngsters have a multiplicity of problems that their "advantaged" peers do not have to face, so that, while they may be concerned with identity issues, these problems appear as lower percentages of the spectrum.

Alternatively, the explanation may lie in the nature of youngsters' identity problems: Most of those identity problems suggested by Turkish subjects related to esteem needs as defined by Maslow (1970). "Nonadvantaged" Turkish youngsters were, more often than their "advantaged" counterparts, in the position of having to fulfil needs of a lower order than identity concerns, while, at the same time, trying to meet the high expectations of their parents. School achievement was made more difficult for them by the crowded classrooms and few amenities offered by the public school; fathers of "nonadvantaged" youth, whose income was lower than those of "advantaged" children, could provide fewer comforts at home and, because of their lower educational levels, were less able to assist their children at their school tasks.

Coping

In coping with their problems, Turkish adolescents' responses were similar to those of their age-mates from around the world in their preference for individual problem-solving strategies. Planning and trying harder, the most commonly reported ways of coping, indicate assessment and analysis as well as persistence. This study did not enquire as to the effectiveness of chosen strategies, unfortunately. Youngsters may be choosing to persist in behaviors which are not helpful in overcoming the problem.

The frequent reporting of resignation as a coping strategy by Turkish adolescents, second in rank only to individual problem-solving, is an important finding that sets Turkish adolescents apart from the multinational sample. Surrendering to the conclusion that the problem cannot be solved may reflect a fatalistic orientation which is common in Eastern and/or Muslim cultures. However, given that turning to religion was a very low occurring response for these adolescents, it is more likely to indicate a general passive orientation or internal locus of control. The reported expectation that time may take care of the problem could be interpreted as an optimistic outlook that a solution will be found. Conversely, it might reflect a belief that although the problem will still be there, one will be less bothered about it. In either case, a responsible and assertive reaction to one's situation appears to be missing. Adolescents who are inclined to cope with their problems by doing nothing about them and "leaving it to time" may later experience depression.

Helpers

Turkish adolescents were like their adolescent peers around the world in consistently turning to their friends and mothers first for help.

Turkish adolescents differed from multinational adolescents in terms of the helper qualities they preferred, with multinational subjects indicating preference for helpers to be knowledgeable about the specific problem and Turkish youngsters worrying more about personal characteristics such as being caring, loving or understanding. It is significant that both studies clearly indicated the desire to be counseled (offered advice and given directions about what to do).

Neither Turkish nor multinational adolescents were likely to seek out professional counselors as sources of help, although they were somewhat inclined to consult teachers. (Other studies with Turkish adolescents have results consistent with this finding (Gökçe, 1984; Nirun, 1986).) It is unfortunate that this is the case. The explanation is beyond the scope of this study, although a number of factors such as youngsters' perceptions of counselors, their position in the schools, actual counseling approaches used and availability to students might be hypothesized.

Implications for Counseling

The findings of this study have a number of implications for counseling in Turkey. The high frequency of schooling and family problems suggests the need for programs that could be carried out in schools as part of their counseling services. The Turkish findings suggest that the model for these programs be specific to Turkish values and expectations, rather than following the US-oriented guidance and counseling models that give high priority to individual differences. Through a truly Turkish model, it might be possible to modify the profession in such a way as to make it easier for Turkish educators, students and the public to understand and accept.

A proposed Turkish model for educational counseling

A three-dimensional model that would make counseling practice relevant and meaningful in the Turkish educational system is proposed. Based specifically on a Turkish problem-oriented school culture that offers problem-solving strategies over and beyond what the social support agencies (parents, relatives, friends and confidants) provide and that is designed to simplify and encourage implementation of these strategies, this model is designed to respond to immediate and real needs of students and their families. It includes:

1. Preventive programs dealing with academic learning problems: The problem of school failure as well as the high rate of coping that indicate resignation suggest a need for programs that aim at failure reduction and, more optimistically worded, achievement enhancement. Study skills, time management and anxiety, such as those that are included in Öner's (1992) counseling model are possible content areas, needed, according to this study, at a nationally inclusive level.

2. Parent education programs designed to impart information concerning both developmental characteristics and needs of adolescents as well as to improve communication skills within the family. Although some parent education programs already have been devised and employed in Turkey under the direction of Kağıtçıbası (1982), these are aimed primarily at parents of preschoolers. The Turkish findings demonstrate that programs targeting adolescence and parents of adolescents are also needed.

3. Programs designed to assist parents, friends and teachers at the helping tasks with which they are already involved. Since it is clear that parents, friends and teachers already are serving helping roles, a new counseling role might be designed to assist these individuals to become more effective at their activities. Since adolescents in this study have expressed desire for a directive approach on the part of their helpers, this clearly needs to be given serious consideration. One should not conclude from the messages provided by our young subjects that counselors ought to take authoritarian stands. However, programs that do not consider the desires and expectations of their clients are not likely to succeed.

While there are many reasons why Turkish youngsters might rarely seek professional help, use of a model designed so well to answer their specific needs and desires may go a long way toward changing this view.

15

Continental United States[1]

GEORGE W. ONDIS

Health America

JANICE GIBSON-CLINE

University of Pittsburgh

MARION DRAGOON

Teachers College, Columbia University

CARLOS JONES

California Department of Mental Health

A private school student: "I mess up on tests."

Fourteen-year-old **Jonathan** is soon entering the ninth grade. His father is an insurance broker. His mother does volunteer work for a child health agency.

"In the future, I want to be doing something with art or in the movies, such as a comic book or story-board artist. I do **not** want to be "in a soup line" and I don't want to be doing the boring "businessman thing".

"My main problem is doing good in academic subjects. Sometimes I mess up on tests . . . This might get me kicked out of school and prevent my going to college. I don't want people to think that I'm stupid. My problem . . . is just that I'm a little nervous.

"I do try to study more . . . Sometimes I try to make myself feel better by telling myself that I am at least smarter than **some** other people. If I'm smarter than half the people then that's ok. My friends understand because they are going through the same thing.

"My wish for the future? To be recognized for my art work and to have a chance to become some kind of artist when I grow up".

[1] The following individuals have contributed to the research in this chapter: C. Baker, I. Ivory, L. Nguyen, C. Pietronuto, S. Showalter and F. Sun.

Introduction

The Continental United States, its citizens and its problems

The US is a multicultural nation embodying more than 100 ethnic and racial backgrounds. The majority of US citizens are White; major minority groups are African-Americans and Hispanics (representing approximately 12% and 9%, respectively, of the population) and Asian-Americans (approximately 3%). The US satisfies the dreams of many for a high standard of living. The median annual income is $30 126; 79% of the population complete high school and 21% graduate from college; life expectancy is approximately 72 years for males and 79 for females (US Bureau of the Census, 1993).

Life is not ideal for everyone, however. Approximately 50% of US marriages end in divorce; more than 14% of Americans and a far higher percentage of minority Americans live on incomes below poverty level; many of these come from single-parent homes. Illicit drugs and violent crime affect ordinary citizens today more than ever before in the country's history; 74 million adults remain functionally illiterate (see Brough, 1990; Davidson and Koppenhaver, 1988; Grant et al., 1991; Lawrence, 1994; National Commission on Children, 1991; National Institute on Drug Abuse, 1988; US Bureau of the Census, 1993).

The problems of the US are reflected in its youth: More than 20% of teenagers admit to drug or alcohol abuse; increasing numbers perpetrate or are victims of crimes ranging from theft to violent attacks on life and property; more than 30% report depressive symptoms and approximately one in ten youngsters has attempted suicide; 25% those who are sexually active contract a sexually transmitted disease before leaving high school; adolescents now account for 15% of pregnancies and 7.5% of the births, many of which produce new single parent homes (see Brough, 1990; Carnegie Council on Adolescent Development, 1989; Garland and Zigler, 1993; Petersen *et al.*, 1993; Sullivan and Englin, 1986; US Bureau of the Census, 1993; US Congress, 1987; Windle, 1991).

The sites of our study

The US study was conducted in the east coast city of Pittsburgh and its environs (population 2.4 million) and in the boroughs of the Bronx and Manhattan in the New York City metropolitan area (population: 17.9 million). Pittsburgh includes a higher percentage of White and a lower percentage of minority residents than the nation as a whole, with a minority population comprised primarily of African-Americans. New York City, by contrast, includes large numbers of African-Americans, Hispanics and Asians, with a myriad of ethnic and racial groups creating an ethnic diversity that has led to complex interactions associated with racism, prejudice and acculturation (Slater and Hall, 1992; US Bureau of the Census, 1993).

TABLE 15.1 *US study: percentages of races represented in the US population as a whole, and in the Metropolitan areas of New York City and Pittsburgh, Pa. as reported by the US Bureau of the Census (1993) and Slater and Hall (1992)*

	United States	*New York City*	*Pittsburgh*
White	80.3	70.0	91.0
African-American	12.1	18.3	8.0
American Indian	.8	2.6	.1
Asian/Pacific Islander	2.9	4.9	.7
Hispanic	9.0	15.5	.6

Note: Hispanic may be of any race.

Table 15.1 details the racial and ethnic makeup of the country as a whole as well as of the sites of the US study.

The social and economic problems of our sites mirror other US urban centers. In the early 1980s, Pittsburgh lost thousands of jobs due to the closing or cutting of production in its steel mills. Unemployment and underemployment remain high, especially among African-Americans and youth (Bangs, 1989). New York City's garment industry lost many low-skill jobs to overseas factories, with resulting unemployment and underemployment that affects poor and minority populations particularly. Illegal sweatshops that employ people desperate for work at salaries below minimum wage have proliferated in poor areas of the city. In such neighborhoods, violent crime affects a higher percentage of the population than in the nation as a whole (Garbarino, 1992, p. 49). Decreased funding in the financially strained cities has reduced income to public schools, resulting in lowered achievement in already economically distressed districts, a situation movingly documented in the US by Jonathon Kozol in *Savage Inequalities* (1991).

School counseling services

Preventive and crisis counseling services in the Pittsburgh and New York City schools include career counseling as well as counseling for emotional and school learning problems. Both cities include school programs dealing with alcohol abuse, child abuse and sexually transmitted diseases. Unfortunately, however, youth often fail to utilize these services (see Christopher *et al.*, 1989; Ondis and Gibson, 1992; Greenspan, Seeley and Niemeyer, 1993, p. 41; Pennsylvania Student Assistance Program Interagency Management Committee, 1991).

Research questions

The Continental US study surveyed male and female adolescents from "advantaged," "nonadvantaged" and "poverty" backgrounds as defined in the multinational study (Chapter 2) as to the problems that cause them stress, the coping mechanisms they use and the persons to whom they go for help. This chapter explores two broad questions:

1. How do the responses of our male and female subjects in the three socioeconomic groups compare with one another and with those of their peers in the multinational study?

2. Do their responses suggest an influence of socioeconomic status and gender?

The Study and Its Methodology

Subjects: "advantaged," "nonadvantaged" and "poverty" Americans

The US sample consists of 780 youngsters ages 13—15 years, 580 of whom formed part of the multinational study. Of these, 380 (159 males and 221 females) were classified as coming from "advantaged" and 207 (102 males and 105 females) from "nonadvantaged" backgrounds as defined in Chapter 2. These two groups were surveyed in 1990—91 in Pittsburgh. There were, in addition, 193 "poverty" subjects (89 males and 104 females) who were surveyed a year later in New York City and, for this reason, were not included in the multinational study.

"Poverty" background of the 193 New York City subjects was inferred from the fact that the schools in which data was collected were in severely economically depressed neighborhoods in which 75% or more of students qualified for governmentally subsidized lunches. School dropout rates in the community are the highest in New York City (Mann, 1986); drugs are a constant plague. The "poverty" group differs from its "advantaged" and "nonadvantaged" peers in several ways: Because of the difficulties of identifying poor adolescents and obtaining the data, this sample is smaller in size than other groups. Sample size, difference in locale and the dates of data collection are all possible influences on the differences that emerged. The "poverty" sample was not included in the international study.

Racial and ethnic composition of the sample

Racial and ethnic composition was estimated by the authors from their knowledge of the specific school populations and background neighborhoods for the "advantaged" sample (90% White and 10% minority (African-American)) and "poverty" sample (5% White and 95% minority (Hispanic or African-American)). A question concerning racial background given subjects on the demographic portion of the survey showed the "nonadvantaged" sample to include 50% White and 50% African-American students.

Procedure

The study followed guidelines of the multinational study as described in Chapter 2. Data was collected from "advantaged" students by teachers, "nonadvantaged" by research team members and "poverty" by a trusted counselor and research team member. Subjects' responses were coded into classes and categories-within-classes. Interrater reliability of coding as measured by the percentage of agreement with a master code ranged between 80% to 90% for category and 90% to 95% for class.

Study Results

Responses to our survey from male and female "advantaged," "nonadvantaged" and "poverty" adolescents compared with one another and with those of their peers in the multinational study.

TABLE 15.2 *US study: percentages of total responses falling into classes and categories of problems*

(a) Classes

	Advantaged				*Nonadvantaged*				*Poverty*			
	Male		*Female*		*Male*		*Female*		*Male*		*Female*	
	%	*Rank*	*%*	*Rank*	*%*	*Rank*	*%*	*Rank*	*%*	*Rank*	*%*	*Rank*
Extreme poverty	0.0	(12)	0.0	(13)	0.0	(12.5)	0.0	(12.5)	0.0	(12)	0.0	(12)
War	0.0	(12)	0.2	(12)	0.7	(10)	0.8	(10)	0.0	(12)	0.0	(12)
Catastrophe	0.2	(10)	0.5	(11)	1.6	(8)	2.4	(7)	0.0	(12)	0.0	(12)
Material desires	3.4	(6)	0.7	(9.5)	2.3	(6)	0.4	(11)	7.5	(4)	2.4	(9)
Family issues	8.0	(4)	18.6	(3)	14.7	(3)	23.7	(2)	18.8	(3)	29.9	(1)
Schooling issues	48.9	(1)	26.9	(1)	42.4	(1)	25.7	(1)	23.1	(1)	18.5	(2)
Identity	18.3	(2)	19.6	(2)	22.9	(2)	18.8	(3)	22.5	(2)	11.4	(4)
Sexuality	1.0	(9)	2.0	(8)	2.0	(7)	4.1	(6)	6.9	(6)	12.3	(3)
Courtship/dating	1.7	(8)	8.6	(5)	4.3	(4)	8.4	(5)	5.6	(8)	8.1	(6)
Interpersonal	8.4	(3)	13.1	(4)	2.9	(5)	11.6	(4)	6.9	(6)	8.5	(5)
Emotions	7.2	(5)	5.0	(6)	0.0	(12.5)	1.8	(8)	1.3	(9)	2.8	(8)
Self-fulfilment	0.0	(12)	0.7	(9.5)	0.9	(9)	0.0	(12.5)	0.6	(10)	0.5	(10)
Altruism	2.7	(7)	4.2	(7)	0.5	(11)	1.4	(9)	6.9	(6)	5.7	(7)

*(b) Categories**

	Male		*Female*	
	Category	*%*	*Category*	*%*
Advantaged	Academic achievement	9.4	Friendship	11.1
	Academic failure	9.2	Academic failure	7.1
	Time pressure	9.2	Academic achievement	6.0
	Extra curricular activity	7.0	Self-confidence	5.3
	Behavioral issues	6.3		
Nonadvantaged	Academic achievement	13.8	Academic achievement	10.8
	Academic failure	9.3	Friendship	10.0
	Behavioral issues	9.1	Behavioral issues	7.8
			Academic failure	7.2
Poverty	Self-destructive behavior	10.6	Welfare or family members	7.6
	Academic failure	8.1	Academic failure	7.1
	Behavioral issues	6.3	Self-destructive behavior	6.6
	School (other)	6.3	Becoming sexually active	6.2
	Crime/drugs in neighborhood	6.3	Crime/drugs in neighborhood	5.2
	Money	5.6	Domestic quarreling	5.2
	Welfare of family members	5.0	Intergenerational disagreement	4.7

* Representing 5% or more of responses.

Tables 15.2—15.6 describe responses by class and category-within-class for the two genders and three socioeconomic groups of subjects. Corresponding sets of responses from the multinational study appear in Chapter 3.

Problems

Problems most frequently noted by all groups of US subjects and accounting for more than 60% of all responses fell into the classes of **schooling, family** and **identity** (Table 15.2(a)). This was similar to the findings of the multinational study. US problems related to schooling reported most frequently:

> "I get nervous when I take tests and fail."

> "My grades are not what you would call bad but are not great ... I just can't seem to get 'A's or many 'B's ..."

(Two exceptions: "Advantaged" males reported interpersonal concerns more frequently than family problems and "poverty" females more sexual than identity problems.)

It is important that our "poverty" group stands out from all US and multinational groups in its frequent reporting of "self-destructive behavior" Approximately 11% of male responses and 7% of females:

> "I drink to get drunk ... to make friends laugh and think I'm funny."

> "I smoke and I know I am endangering my health."

Females alone in the US study reported concerns related to "friendship" and "self-confidence" (Table 15.2(b)). Problems representative of 11% of the responses of US "advantaged" females and 10% of US "nonadvantaged" females:

> "Sometimes my friends are really nice to me and at other times I think they hate me."

> "A guy I like doesn't seem to like me."

> "Sometimes I'm not sure of myself and how I make decisions."

Coping strategies

Individual problem-solving is the coping strategy of choice for both the multinational and US samples (Table 15.3(a)). US females report this strategy less frequently and **seeking assistance** more frequently than do their male SES counterparts.

TABLE 15.3 *US study: percentages of total responses falling into classes and categories of coping strategies*

(a) Classes

	Advantaged				*Nonadvantaged*				*Poverty*			
	Male		*Female*		*Male*		*Female*		*Male*		*Female*	
	%	*Rank*	*%*	*Rank*	*%*	*Rank*	*%*	*Rank*	*%*	*Rank*	*%*	*Rank*
Seek/give assistance	7.8	(5)	17.0	(2)	11.6	(4)	20.8	(2)	20.9	(2)	20.9	(3)
Interpersonal	12.0	(4)	14.7	(4)	12.4	(3)	19.6	(3)	17.8	(3)	21.8	(2)
Individual problem-solving	46.6	(1)	36.6	(1)	44.0	(1)	29.8	(1)	32.5	(1)	23.1	(1)
Stress management	4.0	(6)	2.8	(6)	4.4	(6)	1.5	(7)	1.2	(7.5)	1.3	(9)
Crying	0.2	(9)	1.3	(7)	0.6	(8)	2.9	(6)	0.0	(9)	4.0	(6)
Religious	0.4	(7.5)	0.8	(8)	1.2	(7)	0.6	(9)	1.2	(7.5)	3.1	(7)
Resignation	12.7	(3)	11.4	(5)	10.0	(5)	7.7	(5)	7.4	(5)	8.0	(5)
Disengage	15.9	(2)	15.0	(3)	15.6	(2)	16.0	(4)	14.1	(4)	16.0	(4)
Anti-social	0.4	(7.5)	0.4	(9)	0.2	(9)	0.9	(8)	4.9	(6)	1.8	(8)

*(b) Categories**

	Male		*Female*	
	Category	*%*	*Category*	*%*
Advantaged	Try harder	22.0	Try harder	17.7
	Planning	17.4	Planning	16.2
	Seeking support	11.2	Seek support	13.4
	Assertive cope	6.8	Assertive cope	9.0
Nonadvantaged	Try harder	27.0	Try harder	19.7
	Planning	17.1	Seek support	18.2
	Seek support	11.6	Planning	11.8
	Offer help	6.3	Assertive cope	9.8
	Assertive cope	5.4	Escape/avoid	5.1
			Psychological distance	5.0
Poverty	Planning	18.3	Planning	14.2
	Seek support	15.2	Assertive cope	11.9
	Try harder	13.8	Seek support	11.5
	Assertive cope	8.2	Try harder	11.5
			Offer help	5.3

* Representing 5% or more of responses.

It is significant that US subjects report **disengaging** more frequently than their multinational peers. More than 14% of the responses of all US subject groups suggest this strategy.

Helpers

US adolescents, as adolescents in the other countries of our study, are most likely to go to a **family member** (Table 15.4(a)) or "personal friend" (Table 15.4(b)) for help. Smaller percentages of responses went to "teachers," and only rarely, according to our data, was a "professional counselor" considered.

Like their multinational peers, US adolescents reported **concern, knowledge** and **personal qualities** as the most frequently desired attributes of their helpers (Table 15.5(a)). Also similar to the multinational subjects, their responses

TABLE 15.4 *US study: percentages of total responses falling into classes and categories of desired helpers*

(a) Classes

	Advantaged				*Nonadvantaged*				*Poverty*			
	Male		*Female*		*Male*		*Female*		*Male*		*Female*	
	%	*Rank*	*%*	*Rank*	*%*	*Rank*	*%*	*Rank*	*%*	*Rank*	*%*	*Rank*
Family	47.2	(1)	43.8	(2)	57.5	(1)	51.8	(1)	58.6	(1)	51.4	(1)
Non-family	43.9	(2)	52.3	(1)	38.9	(2)	44.8	(2)	38.6	(2)	44.8	(2)
Offender	0.6	(4)	0.3	(6)	0.5	(5)	1.3	(3)	0.3	(3)	0.6	(3)
Supernatural	0.4	(5)	0.4	(5)	0.8	(4)	0.2	(5)	0.0	(5)	1.5	(4)
Creatures/objects	0.3	(6)	0.8	(4)	0.0	(6)	0.2	(5)	0.0	(5)	0.0	(6)
Non-specific	4.9	(3)	1.3	(3)	0.9	(3)	0.2	(5)	0.0	(5)	0.2	(5)
Nobody	2.6	(X)	1.1	(X)	1.4	(X)	1.5	(X)	2.5	(X)	1.5	(X)

*(b) Categories**

	Male		*Female*	
	Category	*%*	*Category*	*%*
Advantaged	Personal friend	17.3	Personal friend	24.0
	Mother	15.6	Mother	16.1
	Father	13.4	Father	6.6
	Teacher	6.7	Family member	5.9
	Family member	6.3	Sister	5.9
			Counselor	5.4
			Teacher	5.0
Nonadvantaged	Personal friend	21.4	Personal friend	24.3
	Mother	20.0	Mother	18.2
	Father	14.1	Father	7.0
	Teacher	6.0	Sister	6.8
			Teacher	6.0
			Schoolmate	5.7
Poverty	Personal friend	23.5	Personal friend	21.2
	Mother	12.7	Mother	14.2
	Father	8.6	Family member	7.9
	Family member	8.6	Father	7.2
	Teacher	7.3	Sister	5.3
	Brother	6.1	Aunt	5.2

* Representing 5% or more of responses.

suggested the desire for **counseling** (Table 15.6(a)) and, with it "advice," "direction," and "problem-solving" assistance, as well as "comfort" and "encouragement" (Table 15.6(b)). "Poverty" Hispanic- and African-American subjects appear to desire being advised with far greater frequency than their "advantaged" and "nonadvantaged" counterparts. More than 50% of "poverty subjects indicated this need.

Influence of SES and gender on reported problems

Figure 15.1 (page 223) compares graphically US responses by gender and socioeconomic status for problems related to **schooling** and **family**. It reveals noteworthy trends similar to those shown in the multinational results: The per-

TABLE 15.5 *US study: percentages of total responses falling into classes and categories of desired helper qualities*

(a) Classes

	Advantaged				*Nonadvantaged*				*Poverty*			
	Male		*Female*		*Male*		*Female*		*Male*		*Female*	
	%	Rank	%	Rank	%	Rank	%	Rank	%	Rank	%	Rank
Powerful	4.9	(4)	2.2	(4)	6.2	(4)	3.3	(4)	8	(4)	6.4	(4)
Knowledgeable	28.0	(3)	28.2	(3)	37.6	(1)	29.6	(2)	43.2	(1)	29.1	(3)
Available	2.3	(5)	1.9	(5)	0.7	(6)	2.8	(5)	0	(5)	1.6	(5)
Personal qualities	30.9	(1)	31.4	(2)	29.3	(2)	32.9	(1)	32.1	(2)	29.5	(2)
Concern	30.8	(2)	34.7	(1)	20.0	(3)	28.7	(3)	16.7	(3)	32.7	(1)
Uncertain	0.2	(6)	0.9	(6)	2.8	(5)	1.2	(6)	0	(5.5)	0.8	(6)
No listing	3.0	(X)	0.8	(X)	3.4	(X)	1.5	(X)	0	(X)	0	(X)

*(b) Categories**

	Male		*Female*	
	Category	%	*Category*	%
Advantaged	Understanding	14.8	Understanding	19.9
	Caring/loving	13.1	Approachable/good listener	14.4
	Approachable/good listener	10.8	Caring/loving	11.7
	Generous/willing to help	8.9	Similarity to subject	8.8
	Similarity to subject	7.0	Generous/willing to help	8.6
	Content area knowledge	6.5	Gives advice	7.0
	Trustworthy	5.9		
Nonadvantaged	Similarity	11.7	Understanding	14.5
	Generous	10.4	Approachable/good listener	12.8
	Understanding	9.5	Generous	11.0
	Approachable/good listener	8.1	Caring/loving	10.6
	Gives advice	8.0	Gives advice	10.4
	Caring/loving	7.4	Content area knowledge	5.8
	Experienced	6.5	Experienced	5.1
	Content area knowledge	6.0		
	Intelligent/wise	5.1		
Poverty	Gives advice	13.0	Understanding	21.1
	Similarity to subject	11.7	Gives advice	16.3
	Trustworthy	9.9	Approachable/good listener	8.0
	Understanding	9.3	Trustworthy	6.0
	Content area knowledge	9.3	Supportive	6.0
	Approachable/good listener	7.4	Generous/willing to help	5.6
	Can exercise authority	6.2	Caring/loving	5.2
	Appealing personal qualities (other)	6.2		

* Representing 5% or more of responses.

centage of reported **school** problems decreases with decreasing socioeconomic status when gender is held constant, while that of **family** problems increase. Within each socioeconomic group, **school** problems are reported more and **family** problems less by males than by females. "Advantaged" and "nonadvantaged" males report considerably higher percentages of **school** problems than their "poverty" and female peers—more than twice as high for "advantaged" than for "poverty" males!

In addition, the percentage of responses indicating **individual problem-solving**

TABLE 15.6 *US study: percentages of total responses falling into classes and categories of desired helping modes*

	Advantaged				*Nonadvantaged*				*Poverty*			
	Male		*Female*		*Male*		*Female*		*Male*		*Female*	
	%	Rank	%	Rank	%	Rank	%	Rank	%	Rank	%	Rank
Direct satisfaction	0.9	(7)	1.0	(7)	2.4	(7)	1.4	(7)	5.1	(5)	7.9	(3)
Exercise power	8.0	(3)	4.7	(4)	7.1	(3)	4.7	(3)	6.8	(3)	3.9	(4)
Intercede	3.2	(5)	2.2	(6)	4.8	(5)	4.3	(4)	5.9	(4)	2.2	(5.5)
Counsel	51.6	(1)	48.8	(1)	50.4	(1)	51.8	(1)	60.2	(1)	61.8	(1)
Attend to	23.0	(2)	33.9	(2)	22.9	(2)	29.4	(2)	21.2	(2)	21.3	(2)
Help evade problem	2.0	(6)	2.6	(5)	2.8	(6)	2.8	(6)	0.8	(6)	0.0	(7)
Uncertain	3.6	(4)	5.1	(3)	5.6	(4)	3.3	(5)	0.0	(7)	2.2	(5.5)
No listing	2.7	(X)	1.7	(X)	3.9	(X)	2.3	(X)	0.0	(7)	0.6	(X)

*(b) Categories**

	Male		*Female*	
	Category	%	*Category*	%
Advantaged	Advise	16.7	Advise	17.4
	Help	12.1	Help	11.8
	Direct	11.3	Comfort	11.8
	Comfort	9.7	Encourage	8.6
	Encourage	6.4	Direct	7.3
Nonadvantaged	Advise	19.5	Advise	16.4
	Help	12.9	Comfort	16.3
	Comfort	11.1	Help	12.8
	Direct	10.5	Direct	8.2
	Encourage	7.3	Encourage	7.0
	Solve problems	5.9		
Poverty	Advise	20.4	Advise	22.6
	Direct	16.1	Direct	14.3
	Solve problems	9.5	Mediate	9.3
	Give something	8.5	Help	6.8
	Mediate	6.1	Encourage	6.5
	Help	5.5	Comfort	6.2
	Encourage	5.4	Give something	6.2
			Solve problems	5.8

* Representing 5% or more of responses.

decreases with decreasing socioeconomic status and males within each SES group report more **individual problem-solving** strategies than females (Figure 15.2). These trends are also similar to those found in the multinational study.

Discussion

What do these findings imply?

Since education is compulsory through age 16 in the US, it is no surprise to find that schooling is a major source of concern for our youngsters, probably reflecting increased understanding among youngsters of all SES backgrounds of

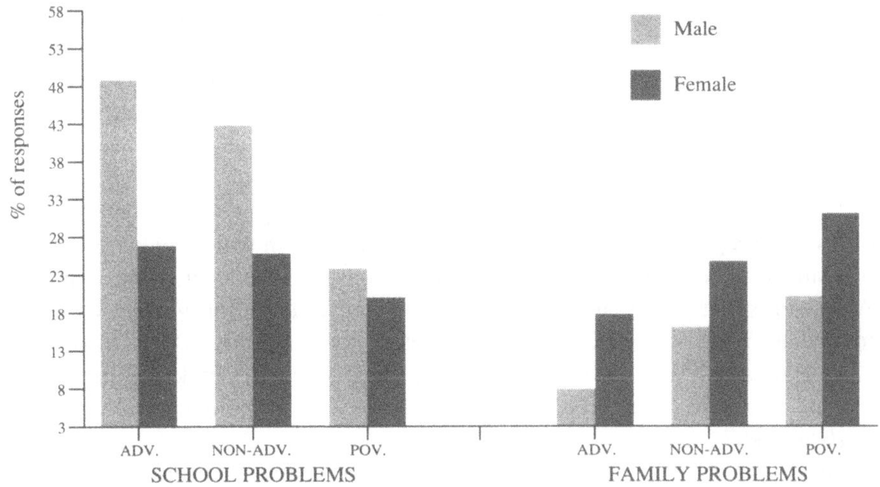

Figure 15.1 Percentages of reponses referring to school problems and family problems reported by gender and SES (advantaged, non-advantaged and poverty) for US subjects.

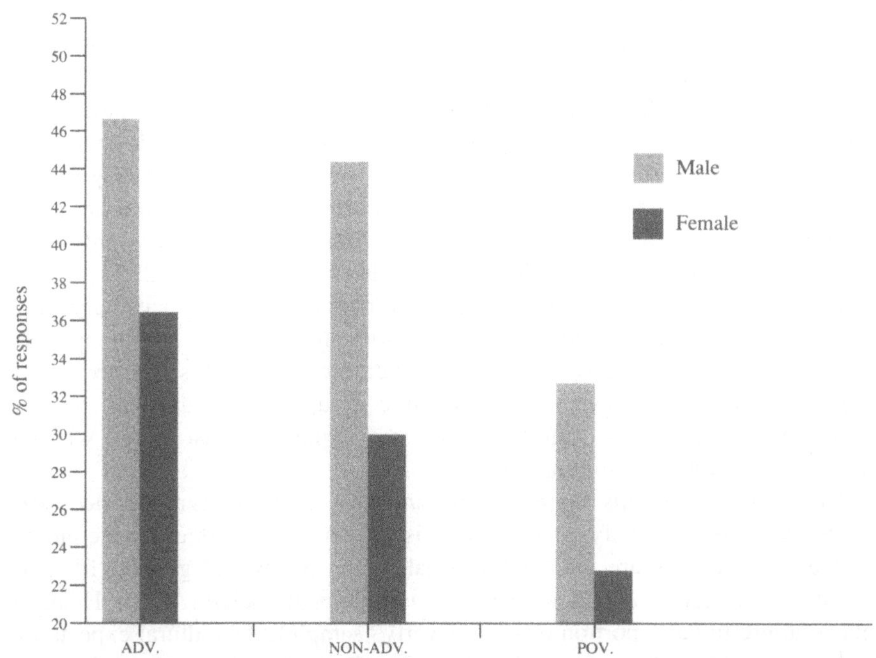

Figure 15.2 Percentages of reponses referring to individual problem-solving strategies reported by gender and SES (advantaged, non-advantaged and poverty) for US subjects.

the importance of education to their futures. However, the dip in its reporting by "poverty" youngsters is intriguing, particularly since studies have consistently shown that poor African-American and Hispanic children (approximately 90% of our "poverty" group) are far more likely to perform poorly in school and to drop out than more "advantaged" and non-Hispanic children, and that nearly 50% of poor Hispanic youth drop out before completing high school (Church *et al.*, 1985; Pallas, 1989).

There are a number of possible explanations. One might be that the responses of lower SES groups reflect a "here and now" attitude in which higher education is assumed to be beyond reach, thus making high school education meaningless. A second is that poor youngsters may have opted early on for work to satisfy an immediate need for money for themselves or their families. Poor "at-risk" or "non-graduates" have been shown to be more likely to look for immediate income rather than to prepare for long-range career options (*The Research Bulletin*, 1987).

Finally, all adolescent groups tend to be concerned with acceptance by peers and being "one of the gang." Among "poverty" youth, acceptance usually is unrelated and often not conducive to academic learning

> "When your friends smoke blunts [marijuana] and then they want me to smoke some, too ..."

At the same time, role models in impoverished street subcultures demonstrate instant success and material achievement (i.e. ball players and drug dealers), increasing the likelihood that these youngsters will try to do the same, while unemployed adults who congregate on streets near school, provide them with negative messages about the possibilities of work as an accepted way of life. Minority youngsters learn early that, for those who find jobs, salaries are lower for minorities and that, on average, African-American college graduates earn salaries equivalent to White high school graduates (Fine, 1986, p. 395).

The fact that the family is among the top worries of US adolescents, regardless of SES background, is reflective of difficulties in US family life today. That family concerns increase with decreasing socioeconomic status, are greater for females than males in every socioeconomic group and are greatest for poor (minority) females is also significant and may explain at least in part why the reverse is true for schooling problems.

That family concerns appear increasingly as SES background decreases probably reflects family stress and disruption exacerbated by economic problems. That they are greater for females than males and greatest for poor females is reflective of US as well as multinational society. In the Hispanic microculture (a large portion of our "poverty" sample), the cultural expectation for females is that they assume family responsibilities including housekeeping, childrearing, caregiving and other family activities. This is certainly true for poor Hispanic female adolescents in the US who often accompany family members as translators to public agencies and hospitals and fill in as surrogate mothers in time of illness or emergency. Being concerned about family life is not surprising among this population: 50% of Hispanic girls in the previously cited survey expected to be married by age nineteen (*The Research Bulletin*, 1987, p. 16).

Problems **not** reported by our subjects may be as important as those that are. Few adolescents other than those in our "poverty" sample noted feelings of depression or concerns about sexuality, an alarming fact when the rates of adolescent depression and suicide as well as teenage pregnancy and sexually transmitted diseases are high.

"Poverty" youth constituted the sole US group to reveal frequent alarming concerns regarding "self-destructive" behavior and crime/drugs in their neighborhoods.

"When people get killed ... it seems that it is happening every day ..."

"Drugs are making people do crazy things like killing, mugging."

Among "poverty" males, these issues were reported more frequently than any other problem category! It is sobering to note that data for this study was collected in 1990 (the Pittsburgh samples) and 1992 (the New York sample), prior to a major increase in adolescent drug use and gang violence in all major US cities. Recent 1994 surveys of Pittsburgh "advantaged" and "nonadvantaged" adolescents using our questionnaire (Maccarelli, 1994) found that gang violence and drug problems accounted for from 15% to 26% of subjects' responses!

How do US youngsters cope?

All US groups chose **individual problem-solving** before other coping strategies. It is in the categories-within-classes of **individual problem-solving**, however, that important differences emerge. "Advantaged" and "nonadvantaged" males chose trying harder and planning solutions. "Advantaged" females reportedly cope most often by "trying harder," while their "nonadvantaged" female peers and their "poverty" male and female peers both "seek support" as their most frequent method of coping. One could say that as the economic level drops, or if one is female, there is less of a sense of personal power and of the ability to handle problems on one's own.

The fact that, when adolescents do seek help for their problems, they tend to prefer friends and family to teachers, and almost none choose professional counselors, is extremely important. However, that this was true even though counseling services are offered in all schools in the study needs to be given serious consideration. It may be that, for youngsters at this age, family and friends are a more immediate and less formal source of help and support. Particularly among the "poverty" populations, crises often are so personal, deep and pressing that it is easier and more comforting to seek help from those closest than from counselors who often are overwhelmed by the numbers of young people needing help and by the severity of the problems they present (Greenspan, Seeley and Niemeyer, 1993, p. 42).

Implications for US Counseling Theory and Practice

Similarities in the reported problems and coping of our young subjects support developmental theories that suggest universal qualities to this stage of life, probably related both to the physiological stage of this age group coupled with common developmental tasks imposed by their cultures. At the same time, gender and SES group differences also suggest the strong influences of environment and learning experiences.

Because the Continental US study is the sole within-country study to incorporate three socioeconomic groups, our results are particularly useful in hypothesizing the influences of SES independent of nationality. As we can also describe minority group composition within all SES groups, we have taken the liberty to use this to make some conjectures related to counseling of minorities.

We suggest the following implications of our results for counseling and the training of counselors in the US:

1. To respond to the needs of all SES as well as minority groups, counseling must be sensitive to and accepting of different patterns of behavior. It must be flexible and embrace diversity. In this regard, the more frequent desires for directive assistance from some youngsters in our study are consistent with the findings of other researchers (Sue, 1981). Helpers need to be attuned to the fact that some youngsters may worry primarily about stereotypic adolescent worries such as friendship while others may be more concerned with basic day-to-day survival. One-on-one counseling strategies based on the assumption that problems lie within the individual are not sufficient alone. A counseling orientation toward locating problems in a system (classroom, family, etc.) and in actively assisting young people in coping with, managing and possibly changing the context and/or environmental interaction is essential as well.

2. Our subjects, regardless of background, reported coping by disengaging far more frequently than their peers in most countries of our study. Among poor and minority Americans, this might speak to feelings of helplessness. It might also speak to lack of concern about self or inability to conceptualize cause—effect relationships. Decision-making can be a focus of a psycho-educational effort, but the counselor must address the issue of empowerment, participation and responsibility.

3. The fact that our subjects indicate that they turn to peers and family members for help in solving problems strongly suggests the use of ongoing counseling groups and the utilization of peer counselors and paraprofessionals to lead them. In this kind of supportive environment, youngsters help one another with the assistance of peers and adults who are trained to recognize more serious problems should they emerge.

4. Preventive outreach that includes specific empowering strategies such as teaching effective study skills, time management, stress management, etc. would be useful. At the same time, because feelings of powerlessness and subjugation form regular parts of the daily experience of many "nonadvantaged" and "poverty" youngsters, helpers would do well to demonstrate to these youngsters how to deal with their feelings of powerlessness by working with them to conceptualize their own solutions within the context of solving an immediate need individually and through organized, purposeful group activities. Not to do so might instead help perpetuate the helplessness and powerlessness characteristic of poverty populations (Katz, 1989; Ropers, 1991).

5. In dealing with the problems associated with poverty, a coordinated and collective societal effort is needed. In addition to nontraditional services now offered by schools, such as family support, health information and drug and alcohol prevention and treatment, a systems-based focus that encompasses intervention with families, schools and society needs to be implemented. Examples of effective efforts might include increasing parental involvement in the educational process (a difficult process at the secondary level) and integrating community resources into the schools. Active outreach into the community may help link the school, parents and community resources. Indigenous paraprofessional helpers who are trained in the basic helping skills and are knowledgeable about available agencies and community resources may be an invaluable support to parents.

6. The types of activities described above dictate an expanded role for counselors that requires efforts that transcend conservative or liberal political agendas. In becoming change agents, ombudspersons and facilitators of indigenous support systems, however, they must also become consultants to school staff and parents, trainers and supervisors [in the clinical sense] (Atkinson, Morton and Sue, 1989, p. 272).

Sadly, just as the recent recession in the US brought a need to increase counseling roles, it simultaneously depleted resources for funding and staffing in educational and community agencies. One solution now being tested involves using public and private monies to create family centers to undertake neighborhood crime-prevention and form volunteer programs in the schools and community that create support systems for parents and children. This approach has become increasingly popular in the past several years (Louv, 1994).

Working with the community to establish these programs and to meet shared goals is one way that professional counselors may exert influence to create change. We believe that the way they choose to respond to this opportunity is of critical importance both to the community and to the counseling profession.

16

Venezuela

MARIA EUGENIA FELCE DI PAULA

National Experimental University "Simon Rodriguez"

FREDDI DI PAULA

University and Technical Institute of the Venezuelan Armed Forces

A squatter: "I would like a scholarship, a good job for my mother and a nice place to live."

Luis is fourteen. His mother works as a cleaning lady in different houses. His father left the family five years ago. Luis is the second of seven brothers.

I want someday to live in a nice apartment building in Caracas with my wife and two children. I want to have my own business as a car mechanic. My children will be going to good private schools. I don't want to live in squatters housing; I don't want to be working in a factory with no opportunity to improve. I don't want my wife to be working as a maid. For sure, I do not want many children.

"What worries me most right now is that my mother does not have a good job and there is not enough money . . . My father doesn't help us . . . I try not to cause my mother problems . . . I am thinking of looking for a part-time job packing at a supermarket or cleaning cars . . . My mother does not want me to do this; she wants me to study. But I know she will be happy if I can get some money . . . My teacher is going to help me find a week-end job.

"If I had three wishes, I would ask for scholarships for me and my brothers, a good job for my mother and a nice and secure place for all of us to live."

Introduction: Country, Culture and Economic Crisis

The small nation of Venezuela (population approximately 19 735 000), is a paradox to those who observe it. Situated in northern South America facing the Caribbean Sea, its coastland enjoys a warm climate all year with temperatures that average 70°F. Such is the case of the northern city of Caracas (population: 7600000), the site of our study. At the same time, its mountain regions suffer biting cold. Venezuela is an OPEC country, rich in oil and other natural resources. At the same time, it suffers from a wide range of maladies ranging from severe poverty and malnutrition to violence and civil unrest. Children and youth comprise almost half of Venezuela's population (some 9 200 000 persons) today (Central Statistics and Information Office, 1990). It is this population that will determine the country's future.

Population

The Venezuelan population is racially heterogeneous. Mestizos (a mix of White, Indian and Negro) comprise 65% of its inhabitants (Central Statistics and Information Office, 1990). Another approximately 25% considers itself White and consists primarily of descendants of early Spanish settlers, although other peoples are also included in this group. These include 340 000 immigrants from Italy, Spain, Portugal, France, Austria and Latin American countries, invited to the country as skilled workers during Venezuela's 1950s economic expansion. Other small percentages include Indians (5%) who inhabit southwest and northeast Venezuela and continue the poverty lifestyle that existed in the past, and Negroes (5%) whose ancestors were brought from Africa by the fifteenth-century conquerors to do heavy manual labor together with Indians. Most Negroes still dwell in small towns on the east coast under marginal conditions, although many have migrated to the cities (Ministry of the Family, 1988).

At least 90% of Venezuelans are Roman Catholic; the official language is Spanish.

Historical background

Like other oil-rich nations, Venezuelan history—and its current problems—can be described in distinct phases: "pre-oil," "oil" and "current economic transition."

Before its "oil age," Venezuela was a poor, rural nation with a population that was three-quarters nonliterate and that had a life expectancy of 34 years (Dehollain and Perez, 1990).

The discovery of oil in the twentieth century changed the country in irreparable ways. At first, it opened the door to a new and affluent way of life, and permitted the emergence of a new urban entrepreneurial middle class. Venezuelan oil appeared to assure social, health and educational development for all.

Unfortunately, the government (democratic since 1958) was unable to contain the over-rapid national economic development that followed the new affluence. One result was the creation of increasingly noticeable inequalities in income distribution that presented problems both for the poor and new middle class. Within a short time it became clear that wealth was being increased only for a small, already wealthy Venezuelan upper class at the expense of the rest of Venezuelan society.

The toll in the past several decades has been great, and has included monetary inflation, falling health social and educational indicators and increasing malnutrition across the country (Ministry of the Family, 1988; Cartaya and d'Elia, 1991).

While the nation actually increased its literacy rate from 25% in the pre-oil period to more than 90% in the early years after the discovery of oil, national literacy then began a steady decline which still continues. As Venezuela entered the 1990s when this study was being conducted, 25% of her rural poor and 13% of her urban poor were nonliterate (Dehollain and Perez, 1990).

The economy today

While Venezuela remains rich in natural resources today, their inefficient use, coupled with years of governmental corruption and a gradually decreasing value of petroleum, has created a national debt of crisis proportions. The government continues emergency remedies, that have ranged in the past from devaluation of currency, free pricing and increased prices of services (light, telephone, and others) to privatization of corporations and decentralization of policy (designed to give greater autonomy to the states). Most, unfortunately, have been unsuccessful. Currently, the government is attempting to improve the increasingly abysmal conditions of the poor through projects aided by the World Bank, such as development of daycare facilities, programs to decrease teenage pregnancy and to increase breast-feeding of infants and the like. All are sorely needed in the slums surrounding Caracas, but they are not, by themselves, stemming the tide (Banco Mundial, 1990; Delgado, 1993). A dissatisfied middle class and an increasingly impoverished lower class threatens Venezuela with widespread civil unrest as well as government coups, both in the name of the need for a better life for Venezuelans.

At this point in time, living expenses still continue to rise while income for the masses falls. Increasing numbers of rural poor continue to leave the countryside in search of work. Approximately 40% of Venezuelans—primarily families from rural areas—now live marginally in squatter camps in the mountains surrounding the country's urban centers (Ministry of the Family, 1988; Central Statistics and Information Office, 1990). These same camps house a growing population of those now impoverished immigrants from other Latin American countries who began arriving twenty years ago in search of the "oil dream." Unfortunately, few found what they came for.

Dwellers of squatter camps in the mountains surrounding Caracas—usually Mestizos and Negroes—live today under squalid conditions in *"ranchos"* (small houses, usually constructed inadequately with often no more than two rooms to house five or more people). While many camps are supplied electricity at no cost to the inhabitants, there is usually no indoor supply of water, which must be carried from long distances. Most squatters work as day laborers. The poor living conditions and economic difficulties of these people not only increase delinquency in these areas but make them dangerous for visitors and inhabitants alike.

The "poverty" subjects of our study come largely from this group. They and their middle-class counterparts from Caracas were surveyed in 1989—90, just prior to the onset of the major civil unrest that led to fall of the government then in power. The responses of our "poverty" subjects proved to be indicators of the problems that produced the social, political and cultural crisis affecting Venezuelan society today (Bethencourt, 1989).

Venezuelan education

Officially, 11 years of education are free of charge to all Venezuelans, with the first nine grades compulsory for all. With the recent opening of new private technical institutions and universities, the country now has approximately fifty institutions of higher education for those who complete this schooling.

Regardless of the free programs formally in place, however, it is difficult for impoverished classes to obtain adequate education. For one thing, rapid growth of poverty populations in urban areas has created severe shortages of schools, teachers and teaching materials (National Conference on the Rights of Children, 1991). Public schools currently available to the poor provide few frills and poor students have minimal access to many activities, most importantly, vocational guidance.

In addition, impoverished youngsters often cannot attend classes. There are a variety of reasons that include malnutrition-related illnesses, the need to care for siblings or handle household chores while their mothers work and the need to give up schooling so as to enter the workforce at an early age (Dehollain and Perez, 1990). Although Venezuelan law officially prohibits child labor and requires children to remain in school until age 18 years, almost 5% of impoverished 10—14-year-olds and 70% of 15—18-year-olds are in the workforce and not in school. For all of these reasons, only one in eight impoverished young children reach 3rd grade (National Conference on the Rights of Children, 1991).

Unfortunately, lack of formal education decreases the earning ability of these youngsters throughout their lives and keeps them in this cycle of poverty.

Venezuelan family life

Venezuelan family life, as all aspects of life, has been affected by the country's socioeconomic crisis. In the past, fathers used to work outside the home and mothers were responsible for household chores, children's socialization and education. Today, in all segments of society, economic need places both parents in the workforce. While young children of middle and upper classes may stay home with a maid or go to daycare or preschool centers, advantages such as daycare are not usually available to their impoverished peers who are often left to care for themselves in fatherless homes while mothers work. Daycare is currently unavailable to half of preschool-aged Venezuelan children, with a disproportionate number coming from rural and urban poverty areas (National Conference on the Rights of Children, 1991).

A major problem affecting Venezuelan families today is divorce, as of 1988 officially affecting 40% of families (Leighton *et al.*, 1988). This statistic does not include families from marginal and extreme poverty populations who often live together without legal register. Research concerning the effects of childrearing patterns and marginality suggests that fathers' absence, lack of economic resources and changing social patterns that have reduced affection available to poverty children in impoverished families, together make excellent predictors of crisis (Recagno, 1982). The dangers that loomed heavily a decade ago for poverty families and portended serious difficulties for middle-class families reached their apex in the 1990s.

Increasing delinquency

Another indicator of the crises facing Venezuelans is the increase in juvenile delinquency. Police reports show an increase in serious crimes committed by adolescents and children, with a rise from 60% to 79% of infractions committed by juveniles in the last few years including not only robbery but homicides and drug related crimes (Rosenberg, 1990). The problem has been exacerbated by Venezuelan TV, which provides models of aggression and criminality with whom young people easily identify (Barrios, 1989). TV programming now includes soap operas in which adolescents are often negatively characterized as gang members who use weapons and commit robbery or murders.

Counseling in Venezuela

Professional counseling was introduced in Venezuela approximately forty years ago. Since that time, the profession has increased its responsibilities to youth and to the educational process. The first National Counseling Program was designed to assist public school students with educational, vocational, health and personal problems in order to enhance their development and facilitate their adjustment. Reforms of educational law in 1983 added that counseling should also be considered as one role of teachers, implying by this that care should be provided for the welfare of students' families and community members as well as students. In 1991, the National Conference on the Rights of Children affirmed the need of guiding adolescents not only in problems related to academic achievement but also to family, sexual issues and drugs. Preparation for counselors to take on all of these tasks today requires post-graduate training that focuses on family, vocational and educational counseling as well as human development.

School counselors are assigned to public schools on the basis of enrolment, with the few largest urban schools having guidance departments that employ psychologists, social workers and counselors to assist with problems related to students' achievement and vocational guidance. Most other schools refer students in need to the Center for Integral Welfare of Students in their region, which provides an extensive multidisciplinary staff (physician, counselor, dentist, psychologist, social worker) to attend to student needs. These centers are considered extremely useful but are insufficient to attend to all populations in need.

Private schools provide greater numbers of counselors who work according to the schools' policies and philosophy.

The Present Study and Its Methodology

This study describes the reported problems, coping strategies and desired help of two groups of Venezuelan "advantaged" middle class and "poverty" youth.

Subjects

Subjects included 399 male and female adolescents, 13—15 years old, from urban "advantaged" and "poverty" communities in and around Caracas. Characterization as "advantaged" or "poverty" matched definitions used in the multinational study (see Chapter 2).

The 201 "advantaged" youngsters (100 males and 101 females) came from middle-class families with an average of two children per family in which parents were usually highly educated and professionally employed. Children lived in comfortable homes where they enjoyed their own bedrooms or shared them with one other sibling. There was usually a maid to do the housework. "Advantaged" children attended private schools and had access to art and/or sports activities after school. Most had opportunity to travel abroad for holidays and planned to go to a private university after completion of high school.

The 198 "poverty" subjects (80 males and 118 females), by contrast, came from families with an average of six children in which most parents had not finished primary education and worked as day laborers or in factories with minimum-wage salary. Most "poverty" subjects lived in squatters' quarters that provided inadequate construction and lacked services such as water. Some lived in government housing projects for the poor that contained one or two bedrooms for the entire family. These youngsters did not have their daily needs met for food, shelter and health care. They attended public schools that usually lacked recreational facilities and counseling services, but did provide access to models of delinquent behavior.

Procedures for data collection and coding

Data collection and coding procedures matched those of other countries in the multinational study (see Chapter 2). Questionnaires that had been translated into Spanish were distributed to small groups of students (15—20) in their classes by teachers or counselors known to the students and trained for this purpose. Coding

TABLE 16.1 *Venezuelan study: percentages of total responses falling into classes and categories of problems*

(a) Classes

	Advantaged				*Poverty*			
	Male		*Female*		*Male*		*Female*	
	%	*Rank*	*%*	*Rank*	*%*	*Rank*	*%*	*Rank*
Extreme poverty	0.5	(11)	0.4	(11)	7.0	(4.5)	8.8	(3.5)
War	0.5	(11)	0.9	(9.5)	8.2	(3)	0.7	(10)
Catastrophe	0.0	(13)	0.0	(12.5)	0.6	(12)	0.0	(13)
Material desires	2.8	(7.5)	2.6	(7)	7.0	(4.5)	7.1	(5)
Family issues	15.2	(2)	25.0	(2)	31.6	(1)	35.7	(1)
Schooling issues	40.6	(1)	28.4	(1)	17.5	(2)	17.5	(2)
Identity	6.9	(4)	9.1	(4.5)	4.7	(7)	2.7	(7)
Sexuality	3.2	(6)	0.9	(9.5)	0.6	(12)	0.3	(11.5)
Courtship/dating	2.8	(7.5)	9.1	(4.5)	1.8	(9)	2.7	(7)
Interpersonal	5.1	(5)	9.9	(3)	5.3	(6)	8.8	(3.5)
Emotions	1.8	(9)	2.2	(8)	1.2	(10)	1.0	(9)
Self-fulfilment	0.5	(11)	0.0	(12.5)	0.6	(12)	0.3	(11.5)
Altruism	7.4	(3)	6.0	(6)	4.1	(8)	2.7	(7)
No problem	12.9	(X)	5.6	(X)	9.9	(X)	11.8	(X)

*(b) Categories**

	Male		*Female*	
	Category	*%*	*Category*	*%*
Advantaged	Academic failure	19.2	Academic failure	12.9
	Academic achievement	10.0	Friendship	8.6
	Time pressures	5.0	Intergenerational disagreement	6.9
			Domestic quarrels	6.5
			Academic achievement	5.6
Poverty	Fear of delinquency	8.1	Domestic quarrels	7.7
	Academic failure	7.0	Academic failure	7.4
	Physical needs	6.4	Physical needs	6.7
	Domestic quarrels	5.8	Money	6.7
	Welfare of family	5.2	Welfare of family	5.1

* Representing 5% or more of responses.

followed standardized procedures used by all countries. Interrater reliability as measured by comparison of coders' responses with that of a master code showed 95% agreement for classes and 80% for categories.

Study Results

Results are reported in terms of percentages and rank order of responses given by gender and SES group for reported problems, coping strategies and chosen helpers.

Problems

Table 16.1(a) demonstrates that the problems most frequently reported by youngsters in our study relate to **schooling** and **family**, just as in the multinational study. The responses of our Venezuelan subjects match those in the multinational study. also, in the following trends:

1. Reported **schooling** problems decrease while family problems increase with decreasing SES.

2. Females within each SES group report more **family** problems than males.

Extreme poverty was an important issue for "poverty" youth.

Examination of categories-within-classes into which responses fell (Table 16.1(b)) suggests qualitative differences between the responses of our "advantaged" and "poverty" subjects: The academic problems of "advantaged" subjects were related frequently to "failure" to achieve high and, often, long-range goals or impediments such as "time pressures" that affect their academic work:

> "I want to keep my grade point average; I want to study medicine and they require very good grades."

> "I study hard but my grades are not good enough to be in the first five students of my class."

> "Two afternoons a week I attend English classes and afternoons I go to play baseball. There are only two afternoons left and they are not enough to study all the subjects."

By contrast, when "poverty" subjects reported **school** worries, they tended to emphasize lower expectations:

> "I'm afraid I'll have to repeat my school grade if I don't study harder."

Family concerns as reported by "advantaged" youngsters tended to be related to "intergenerational disagreements" or "domestic quarrels." Typical:

"My mother thinks I have to do things like she did forty years ago."

"My grandmother is staying with us and we are always arguing because she wants to control our dating."

"My parents are always fighting for nonsense issues."

"At home we are always fighting, especially my sister and my mother."

"My father is always yelling at my fifteen year old brother."

Family problems of "poverty" youth, although they also dealt frequently with "domestic quarrels" were often related to "family welfare." Typical worries:

"My mother is sick at home. We have to go to friends' houses for food and medicines."

"My father is sick, his heart is tired, I am afraid he will get worse."

"Our 'rancho' is small, we all have got a virus and are coughing constantly, my little brother is coughing too much."

"I live with my mother and four brother and sisters. I do not know who my father is. My mother works hard, sometimes she cries a lot. I don't know what to do. It makes me afraid something will happen to us."

In contrast to their "advantaged" peers, "poverty" youngsters had many worries concerning "money" and "physical needs":

"There is not enough money for food for all my family members. Many times we go to school without food."

"Every day things are more expensive. We have trouble getting enough to eat, so my mother cannot buy shoes for me to go to school."

"We do not have food for everyone at home, so I go to my aunt's house for lunch."

"Poverty" males stand out in their concern about **war** (similar to Israeli "advantaged" youngsters, Chapter 9). However, in the case of Venezuelan

TABLE 16.2 *Venezuelan study: percentages of total responses falling into classes and categories of coping strategies*

(a) Classes

	Advantaged				Poverty			
	Male		Female		Male		Female	
	%	Rank	%	Rank	%	Rank	%	Rank
Seek/give assistance	14.0	(3)	10.8	(3)	22.2	(2)	20.2	(3)
Interpersonal	16.9	(2)	26.7	(2)	20.9	(3)	22.4	(2)
Individual problem-solving	47.0	(1)	37.2	(1)	28.5	(1)	27.7	(1)
Stress management	5.1	(5.5)	4.7	(6)	3.8	(6)	3.6	(6.5)
Crying	0.4	(8)	2.2	(7)	2.5	(7)	3.6	(6.5)
Religious	0.4	(8)	0.4	(8)	0.0	(9)	0.0	(8.5)
Resignation	5.1	(5.5)	10.5	(4)	10.1	(5)	11.8	(4)
Disengage	10.6	(4)	7.6	(5)	11.4	(4)	10.6	(5)
Anti-social	0.4	(8)	0.0	(9)	0.6	(8)	0.0	(8.5)
Do nothing	0.0	(X)	0.0	(X)	0.0	(X)	0.0	(X)

*(b) Categories**

	Male		Female	
	Category	%	Category	%
Advantaged	Try harder	20.8	Assertive coping	19.9
	Plan solution	14.8	Plan solution	9.4
	Assertive coping	11.9	Try harder	14.1
	Seek support	11.4	Accepting responsibility	5.4
	Escape/avoidance	5.9		
	Accepting responsibility	5.1		
Poverty	Seek support	17.7	Assertive coping	15.1
	Assertive coming	13.9	Try harder	12.3
	Try harder	12.0	Offer help	10.6
	Plan solution	7.0	Seek support	9.5
	Accepting responsibility	5.7	Escape/avoidance	7.0
	Seek company	5.1	Plan solution	6.4
			Seek company	5.3

* Representing 5% or more of responses.

subjects, **war** relates to street violence and delinquency rather than to national conflict.

> "I am afraid I might be killed if I go out."

Our subjects, particularly "advantaged" males, also expressed **altruistic** concerns (societal level concerns regarding hunger, poverty, justice and equal rights). For "advantaged" subjects, this probably reflects increasing media coverage of the country's socioeconomic and political crises, as well as changes in their own situations:

> "I worry for the starving people in my country, especially the children in the Andean Mountains, because they have cold weather."

TABLE 16.3 *Venezuelan study: percentages of total responses falling into classes and categories of desired helpers*

(a) Classes

	Advantaged				Poverty			
	Male		Female		Male		Female	
	%	Rank	%	Rank	%	Rank	%	Rank
Family	59.7	(1)	49.2	(1)	74.3	(1)	57.9	(1)
Non-family	35.8	(2)	46.5	(2)	23.7	(2)	37.1	(2)
Offender	0.2	(6)	1.7	(3)	0.3	(4.5)	1.0	(3)
Supernatural	0.4	(4.5)	0.0	(6)	0.3	(4.5)	0.3	(5)
Creatures/objects	0.4	(4.5)	0.2	(5)	0.0	(6)	0.6	(4)
Non-specific	1.1	(3)	0.9	(4)	0.6	(3)	0.2	(6)
Nobody	2.3	(X)	1.5	(X)	0.9	(X)	2.9	(X)

*(b). Categories**

	Male		Female	
	Category	%	Category	%
Advantaged	Mother	19.5	Personal friend	22.5
	Father	16.1	Mother	19.3
	Personal friend	14.4	Father	8.3
	Teacher	6.4	Teacher	5.3
	Parents/family	5.7		
Poverty	Mother	20.4	Mother	18.6
	Father	16.6	Personal friend	17.3
	Personal friend	7.1	Father	7.5
	Teacher	5.6	Sister	6.9
	Parents/family	5.6	Aunt	5.8
	Grandmother	5.3	Teacher	5.0
	Brother	5.3		
	Uncle	5.0		

* Representing 5% or more of responses.

"There is a big problem with the water . . . Why is there a lack of water if it is a necessity of life?"

"The economic situation must change, so everyone will have money for food and clothes."

"While politicians get so much money and spend it in parties, there is nothing for the poor people. It is not fair!"

"We need justice so that corrupt persons (mostly the politicians) will go to jail. They are robbing the people who work every day."

TABLE 16.4 *Venezuelan study: percentages of total responses falling into classes and categories of desired helper qualities*

(a) Classes

	Advantaged				Poverty			
	Male		Female		Male		Female	
	%	Rank	%	Rank	%	Rank	%	Rank
Powerful	4.0	(4)	2.9	(4)	8.7	(4)	6.8	(4)
Knowledgeable	39.2	(1)	38.2	(1)	39.0	(1)	35.0	(1)
Available	0.3	(6)	1.6	(5)	3.5	(5)	2.0	(5.5)
Personal qualities	26.6	(3)	28.6	(2)	23.3	(2)	19.8	(3)
Concern	27.6	(2)	26.3	(3)	22.7	(3)	29.3	(2)
Uncertain	1.3	(5)	0.3	(6)	0.6	(6)	2.0	(5.5)
No listing	1.0	(X)	2.1	(X)	2.3	(X)	5.3	(X)

*(b) Categories**

	Male		Female	
	Category	%	Category	%
Advantaged	Gives advice	19.1	Similar to subject	15.6
	Understanding	15.9	Understanding	15.6
	Experienced	12.6	Trustworthy	9.5
	Similar to subject	10.3	Experienced	8.8
	Trustworthy	8.6	Gives advice	5.3
	Supportive	6.3	Approachable	5.3
			Supportive	5.3
			Caring/loving	5.0
Poverty	Understanding	16.9	Understanding	18.5
	Experienced	14.5	Experienced	11.8
	Gives advice	12.2	Gives advice	10.8
	Trustworthy	5.8	Caring/loving	6.3
	Approachable	5.2	Similar to subject	5.8
			Approachable	5.3

* Representing 5% or more of responses.

Coping strategies

Among all groups of our youthful subjects, **individual problem-solving** (Table 16.2(a)), including strategies such as "trying harder" and "planning" (Table 16.2(b)), was the most frequent type of coping reported. As in the multinational study (Chapter 3), there is a trend for the percentage of responses indicating **individual problem-solving** to decrease with decreasing SES and from male to female. **Interpersonal coping**, utilizing strategies such as "assertive coping" and "seeking support", was also popular.

Helpers

Family members were chosen as helpers more frequently than others (Table 16.3(a)), with "mothers" the single most popular choice of both SES groups, with

TABLE 16.5 *Venezuelan study: percentages of total responses falling into classes and categories of desired helping modes*

(a) Classes

	Advantaged				*Poverty*			
	Male		*Female*		*Male*		*Female*	
	%	*Rank*	*%*	*Rank*	*%*	*Rank*	*%*	*Rank*
Direct need satisfaction	1.4	(7)	1.4	(7)	9.0	(4.5)	6.4	(5)
Exercise power	7.4	(4)	6.4	(4)	9.0	(4.5)	8.4	(4)
Intercede	7.8	(3)	9.3	(3)	15.2	(2.5)	13.5	(3)
Counsel	54.4	(1)	37.5	(1)	40.7	(1)	35.7	(1)
Attend to	24.0	(2)	34.3	(2)	15.2	(2.5)	19.9	(2)
Evade problem	1.8	(5.5)	2.5	(6)	0.7	(7)	3.0	(7)
Uncertain	1.8	(5.5)	4.6	(5)	6.9	(6)	6.1	(6)
No listing	1.4	(X)	3.9	(X)	3.4	(X)	7.1	(X)

*(b) Categories**

	Male		*Female*	
	Category	*%*	*Category*	*%*
Advantaged	Advise	18.9	Advise	14.3
	Direct	17.1	Comfort	11.4
	Help solve problems	16.6	Direct	10.0
	Comfort	10.1	Mediate	9.3
	Mediate	7.8	Help solve problems	9.3
			Encourage	7.1
			Understand/empathy	7.1
Poverty	Advise	17.6	Advise	18.2
	Mediate	14.2	Give something	15.5
	Direct	10.1	Mediate	13.5
	Give something	8.8	Direct	10.1
	Help solve problems	8.8	Comfort	9.4
	Does not know	6.8	Help solve problems	6.4
	Understand/empathize	5.4	Does not know	6.1

* Representing 5% or more of responses.

the exception of "advantaged" females who chose a "personal friend" more frequently than any other individual (Table 16.3(b)). "Teachers" were chosen less frequently than either parent or "personal friends," and "counselors" were chosen so infrequently as not to appear in the category listing for Table 16.3.

Table 16.4 shows that, just as their peers in other countries, Venezuelan adolescents seek **knowledgeable** helpers ("experienced" in ways "similar" to them). They also want helpers to be **concerned** ("understanding") and to have **appealing personal qualities** such as "trustworthiness." They want helpers to **counsel** them (to "give advice" upon request) (Table 16.5). This is important.

Implications of These Findings for Counseling in Venezuela

The great disparity in some problems reported by our "advantaged" and "poverty" subjects (concerns related to basic needs, family welfare and inability to achieve education by "poverty" subjects vs. multigenerational disagreements, parental control and desire to succeed academically by "advantaged" youngsters) is indicative of the crisis in which Venezuela finds itself today.

As the difference between high and low socioeconomic groups continues to increase, the problems of the country's "poverty" population can be expected only to increase. Inability of this group to utilize education in changing its coping strategies is one major problem. As economic conditions and opportunities for the middle class continue to fall, problems will be heightened for this group as well. Until the government succeeds in closing the gap between the middle and poverty classes on the one hand and the upper class on the other, these problems are not likely to be diminished.

In the meantime, some directions that might be taken by professional counselors to begin assisting adolescents to deal more effectively with existing problems are presented here.

1. The first concern of "advantaged" and the second of "poverty" subjects relates to schooling, most frequently, academic failure. This, together with the extremely high rates of failure and school desertion among "poverty" groups in Venezuela reported earlier in this chapter, suggests that counselors and teachers should focus efforts on teaching effective learning strategies, beginning with techniques.

   Since school learning is made easier by feelings of self-esteem and self-confidence, additional focus on personal counseling and empowerment should be of help to all youngsters, "advantaged" and "poverty" alike.

   This is far from a simple task, especially for counselors working with impoverished youngsters: To enhance feelings of self-esteem among "poverty" children, counselors and teachers should work together with their clients to reduce the physical needs that serve as impediments to learning. In some cases, this may require helping youngsters to avail themselves of services provided by already operative social programs instituted by governmental and other institutions. In others, it may involve empowering them by providing information about the systems in which they live and how to use them to access what they need.

   These approaches are discussed further in Chapter 18.

2. The types and numbers of family problems reported by both groups of our subjects suggest that the Venezuelan family is, indeed, in crisis! Professional helpers should assist youngsters and their families to develop more effective personal skills to reduce domestic quarreling and intergenerational disagreement and to commit themselves to sharing of responsibilities. To succeed at these efforts, they will need to explore ways to motivate family members to participate. They will need to provide information regarding children's expected characteristics at different ages in order to assist parents to comprehend their children's development in such a way as to increase their social,

emotional and intellectual growth. Counselors need also to assist parents to help their children deal satisfactorily with modern issues such as drugs and sexuality, a difficult task since these were not emphasized as problems by youngsters.

3. It is apparent from crime statistics as well as the concerns reported in our study that street violence and delinquency constitute major threats, particularly to young "poverty" males. This problem is exacerbated by the TV, which emphasizes violence and provides violent models with whom youngsters can identify.

   The problem is not likely to be solved without a national economic recovery. Until this occurs, counselors may provide some help by dealing within the system that now exists. Some small steps have already been taken. Concern regarding the important negative role played by TV has led to a political movement against TV violence. Venezuelan counselors have backed this movement as part of their counseling functions, speaking out and educating both students and parents. Some programs displaying violence have been rescheduled to times when children are less likely to be watching or when parents are more likely to be available to monitor. In addition, more effort has been expended by the media to display children in more socially acceptable roles and a group of professionals has been working with the media to produce more interesting pro-social programming. While clearly not a solution to the country's crime and violence, it is a beginning.

4. Our study shows that Venezuelan children are more likely to seek help from teachers than from professional counselors in solving their problems. Since teachers already interact regularly with youngsters in teaching and learning situations, it might be useful for the Ministry of Education to provide counseling training to teachers to assist them to work effectively with youngsters on these issues. Such a program has been established in other countries in our multinational study, as, for example, the Netherlands and Israel.

5. Given our finding that most youngsters prefer to obtain help from their close friends, mothers or other family members before going to teachers or other professional helpers, another effective approach might be to provide programs for family members and peers that assist them in guiding adolescents and provide information concerning where to go for help. In designing these programs, it will be important for counselors to note the desire of young people for advice and to plan strategies that take this into consideration.

6. Finally, a useful and cost-effective approach to providing information important to young people in developing countries is the group information workshop offered within schools and communities in which activities are

planned by young people in coordination with teachers, counselors or other relevant adults. Since 1993, this approach has been used in Venezuela through national workshops on topics vital to youth, such as teenage pregnancy, family living, improving health and so on.

The key to effectiveness workshops is using group commonalities such as age, SES and family type to bring the group together and to show how the various possible solutions to problems are relevant to the particular group. The approach works effectively, not only with adolescents, but also with parents and others responsible for the care of adolescents (for example, managers of sports teams, directors of music groups at churches and so on). If conducted professionally with understanding of participants' needs, it can help participants to become sufficiently secure to discuss even their most personal problems with peers and personal friends and work out solutions. This includes even delicate issues such as those related to the very real and serious problems regarding sexuality, about which almost none of our subjects even commented. Until issues such as teenage pregnancy can be discussed openly, government programs to combat the problems will have difficulty succeeding.

While this short list does not pretend to represent the solution to Venezuela's crisis, it does suggest some steps that counselors may utilize to initiate resistance to some of the problems faced by Venezuela's youth. Chapter 18 continues the discussion, utilizing these suggestions as well as others suggested by the many national studies that comprise our ERT project.

Part 4

Minority Populations

Part 4 gives special attention to five groups of minority youngsters surveyed in four countries of the ERT study. Chapter 17 details the responses to the ERT questionnaire of "nonadvantaged" Antillian, Moroccan, Surinamese and Turkish migrant youngsters in the Netherlands; "nonadvantaged" Arabs in Israel; "non-advantaged" African-Americans in the Continental US; "poverty" gypsies in Greece; and "poverty" Hispanic- and African-Americans in the Continental US.

The small and sometimes discrepant sizes of samples as well as methodological limitations inherent in the multinational study preclude making more than conjectures as to the meaning of the findings. However, the data permits the authors to generate hypotheses important to the understanding of minority status in problem-solving as well as to raise important research questions.

17

Minority Populations

MARIA DIKAIOU, JANICE GIBSON-CLINE, PETER DE WEERDT, MARION DRAGOON AND CARLOS JONES WITH MAHMOD SALEH[1]

> **"People don't buy flowers like they used to . . ."**
>
> Fifteen year old **Sultana** is a Gypsy girl. Her parents are nonliterate.
>
> "Ten years from now, I want my own caravan so I can travel with my children. We'll be in one place as much as we would like and then go off to the next . . . I don't want to stay in one place because we would have to compromise . . . behave like others (non-Gypsies). I would not like to have to cook, send children to school. I would like to be free.
>
> "My grandmother is very sick. We don't have heating in the caravan . . .We don't have money to buy a proper caravan to live in . . . My brothers often come home without having earned any money. People don't buy flowers as they used to. I sell flowers in the shop so I can help out with money . . . Sometimes we sit down with other children and start singing.
>
> "I talk about these problems with my mother, my brother and my friend. They are also concerned about my grandmother and they love me. They try to think of ways we can work together and collect money. I don't want them to say that my grandmother . . . will die. I don't want them to think I don't try hard enough to bring money home.
>
> "I would like my family to have our own caravan. I would like to sell more of our goods and be able to buy nice clothes."

[1] The Israeli Arab study was conducted by Mahmod Saleh of Mesgave, Israel who organized the project, collected and coded the data and submitted it for inclusion in the multinational study. Attempts by the other authors to reach Dr Saleh for interpretation of his results during the two years prior to book publication failed, however. For this reason, interpretations reported in this chapter had to be made without his input and are the responsibility of the remaining authors.

Catherine Pretrowito and India Ivory contributed to the study by collecting and coding responses of minority youngsters.

The Minority Populations study describes responses of five minority groups surveyed as part of the ERT study. It is presented as a pilot project which, the authors hope, will provoke creative problem-solving and further research.

Introduction

Minority populations: a working definition

The term, "minority populations," has often been used by social pychologists and others to refer to groups of people who occupy subordinate positions within their societies (see, for example, Simpson and Yinger, 1985; Berry et al., 1992). "Minority status" is determined by two sets of factors: "objective" indices related to housing, employment, health and education as compared with those associated with the "majority" population of that society; and "subjective" considerations such as the extent to which the group in question regards itself or is regarded as different, usually in negative fashion, from the "majority" group in characteristics such as religion, language, race, ethnicity, cultural background or behavior.

This approach makes two assumptions: First, while many minority group members are economically deprived, economically deprived individuals are not necessarily minorities (i.e. they may come from low socioeconomic backgrounds but not meet other requirements of our definition); second, minority status may be conferred on a people who constitute a numerical majority in their country. (Although South African Blacks constituted a minority population in South Africa when they lived under apartheid, majority status is presumed under their new government.)

For the purposes of this chapter, the authors define "minority population" as follows:

A minority population is a group of people who carry low socioeconomic status when compared the majority society. In addition, both the members of the minority group and others consider it ethno-culturally different in some way, lacking in power and influence and, often, subject to differential treatment and discrimination or prejudice, perhaps over generations.

The specific minority populations examined include:

1. "nonadvantaged" migrants in the Netherlands from Morocco, Surinam, Turkey and the Antilles;
2. "nonadvantaged" Arabs in Israel;
3. "nonadvantaged" African-Americans in Continental US;
4. "poverty" Gypsies in Greece;
5. "poverty" Hispanic- and African-Americans in Continental US.

Models designed to explain minority problems and coping

The mainstream-minority model

The study of minority problems and coping has most often been approached from the perspective of the mainstream-minority model in which the minority population interacts with a single dominant society (Simpson and Yinger, 1985; Oudenhoven and Willemsen, 1989). This approach suggests that our adolescent minority subjects actually live in two cultures, their own and that of the majority society and that minority problems need to be seen in terms of the need to adjust to both of these cultures simultaneously.

The social identity model

Social identity theory posits that:

1. individuals identify with what they consider to be their own group and
2. they choose to behave in ways they perceive their group to behave.

This model has often been used to explain adjustment of minority immigrants. Bond and King (1985), for example, studied the adjustment strategies of immigrant groups and related them to perceptions of appropriate behavior derived by subjects from their ethno-cultural backgrounds as well as from other, more personal, factors.

With what groups do minority populations identify—their minority group, their socioeconomic background or both? This is a difficult question to answer since most minority groups, by definition, belong to lower socioeconomic groups as well.

Studies have shown that differences in coping strategies may be related to either or both (see, for example, Pearlin and Schooler, 1978; Hallahan and Moos, 1987; Billings and Moos, 1981; Dikaiou and Kiosseoglou, 1994). In our own ERT research, the Continental US study (Chapter 15) demonstrates that individual problem-solving approaches such as trying harder and planning are used more frequently by "advantaged" youngsters, 95% of whom are White and 5% minority, than by "poverty" youth, 95% of whom are minority and 5% White. The reverse is true for escape/avoidance coping.

These studies suggest that, to understand minority coping behavior, research is needed to distinguish effects of socioeconomic background from those of minority status. The present pilot study is designed to explore this issue.

Choices of helpers: evidence from non-minority studies

A large literature regarding the choices of helpers by non-minority adolescents suggests that young people most often bring psychosocial problems to their families or close friends and only rarely use formal helpers (see, for example,

DePaulo, Nadler and Fisher, 1983 and Veroff, Kulka and Douvan, 1981). Our multinational study results (Chapter 3) confirm the cross-national validity of this finding, but do not respond to the question of how minority subjects choose helpers in contrast to their non-minority peers.

The Study: Research Questions and Methodology

Research questions

To begin exploring possible differential effects of minority status and poverty status of young people on their problems and coping strategies, this study asks the following questions:

1. Among the five populations of minority adolescents surveyed for this study, how do "nonadvantaged" and "poverty" groups compare as to problems, coping strategies and choices of helpers?
2. How do they compare with their non-minority socioeconomic counterparts in the multinational sample?

Subjects

The five groups of young people represented here tend to be regarded and regard themselves as different from the "majority" population in terms of religion, language, race, ethnicity or cultural background. At the same time, they vary greatly from one another in cultural and socioeconomic background as well as life experiences.

All youngsters were 13—15 years of age at the time of the study. As reported earlier, the numbers of subjects in our groups vary considerably in size and some samples are extremely small. Groups and the characteristics used to define them as minorities include:

1. "Nonadvantaged" migrants in the Netherlands: The 23 migrant subjects attended high schools in and around Utrecht and differed racially from the majority population. Parents were born in Surinam, Turkey, Morocco and the Antilles islands and migrated to the Netherlands in search of employment. Parents tended to have less than average educational level when compared with their Dutch peers, usually having reached a maximum of elementary school in their home countries. Their occupational level in the Netherlands usually was that of unskilled factory worker. Minority status is confirmed by relevant studies (e.g. Eldering and Kloprogge, 1989). Because of the small size of this sample, no effort was made to distinguish males from females. The sample itself forms part of the "nonadvantaged" group in the Netherlands study (Chapter 11).

2. "Nonadvantaged" Israeli Arabs. At the time of the study, the 123 subjects (76 males and 47 females) were enrolled in middle schools and high schools in and around Mesgave, Israel. They came from families representing the lower 50% of income levels in Israel and had parents who usually had obtained low educational and occupational levels (unskilled labor) in that country. Israeli Arabs have been considered a minority population in Israel since the State of Israel came into existence. Just as for Jewish Israelis, concern for individual rights as well as pressures coming from political violence have affected this population (Punamaki and Ramzi, 1990).

3. "Nonadvantaged" African-Americans (Americans of African descent) in the Continental US. This population is composed of 103 students (51 males and 52 females) from in and around Pittsburgh, Pennsylvania. The majority resided in economically depressed (lower than the US average) urban, inner-city and rural areas and moderate-low-to-low-income level households, some in public housing facilities. Parents tended to be high-school graduates, with a small number reportedly having received some college education. Parents' occupations included primarily low-skilled labor, with some moderately skilled and fewer skilled labor positions. While this group is "nonadvantaged" as defined in the multinational study, 48% of African-Americans in the US had incomes below the poverty level as compared with 13% for White Americans at the time the data were collected (US Bureau of the Census, 1991). The "nonadvantaged" African-American minority group is also included in the US study in which it represents 50% of the "nonadvantaged" sample.

4. "Poverty" Gypsies in Greece. This 200 subject sample (100 males and 100 females) comes from an underprivileged area on the outskirts of Salonica in which residents live under conditions of extreme poverty. Greek Gypsies do not always meet their needs as regards food, shelter and medical care. Housing conditions are below accepted standards with at least five persons per room. 65% of the Gypsy population in Greece are illiterate, with most adults employed at temporary occupation that include craft sales and/or unskilled workers, requiring most families to move at least twice per year in search of employment. Half are under 16 years of age, of which only 30—40% have ever attended school and only 1% has achieved any secondary education (Dikaiou, 1990). Traditions of mistrust and suspicion exist between this group and Greeks, influencing their interactions. Most of our Gypsy subjects had never attended any formal school and those who had were unable to read or write.

5. "Poverty" Hispanic- and African-Americans in the Continental US. This 193 subject sample (89 males and 104 females), representing approximately 50%

Hispanic- and 50% African-Americans, attended two local neighborhood schools in New York City in areas more severely economically depressed than for the "nonadvantaged" African-American minority sample. Almost 75% of students in these schools qualified at the time of the study for US government subsidized lunch program for financially needy children. Most of their families lived on US public assistance programs (welfare, aid to dependent children, medicaid, etc.). Those who worked were employed at low-paying jobs. Families did not always meet their food, shelter and medical needs. This sample is also included as the "poverty" population in the US study (Chapter 15).

Instruments, data collection and data coding

Data was collected by means of the instruments used in the larger multinational study. Data collection and coding procedures also matched those of the larger study, with the following exceptions:

1. In order to separate "nonadvantaged" African-American students from a classroom population of both African-American and White youngsters, the questionnaire used with "nonadvantaged" African-Americans included an item concerning race in its demographic section. Because this question was not asked of the "poverty" minority sample in the Continental US, responses of African-American and Hispanic youngsters in that sample cannot be distinguished from one another.

2. Questionnaires turned in by the few Caucasians in the US "poverty" groups studied were noted and eliminated by the data collector when questionnaires were submitted.

3. Responses were collected from the Gypsy population by interview because these subjects were non-literate and could not complete a written questionnaire. This procedure followed guidelines for other non-literate populations in the larger study (see Chapter 2).

TABLE 17.1 *Reliability of coding established for coders of each minority group and measured by percentage of agreement between each coder and the master code*

Minority Group	*Classes*	*Catgories-within-classes*
"Nonadvantaged" migrants to the Netherlands	.83	.94
"Nonadvantaged" Israeli Arabs	.85	.90
"Nonadvantaged" African-Americans	.84	.95
Greek Gypsies	.77	.93
"Poverty" Hispanic- and African-Americans	.90	.97

Reliability of coding for each subject group, measured by percentage of agreement between the coder and the ERT master code appears in Table 17.1.

Limitations of the sampling and methodology

1. Although the Minority Populations study separates "nonadvantaged" from "poverty" subjects and identifies by name the cultural/ethnic backgrounds they represent, it does not distinguish among the common or unique characteristics defining these cultural/ethnic groups, the other factors that form part-and-parcel of minority status or the possible interrelationships that exist among these.

2. Subject samples are varied and often small in size, due to the difficulties of gathering information from these populations.

3. While data collectors took precautions to decrease mistrust and suspicion inherent in these populations and to increase cooperation, the possibility nevertheless remains that these subjects "protected" themselves in their responses and were not altogether open. Some minority youngsters, the Dutch migrant youth for example, in fact demonstrated some discomfort in expressing their own opinions on the questionnaire and required special encouragement by the data collector before doing so.

While these problems prohibit more than conjectures as to the meaning of our young subjects' responses, the study nevertheless permits generation of hypotheses and raises important research questions, as discussed later.

Study Results

Results are reported for minority groups by cultural/national background and gender.[2] Tables 17.2—17.6 list findings by classes and categories-within-classes accounting for 5% or more responses. Highlights are described in the text. Readers are reminded of the study limitations when interpreting the data.

Problems

Schooling and **family** appear among the top three classes most frequently reported by both our "nonadvantaged" and "poverty" minority groups, just as in the multinational study. **Identity/self-concept** issues are cited less frequently (Table 17.2(a)).

Schooling categories "academic failure" or "inability to learn" were reported by minority and non-minority groups in both studies, the one exception being Gypsies who did not attend school (Table 17.2(b)).

[2] Subjects were not broken down by gender for the Dutch migrant group because of the small sample size.

TABLE 17.2 *Minority group study: percentages of total responses falling into classes and categories of problems*

	"Nonadvantaged' migrants in Netherlands Male and Female		*"Nonadvantaged" Arabs in Israel*				*"Nonadvantaged" African-Americans*				*"Poverty" gypsies in Greece*				*"Po*	*a*
			Male		*Female*		*Male*		*Female*		*Male*		*Female*		*Male*	
	%	*Rank*	*%*	*Rank*	*%*	*Rank*	*%*	*Rank*	*%*	*Rank*	*%*	*Rank*	*%*	*Rank*	*%*	*Ra*
	—	—	—	—	0.6	(11)	—	—	—	—	—	—	—	—	—	-
	—	—	1.5	(9.5)	1.3	(9.5)	—	—	—	—	—	—	—	—	—	-
	—	—	26.5	(1)	6.5	(5.5)	2.1	(9)	3.1	(7)	—	—	1.3	(9)	—	—
	1.6	(7.5)	2.9	(8)	5.2	(7)	2.1	(9)	0.4	(11)	5.8	(5.5)	1.3	(9)	7.5	(4
	33.9	(1)	20.6	(2)	24.7	(2)	17.5	(3)	29.3	(1)	32.7	(1)	37.3	(1)	18.8	(3
	22.6	(2)	19.1	(3)	29.2	(1)	40.2	(1)	21.8	(2)	19.2	(3)	16.0	(2)	23.1	(1
ept	12.9	(3.5)	8.8	(5.5)	1.9	(8)	18.6	(2)	16.6	(3)	23.1	(2)	12.0	(3)	22.5	(2
	—	—	1.5	(9.5)	—	—	3.1	(6)	7.4	(5)	3.8	(7)	9.3	(4)	6.9	(6
	3.2	(6)	5.9	(7)	12.3	(3)	3.6	(5)	6.6	(6)	5.8	(5.5)	8.0	(5.5)	5.6	(8
ialization	12.9	(3.5)	8.8	(5.5)	10.4	(4)	2.6	(7)	9.6	(4)	7.7	(4)	8.0	(5.5)	6.9	(
s	3.2	(7)	—	—	6.5	(5)	1.5	(11)	1.3	(9)	1.9	(8)	5.3	(7)	1.3	(
	—	—	—	—	—	—	2.1	(9)	—	—	—	—	1.3	(9)	0.6	(10
	8.1	(5)	11.1	(4)	1.3	(9.5)	0.5	(12)	0.9	(10)	—	—	—	—	6.9	(
	1.6	(7.5)	—	—	—	—	6.2	(4)	1.7	(8)	—	—	—	—	—	—

	%	*Sex*	*Category*	*%*	*Category*	*%*	*Category*	*%*	*Category*
' rlands			*"Nonadvantaged" Arabs in Israel*		*"Nonadvantaged" African-Americans*		*"Poverty" gypsies in Greece*		*"Poverty" Afri Hispanic-Amer*
:	14.5	Male	Disaster	17.6	Academic achievement	10.8	Employment	18.7	Self-abuse
s	9.7		Welfare of family	8.8	Academic failure	9.8	Prejudice/discrimination	10.7	Academic failu
her	9.7		Inability to learn	8.8	Behavioral	6.7	Unmet physical needs	9.3	Behavioral
	8.1				Self-abuse	5.2	Family move	6.7	School: other
							Unmet physical needs	5.3	Concern about
							Personal health	5.0	in the neighbo
							Intergenerational disagreement	5.0	Money Welfare of fam
		Female	Inability to learn	13.6	Academic failure	8.3	Unmet physical needs	12.7	Welfare of fam
			Disaster	5.2	Friendship	7.4	Money	12.0	Academic failu
			Money	5.2	Academic achievement	7.2	Employment	9.3	Self-abuse
					Behavioral	5.7	Welfare of family	9.3	Becoming sexu
							Domestic quarrelling	7.3	Concern about
							Family status	6.7	in the neighbo
							Child rearing	6.7	Domestic quar

% or more of responses.

"Poverty" subjects, interestingly, did not report a higher incidence of problems related to "money" or "unmet physical needs" than their economically wealthier counterparts. This was also true in the multinational study.

Problems related to "becoming sexually active" were addressed only by one group, minority "poverty" Hispanic- and African-Americans (Table 17.2(b)). This was the sole group in the multinational study expressing this concern!

Comparing "nonadvantaged" and "poverty" minority youngsters, by and large, **schooling** problems decrease and **family** problems increase with decreasing SES status. Again, this was true of non-minority subjects in the multinational study.

A gender-related difference was also found, just as in the multinational study: Taking into consideration the four subject groups for which gender is provided in Table 17.2(a), it can be seen that males report a higher percentage of **schooling** problems and a lower percentage of **family** problems than do females (the "non-advantaged" Israeli Arab group constitutes an exception).

In addition to these similarities to the multinational non-minority youth, some potentially important differences are suggested by the data:

1. "Poverty" minority youth did not report concerns related to "growing up" (becoming an adult; attaining physical or social maturity).
2. While **schooling** and **family** problems concerned both minority and non-minority youth, young minority subjects often gave reports reflective of the immediate situations in their countries. Some Arab Israeli youngsters, for example, discussed fear of an immediate **catastrophe** in their country. Others worried about what was happening in their classrooms. A 14-year-old Arab boy:

"My teacher ignores me. Whenever I try to say what I think, he does not take it seriously."

Hispanic- and African-American youngsters in the US reported:

"I wish for nobody else to die, to be killed."

"I don't want to be sent to jail."

Hispanic- and African-American youngsters also reported numbers of problems related to self-abuse, primarily drugs.

Coping strategies

Individual problem-solving is the first choice of coping strategy of most minority groups in this study, regardless of their socioeconomic status, just as in the non-minority multinational study (Table 17.3). The one exception is our

Table 17.3 *Minority group study: percentages of total responses falling into classes and categories of coping strategies*

	"Nonadvantaged" migrants in Netherlands Male and female %	Rank	"Nonadvantaged" Arabs in Israel Male %	Rank	Female %	Rank	"Nonadvantaged" African-Americans Male %	Rank	Female %	Rank	"Poverty" gypsies in Greece Male %	Rank	Female %	Rank	"Po Male %	R
nce	13.2	(3)	21.2	(3)	24.7	(2)	11.5	(4.5)	20.3	(2)	16.0	(2)	11.0	(4)	20.9	
	25.0	(2)	7.6	(5)	6.3	(5)	13.4	(3)	19.2	(3)	3.0	(5)	16.0	(2.5)	17.8	
n-solving	40.8	(1)	15.2	(4)	35.4	(1)	42.1	(1)	26.1	(1)	64.0	(1)	49.0	(1)	32.5	
ent	2.6	(6)	—	—	1.3	(7.5)	4.3	(6)	1.4	(8)	1.0	(7)	1.0	(6.5)	1.2	(
	2.6	(6)	1.5	(7)	2.5	(6)	1.0	(7.5)	4.0	(6)	—	—	—	—	—	
ıse	—	—	1.5	(7)	1.3	(7.5)	1.0	(7.5)	1.1	(9)	—	—	—	—	1.2	(
	11.8	(4)	21.5	(2)	13.9	(4)	11.5	(4.5)	8.7	(5)	4.0	(4)	6.0	(5)	7.4	
	2.6	(7)	30.3	(1)	14.6	(3)	15.3	(2)	17.4	(4)	8.0	(3)	16.0	(2.5)	14.1	
onses	1.3	(8)	1.5	(7)	—	—	—	—	1.8	(7)	3.0	(5.5)	1.0	(6.5)	4.9	
	—	—	—	—	—	—	—	—	—	—	—	—	—	—	—	

	%	Sex	Category	%	Category	%	Category	%	Category
l" erlands			*"Nonadvantaged" Arabs in Israel*		*"Nonadvantaged" African-Americans*		*"Poverty" gypsies in Greece*		*"Poverty" Af Hispanic-Am*
;	21.1	Male	Distancing	15.2	Planning	22.5	Try harder	42.0	Seek support
	21.1		Seek support	15.0	Try harder	15.8	Seek support	15.0	Planning
	14.5		Escape/avoidance	13.6	Seek support	10.5	Planning	7.0	Try harder
	13.2		Do nothing	7.6	Escape (behavioral)	8.6	Mental preoccupation	6.0	Escape/avoid
	10.6				Assertive cope	7.7	Escape/avoidance	6.0	Assertive cop
					Distancing	6.4			Do nothing
					Do nothing	5.7			
					Hostile-aggressive	5.3			
		Female	Seek support	18.4	Seek support	18.8	Try harder	31.0	Seek support
			Try harder	17.7	Planning solution	12.0	Assertive coping	11.0	Assertive cop
			Planning	9.5	Assertive coping	14.5	Seek support	10.0	Escape/avoid
			Escape/avoid	7.0	Escape (behavioral)	11.2	Escape/avoidance	10.0	Try harder
					Try harder	7.6	Distancing	6.0	Planning
					Distancing	6.2	Planning	6.0	Do nothing
					Do nothing	5.8			Distancing
					Hostile-aggressive	5.3			Offer help to

5% or more of responses.

sample of Israeli Arab males for whom **disengaging, resignation** and **seeking and giving assistance** appear more frequently (Table 17.3(a)).

However, minority groups do not replicate the multinational SES trend in which **individual problem-solving** decreases with decreasing socioeconomic status. "Poverty" minority groups actually tended to report higher percentages of **individual-problem-solving** strategies than "nonadvantaged" groups. There also appeared to be no difference in responses of males and females. In some cases, females reported taking more active coping strategies than males. A 15-year-old Moroccan girl living in the Netherlands who was worried that she was might be "forced to marry someone that I don't know at all," is an example:

> "If my parents try to make me do that, I will talk to them and make it clear that they cannot . . . I will just keep talking to [them] until the problem is solved. I will also talk to my sister and best friend."

Another potentially important difference between our minority subjects and their multinational non-minority peers is that all "poverty" minority groups reported frequent use of "escape/avoidance." In the non-minority multinational group, "escape/avoidance" was reported only by "nonadvantaged" females.

Helpers

Minority adolescents, as their non-minority counterparts, seek help from **family** or "personal friends," first. Mothers are first choice.

A thirteen-year-old African-American boy in the US:

> "What worries me is when I lose my temper. I talk about this to my mother, nobody else. She tells me how [it was like] when she was younger, helps me see a different picture ..."

While "teachers" are also mentioned by some groups (Israeli Arabs, male African- and Hispanic-Americans and female African-Americans), they were not reported by others (migrants in the Netherlands or Gypsies), (Table 17.4). "Professional counselors" were not among the choices made by any group.

Discussion

A comparison of minorities and non-minority peers

Problems

While schooling and family problems concerned both minority and non-minority youth, it appears the problems of some minority youth might have been affected by their immediate national/ethnic environments. At the same time, it

TABLE 17.4 *Minority group study: percentages of total responses falling into classes and categories of desired helpers listed by gender and SES grouping of sul*

"Nonadvantaged" migrants in Netherlands, Male and female %	Rank	"Nonadvantaged" Arabs in Israel, Male %	Rank	Female %	Rank	"Nonadvantaged" African-Americans, Male %	Rank	Female %	Rank	"Poverty" gypsies in Greece, Male %	Rank	Female %	Rank	"Pov… Male %	Ra…
46.9	(1)	51.5	(1)	57.3	(1)	61.3	(1)	57.8	(1)	40.0	(2)	30.0	(2)	58.6	(1
35.7	(2)	41.8	(2)	37.8	(2)	35.2	(2)	39.1	(2)	60.0	(1)	70.0	(1)	38.6	(2
1.4	(5)	1.5	(4)	0.6	(4)	—	—	1.8	(3)	—	—	—	—	0.3	(4
—	—	—	—	0.3	(5.5)	1.2	(4)	0.2	(5)	—	—	—	—	—	—
—	—	—	—	—	—	0.9	(5)	—	—	—	—	—	—	—	—
14.0	(3)	0.7	(5)	0.3	(5.5)	—	—	—	—	—	—	—	—	—	—
2.1	(4)	4.5	(3)	3.7	(3)	1.4	(3)	1.1	(4)	—	—	—	—	2.5	(3

%	Sex	Category	%	Category	%	Category	%	Category
'ands		"Nonadvantaged" Arabs in Israel		"Nonadvantaged" African-Americans		"Poverty" gypsies in Greece		"Poverty" Afri… Hispanic-Amer…
19.6	Male	Personal friend	19.4	Personal friend	20.4	Mother	53.0	Mother
10.5		Mother	13.4	Mother	19.4	Personal friend	44.0	Personal friend
9.8		Father	12.7	Father	13.4	Father	26.0	Cousin
8.4		Brother	9.7	Teacher/instructor	8.0	Brother	19.0	Sister
		Teacher	6.0	Grandmother	6.6			Teacher
		Personal friend	23.6	Personal friend	26.5	Personal friend	31.0	Personal friend
		Mother	18.6	Mother	20.1	Mother	29.0	Mother
		Father	11.5	Teacher/instructor	5.9	Sister	8.0	Cousin
		Sister	6.8	Father	5.6	Grandmother	7.0	Sister
		Parents/family	6.2					
		Teacher	5.6					

› or more of responses.

appears that socioeconomic background plays an important role. The SES trend toward increase of family problems with decreasing socioeconomic backgrounds, similar to that shown in the multinational sample, demonstrates its importance on family life and the increasing economic problems that "poverty" youth and their families must face.

The trend toward decreasing reports of school-related problems with decreasing SES, in turn, is probably also a reflection of the increase of other types of problems that go hand-in-hand with poverty. While many minority youth may understand the need for education if they are to better their lives, they may feel incompetent. The fact that, unlike their non-minority peers, they rarely reported concerns related to their growing up may, in addition, suggest a loss of faith in the future.

Does discrimination play a role in our subjects' problems and/or behavior? Gypsy males are, interestingly, the only group in the Minority Populations study who indicated concerns regarding discrimination. It may be that these young people are simply unconcerned about discrimination, that they have internalized their feelings or that they do not recognize them as problems external to themselves.

There are additional possible explanations: Minority youth may be concerned about discrimination, but have chosen to avoid discussing the problem because it requires them to address unpleasant emotions. Because they are at the stage of adolescence in which the need for belonging is especially important, they may be uncomfortable suggesting in any way that they are "discriminated against" or are in any way different from their peers. Unfortunately, this study does not address these separate possibilities. It was interesting that some minority youngsters, as for example, the Dutch migrant youth, had difficulty expressing their opinions on the questionnaire, as noted earlier.

Coping

Our results do not support theories that would suggest that "poverty" minority groups should act more passively than other groups, or that "passive" coping is dysfunctional, as some researchers have suggested (Bosma and Jackson, 1990). To the contrary, our minority "poverty" subjects reported strategies that involved disengagement and resignation less frequently on average than either our "non-advantaged" minority subjects or their multinational non-minority peers.

The fact that our "nonadvantaged" Israeli Arab subjects constitute the single minority group reporting these two strategies frequently may be reflective of cultural background. It may also be an indication that this group is coping through multiple strategies, an approach that Hallahan and Moos (1987) suggest is functional in dealing with threatening situations and when personal and contextual resources are scarce. Individual problem-solving was also frequently reported by our Israeli Arab subjects, ranking third among their chosen coping strategies.

The specific coping strategies reported by our subjects may have been chosen because of the immediacy of serious problems coupled with real lack of power to resolve them. Previous research indicates that coping serves two major functions: emotion-focused coping regulates emotions whereas problem-focused coping concentrates on activities designed to resolve the problem itself (Lazarus and Folkman (1984). Although "constructive" coping concentrates on problem resolution, success is ultimately determined by options within each situation. We found in this study that minorities apparently are not less active in this pursuit than non-minorities. For instance, while Israeli Arabs reported disengagement with greater frequency than other minority groups, the immediacy of dangerous conflict and the lack of opportunity to resolve it, rather than apathy, may have triggered this response. Similarly, Hispanic- and African-American youngsters, who might expect their lives to be shortened by the violence in their immediate neighborhoods, recognize at the same time their inability to change their environments. This, together with the fact that these youngsters do not search out professionals to help them, have important implications for counseling.

Implications

For counseling: creating effective helpers

1. To increase the possibility that minority youngsters will utilize the services that professional helpers provide as well as to increase the efficacy of counseling which some researchers in the past have suggested is low (Durlak, 1979), counselors should focus on immediate concerns. Since school achievement poses major problems, for example, they should prepare themselves to help youngsters deal with immediate curriculum-oriented issues by teaching study skills, as Eilering (1987) suggested. Since family problems are also of paramount importance, professionals need to become well versed in family counseling techniques.

2. While our results suggest that minority adolescents actively influence their lives, it is clear that they differ in their opportunities to become engaged in solving problems. When youngsters fail to engage themselves in productive problem-solving, a major goal of counseling should be to empower them by teaching that options to effect change are available and how they might create change by using resources available to them. In this regard, a useful counseling service would be the tapping into the community and public services for resources and then communicating to clients relevant information. Having the counselor take on the role of "resource broker" might then serve not only to empower minority youngsters but, in addition, increase the currently low probability that they will consider going to professional counselors as potential helpers in the first place.

3. Another way to deal with the fact that minority adolescents bring their problems to informal rather than professional helpers and that they prefer family and friends to counselors is for counselors to identify potential informal helpers to whom adolescents are likely to turn and offer these lay people training and support to provide effective help. In the schools, students from upper grades might serve as effective lay helpers. In the community, they might be peers, family members or other adults who are approachable as well as experienced in the problems of minority youth. The professional counselor who takes on the task of identifying lay helpers could then work in tandem with these paraprofessionals.

4. It is interesting that few minority youth expressed concerns related to prejudice or discrimination. If we assume that their responses imply a hesitance to discuss the issue rather than nonexistence of discrimination, another arena in which counselors might assist young minority could be to sensitize them to the sociopolitical and economic implications of their minority status. Counselors might help them to press for changes which will lead to the diminishing of discrimination. This type of social action counseling is discussed in some detail in Chapter 18.

For future research: answering unanswered questions

1. What factors play important roles in determining the problems and coping strategies of minority youngsters and how do they interact? The importance of minority populations to the world's future suggests the importance of further research to answer these questions. The results of our study suggest that further research should include systematic study of these and other minority and non-minority populations, matched for SES and national/ethnic situation and with larger numbers of subjects.

2. This study did not ask important questions regarding the social and psychological processes by which minority groups come to adopt one particular type of coping as against others. Most probably, macro-social processes such as forced assimilation policies as well as micro-phenomena such as learned helplessness are worth looking into if we are to understand minority adolescents' behavior.

3. Another question left unanswered concerns the relationship between wider cultural processes and specific types of problems. Further research needs to be done to determine effects on the problem-solving behavior of minority youth under conditions of increased educational opportunities. Would improving education enhance relations with parental figures and with school? Might it lead to changes in styles of coping and/or help-seeking and if so, what styles and in which directions?

4. Finally, questions need to be asked about the relationship between patterns of coping of minority youth during adolescence and those which occur in early adulthood. Do the coping strategies of youngsters influence coping in their adult years? If so, we cannot underestimate the importance of improving intervention strategies.

This pilot study has provided a beginning to the understanding of problems and coping of minority youth. The answers to these and other research questions are not only important to the understanding of this important population but can also be used to suggest directions that effective counseling should take.

Part 5

Conclusions and Implications for Theory and Practice

Multinational Counseling for the Helping Professions: A Model for the Twenty-first Century

Part 5 moves from crisis to coping as it provides the conclusions of the Energetic Research Team and the implications of the ERT research.

Chapter 18 reviews the findings of our multinational, national and minority population findings and outlines models for crossnational counseling for the twenty-first century as well as preparation for developing needed necessary skills.

18

Implications for Theory and Practice

JANICE GIBSON-CLINE, MARIA DIKAIOU, MARION DRAGOON, MARIA HARITOS-FATOURAS, BENJAMIN SHAFRIR, ISAURA GUIMARAES, ELIZABETE PEREIRA, PETER DE WEERDT AND LINA KASHYAP
with the assistance of
QASEM AL-SARRAF and GUNDELINA VELAZCO

Introduction

The ERT portrait of adolescence

At a macro level, the ERT portrait of adolescent concerns and coping strategies is less of similarities than of differences. Most youngsters across the nations and backgrounds of our study were similar in this concern, the primary source of which was related to schooling and grades, this fact should not be surprising, given today's technological world and the increased need in all countries to learn new skills. Problems related to family issues were a close second.

Some typical statements:

"My problem is my grades" (China)
"I have serious problems in class" (Turkey)
"I'm afraid I might fail ..." (Brazil)
"My parents keep arguing" (India).

Our respondents gave little indication of worry concerning sexually related disease or pregnancy even when they are from countries in which the seriousness of these dangers is highly publicized. Whether adolescents don't worry about sexuality or are too uncomfortable to discuss it openly, this might suggest that they probably cannot cope effectively with this issue. ERT youngsters also appear unconcerned about poverty, war and civil unrest, with the exception of those affected personally. By contrast, many speak freely about fear of drug-motivated crime and violence. Recent studies confirm that these realistic fears are on the increase (Maccarelli (1994).

According to our young subjects, they handle their problems primarily by themselves; when they require help, they go first to close friends or their mothers. Most seek counsel and direction, a fact with implications for help-giving. Not all adolescent responses in our study were the same, however.

A micro-level examination: external factors that affect our portrait

Socioeconomic background

Subjects' socioeconomic status clearly played a role in determining reported problems and coping strategies; the percentages of worries regarding schooling and their choices of individual problem-solving strategies decreased—and worries about family increased—with decreasing SES.

Poverty proved a special case. While our studies portrayed adolescents as often more similar than different regardless of national background, "poverty" youth (youngsters unable to satisfy their basic needs for food, adequate shelter and medical care on regular bases) were distinguishable from others both by their problems, a higher percentage of which were related to family issues and a lower percentage to schooling—and their coping strategies, a lower percentage of which indicated individual problem-solving (see Chapter 3). The concerns of "poverty" youth were far more situation-specific than those of their peers: They worried about material needs while more advantaged youngsters worried about identity; they agonized over their own impoverishment and worried about their "inability to succeed" while youth who were economically more advantaged fretted about emotions and feelings (loneliness, boredom, stress and the like).

Our results suggest that impoverished youth may be more similar to each other than they are to their more advantaged same-nationality peers. Since the ERT study includes "poverty" samples from only five countries (Brazil, India, Philippines, Continental US and Venezuela), however, and some of these are small in size (see Appendix III), it is possible only to conjecture as to the meaning of these results. Should further research with larger samples and a greater diversity of nationalities demonstrate the same findings, it will support the position that conditions of poverty may, in fact, create cultural norms that are stronger than those associated with national backgrounds. **This is important!**

The poor young people of our study worked actively to solve their problems:

> "I go to an institute for homeless street-children ... and talk to a social worker or Brother Francisco ..." (Filipino street-boy).

> "I am looking for a part-time job packing st a supermarket or cleaning cars . . . My mother does not want me to do this. But I know she will be happy if I can get some money" (Venezuelan boy).

It is also important that their coping strategies do **not** commonly include "inactive" coping strategies and our data do **not** support hypotheses of Bosma and Jackson (1990) that suggest that "active" coping decreases with decreasing SES. Although our separate studies indicated that individual problem-solving occurred least frequently among poverty subjects, this class of coping actually encompasses a wide range of activities that implies both active coping ("assertive coping," "planning toward a solution," "trying harder") as well as nonactivity ("mental preoccupation," "anxiety without planning," "hope"). In fact, our "poverty" populations gave far more reports of "assertive coping" than did our advantaged groups!

Nationality

While there were fewer differences among the various nationality groups of our study than we had initially anticipated, a number of coping strategies appear to be situation-specific and idiosyncratic to specific national backgrounds: Filipinos coped by praying, for example, while Brazilians distanced themselves psychologically and Jewish Israelis sought professional helpers (the only group in our study to do this with any frequency).

Minority status

While minority youngsters may have been influenced in some of their decision-making by their minority status, most were simultaneously affected by their lower socioeconomic backgrounds. It is important that many minority poverty subjects worried about "inability to learn". This suggests that poverty and minority status contribute together to lower self-images.

Gender

We find it a fascinating comment on gender that females responded in some ways more like lower than higher SES groups and more like minority than majority groups! This occurred within all socioeconomic groupings and most countries, with females giving higher percentages of reports that described family issues than males and lower percentages that described school problems, just as was found when lower and higher SES groups were compared. When problems related to sexuality were reported, as, for example, pressure to become involved sexually, they appeared far more frequently in the statements of females and lower SES groups than of males and higher SES groups.

Implications for Theories of Adolescence

Traditional theories of adolescence describe this stage of life as one of crisis and are often construed to imply that it is the stage of adolescence that generates these crises. To the contrary, while our subjects provided many indications of involvement in crises, with few exceptions, these were rooted in the external situations in which these youngsters found themselves, rather than in their own internal psyches.

It is sad that adolescents admitted abusing themselves with drugs or alcohol or with attempted suicide. While this behavior contributes to problems, it is important that these youngsters reported it as a problem rather than a solution. A systems-theory approach would suggest that this is a first step toward a productive solution. (Systems theory is discussed in some detail both in Chapter 11 and later in this chapter.)

Some coping responses reported by our subjects may be construed as non-productive, at least in terms of bettering their long-term situations. Examples include coping by disengaging, giving up or resigning themselves to their situations, although, in some cases, these views reflected realistic views of their options.

> "I realize there isn't much I can really do, so I try not to think about it" (Australia)

> "When I worry about school, I go listen to music or stay alone at home" (Israeli Arab)

> "Sometimes when I do badly, I make myself feel better by telling myself that I am at least smarter than **some** people" (Continental US).

The only subjects to report antisocial hostile-aggressive behavior directed at their offenders were Russian males and immigrant males in the Netherlands. Both groups were dealing with political problems out of their control.

What external crises generate problems for adolescents? We suggest that, throughout the ERT countries, from the Peoples' Republic of China to Kuwait, educational systems are in crisis and unable to provide adequate learning environments to teach skills needed by many students.

Family institutions are also in crisis and increasingly ill equipped to provide children needed support.

> "My parents don't give me freedom . . ." (India)

> "I'm so worried about my mother. She has been ill and doesn't take care of herself" (Netherlands)

> "My father went away. My mother cleans houses, but she cannot find a good job. I worry that we will not be able to go to school" (Venezuela)

Governmental and political crises stemming from ills that range from economic problems to corruption increase the problem.

"Entrance examinations to university are not fair and I'm afraid I won't have a chance to get a good education." (Soviet Russia)

Venezuelan and Brazilian subjects worried about street violence, and Arab Israelis about "catastrophes."

We suggest that adolescents, although particularly vulnerable to all of these external crises at their stage of life, are capable of coping actively and using resources available to them in effective ways—so long as they are helped to understand their situations and are given appropriate support by the adult world. When Sultana, the Greek Gypsy girl (p. 247) understands that the causes for her lack of money are more complex than the fact that people "don't buy flowers as they used to," she may be more likely than now to explore new coping strategies. So long as her poverty narrows her view of the causative factors related to her impoverished condition, however, she is not likely to search for more daring solutions than to "sit down with the children and start singing."

For those youngsters whose problems are related to drug or alcohol abuse—an increasing world plague—the first step, similarly, is understanding the cause of the problem. Appropriate counseling **can** help.

Implications for a Multinational Approach to Counseling Adolescents: Addenda to the classical approaches of counseling

The ERT authors agree with the classical view regarding the importance of helping youngsters to deal with personal and acute crises affecting them. To validate new needs of youth, we suggest the following additions to our current approaches to counseling:

1. Eclectic and flexible approaches to meet the needs of different peoples

Professional counseling was initially designed to aid clients of "advantaged" middle-class backgrounds who sought advice regarding education and career choices. While this clientèle remains important today, a new clientèle from a variety of backgrounds and with different problems and coping strategies has expanded the tasks of the profession. Today's counselors must not only be flexible, but must embrace diversity, respecting and understanding both the problems and coping strategies of their new clients and utilizing their culturally derived desires, such as the desire for directive assistance, in planning interventions.

2. Special responsibility as advocate for the poor and downtrodden, wherever they exist

To counsel the poor of the world requires additional specialized roles. Counselors working with impoverished peoples, regardless of their national backgrounds, must be prepared to assist them to fight, first, for basic survival for themselves and their families, and then for educations that will afford them opportunity to better their lives. We believe that the ultimate goal should be that all youngsters, regardless of background or gender, reach the highest level of functioning possible. While this point of view does not negate the classical roles of counseling, it does suggest new priorities.

Reinventing and transforming society

Paulo Freire argued (1984) that the highest priority of helping professionals should be to assist clients in "reinventing" and "transforming" their societies and the institutions they encompass. We believe that this task is important everywhere and for everyone—not only in Third World countries and impoverished populations.

Followers of Freire suggest that, productive coping requires an initial "critical" perspective of problem causation. Using schooling problems as an example, teachers and counselors can best assist youngsters with a fear of failure by first helping them to understand the causes of their inability to succeed academically and then assisting them to empower themselves to cope productively. To do so, helping professionals must begin with "macro" realities such as the "true" social causes of the problems their clients face as well as their perceptions of these problems. Building on these, counselors and clients must then work together to develop plans that avoid blaming (inappropriately) the victims. The final step is to construct (together) realistic and meaningful coping responses, utilizing the clients' available resources. According to Freire, counselors should serve in this process as models for their clients and be prepared to engage with them in struggle for the betterment of society.

3. Developing preventive approaches that emphasize coping: a systems theory approach

Freire's arguments apply to the counseling of advantaged youngsters as well as to the poor and oppressed of the world. Our many subjects from affluent backgrounds who reported fear of school failure and responded by "trying harder" (in De Weerdt's words (p. 166), "maintaining a 'more of the same' scenario") are a case in point. Both Freire's approach and that of systems theorists Watzlawick, Weakland and Finch (1973) would assert in this case that the solution contributes to the problem. What is needed is change of the system (defined by Freire to be societal or political institutions and by systems theory to be a collection of elements, in this case, attitudes of the group of students existing in the situation).

With the system by definition possessing inherent tendency to resist change, options for reducing fear include dealing with it either as it affects individual students or as it exists throughout the system. When "trying harder" fails to reduce fear of failure for individual students, for example, their most productive coping strategy should involve locating the "real" roots of the problems in order to change the situation. In this case, the most productive intervention strategy would probably be to assist them to change the context of their perceptions. As an example, "poverty" subjects in our study worried about what they perceived to be an (intrinsic) inability to "learn." In this situation, resulting feelings of helplessness kept them from changing their situations. Until these youngsters understand the relationship of their external situation (that they had been unable to attend school regularly, or to learn the basics on which all later school learning follows, for example) to their poor achievement, they are not likely to explore their options meaningfully and select productive coping strategies.

Many coping strategies that youngsters might select at this point may increase (rather than reduce) the problem. Those who elect simply to disengage are unlikely to reduce their need. Those who act out in socially unacceptable or self-abusive ways create new problems. In both situations, the solution contributes to the problem.

Helping professionals using this interpretation would teach youth to understand themselves in the context of the systems in which they exist. In this case, they would assist clients to interpret their environments as sources of both their problems and their solutions, and to begin using this understanding to develop productive coping strategies.

This scenario moves the helping professional from crisis to coping by indicating the importance of coping strategies in developing plans for intervention. Just as the problems and the situations that generate them differ for different young people, so does understanding of the situation and the strategies that should be most effective to deal with them. Implementation of specific types of programs is discussed later in the chapter.

Multinational Counseling: a Model for the Twenty-first Century

We propose for the twenty-first century Bronfenbrenner's (1979) cross-national "ecological" perspective of counseling which suggests that counselors must be sensitive to the individual concerns and coping strategies of all socioeconomic and cultural groups while, at the same time, anticipating their similarities.

Needed roles of helping professionals in the twenty-first century

In response to these suggested additions to current counseling approaches, we suggest that helping professionals should serve as the following:

1. Conductors of individual (one-on-one) and group counseling. These activities should be designed to provide clients emotional support to deal with personal crises, assist them to enlarge their repertoire of strategies and to replace

ineffective ones; impart information to assist clients to develop new perspectives on their problem-solving; and utilize other sources of help available in the indigenous communities of the clients.

2. Directors and/or participants in programs for preventive outreach, designed to reduce problems before they result in acute client distress. Preventive outreach for many school-related problems reported by our ERT subjects might include time management and stress management counseling as well as workshops to increase study skills. Outreach programs to deal with family problems (another major concern of our subjects) might be designed along the lines of the Family Centers described in the India study to include assisting children in their decision-making abilities, increasing communication and understanding among all family members and teaching skills necessary for successful adult life. Helping females is particularly important here.

   "I wish ... I would be allowed (by my parents) to study as much as I am capable of doing, so that I could have an opportunity for a better life" (an Indian girl).

   In some countries, preventive outreach already includes counseling regarding gender and sexuality that includes topics such as developing self-assertiveness and decreasing feelings of helplessness as regards social pressure on females (suggested for implementation in the Australian and Chinese studies). In this regard, one innovative prevention program that has worked effectively in Venezuela (Chapter 16) is the group information workshop run through schools and communities that deals with topics vital to youth, as, for example, teenage pregnancy. The key to success of this cost-effective program is that activities are planned and conducted by young people, themselves, with the help of teachers, counselors or other relevant adults. Commonality of the group utilizes adolescent needs for peer approval and increases feelings of security in discussing feelings related to issues as sensitive as sexuality.

3. Directors and/or participants in programs for crisis management designed to reduce existing severe client distress. Since crises and client distress are often situation-specific, the composition of crisis management teams as well as the most effective procedures to reduce them vary according to the situation, making flexibility an important quality of helping professionals.

   Theoretically, if preventive outreach is successful, crisis management should not be necessary. In practice, however, preventive outreach and crisis management often merge because of circumstances. For example, preventive programs such as those discussed in the Brazil study to teach viable skills for the poor might be considered crisis management, given Brazil's already-existing crisis regarding its poverty population.

4. Directors or members, together with paraprofessionals and/or professionals representing other disciplines, of a multidisciplinary team.

Using the chosen helpers of adolescents as paraprofessionals

The possibility of using peers or family members as paraprofessionals to work directly with clients has been suggested in a number of ERT studies. Indication given by our subjects that they prefer the help of peers and family—and seek help from professional help-providers only later (often as a last resort)—suggests that peers and family members who have the advantage of being close to these clients might reach potential clients who now are not benefiting from available services. This strategy has already proved successful in some situations, as, for example, with self-help groups such as Alcoholics Anonymous, although it has sometimes proved difficult to implement in schools when members of the school community have disagreed as to the utility of paraprofessional activities and the appropriate relationship between paraprofessional and professional roles. For paraprofessionals to work effectively in school situations, these issues must be resolved in advance, paraprofessionals must receive adequate training and must work as members of a team rather than alone, together with trained professionals who monitor activities and consult on regular bases and whenever needed.

Working with professionals in other disciplines

Member of multidisciplinary intervention teams may include a variety of professionals such as social workers, health professionals, teachers, businesspeople, etc., depending on the situation. To assist families in crisis, for example, family centers might be developed along the lines of those in India, using medical personnel to encourage behaviors that increase physical health as well as psychologists and/or counselors to assist in helping family members to reduce domestic quarreling and increase communication, issues of concern of our subjects. Programs—and team personnel—vary with the situation. In some countries, programs might include neighborhood crime prevention monitored by police personnel; in others, they might supply support systems for immigrant families and so on.

5. Challengers of injustice with roles of assisting the poor, migrants, minorities and females. Helping professionals might consider these roles as transformers of society, teachers of empowerment or reducers of feelings of helplessness, three roles that require political awareness. We believe that effective counseling, however, should transcend usual political agenda. And, while these roles may be used to assist "poverty" and minority groups, they are also important in developing intervention strategies for advantaged youth.

Teaching empowerment

Adolescents, classically described as a group for whom peer approval is an important source of feelings of psychological well being, are particularly vulnerable to peer pressure (see Chapter 1), making it difficult for them to avoid harmful behaviors sanctioned by their peers, as, for example, drug abuse or dangerous sexual behavior. Our study suggests that the teaching of empowerment should be useful for all adolescents, regardless of gender or background. Females are a particular case in point: While minority male youth are the focus of greatest concern in many countries, females in our study also reported a lack of self-confidence in dealing with social pressure as well as serious concern that they were powerless to avoid pressures dangerous to themselves.

6. Mediators between organizations and governmental agencies that can provide help on the one hand, and individuals and communities needing assistance on the other. Success at this role requires sensitivity to a variety of institutions, awareness of effective approaches to communication and "political tact." It demonstrates to clients that professional helpers can assist effectively in changing adverse situations. Together with the teaching of empowerment, it may provide clients needed incentive to seek professional counselors for assistance.

7. Developers of indigenous philosophies of counseling wherever traditional philosophies do not meet the needs of the communities or, as described in our chapters describing Filipino and Turkish youth.

8. Counselor-researchers who conduct theoretical and practice-based research to determine conditions under which effective intervention can take place. In this role, helping professionals function along the lines of the American Psychological Association scholar-practitioner model in which their practitioner activities permit them to ask questions important to the professional field and their scholarly backgrounds permit them to design valid studies to provide answers.

Professional skills needed in the twenty-first century

The roles listed above require specific abilities and awareness if counselors are to be prepared for the future. These include:

1. Ability to anticipate correctly similarities and differences in the problems and coping strategies that exist between and within groups of clients, differentiated by national or socioeconomic background or by other factors. According to Bronfenbrenner (1979), this is best learned from first-hand experience, requiring training programs to set up supervised field studies or programs that are broad and inclusive.

2. Ability to utilize effectively both individual and group techniques, including those in which paraprofessionals and professionals in other disciplines may play major roles, necessitating supervisory skills as well.

3. Ability to serve on multidisciplinary teams, making use of knowledge in other disciplines, e.g. economics, sociology; sharing some activities and dividing responsibility for others.

4. Awareness of the effects of the power structure of institutions, communities and the social processes of change as they affect client problems and the effectiveness of various coping strategies. In addition, the knowledge of organizational change strategies and the sensitivity and "political tact" necessary to deal successfully with institutions as well as clients and members of their communities.

5. Ability to access support systems available in the communities of clients and to mediate between these systems and clients. This may require sensitizing governmental agencies and functionaries of non-governmental organizations as well as counselors to the real issues at hand.

6. Ability to convey honesty, openness, positive regard and unconditional acceptance; ability to listen and to become emotionally involved, to care and to feel for the client; ability to understand oneself in order to be able to achieve understanding in others; ability to provide the type of help wanted in ways that demonstrate immediately what is likely to take place. Male and female subjects from all countries and socioeconomic backgrounds of our study regarded these abilities as extremely important in their choices of helpers. This suggests that, to assist clients effectively with their problems, particularly when they involve sensitive issues, counselors must quite literally get out of their offices, keep in constant touch with their clients and their clients' environments, reach out to those most in need using a multifaceted approach, and, above all, be caring and loving (see Kashyap, 1994 and Shafrir, the Israeli study (above, Chapter 9).)

7. Ability to assess needs of clients and use these assessments to provide a form of directive counseling that maintains a delicate balance between being overly prescriptive and non-directive. Subjects from every country of the ERT study made clear their desire for some form of direction; on which side balance should occur depends on many factors, including cultural, national and ethnic backgrounds.

8. Ability to assess outcomes of counseling. The new needs of the twenty-first century suggest the value of continual evaluation of alternative approaches to providing help. Information thus obtained should be used to change future practice.

Figure 18.1 incorporates these abilities in a model describing the roles and strategies needed for counselors in the twenty-first century.

Figure 18.1 Roles and strategies: a model for helping professionals for the twenty-first century

Roles		Strategies
Counselor-providers of emotional support; of information to develop new perspectives and to access support	→	Individual and group counseling
Counselor-teachers of coping strategies	→	Individual and group counseling
Counselor-team members; Crisis intervention; Preventive outreach	→	Selecting/training/consulting paraprofessionals; teaming with professionals in other disciplines, institutions and agencies
Chalengers of injustice working with poor, migrants, minorities, females	→	Individual and group counseling; team members working to transform society and teach meaningful coping strategies
Counselor-mediators between organizational and governmental institutions, individuals and communities	→	Mediation, team administration, communication
Counselor-researchers	→	Evaluating theory and practice

Figure 18.2 describes the knowledge base and skill-training to prepare helping professionals for the above roles. We do not suggest the academic level at which this preparation should be given or the type of institution where it will take place, as these should be expected to vary considerably from country to country.

Using adolescents as an example clientèle, these include:

1. **Knowledge base:** Age/stage knowledge regarding adolescence as well as the pre- and post-years of this stage is necessary both in general and specific terms as regards various national, cultural and ethnic groups. Knowledge is needed, in addition, of the effects of cultural, ethnic and socioeconomic background on youngsters as well as personal experience within these settings; knowledge regarding power structures and social processes of change and

how these operate; and knowledge regarding existence and functions of support systems available and particular to the community.

2. **Professional skill-training:** The need for flexibility required by a wide variety of situations and clients call for hands-on experience with diverse problems and clients both prior to and during professional education.

Pre-education experience

This should include practice in some capacity (preferably for at least a year) as part of a team of professional help-providers who work with clients from varied backgrounds and who present a variety of symptoms.

Professional education experience

This should include experiential group training as well as laboratory experience in which one's own cultural, ethnic and racial attitudes are explored. Practicum/field work experience should involve counseling experience with

Figure 18.2 Preparing helping professionals for the twenty-first century: necessary learning and experience for counselors

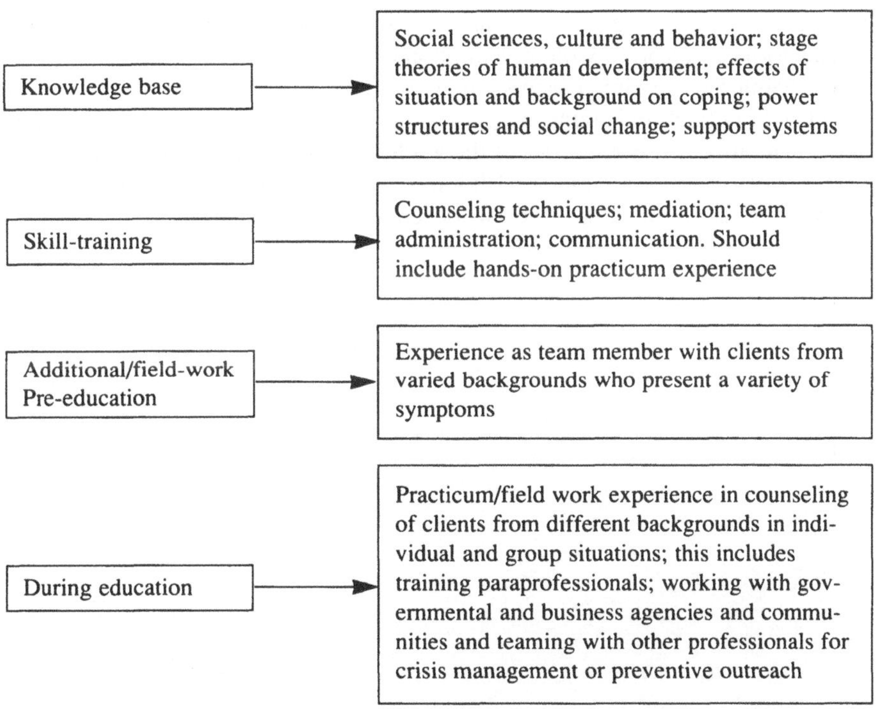

clients from different cultural/ethnic/SES backgrounds in both one-on-one individual and in group situations. Experience training paraprofessionals, working with governmental/business/agencies/community and teaming with other professionals at a crisis management or preventive outreach should be included.

A Postscript: Migration and the Changing Faces of Nations

Today, as more and more families seek to escape trauma and to better their lives by migrating across national boundaries, the multicultural composition of many countries is increasing at dramatic rates and making information about these populations essential to planners. Impoverished minority immigrants are already having major impact on daily life and on national institutions across the world. The expectation is that these migrations will continue to increase as we approach the twenty-first century.

Today, teachers in countries across the world no longer can expect students who enter classrooms necessarily to speak the national language; police cannot expect young people necessarily to have learned national values or to know how to behave according to the norms of the dominant culture. Successful adjustment of these arrivals and their families to their host communities and their new social realities are not only important to the betterment of life everywhere; recent events throughout the world suggest that failure of these potential new citizens to adjust satisfactorily can lead to violent disruption of society.

As helping professionals across the world take over the new task of multinational and multicultural counseling, the importance of learning how backgrounds and situations affect perceptions of the worlds and how to cope in it will increase dramatically in all societies. The ERT research—and this book—have provided an introduction to this task. Much work remains.

Appendix I Classes and Categories within Classes Listed in Taxonomy of Problems, Coping Strategies, Desired Helpers, Desired Helper Qualities and Desired Modes of Helping[1]

1. PROBLEMS

EXTREME POVERTY (inability to meet basic physical or psychological needs).
Unmet basic physical needs
Unmet basic psychological needs
Other

WAR (impact of war on subject's life).
Physical harm
Fear of war
Loss
Other

CATASTROPHE (impact on subject's life; other than war).
Sudden disaster-causing event (apart from war)
Fear of catastrophe
Other

MATERIAL DESIRES (unsatisfied desires for other-than-basic needs).
Money
Tangible items
Other

FAMILY ISSUES (families or relationships within families).
Marriage
Divorce/separation/melded family
Intergenerational disagreement
Domestic quarreling
Domestic violence
Sexual abuse (within the family)

[1] See *Human Problems and Methods of Help-seeking across Cultures: A Coding Manual*, Pittsburgh, Pa.: University of Pittsburgh (copyright J. Gibson, S. Showalter) for definitions of categories-within-problems and examples of responses fitting these categories, together with instructions for using the coding scale.

Family status or honor
Psychological estrangement from family members(s)
Lack of privacy
Parental strictness
Childrearing
Lack of love, feelings or responsibilities
Physical isolation from family
Family move
Self-abuse among family members
Welfare of family members
Misconduct
Other

SCHOOLING (school, academic learning, social learning and socializing in school settings).
Academic achievement
Academic failure
Time pressures
Inability to learn
Language barrier
Subject's misconduct
Teacher-related
Social success/failure
Extracurricular activities
School related abuse
Other

PERSONAL IDENTITY/SELF-CONCEPT (human development or perceptions of self)
Self-confidence
Growing up (assuming adult roles)
Aging (adulthood)
Physical appearance
Behavioral issues (non-school related)
Individuality vs conformity
Self-expectations
Personal health
Physical disability
Self-abuse
Other

SEXUALITY (sexual activity).
Becoming sexually active
Sexual knowledge
Sexual inhibition
Sexual abuse (non-family and non-school)
Sexual dissatisfaction (sexual dysfunction)

Birth control
Pregnancy
Sexually transmitted diseases
Other

COURTSHIP AND DATING (courtship, dating and selection of marriage partner).
Dating/marriage restrictions
Choice of marriage partner
Unrequited feelings
Not dating
Relationship pressures and fears
Separation
Other

INTERPERSONAL PROBLEMS/SOCIALIZATION (immediate concerns related to working and interacting with others on daily bases). (Non-family and non-school related)
Employment
Friendship
Role conflict
Sharing of living space
Prejudice/discrimination
Time pressures
Other

EMOTIONS/FEELINGS (not described in association with specific life event).
Loneliness
Generalized fear or anxiety
Grief
Serious depression
Boredom
Stress
Envy
Guilt
Anger
Other

SELF-FULFILLMENT (desire to understand life and play a meaningful role in it).
Search for knowledge, understanding or wisdom
Struggle between good and evil
Creativity
Search for meaning/purpose in life
Having adequate time for religion and spirituality
Seeking a fundamentalist religious experience
Seeking a liberating religious experience
Other

ALTRUISM (concerns regarding humanity and society).
Concern about war
Concern about the environment
Concern about hunger in the world
Concern about materialism
Concern about poverty in the world
Concern about justice and equality in the world
Other

NO PROBLEM
NO RESPONSE/NO LISTING

2. COPING STRATEGIES

SEEKING OR GIVING ASSISTANCE (asking for or giving direct help).
Offer help to others
Seek support from others
Other

INTERPERSONAL INTERACTIONS (interacting with another person in order to solve a problem).
Assertive coping
Hostile-aggressive
Seeks company of others as way of problem-solving
Other

INDIVIDUAL PROBLEM-SOLVING (attempting to solve problem by oneself).
Planning toward a solution
Trying harder
Reframing
Mental preoccupation
Accepting responsibility
Anxiety without definite plan for solution
Hope
Other

STRESS MANAGEMENT (adaptive attempts to reduce impact of a problem).
Doing something of a comforting nature
Relaxation
Meditation
Other
CRYING (sobbing or shedding tears).
Crying
Other

RELIGIOUS EXPERIENCE (seeking religious support).
Prayer or religious ceremony/ritual
Seek support from clergy
Animism
Other

RESIGNATION (surrender to a conclusion that problem cannot be solved).
Anger or depression
Take a fatalist view
Giving up
Do nothing or make no attempt to find a solution
Other

DISENGAGEMENT (avoiding or distancing oneself from the problem).
Escape-avoidance (behavior)
Psychological distancing (thinking)
Unrealistic response
Other

ANTI-SOCIAL RESPONDING (behaving in socially unacceptable ways)
Steal
Cheat
Other

DO NOTHING
NO RESPONSE/NO LISTING

3. DESIRED HELPERS

FAMILY (related through birth or marriage).
Mother
Father
Grandmother
Grandfather
Sister
Brother
Sibling
Spouse
Child
Step-parent
Mother-in-law
Father-in-law
Aunt

Uncle
Niece
Nephew
Cousin
Other extended family members
Parents/family
Children
Other

NON-FAMILY (not related through birth or marriage).
Personal friend
Schoolmate/ classmate
Gangmate
Friend of family
Acquaintance
Paramour/fiancé(e)/boyfriend/girlfriend
Teacher/instructor
Clergy person
Boss/employer
Political leader
Professional counselor
Person possessing desired qualities necessary for help
Other

OFFENDER (person causing the problem).
Person who is source of problem
Other

SUPERNATURAL (God or other (non-animal) deities).
God
Other

ANIMATE CREATURES/INANIMATE OBJECTS (animal, element or object)
Animal, bird
Earth/sky/ocean
Natural element (wind, rain, sun, etc.)
Natural object (rock, tree, etc.)
Other

NON-SPECIFIC RESPONSE
NOBODY
NO RESPONSE/NO LISTING

4. DESIRED HELPER QUALITIES

POWERFUL (has strength to solve problem). Can exercise authority or change a situation
Can fulfil a material need
Other

KNOWLEDGEABLE (Has information that can provide help).
Experienced
Similarity to subject
Content area knowledge
Intelligent/wise
Informative
Gives advice
Other

AVAILABILITY (Physical proximity/accessibility to subject).
Available
Distant
Other

APPEALING PERSONAL ATTRIBUTES (Includes personality description).
Trustworthy
Loyal
Honest
Approachable/good listener
Patient
Generous/willing to help
Sense of humor
Mature
Stable
Objective
Moral
Religious/spiritual
Other

CONCERN FOR OTHERS (personal characteristics that relate to ability to care).
Understanding/attentive/empathetic
Caring/loving
Supportive
Other

DOES NOT KNOW/UNCERTAIN
NOTHING
NO RESPONSE/NO LISTING

5. DESIRED HELPING MODES

DIRECT SATISFACTION OF A NEED (Gives something).
Gives something
Other

EXERCISES POWER (Solves problem for subject).
Change the situation
Prevent problem or prevent subject from engaging in problem
Solve the problem for the subject
Other

INTERCEDE WITH OTHERS
Mediate
Other

COUNSELS (Provides counseling assistance).
Direct
Advise
Refer
Share
Reveal self-knowledge
Admonish
Help subject to problem-solve
Other

ATTENDS TO (Pays attention, inspires or comforts).
Encourage
Care
Comfort/reassure
Understand/empathize/sympathize
Listen
Accept
Approve
Agree
Other

EVADES (Helps subject to escape or avoid).
Help subject to escape or avoid
Other

DOES NOT KNOW/UNCERTAIN
NOTHING
NO RESPONSE/NO LISTING

Appendix II Percentage of Agreement between Responses of Researcher-Coders and "Master Code" on Sample Responses from Fifteen Multinational Subjects

		Category	*Class*
AUSTRALIA	(Robertson)	.84	.94
BRAZIL	(Guimaraes)	.80	.89
GREECE[1]	(Dikaiou)	.77	.93
INDIA	(Kashyap)	.80	.93
ISRAEL	Jews (Shafrir)	.83	.95
	Arabs (Saleh)	.85	.90
KUWAIT	(Al-Sarraf)	.84	.95
NETHERLANDS[2]	(de Weerdt)	.83	.94
PHILIPPINES	(Velazco)	.89	.97
RUSSIA	(Gabay)	.70	.89
TURKEY	(Arsoy)	.83	.95
UNITED STATES			
Advantaged	(Showalter)	.88	.97
	(Sun)	.82	.94
Nonadvantaged[3]	(Jones)	.84	.95
Poverty[4]	(Ondis)	.90	.97
VENEZUELA	(di Paula)	.80	.95

[1] Greeks and Greek gypsies.
[2] Dutch and migrants.
[3] Whites and African-Americans.
[4] Hispanic and African-Americans.

Appendix III Numbers of subjects Included In: (a) Multinational Results; (b) National and Minority Results Only; and (c) Minority and Multinational Results

(a) Subjects included in multinational study

Country	*Socioeconomic grouping*						*Subtotals*
	ADV.		*NONADV.*		*POV.*		
	M	*F*	*M*	*F*	*M*	*F*	
Australia	99	59	55	78			291
Brazil	94	130			34	31	289
China	73	75	69	80			277
Greece	100	100	100	100			400
India	100	100			100	100	400
Israel	145	160					305
Kuwait	57	40	11	12			120
Netherlands	171	183	33	64			451
Philippines	100	100			100	100	400
Turkey	96	99	121	112			428
US[2]	159	221	102	105			587
Venezuela	100	101			80	118	399
Subtotal	1294	1368	491	551	314	349	4367

(b) Subjects included in national and minority results only

Cultural group	*Socioeconomic grouping*								*Subtotals*
	ADV.		*NONADV.*		*POV.*		*OTHER*		
	M	*F*	*M*	*F*	*M*	*F*	*M*	*F*	
US Pov.Hisp-Afr.-Amer.[3]					89	104			193
Israeli Arabs			76		47				123
Greek Gypsies			100		100				200
Russia[4]							78	106	184
Subtotals			176	147	89	104	78	106	700
TOTAL Ss	1294	1368	667	698	403	453	78	106	5067

(c) Subjects included in both minority and multinational results

Dutch migrants included in Dutch "nonadvantaged" sample: 23

US African-Americans included in US "nonadvantaged" sample: 103

[2] US poverty subjects reported in minority and US chapters only.

[3] Reported in US and minority chapters.

[4] SES backgrounds of Russian subjects not reported.

Glossary

Active coping *See* Coping, types.
Adolescence, theories of Behavioral, explains adolescent behavior in terms of effects of environmental reinforcers; cognitive-behavioral, considers both environmental (external) and psychological (internal) variables or reinforcers; psychoanalytic-traditional, assumes a psychological struggle characterized by storm, stress and crisis necessary in order for youth to assume adult roles and responsibilities; psychosocial, explains behavior in terms of day-to-day interactions within the family, school and cultural environments.
Adolescence Stage of human development that falls between pubescence and full physical and emotional security. *See* Adolescence, theories of.
Advantaged group *See* Socioeconomic status group.
Altruism In this study, societal level concerns regarding hunger, poverty, justice and equal rights; in some cases, political freedom and justice (coded "other").
Antisocial coping In this study, includes activities deemed unacceptable by the society in which individuals live; categories including stealing, cheating and "other" which, in this study includes violent, hostile aggressive behavior.

Banzhuren In People's Republic of China, class and homeroom teacher responsible for teaching and evaluation, moral education and assisting students in academic and personal problem-solving.
Behavioral counseling *See* Counseling approaches.
Behavioral theories *See* Adolescence, theories of.
Burt Table Table used in early steps of multiple correspondence analysis to portray relationships between and among variables. *See* Multiple correspondence analysis.

Categories For purposes of this study, narrow descriptions of groups of responses given by subjects that can be grouped together into larger classes.
Children's House On a kibbutz, place in which kibbutz children spend time being reared, together with their peers and metaplot.
Classes For purposes of this study, broad descriptions of groups of responses given by subjects that can be broken down into narrow categories.
Client-centered/nondirective counseling *See* Counseling approaches.
Coding *See* Research, procedures.
Coding reliability *See* Interrater reliability; Master code; Research procedures.

Cognitive-behavioral theories *See* Adolescence, theories of.
Collaborative model for research *See* Research, collaborative model for.
Coping types In this study, includes active, involves action; emotion-focused, related directly to reducing unpleasant feelings or emotions; individual problem-solving, attempting to solve a problem by oneself, referred to by cognitive-behaviorists as goal-directed "planful behavior"; interpersonal problem-solving, interacting with another person in order to solve a problem; passive, involves little or no activity; problem-focused, related directly to reducing the problem.
Coping According to the psychosocial approach, problem-solving which involves a transaction between individuals and their environments and that has specific characteristics, e.g. demands, constraints and resources; may involve help-seeking. *See* coping types.
Counseling Interaction between a helper and a client to assist individuals in distress.
Counseling approaches In this study, include behavioral/cognitive-behavioral, working toward the change of behavior through use of reinforcement, emphasizes coping with a focus on actions and behaviors; group, providing counseling to groups of clients simultaneously; indigenous, philosophical approach that utilizes the national or cultural backgrounds particular to a group of clients in designing strategies to meet client needs, normally developed within the community, culture or nation by counselors of the same background/socioeconomic status; multinational/crossnational, designed to assist clients of different national backgrounds (across nationalities); nondirective or client-centered, utilizes client/ helper relationship; one-on-one, involves one client and one counselor working together; psychosocial, considers day-to-day interactions with the family, school and cultural environment; psychotherapy/psychoanalytic/psychodynamic, utilizes psychoanalytic approaches, often emphasizing personality organization, defense mechanisms and developmental stages.
Counseling psychologist Psychologist who provides psychotherapeutic assistance to clients whose problems are not physiological in origin, not a psychiatrist.
Counseling types In this study, include crisis-intervention, assisting of clients in immediate crisis situations, often by interdisciplinary teams; economics, utilizing intervention strategies to assist with economic issues, particularly for use in Third World countries; guidance counseling, differs from other types of counseling by virtue of its specialization in academic or vocational planning and placement; outreach, going out into the community to assist clients; preventive outreach, going out into the community to assist clients to prevent, rather than reduce problems that already exist; psychological counseling, assistance with problems of a psychological nature. *See* Counseling psychologist.
Crisis Situation requiring immediate attention to alleviate dire conditions. *See* Psychoanalytic theories of adolescence.
Crisis-intervention *See* Counseling types.
Crosscultural research *See* Research types.

Crossnational counseling *See* Counseling approaches.
Crossnational research *See* Research types.
Crossnational counseling *See* Counseling approaches.
Cultural bias Attitudes toward groups of individuals that affect interpretation of their behaviors. *See* Research types, culture-fair.
Cultural group *See* Culture.
Culture-fair research *See* Research types.
Culture In this study, the sum total of belief systems, values, life styles, child-rearing approaches, marriage and family patterns and childrearing patterns built by a group of people and transmitted from generation to generation.

Developmental tasks Societal-determined age-referenced tasks that involve expectations of acceptable behavior of individuals at different stages of development.
Disengagement Avoiding or distancing oneself from a problem.

Economics counseling *See* Counseling types.
Emotion-focused coping *See* Coping types.
Empowerment In this study, increasing self-confidence of clients by teaching them how to solve their problems, particularly important in intervention with minority youngsters.
Energetic Research Team (ERT) Name chosen by the author-researchers of this book to describe themselves in their publications.
ERT Study The multinational study described in this book. *See* Energetic Research Team.
ERT *See* Energetic Research Team.
Ethnicity/ethnic group In this study, characteristics that describe a group of people, often derived from cultural, racial, or religious traditions.
Extended family *See* Family type.

Family type In this study, includes extended, family unit in which multiple generations of family members as well as other relatives may live together within the same household; nuclear, family unit in which mother, father and children live together, apart from other members of the extended family.
Family In this study, persons related through birth or marriage.

Gender In this study, male or female.
Group counseling *See* Counseling approaches.
Group Information Workshop In Venezuela, program offered within schools and communities, planned by students, teachers and other relevant adults to impart information to young people, beneficial as a means of communication in Third World countries.
Guidance counseling *See* Counseling types.

Help-seeking A form of coping in which individual seeks help in problem-solving.
Helper quality For purposes of this study, personal characteristics that describe a helper.
Helper Person who assists another individual to solve problems.
Helping professional A person whose professional role it is to assist individuals to solve their problems (counselors, psychologists, social workers, teachers, etc.).
Helping mode For purposes of this study, action taken by a helper to assist an individual to solve problems.
Helplessness *See* Learned helplessness.

Identity In this study, perception of self; frequently reported.
Immigrants *See* Migrants.
Indigenous Counseling philosophy/ indigenous counseling. *See* Counseling, approaches.
Individual problem-solving *See* Coping types.
Interdisciplinary team In this study, helping team composed of members from a variety of professional backgrounds with other relevant persons from the community or elsewhere who work together to assist individuals in need.
International Research Seminar International group of psychologists, counselors and other researchers concerned with the helping professions whose members meet annually to design and conduct cross-cultural and cross-national research in response to questions generated by their professions.
International Round Table for the Advancement of Counselling (IRTAC) International association of counselors, psychologists and other helping professionals who meet annually to discuss issues related to their field.
Interpersonal problem-solving *See* Coping types.
Interrater reliability In this study, measured by percentage of agreement of a national rater with the coded responses of a ERT master coder. See Master code; Reliability of coding; Research procedures, coding reliability.
Intervention The act of intervening in a situation so as to cause a change; in the case of counseling intervention, to assist a client to change an internal or external situation creating a problem.
IRTAC *See* International Round Table for the Advancement of Counselling.

Key Schools In People's Republic of China, specialized government schools designed to provide best resources to high achievers; in PRC study, attendance in a Key School defines "advantaged".
Kibbutz Farming collective unique to Israel that provides a specialized socialization process in which members give to and receive from the community according to their intellectual and physical abilities, all within the framework of an elevated regard for the value of productive manual labor.
Kibbutzniks Members of a kibbutz.

Learned helplessness A psychological state in which people tend to attribute failure to global, stable and internal factors; persons with learned helplessness do not perceive that they can control the outcomes of their efforts and are prone to low self-esteem and depression regarding their chances of success.

Mainstream-minority model Model in which a minority population interacts with a single dominant majority culture.
Marathi Indian language.
Master code Set of coded responses for a sample set of multinational data coded by the ERT and used as the basis of comparison for determining reliability of coding in each of the national studies. *See* Interrater reliability; Research procedures, coding reliability.
MCA *See* Multiple correspondence analysis.
Metaplet (plural: metaplot) Member of a kibbutz whose role it is to provide child care in a Children's House; "mothering caretaker".
Migrants In this study, children of parents who were born outside the country in which they live and who are there, usually, for economic or political reasons.
Minority population In this study, a group of persons, often with low socioeconomic status when compared with the majority society and who, together with the majority society, considers itself ethno-culturally different in some way, who lack power and influence and, often, are subject to differential treatment and discrimination or prejudice, perhaps over generations.
Minority status *See* Minority population.
Mode of helping *See* Helping mode.
Multinational counseling *See* Counseling, approaches.
Multinational research *See* Research types.
Multiple correspondence analysis (MCA) Statistical technique that permits exploring possible relationships between and among variables, effective with a limited number of variables simultaneously.

National group A group of people associated with a given territory or government.
Non-family In this study, persons not related through birth or marriage.
Nonadvantaged *See* Socioeconomic status grouping.
Nondirective/client-centered counseling *See* Counseling approaches.
Nuclear family *See* Family types.

One-Child Policy In People's Republic of China, family planning campaign directed primarily to urban areas pressuring married couples to have no more than one child.
One-on-one counseling *See* Counseling approaches.
Outreach In this study, going out into the community to assist clients in need.

Paraprofessional In this study, persons, such as parents or peers, who take on helping tasks without formal educational preparation to do so.
Passive coping *See* Coping types.
Percentage of agreement *See* Research procedures, coding reliability.
Planful Behavior *See* Coping types.
Poverty *See* Socioeconomic status group.
Preventive outreach *See* Counseling types.
Problem In this study, anything that causes worry or feelings of pressure.
Problem-focused Related directly to problem-solving.
Problem-focused coping *See* Coping types.
Problem-solving *See* Coping.
Psychoanalytic counseling *See* Counseling approaches.
Psychoanalytic theories of adolescence *See* Adolescence, theories of.
Psychodynamic counseling *See* Counseling approaches.
Psychological counseling *See* Counseling approaches.
Psychosocial counseling *See* Counseling approaches.
Psychosocial theories of adolescence *See* Adolescence, theories of.
Psychotherapy *See* Counseling approaches.

Reliability of coding *See* Research, procedures.
Research, collaborative model for Approach to cross-cultural or cross-national research that fully involves researcher-participants from all cultures or nations of the study in all aspects of the work.
Research instruments In this study, data collection questionnaire, coding scale for analysis, case history.
Research limitations Aspects of research, research model, research instruments or research design that provide limitations to the interpretation of results.
Research procedures In this study administering questionnaires, conducting interviews, coding of responses into classes and categories-within-classes (*see* Classes; Categories); determining coding reliability from the extent to which researchers from the various countries agree with a "master" code; standardizing methodology by matching all procedures to insure that they have the same meaning across the nations and backgrounds of subjects.
Research types In this study, cross-cultural, involving more than one culture; cross-national, involving more than one national group; culture-fair, uncontaminated by cultural bias.
Resource broker In this study, person who taps into the community and/or public services for resources and then uses these to aid clients.

Schooling In this study, a formalized educational process, usually provided within a special setting; a frequently reported problem-class.
Self-concept In this study, perception of self given a positive or negative value; a frequently reported problem-class. *See* Problem.

Self-expectation In this study, demand on self/ self-criticism of one's behavior and motivation; a category-within-the-problem-class, personal identity and self concept; see problem.

Sexuality In this study, activities of a sexual nature; a rarely reported class of problems in this study. *See* Problems.

Social-identity model Posits that individuals tend to identify with what they consider to be their own group and choose to behave in ways they perceive their group to behave; used to explain adjustment of minority immigrants.

Socioeconomic status group Determined for purposes of this study as advantaged, nonadvantaged and poverty; definitions vary according to attributes determined within each country by national norms, but have the following characteristics in general. Advantaged–subjects, by and large, have literate, well educated parents who are employed in skilled professions, are raised in average-to-above average (for their country) neighborhoods, expect college educations. Nonadvantaged–subjects, by and large, have parents who may be literate but sometimes are nonliterate, possess lower levels of education and professional skills; are raised in average-to-below-average neighborhoods, often hope for college education but are less likely to attain it. Poverty–subjects often have parents who are nonliterate and who have low levels of education and low paying jobs; do not always possess adequate housing, sufficient food or satisfactory medical coverage and have few educational aspirations.

Squatter In this study, person who does not own or rent living quarters, but dwells on property belonging to another, usually in quarters built by hand and under squalid conditions, without adequate necessities for living.

Standardization of methodology *See* Research, procedures.

Storm and stress theory *See* Adolescence, theories of; Psychoanalytic theories of adolescence.

Street-children (also -adolescents, -boys, -girls) Youngsters with no home or family with whom they can live and whose dwelling place is on the street with other children; usually survive by begging, stealing or prostitution; make up a portion of the poverty groups in this study .

Systems theory An approach to intervention in problem-solving situations in which it is asserted that (1) the system in which an individual is operating contributes to the problem and has an inherent tendency to resist change; (2) individuals making up the system fail to change the situation by attempting to do so through repetition of responses proved unsuccessful in the past; and (3) the solution to this problem is to change the larger system rather than by continuing the unsuccessful individual responses.

Theories of adolescence *See* Adolescence, theories of.

Zionism Ideology upon which the Jewish State of Israel was founded, advocating the return of Jews to their homeland in Palestine, which led in 1947 to the UN Partition of Palestine and the creation of Israel.

References

Abramson, L., Seligman, M. and Teasdale, J. (1978). Learned helplessness in humans: Critique and reformulation. *Journal of Abnormal Psychology*, **87**, 49—74.

Abu-Eita, S. and Sherif, N. (1990). Counselor competencies and personality traits at secondary schools in Kuwait. *International Journal for the Advancement of Counselling*, **13**, 27—38.

Agoncillo, T. (1990). *History of the Filipino People*, Quezon City, Philippines: Garcia.

Al-Ebraheem, H. (1984). *Kuwait and the Gulf*, London: Croom Helm.

——— (1991). *Culturegram: State of Kuwait*, Washington, DC: Embassy of the State of Kuwait.

Al-Sarraf, Q. (1990). Sex differences in attitudes of college students in Kuwait toward manual work. *Journal of the Social Sciences*, **18**, 246—55. Kuwait: Kuwait University.

——— (1991a). Perceptions of students and school counselors for guidance and counselling services in credit-system schools in Kuwait. Unpublished paper, University of Kuwait (in Arabic).

——— (1991b). The relationship of mother's education, age and number of children to raising children in Kuwaiti society. *Journal of King Saud University*, **3**, 199—225. Saudi Arabia: King Saud University (in Arabic).

Almeida, C. (1993). *The Voice of the Boys from Brazil*. Sao Paulo: Revista Veja, pp. 46—51 (in Portuguese).

Alon, M. (1973). The youth society. In S. Rabin. and P. Hazan (eds), *Collective Education in the Kibbutz*, New York: Springer Press, pp. 3—11.

Annual Bulletin of the Mercantile Gazette (1994/95). (Gazeta Mercantile, Balano Anual) (in Portuguese).

Arab Times (1992). Kuwait City (English daily paper in Kuwait), #8057.

Atkinson, D., Morton, G. and Sue, S. (1989). *Counseling American Minorities: A Cross-Cultural Perspective* (3rd edn), Dubuque, Iowa: William C. Brown.

Baker, D. (1979). *Chinese Family and Kinship*, NY: Columbia University.

Bakri, B. and Mukhoadyay, B. (1989). *Guidance and Counselling: A Manual*, New Delhi: Sterling Publishers Ltd.

Banco Mundial (1990). *Venezuelan Poverty Studies: From Generalized to Targeted Programs*, Caracas: Banco Mundial.

Bangs, R. (1989). Recent regional economic and demographic trends. In R.

Bangs and V. Singh (eds), *The State of the Region: Economic, Demographic, and Social Trends in Southwestern Pennsylvania,* Pittsburgh, Pa.: University of Pittsburgh Center for Social and Urban Research, pp. 1—17.

Barrios, L. (1989). Family and television in Venezuela: an ethnographic study. Unpublished doctoral dissertation, Columbia University Teachers' College, New York.

Benson, P., Williams, D. and Johnson, A. (1987). *The Quicksilver Years: The Hopes and Fears of Early Adolescence,* San Francisco: Harper & Row.

Benzecri, J. (1973). *Analysis of Numbers: Analysis of Relationships,* Paris: Dunod (in French).

——— (1977). *On the Analysis of Associated Binary Numbers by Correspondence Analysis,* Vol. II, **1**, 9-40. Paris: Dunod (in French).

Berrien, F. (1970). A superego for crosscultural research. *International Journal of Psychology,* **5**, 33—9.

Berry, J., Poortinga, Y., Segall, M. and Dasen, P. (1992). *Cross-cultural Psychology,* Australia: Cambridge University Press.

Bethencourt, L. (1989). Daily living and survival. *Notebooks from the Center for The Study of Development,* No. 10, Caracas: Universidad Central de Venezuela (in Spanish).

Bettelheim, B. (1969). *Children of the Dream,* New York: Macmillan.

Billings, A and Moos, H. (1981). The role of coping responses and social resources in alternating the stress of life events. *Journal of Behavioral Medicine,* **4**, 139—57.

Bond, M. and King, A. (1985). Coping with the threat of westernization in Hong Kong. *International Journal of Intercultural Relations,* **9**, 351—64.

Bosma, H. and Jackson, S. (eds) (1990). *Coping and Self-Concept in Adolescence,* New York: Springer-Verlag.

Brazilian Institute for Geography and Statistics (1992). *Report of the Brazilian Institute for Geography and Statistics,* Brazilia: Instituto Brasileiro de Geografia e Estatistica (in Portuguese).

Broman, C. (1987). Race differences in professional help-seeking. *American Journal of Community Counseling,* **15**, 473—89.

Bronfenbrenner, U. (1970). *Two Worlds of Childhood,* NY: Russell-Sage.

——— (1977). Toward an experimental ecology of human development. *American Psychologist,* **42**(3), 513—31.

——— (1979). *The Ecology of Human Development,* Cambridge, Mass.: Harvard University Press.

Brough, J. A. (1990). Changing conditions for young adolescents: reminiscences and realities. *Educational Horizons,* **68**, 79—81.

Buber, M. (1958). *Paths in Utopia,* Boston: Beacon Press (transl. from Hebrew).

Carnegie Council on Adolescent Development (1989). *Preparing American Youth for the 21st Century: A Report on the Task Force on Education of*

Young Adolescents, Washington DC: Carnegie Council on Adolescent Development.

Cartaya, V. and D'Elia, Y. (1991). *Poverty in Venezuela: Policies and Realities,* Caracas: Centro al Servicio de la Accion Popular (CESAP) (in Spanish).

Census of India, (1991). *Provisional Population Totals,* New Delhi: Government of India.

Central Statistics and Information Office (1990). *Data from Homes.* Caracas: Central Statistics and Information Office.

Chauhan, B. (1989). *India: A Socio-Economic Profile,* New Delhi: Sterling.

Cheniaux, S. (1988). *Street Boys and the Social Workers,* Sao Paulo: Ed. Cortiz (in Portuguese).

Christopher, G., Kurtz, P. and Howing, P. (1989). Status of mental health services for youth in school and community. *Children and Youth Services Review,* **11**, 159—74.

Church, G., Goodgame, D., Leavitt, R. and Lopez, J. (1985). Hispanics: a melding of cultures. *Time Magazine,* **126**, July 8, 36—9.

Conway, R. (1978). *The Land of the Long Weekend,* Melbourne: Sun Books.

Datt, R. (1994). Jobless growth: implications of new policies. *Indian Journal of Industrial Relations,* **29**(4), April, 4.

Dauster, T. (1988). Family code: the significance of the family for the urban middle classes. *Brazilia: Revista Brasileiro de Estudos Populacais,* **5**(1), June, 103—25 (in Portuguese).

Dave, I. (1984). *The Basic Essentials of Counselling,* New Delhi: Sterling.

Davidson, J. and Koppenhaver, D. (1988). *Adolescent Literacy: What Works and Why,* New York: Garland.

Davin, D. (1991). Early childhood education of the only-child generation in urban China. In I. Epstein (ed.), *Education: Problems, Policies and Prospects,* London: Garland, pp. 49—50.

Dehollain, P. and Perez, S. (1990). *Malnourished Venezuela towards the Year 2000,* Caracas: Alfadil Editions (in Spanish).

Delgado, C. (1993). Update. *Ambiente y Ecologia,* **2**(12), June 30, 8 (in Spanish).

DePaulo, B., Nadler, A. and Fischer, J. (eds) (1983). *New Directions in Helping: Help-seeking,* New York: Academic Press.

De Weerdt, P. (1988). School counsellors' perceptual sex role differences in Dutch secondary education. *International Journal for the Advancement of Counselling,* **11**, 183—95.

Digest of the Soviet Press (1977). Sukhomlinsky's education views get top OK, *American Association for the Advancement of Slavic Studies,* **9**, (40), Nov. 2.

Dikaiou, M. (1990). Illiteracy and Tsigani minority children in northern Greece: an exploration of parents' and children's views. *International Migration,* **28**, 47—68.

——— and Kiosseoglou, G. (1994). Identified problems and coping strategies:

Gypsy minority versus non-minority adolescents. *International Migration*, **31**, 473—95.

Dragona, T. (1983). The self-concept of pre-adolescents in the Hellenic context. Unpublished doctoral dissertation, University of Aston.

Durlak, J. (1979). Comparative effectiveness of paraprofessional and professional helpers. *Psychological Bulletin*, **86**, 80—92.

Eilering, R. (1987). Intervention programs for the training of adequate coping strategies with adolescents. Unpublished master's thesis, State University, Groningen.

Eldering, L. and Kloprogge, J. (eds) (1989). *Different Cultures, Same School*, Amsterdam: Swets & Zeitlinger.

Elgaard, B., Langsted, O. and Sommer, D. (eds) (1989). *Research on Socialization of Young Children in the Nordic Countries*, Denmark: Aarhus University Press.

Emke-Poulopoulou, I. (1986). *Problems of Migration and Returning Home*, Athens: Greek Society of Demographic Studies.

——— (1994). *Demographics*, Athens: Hellin (in Greek).

Encyclopedia Americana, The (1991). Conn.: Grolier.

Erikson, E. (1950). *Childhood and Society*, NY: Norton.

Erikson, E. (1968). *Identity, Youth and Crisis*, NY: Norton.

Fine, M. (1986). Why urban adolescents drop into and out of public high school. *Teachers College Record* (IC Record), **8**(3).

Fischer-Ferreira, M. (1980). *Street Boys*, Sao Paulo: Cedec (in Spanish).

Fishman, E. and Stuftal, S. (1978). *The School Counsellor, Report No. 1: Role Analysis*, Holon, Israel: Exploratory Research Center for Technological Studies.

Folkman, S. and Lazarus, R. (1980). An analysis of coping in a middle-aged community sample. *Journal of Health and Social Behavior*, **21**, 219—39.

——— and ——— (1986). Stress processes and depressive symptomatology. *Journal of Abnormal Psychology*, **95**(2), 107—13.

Freire, P. (1983). *Pedagogy for the Oppressed*, Rio de Janeiro: Ed. Paz e Terra (in Portuguese).

Friedman, I. (1989). *Adolescent Decision Making: Issues and Processes*, Jerusalem: The Henrietta Szold Institute and National Institute for Research in the Behavioral Sciences.

Frydenberg, E. and Lewis, L. (1991). Adolescent coping: the different ways in which boys and girls cope. *Journal of Adolescence*, **14**, 119—33.

Foundation for the study of Growth and Development of Venezuela. (1984). *Report on the Caracas Urban Area*, Caracas: Fundacredesa (in Spanish).

Galvin, M. and West, P. (1988). *A Changing Australia: Themes and Case Studies*, Sydney: Harcourt Brace Jovanovich.

Gandevia, K. (1989). An Assessment of Drug Abuse, Drug Users and Drug

Prevention Services in Bombay. Unpublished report, Tata Institute of Social Sciences, Bombay.

Garbarino, J. (1991). The young victims: Kuwaiti children bear psychic scars of conflict in Gulf. *Psychology International,* **2**(1—3), Washington, DC: American Psychological Association Office of International Affairs.

——— (1992). Children in Danger, San Francisco: Jossey-Bass.

Garland, A. and Zigler, E. (1993). Adolescent suicide prevention. *American Psychologist,* **48**, 169—82.

Gao, M. (1987). Child Development in Urban China: Yesterday and Today. Unpublished paper, University of Pittsburgh.

Garmezy, N. (1981). Overview. In C. Moore (ed.), *Adolescence and Stress,* DHHS Publication No. ADM 81-1098, Washington, DC: US Government Printing Office, pp. 1—10.

Gerris, J. (1992). *Childhood as a Social Phenomenon: Report of the Conference, "Child, Family and Society,"* held in Luxemburgh, May 27—9, 1991. Brussels: Commission of the European Communities.

Gibson, J. (1984). Comparative views on education of students with special needs: American and Soviet approaches. *School Psychology International,* **5**, 189—94.

——— (1988). Sex roles in the family, school and workplace: The Soviet example. *International Journal of Counseling,* **11**, 209—18.

———, Baker, C. *et al.*, (1992). Gender and culture: reported problems, coping strategies and selected helpers of male and female adolescents in fifteen countries. *International Journal for the Advancement of Counselling,* **15**, 137—49.

——— and Showalter, S. (1989). *Human Problems and Methods of Coping: A Taxonomy and Coding Manual,* Pittsburgh, Pa.: University of Pittsburgh.

——— , Westwood, M., Ishiyama, I. et al. (1990) Youth and culture: A seventeen nation Study of perceived problems and coping strategies. Address to the International Research Seminar, *International Round Table for the Advancement of Counselling,* Helsinki, Finland.

——— , Westwood, M., Ishiyama, I. *et al.* (1991). Youth and culture: A seventeen nation study of perceived problems and coping strategies. *International Journal for the Advancement of Counselling,* **14**, 203—16.

———, Wurst, K. and Cannonito, M. (1984). Observations on contact stimulation provided young children in selected areas of Greece, U.S. and USSR. *International Journal of Psychology,* July, 36—46.

Gille, M., Hoffmann-Lange, U. and Schneider, H. (1993—4). Is German youth violent? *Deutsches Jugendininstitut Bulletin,* Munich: Deutsches Jugendininstitut, 8—14.

Gökçe, B. (1984). Problems and Expectations of Youth in Secondary Education, Ankara: Ministry of Education, Youth and Sports (in Turkish).

Gordon, E. and Saa Meroe, A. (1991). Common destinies—-continuing dilemmas. *Psychological Science,* **2**, 23—9.

Gore, M. 1977). *Indian Youth: Process of Socialization,* New Delhi: Vishwa Yuvak Kendra.

Grant, B., Harford, T., Chou, P., Pickering, R., Dawson, D., Stinson, F., and Noble, J. (1991). Prevalence of DSM-III-R Alcohol Abuse and Dependence: United States, 1988. *Alcohol Health and Research World,* **15**, 91—6.

Greenspan, R., Seeley, D. and Niemeyer, J. (1993). *Principals Speak: The Vital Importance of Mental Health Social Services to School Reform,* NY: CUNY Principals Speak Project.

Grinspun, M. (1987). The historic background of guidance counselling services: an analysis. *Brazilia: Revista de Educaao da AEC,* **16**(64), June, 7—30 (in Portuguese).

Guide to the Brazilian Economy (1991). *Guide to the Brazilian Economy,* Brazilia: Companihia Brasileira de Mineraao e Minerio (in Portuguese).

Hakim, S. (1984). *On Education,* Kuwait: PO Box 20579, Safat.

Hallahan, C. and Moos, R. (1987). Personal and contextual determinants of coping strategies. *Journal of Personality and Social Psychology,* **52**, 946—55.

Haritos-Fatouros, M. (1981). Educational and vocational guidance in Greece. In H. Z. Hoxter (ed.), *The Forms, Methods and Techniques of Vocational and Educational Guidance: International Case Studies,* Paris: UNESCO, 22—30.

Herr, E. (1987). Cultural diversity from an international perspective. *Journal of Multicultural Counseling and Development,* **15**, 99—109.

Hofstede, G. (1984). *Culture's Consequences: International Differences in Work-Related Values,* Beverly Hills, Cal: Sage.

Hooper, B. (1991). Gender and education. In I. Epstein (ed.), *Chinese Education: Problems, Policies and Prospects,* NY: Garland, 352—74.

Horne, D. (1987). *The Lucky Country Revisited,* Melbourne: Dent.

Hoxter, H. (1981). *The Forms, Methods and Techniques of Vocational and Educational Guidance: International Case Histories,* Paris: UNESCO.

Hsu, F. (1981). *Americans and Chinese: Passage to Differences,* 3rd edn, Honolulu: The University Press of Hawaii.

Ianni, O. (1987). *Racial and Social Classes in Brazil,* Sao Paulo: Ed Brasiliense (in Portuguese).

Israeli Ministry of Education and Culture (1991). *Statistic Fact Sheet,* Jerusalem: Ministry of Education and Culture Psycho-guidance Services.

Israeli Statistical Abstracts (1993). Jerusalem: Government of the State of Israel.

Ivey, A. (1990). *Developmental Counseling and Therapy,* Pacific Grove, Cal.: Brooks/Cole.

Jaffe, C. (1991). Psychoanalytic approaches to adolescent development. In J. Gold (ed.), *Adolescent Psychotherapy,* Washington, DC: American Psychiatric Press, 11—40.

Jatoba, J. (1994). *Inequalities and Education,* Sao Paulo: Folha de Sao Paulo, July 10 (in Portuguese).

Kagıtçıbası, Ç. (1982). Sex Roles, Family and Community in Turkey. Indiana: Indiana University Turkish Studies 3.

Kanitz, O. (1994). *Brazil Can Work: The New Cycle of Growth,* 1994—2000. Sao Paulo: Ed. Makron (in Portuguese).

Kashyap, L. (1994). Counselling the family under pressure of modernization: a Third World perspective, Invited Plenary Address before the *International Round Table for the Advancement of Counselling,* Munich, Germany, April 9.

Katz, M. (1989). *The Undeserving Poor,* NY: Pantheon Books.

Kessler, R., Brown, R. and Broman, C. (1981), The relationship between international student national background and symptoms of stress. *Journal of Health and Social Behavior,* **22**, March, 49—64.

Kozol, J. (1991). *Savage Inequalities: Children in America's Schools,* NY: Crown Publishers.

Kulka, R., Veroff, J. and Douvan, E. (1979). Social class and the use of professional help for personal problems: 1957 and 1976. *Journal of Health and Social Behavior,* **20**, 2—17.

Kuo, S. and Spees, E. (1983). Chinese-American student lifestyles: a comparative study. *Journal of College Student Personnel,* **24**, 111—17.

Kuwait Ministry of Planning. (1990). *Twenty-Five Years of Statistical Data* (Special Issue), Kuwait: Central Statistical Office.

Kuwait University. (1991). *Statistical Bulletin,* Kuwait: Kuwait University Publications.

Laslett, P. (1992). Child, family and society. *Report of the Conference Held in Luxemburgh,* May 27—9, 1991. Brussels: Commission of the European Communities.

Lawrence, C. (1994). Home Sweet Home. *Daily Telegraph Weekend,* May 14, p. B1.

Lazarus, R. (1966). *Psychosocial Stress and Coping Paradigms,* NY: McGraw-Hill.

——— (1981). *The Practice of Multi-Modal Therapy,* NY: McGraw-Hill.

——— and Folkman, S. (1984). Coping and adaptation. In W. Gentry (ed.), *Handbook of Behavioral Medicine,* New York: Guilford Press, 44—68.

——— and Folkman, S. (1987). Transactional theory and research on emotions and coping. *European Journal of Personality,* **1**, 141—69.

——— and Launier, R. (1978). Stress-related transactions between person and environment. In L. Pervin and M. Levis (eds), *Perspectives in International Psychology,* NY: Plenum, 78—95.

Lebart, L., Morineau, A. and Warwick, K. (1984). *Multivariate Descriptive Statistical Analysis: Correspondence Analysis and Related Techniques for Large Matrices,* NY: Wiley.

Leighton, C., Bellorin, M. *et al.* (1988). *Infancy and Family,* Caracas: Family Programs (in Spanish).

Leus, J. (1992). Schooling in the USSR. Unpublished paper, University of Pittsburgh.

Levin, D. (1963). *Soviet Education Today,* London: MacGibbon.

Louv, R. (1994). The new culture of renewal. *The Christian Science Monitor,* Oct 24, 12.

Maccarelli, L. (1994). Problems Reported by Adolescents: A Comparison of Data Collection Methods. Unpublished master's thesis, University of Pittsburgh.

Maccoby, E. and Jacklin, C. (1974). *The Psychology of Sex Differences,* Stanford, Ca.: Stanford University Press.

McGoldrick, M. (1982). Ethnicity and family therapy. In M. McGoldrick, J. Pierce and J. Giordano (eds), *Ethnicity and Family Therapy,* NY: Guilford Press, 3—31.

Macksoud, M. (1992). Assessing war trauma in children: a case study of Lebanese children. *Journal of Refugee Studies,* **5**, 1—15.

Mahale, M. (1987). Adolescents: Their Family Situations and Education, Delhi: Mittal Publications.

Mann, D. (1986). Can we help dropouts? *Teachers College Record,* **87**, 3.

Mansour, T. (1992). Psychological Correlates of the Gulf Crisis in Children and Adolescents of Kuwait and Implications for Counselling. Unpublished paper, Kuwaiti Society for the Advancement of Arab Children (in Arabic).

Markun, P. (1973). *Parenting,* Washington, DC: Association for Childhood International.

Maslow, A. (1970). *Motivation and Personality,* NY: Harper & Row.

Meichenbaum, D. (1977). *Cognitive-Behavior Modification: An Integrative Approach,* NY: Plenum.

Ministry of the Family (1988). *Indicators of Poverty,* Caracas: Ministry of the Family (in Spanish).

Morais, R. (1980), Dimensions of Interpersonal Relationships in a Lowland Philippine Town. Unpublished doctoral dissertation, University of Pittsburgh.

Moussourou, L. (1985). *Family and Child in Athens,* Athens: Hestia (in Greek).

Naltao, W. (1986). Dealing with the spoiled brat. *Beijing Review,* **29**(19), 26—8.

National Commission on Children (1991). *Beyond Rhetoric: A New American Agenda for Children and Families (Final Report of the National Commission on Children),* Washington, DC: US Government Printing Office.

National Conference on the Rights of Children (1991). *The Children: The 1990's Compromise,* Caracas: Comision Presidencial por los Derechos del Nino (in Spanish).

National Economic and Development Authority (1992). *Philippine Statistical Yearbook,* Manila: National economic and Development Authority.

National Institute on Drug Abuse. (1988). *National Household Survey on Drug Abuse*, Rockville, Md.: NIDA.

Newman, B. and Newman, P. (1986). *Adolescent Development*, Columbus, Ohio: Merrill Publishing Co.

Newspaper on Economy, Annual Bulletin (1994/5) (in Portuguese).

Newsweek, Oct 10, 1977, p. 67.

Nirun, N. (1986). Socioeconomic problems of 12—14-year olds. Ankara: Gazi University Press.

Ondis, G. and Gibson, J. (1992). Survey of Counseling Services Available in Pittsburgh Area School Districts. Unpublished study, University of Pittsburgh.

Öner, N. (1992). Turkish Guidance Counseling: In Search for Identity and Model. Unpublished manuscript.

——— (1994). A guidance-counselling model for Turkey. In N. Öner and G. Yıldıran (eds), *Proceedings of the Symposium on Guidance and Career Counselling at the University Level*, Istanbul: Bogaziçi University.

Oudenhoven, J. and Willemsen, T. (eds) (1989). *Ethnic Minorities: Social Psychological Perspectives*, Amsterdam: Swets & Zeitlinger.

Pallas, A. (1989). *Making Schools More Responsive to High Risk Students* (Report # EDO-UD-89-0). Washington, DC: Office of Educational Research and Improvement (ERIC Document Reproduction Service #ED 316 617).

Patterson, C. (1980), *Theories of Counseling and Psychotherapy*, 3rd edn, NY: Harper.

Pearlin, L. and Schooler, C. (1978). The structure of coping. *Journal of Health and Social Behavior*, **19**, 2—21.

Pearson, L. (1990). *Children of the Glasnost: Growing Up Soviet*. Seattle: University of Washington Press.

Pedersen, P. (1987). Ten frequent assumptions of cultural bias in counseling. *Journal of Multicultural Counseling and Development*, **15**, 16—25.

Pennsylvania Student Assistance Program Interagency Management Committee (1991). *Guidelines for Student Assistance Program Implementation*, Harrisburg, Pa.: Pennsylvania Departments of Health, Public Welfare, Education, and Governor's Drug Policy Council.

Pepper, S. (1991). Post Mao reforms in Chinese education: can the ghosts of the past be laid to rest? In I. Epstein (ed.), *Chinese Education: Problems, Policies and Prospects*, NY: Garland, 1—41.

Petersen, A., Compas, B., Brooks-Gunn, J., Stemmler, M., Ey, S. and Grant, K. (19??). Depression in adolescence. *American Psychologist*, **48**, 155—68.

Pompeu, K. (1990). *Generation of the Nineties*. Manchete: Ed Block, 33—45 (in Portuguese).

Powers, S., Hauser, S. and Kliner, L. (1989). Adolescent mental health. *American Psychologist*, **44**(2), 200—8.

Punamaki, R. and Ramzi, S. (1990). Predictors and effectiveness of coping with political violence among Palestinian children. *British Journal of Social Psychology*, **29**, 67—77.

Qu, G. and Li, J. (1994). *Population and the Environment in China* (transl. by Jiang, B. and Gu, R.; Engl. lang. edn ed. R. Boardman)), London: Paul Chapman Ltd.

Recagno, I. (1982) *Childrearing Patterns and Marginality*. Caracas: Publicaciones Universidad Central de Venezuela. (In Spanish).

The Research Bulletin (1987). *Statistics*, NYC and Washington, DC: Hispanic Policy Development Program, Fall.

Revista Veja (1990). *Growth in Pentecostal Churches*, Sao Paulo: Revista Veja (in Portuguese).

Roach, J. (1986). *India — 2000: The Next Fifteen Years*, Riverdale. NY: The Riverdale Co.

Roelandt, T., Roijen, J. and Veenman, J. (1991). *Minorities in the Netherlands*, Den Haag: CBS (in Dutch).

Rogers, C. (1966). A theory of therapy as developed in the client-centered framework. In A. Art, Jr (ed), *Counseling and psychotherapy*, Palo Alto: Science and Behaviour Books.

Ropers, R. (1991). *Persistent Poverty*, NY: Plenum Press.

Rosenberg, C. (1990). *Juvenile Delinquency*, Caracas: El Universal, May 8, 2—18 (in Spanish).

Ryan, L. (1993). *Counselling the Adolescent in a Changing Ireland*, Dublin: Institute of Guidance Counsellors.

Salazar-Clemena, R. (1987). The status of graduate counsellor education in Metro Manila. *Philippine Journal of Counselling Psychology*, **I**, 70—96, Manila: DeLaSalle University Press.

Schwartz, K. (1987). The Relationship between Culture and Stress: A Comparison of Chinese, Saudi and American Student Perceptions Regarding Problems and the Effectiveness of Coping. Unpublished doctoral dissertation, University of Pittsburgh.

Shaw, R. (1976). *Kuwait*. London: Macmillan.

Shipler, D. (1989). *Russia: Broken Idols, Solemn Dreams*, NY: Times Books.

Showalter, S. (1990). Making Sense of Crosscultural Data. Unpublished master's thesis, University of Pittsburgh.

——— (1992). The Relationship of Gender to Types of Self-perceived Stressors among Adolescents. Unpublished PhD dissertation, University of Pittsburgh.

Silveira, L. (1992). *Rebelling Angels: Brazil Shows its Face*, Desfiles: Ed Block, Nov., 21—3 (in Portuguese).

Simpson, G. and Yinger, J. (1985). *Racial and Cultural Minorities*. London: Plenum Press.

Skinner, B. F. (1953). *Science and Human Behavior*, NY: Macmillan.

Slater, C. and Hall, E. (1992). *County and City Extra (Annual Metro, City and County Data Book)*, Lanham, MD.: Bernan Press.

Smith, H. (1976) *The Russians,* NY: Ballantine.

——— (1990). *The New Russians,* NY: Avon.

Soliman, A. (1990). The relationships between choice of helper, type of problem, and sex of helpee of college students in Kuwait. Paper presented at meeting of *The International Round Table for the Advancement of Counselling.* Helsinki, July 1—5.

Sriram, R. (1991). *Research on Marital Violence: Some Trends, Implications and Emerging Issues.* Bombay: Tata Institute of Social Sciences.

Statistical Institute of Turkey. (1992). *Statistical Yearbook of Turkey:* 1990, Ankara: State Statistical Institute (in Turkish).

Stern, E. (1985). A Dutch contribution to counsellor education: an in-service model. *International Journal for the Advancement of Counselling,* **8**: 239—48.

Sue, D. (1981). *Counseling the Culturally Different,* New York: Wiley.

Sullivan, W., and Englin, A. (1986). Adolescent depression: its prevalence in high school students. *Journal of School Psychology,* **24**, 103—9.

Sun, F. (1988). The Role of "Banzhuren" in Chinese Elementary and Middle Schools after 1977. Unpublished paper, University of Pittsburgh.

Taft, R. (1977). Coping with unfamiliar cultures. In N. Warren (ed.), *Studies in Cross-Cultural Psychology,* London: Academic Press, 121—51.

——— (1986). Methodological considerations in the study of immigrant adaptation in Australia. *Australian Journal of Psychology,* **38**, 339—46.

Takiuiti, A. (1990). *The Adolescent Girl is Slightly Pregnant: So What?,* Sao Paulo: Ed. IGLU (in Portuguese).

Timbreza, F. (1982). *Filipino Philosophy,* Manila: Rex Printing (in Tagalag).

Triandis, H. (1972). *The Analysis of Subjective Culture,* NY: Wiley.

Triandis, H. and Vassiliou, V. (1967). Frequency of contact and stereotyping. *Journal of Personality and Social Psychology,* **7**, 316—28.

UNESCO (1960). *Report on Education in the Arab States,* No. 2, NY: UNESCO.

UNICEF (1991). *Children and Women in India: A Situational Analysis,* 1990, New Delhi: UNICEF India Office.

——— (1992). *UNICEF on the World's Children,* NY: UNICEF House.

US Bureau of the Census (1993). *Statistical Abstract of the United States* (113th edn), Washington, DC: US Government Printing Office.

US Congress, House Select Committee on Children, Youth, and Families. (1987). U.S. *Children and their Families: Current Conditions and Recent Trends,* Washington, DC: US Government Printing Office.

Vassiliou, G. and Vassiliou, V. (1970). *On Aspects of Child-Rearing in Greece,* Athens: Athenian Institute of Anthropos.

——— and ——— (1982). Promoting psychosocial functioning and preventing malfunctioning. *Pedetican,* **11**(1—2), 90—8.

Velazco, G. (1991), Development of an Indigenous Counselling Approach to Economic Problems. Unpublished doctoral dissertation, De La Salle University, Manila.

——— (1993). The Filipino culture as it affects child development. *Kaya Tao*, **12**, 1—18, Manila: DeLaSalle University Press.

Veroff, J., Kulka, R. and Douvan, E. (1981). *Mental Health in America: Patterns of Help-seeking from 1957 to 1976*, NY: Basic Books.

Wang, X. and Li, C. (1987). *The Function and Duty of "Banzhuren,"* Heibi: Hebei Peoples' Publisher (in Chinese).

Ward, R. (1958). *The Australian Legend*, Melbourne: Oxford University Press.

Watts, A., Dartois, C. and Plant, P. (1987). Career guidance services within the European Community. *International Journal for the Advancement of Counselling*, **10**, 179—89.

Watzlawick, P., Weakland, J. and Finch, R. (1973). *Change*, Palo Alto.

Werebe, M. (1994). *Riches and Miseries of School Systems in Brazil, Thirty Years after the Revolution*, Sao Paulo: Ed Atica (in Portuguese).

White, T. (1987). Implementing the "one-child per couple" popular program in rural China: national goals and local policies. In D. Lampton (ed.), *Policy Implementation in Post-Mao China*, pp. 46—66, Berkeley: U. of California Press.

Whiting, B. and Edwards, C. (1973). A cross-cultural analysis of sex differences in the behavior of children aged 3—11. *Journal of Social Psychology*, **91**, 171—88.

——— and Whiting, J. (1975). *Children of Six Cultures*, Cambridge, Mass.: Harvard University Press.

Windle, M. (1991). Alcohol use and abuse: some findings from the National Adolescent Student Health Survey. *Alcohol Health and Research World*, 15, 5—10.

Women of China (1987). *New Trends in Chinese Marriage and the Family*, Beijing: Women of China Publications.

Wrenn, G. (1962). *Black Psychology*, NY: Harper & Row.

Xiaotong, F. (1982). Changes in Chinese family structure. *China Reconstructs*, **31**(10), 23—6.

Yıldıran, G. (1990). Turkish Education and its Problems. Istanbul: Report presented to Academy of National Security.

Ying, L. (1985). *Structural Changes in Beijing Families*, **5**, 16—17. Beijing: Women of China.

Ziv, A., Guttman, D. and Green, D. (1980). Exposure to social societies and moral judgement of Israeli adolescents in city, kibbutz, and Arab villages. *Israeli Journal of Psychology and Counseling in Education*, No. 13, Jerusalem: Ministry of Education and Culture Psychological and Counseling Services.

Author Index

Subject Index

For Product Safety Concerns and Information please contact our EU representative GPSR@taylorandfrancis.com Taylor & Francis Verlag GmbH, Kaufingerstraße 24, 80331 München, Germany